2449

Roofing Design and Practice

Stephen Patterson, P.E., R.R.C.
Roof Technical Services, Inc., Fort Worth, Texas

Madan Mehta, Ph.D., M.Bdg.Sc., B.Arch.
University of Texas at Arlington

Prentice
Hall

Upper Saddle River, New Jersey
Columbus, Ohio

Dedicated in the memory of Adren Martin, who sought excellence in every aspect of his professional career,
and one of the first to recognize the need for a true roofing design text.

Library of Congress Cataloging-in-Publication Data
Patterson, Stephen (Stephen L.)
    Roofing design and practice/Stephen Patterson, Madan Mehta
       p. cm.
    Includes index.
    ISBN 0-13-025995-0
    1. Roofs—Design and Construction. 2. Roofing. I. Mehta, Madan. II. Title.

    TH2401.P38 2001
    695—dc21
                            00-049201

Vice President and Publisher: Dave Garza
Editor in Chief: Stephen Helba
Executive Editor: Ed Francis
Production Editor: Christine M. Buckendahl
Design Coordinator: Robin G. Chukes
Cover Designer: Linda Fares
Cover photos: Kimbell Art Museum
Production Manager: Matt Ottenweller
Marketing Manager: Jamie Van Voorhis

The cover was printed by Phoenix Color Corp.

10 9 8 7 6 5 4 3 2 1
ISBN: 0-13-025995-0

CONTENTS

PREFACE

The aesthetic aspects of a roof may or may not be important, but in functional performance, the roof is one of the most critical components of a building. Most energy loss from a building envelope (particularly from a single-story building) occurs through the roof. Disastrous wind-caused damage to a building initiates when the roof fails to function as a structural diaphragm. Inadequate roof drainage may cause excessive water ponding on the roof, leading to its collapse.

Water leakage, the most aggravating aspect of the malperformance of a building envelope, occurs primarily through the roof. In fact, a large majority of owners' complaints with the design and construction of buildings relate to roofs that leak.

Although authoritative data is not available, it is estimated that nearly 65% of building construction lawsuits relate, in one way or the other, to roofing problems. The above statistic assumes significance considering that the roof cover of a typical building is replaced every few years — one estimate gives a 12- to 14-year period. This replacement frequency would be unacceptable for any other envelope component — walls, doors, windows, etc.!

It is the authors' belief that most roof failures and the resulting disputes can be prevented if the architects, engineers, contractors, roofing consultants, and facility managers — all personnel engaged in the design, construction, and maintenance of buildings — have greater knowledge of roofing design and practice. This book has been written to supply that knowledge. It has taken several years to complete this book, during which the authors cotaught (and still continue to teach) a five-week component on roofing design to architecture students at the University of Texas at Arlington, as part of a building construction course.

OBJECTIVES OF THE BOOK

Roofing Design and Practice is a joint undertaking of a roofing consultant, who has been in practice for over 25 years, and a university professor, who has taught building construction courses to architecture students for nearly the same period. Therefore, it combines academic rigor with the meticulousness necessary in contemporary design practice. It is expected that it will serve both as a text for students of architecture and construction, as well as a reference resource for roofing consultants, practicing architects, consulting engineers, construction specifiers, roofing contractors, and facility managers.

The need to undertake this project arose from the relative absence of a suitable publication, which could be adopted as a textbook for the course. An initial survey by the authors indicated that, although there are a few excellent manuals and compendiums dealing with the subject, none address all of the design and practice issues comprehensively in the reader-friendly format of a textbook.

Anyone involved with roofing design and installation knows that the roof in a contemporary building is an extremely complex component. Long gone are the days when a roof in architectural drawings could be represented by a squiggly line atop a wood or concrete deck, indicating a three- or four-ply, gravel-covered, built-up roof. In fact, it is highly inaccurate to refer to a contemporary roof as a mere component, since it consists of an integrated and interactive system of several components.

A typical low-slope roof in today's building consists of a roof membrane, insulation, vapor retarder (and sometimes an air retarder), and a roof deck. All of these components must be physically and chemically compatible with each other. Each component has its own individual design requirements, in addition to those of the system as a whole.

The roof must not only provide a waterproof cover over the building and be durable against all deteriorating environmental elements (such as ultraviolet radiation, exhausts from neighboring industries, kitchens, roof-top mechanical equipment, etc.), but must also be able to withstand wind and hail storms. Additionally, it must be able to protect the building from an internal or an external fire. It must also be designed to drain rainwater rapidly off its surface. It must do all of this in a reasonably economical way, because the roof will be replaced several times during a typical building's life span.

The roof's replacement frequency further complicates an otherwise complex system. Replacement frequency is the primary cause of the roofing industry's relatively large size. According to the National Roofing Contractors Association's annual survey, more than $26 billion was spent on roofing in the United States in 1998 — a figure that is expected to rise by nearly $2 billion in 1999.

The economic dimensions of the industry catalyzes a great deal of research in the development of new materials and application techniques. Consequently, several new roofing systems or new versions of the old systems appear in the market frequently, complicating the situation for architects, roofing consultants, and roofing contractors, who must constantly keep abreast of new products and systems.

An architect or a contractor who does not fully comprehend various roofing design issues will find it difficult to evaluate these innovations. This book promises to provide that comprehension.

A NOTE TO THE READER

The book contains 15 chapters. Chapter 1 is an introduction to roofing, which is generally divided in two parts — low-slope (commercial) roofs, and steep (residential) roofs. Chapters 2 through 10 deal with low-slope roof components (roof membranes, insulation, and roof decks) and design issues (design for drainage, heat and vapor transmission, fire, wind, and hail). Chapters 11 through 13 deal with steep roofs, and Chapter 14 with metal roofs. Chapter 15 discusses roofing manufacturers' warranties and other legal issues in roofing.

The authors' teaching experience indicates that it is not necessary to cover all topics in detail in the classroom. Depending on the time allocated to roofing, some topics should be covered in detail, some briefly, while others could be left for students to read on their own. A large number of drawings, sketches, photographs from construction sites, and commonly used construction details make the book reader-friendly. A chapter-wise list of review questions at the end of the book should be useful to the teacher as well as the reader.

We hope that the architects, engineers, roofing consultants, and roofing contractors will find this book useful in selecting and specifying a roof system. *Roofing Design and Practice* should provide necessary information on the suitability of various systems for a specific project. The chapters on drainage, insulation, water vapor, and wind design will help to design roof drainage, the type of insulation, and the anchorage system needed.

ACKNOWLEDGMENTS

It is impossible to record here the names of every individual who has helped us in completing this undertaking. The following individuals have, however, contributed significantly during the preparation of the manuscript and are thankfully acknowledged.

- James R. Fell, National Account Manager, Southern Region, Firestone Building Products Company, Grapevine, Texas, for reviewing Chapters 1 through 8.
- Joel Lewallen, Architectural Representative, Johns Manville, Fort Worth, Texas, for reviewing Chapters 1 through 5.
- James R. McDonald, Department of Civil Engineering, Texas Tech University, Lubbock, Texas, for reviewing Chapter 8.
- Hollye Fisk, Registered Architect and Practicing Attorney, Dallas, Texas, for reviewing Chapter 15.
- Scott A. Meyer, M.Arch. student, University of Texas at Arlington, for reading the entire manuscript for typographical and other errors.
- James R. Kirby, Director, Technical Services, National Roofing Contractors Association, for answering authors' questions and providing much-needed information.
- Phillip Smith, Senior Engineer, Factory Mutual Research Corporation, for answering authors' questions related to wind uplift resistance of roof assemblies.
- David Tanaka, Project Engineer, Factory Mutual Research Corporation, for answering questions related to fire resistance of roof assemblies.

- Jens Pohl, School of Architecture, California Polytechnic State University, San Luis Obispo, California.
- Steve Martens, School of Architecture and Landscape Architecture, North Dakota State University, North Dakota.
- James Goddard, Department of Architectural Engineering and Construction Science, Kansas State University, Manhattan, Kansas.
- Roger Liska, Department of Construction Science and Management, Clemson State University, Clemson, North Carolina.

The following individuals are recognized for their graciousness in providing timely permissions to use copyright materials under their jurisdiction.

- William J. Woodring, GAF Building Materials Corporation, Wayne, New Jersey.
- John Dillard, Siplast, Irving, Texas.
- James R. Fell, Firestone Building Products, Southern Region, Grapevine, Texas.
- John R. Barker, E.S. Products, Inc., Bristol, Rhode Island.
- Craig D. Porter, Johns Manville, Denver, Colorado.
- Richard P. Kuchnicki, International Code Council, Inc., Falls Church, Virginia.
- Karen Ryan, American Society of Civil Engineers, Reston, Virginia.
- Robert Martell, Factory Mutual Research Corporation, Norwood, Massachusetts.
- Ken Wolford, Single Ply Roofing Institute, Needham, Massachusetts.
- C. Michael Schuerman, MM Systems Corporation, Tucker, Georgia.
- Anne Adams, Kimbell Art Museum, Fort Worth, Texas.

A special acknowledgement is due to Ed Francis, Executive Editor, Prentice Hall for posing his trust and faith in the need for this book. The authors also acknowledge the help of the Production Editor, Christine Buckendahl, and the Copy Editor, Colleen Brosnan.

DISCLAIMER

The information in this book has been derived from several sources, such as the industry associations' manuals, reference and text books, journals, and the authors' professional experience. It is presented in good faith, and although the authors and the publishers have exercised every care to present the information accurately and completely, they do not warrant or assume any liability to that effect. It is the responsibility of the reader to apply his or her professional knowledge in using the information given here and refer to the original sources for detailed information.

1 INTRODUCTION TO ROOFING

The roof is one of the most critical components of a building. It is the primary source of construction litigation and building owners' complaints. One estimate indicates that nearly 65% of all lawsuits brought against architects originate with roofing problems.[1.1] This statistic becomes significant considering that the roof covering of a typical building is replaced every few years — 12 to 14 years on the average. Would we accept replacing other components of a building envelope so frequently — doors, windows, curtain walls, etc.?

A major reason for this situation is the ever-increasing complexity of a contemporary building and, more specifically, that of a contemporary roof. Until the middle of the 20th century, roofing alternatives were very few, and roof design was relatively simple. For a flat roof, the roofing membrane consisted of either a coal tar or an asphalt built-up roof on a concrete or wood deck. For a steep roof, clay tiles or wood shingles were the major alternatives. Not so today.

A relatively sudden spurt in the gross national products of Western economies after World War II introduced large industrial buildings with relatively light steel roof decks. A roof that performed well on a stiff concrete or wood deck failed prematurely on a light and flexible steel deck.

The advent of air conditioning and more efficient heating systems led to urban development in very warm and cold climatic regions, particularly in the United States. A general lack of performance-based data and experience with roofs in these climates complicated issues further. Roof insulation that was seldom used earlier became the norm. The greater degradation of roofs in extremely hot and cold climates and the effect of roof insulation introduced factors whose impact was not realized until several years later.

The oil embargo of 1973 led to significant increases in the cost of built-up roofs, which made single-ply roofs economically competitive for the first time. This, combined with several other market forces including major problems with two-ply built-up roofs, resulted in a significant increase in the market share of single-ply roofs.

Some of the early single-ply roofs had a fairly brief history, and some had a poor history of use, which further increased roofing problems. Although roofing products are generally subjected to several laboratory tests before being introduced in the market, none of these tests can fully simulate the actual field conditions. In other words, it takes several years before we discover the suitability of a new roofing product for a particular climatic region. It also takes a long time to train roofers in proper installation techniques.

This chapter provides a bird's eye view of roofing design and construction issues and forms an introduction to the subsequent chapters in the text.

1.1 ROOF TYPES BASED ON ROOF SLOPE

A discussion of roofing must begin with its classification under two types:

- *Water-shedding roof*, also referred to as a steep roof

- *Water-resisting roof*, also referred to as a low-slope roof

A water-shedding roof typically consists of small individual roofing units (shingles) that overlap each other. The roof surface must be sloped so that the water is shed off the roof by gravity. The slope must generate adequate gravitational force to overcome the forces produced by wind, head pressure, and capillary action that might push the water up the slope between adjacent shingles and cause the roof to leak. Double coverage in shingles and adequate overlap are necessary to prevent roof leakage.

A water-resisting roof consists of a continuous roof membrane over a relatively flat roof surface. Although, water ponding is generally to be avoided, a water-resisting roof has to be designed for a certain minimum depth of ponding (usually a minimum of 2 in. — 50 mm of water) that might collect on the roof if there is a blockage in the roof's drainage system. The roof membrane must, therefore, act as a waterproofing membrane and be able to resist water pressure and water leakage until the drainage system is able to function again. This period may be as long as a few hours or a few days, particularly if the roof drainage system is blocked.

The rate of discharge of water from the roof is not only critical in keeping the roof and the building's interior dry, it is also one of the most important factors in determining the longevity of the roof. There is sufficient long-term data to confirm that — everything else being the same — the durability of a roof increases directly with the slope of the roof. For instance, a built-up roof with 1-1/2 in. per ft slope (generally expressed as 1-1/2:12, or 12.5%) lasts twice as long as one with no slope.[1.2] Water-shedding roofs, in general, outsurvive the water-resisting varieties.

A water-shedding roof is generally referred to as a *steep-slope roof*, or simply a *steep roof*, and is commonly used for residential type (low-rise) structures — individual homes, apartments, motels, etc. It is defined as a roof with a slope of greater than 3:12 (25%) slope. Although 3:12 is the minimum slope for a roof to be classified as a steep roof, some roofing shingles may require a steeper slope, while other shingle varieties may be used on a slope as low as 2:12.

A water-resisting roof is referred to as a *low-slope roof* and is generally used for commercial and industrial buildings. Although a low-slope roof, by definition, has a slope of 3:12 (25%) or less, it is generally a flat roof. However, even a flat roof is mandated by contemporary building codes to have a minimum slope of 1/4:12 (2%).

Despite the greater durability of a steep roof, the market share[1.3] of low-slope roofs is nearly twice as large as that of steep roofs, Figure 1.1. The popularity

Steep roof	Slope > 3:12
Low-slope roof	Slope ≤ 3:12

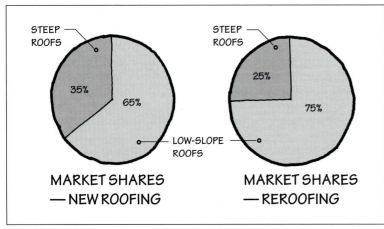

1.1 *Current market shares of low-slope and steep roofs.*

of a low-slope roof is primarily because it provides an easily accessible space for installing HVAC and other equipment. Buildings with flat roofs have their HVAC equipment generally mounted on the roof, while those with steep roofs have the same equipment placed on the ground. A low-slope roof also makes maintenance and reroofing, particularly on high-rise buildings, relatively easy. Imagine reroofing or repairing a steep roof a few hundred feet above the ground!

The design principles and the construction of a steep roof are relatively simple. As shown in Figure 1.2, the basic components of a steep roof are:

- Roof shingles
- Roof underlayment
- Roof deck
- Flashings at roof terminations and around roof penetrations

1.2.1 Roof Shingles

Shingles can be of various types. The more commonly used shingle varieties are:

- Asphalt shingles
- Slate shingles
- Concrete and clay tiles
- Wood shingles
- Metal shingles

Of the shingle types, asphalt shingles (also called composition shingles) have the largest steep roof market share because of their low cost and acceptable life span. They are available in different colors and textures and have a satisfactory aesthetic. With shadow lines added to their surface, some varieties can mimic a wood shingle roof, which is considered to be more attractive than a standard thin, relatively flat, asphalt shingle roof. Another advantage of asphalt shingles is their light weight, which reduces labor and transportation costs and also the cost of the structural components of the roof. Asphalt shingle roofs are covered in detail in Chapter 11.

1.2 STEEP ROOFS

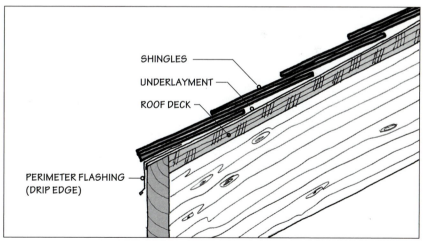

1.2 *Components of a steep roof.*

Most asphalt shingles are reinforced with glass fiber mats although organic fiber reinforced shingles are also available. The use of organic fiber reinforced shingles, which preceded asphalt glass fiber shingles, has decreased substantially since the introduction of glass fiber shingles. Organic shingles are preferred in colder climates because of their greater pliability compared to their fiberglass cousins. The fiberglass mats in fiberglass asphalt shingles render them comparatively more brittle.

More recently, asphalt shingles coated with styrene butadiene styrene (SBS) or attactic polypropylene (APP)[1] have been marketed. They have excellent flexibility, but their performance history is too brief.

Among the contemporary steep roofs, natural slate roofs have the longest history. They have been used in many buildings of historical importance in Europe and the United States. Being a hard and dense natural stone, slate roofs last a long time. They perform quite well when subjected to repetitive freeze-thaw cycles. Well-constructed and detailed, a slate roof can last 75 years or more. Obviously, they are expensive. Imitation slates are also available, but their performance records must be checked before specifying them. Slate roofing is covered in Chapter 12 of the text.

Clay tiles create a handsome roof due to the availability of a large variety of tile shapes. Like slate roofs, clay tile roofs are quite durable. However, it is important to understand that there can be significant differences in the quality of tiles, which can affect the durability of a clay tile roof.

Concrete tile roofs are generally less durable than clay tile roofs. There can also be problems with long-term fading of colors of concrete tiles. However, concrete tile roofs provide good, long-lasting performance. Concrete and clay tile roofs are covered in Chapter 13.

Wood shingles and shakes, once extensively used in the United States due to the country's abundant forest reserves, have a decreasing market share today because of their fire hazard. Although fire-retardant-treated wood shingles are available, their long-term performance history is uncertain.

A large variety of metal shingles are used in contemporary steep roofs. Like wood shingles, their market share is also small. Wood and metal shingle roofs are not covered in this text. However, the design and installation principles of wood shingle roofs is somewhat similar to slate roofs, and those of metal shingle roofs are similar to tile roofs.

---

[1] See Chapter 3 for a discussion of SBS and APP polymers.

1.2.2 Underlayment

In a properly designed and constructed steep roof, rainwater should normally not get under the shingles. However, a water-resistant layer, called *roof underlayment*, is required under the shingles throughout the roof as a second line of protection against water leakage. The requirements for the type of roof underlayment varies with the type of shingles and roof slope.

A valley requires an additional roofing layer, referred to as *valley underlayment*. A valley is more vulnerable to water leakage than the field of the roof because its slope is smaller than the roof itself. The slope of a valley created by two intersecting planes, each with a slope of 4:12, is only 2.8:12 — a 30% reduction in slope. A significant head of water can be present in a long and flat valley. In addition to a smaller slope, the water running through the valley experiences more turbulence because it arrives in the valley from two orthogonal directions.

Another special type of underlayment is called an *ice dam protection membrane*. It is required at the eaves in climates where there is a potential for the formation of ice at an overhanging eave, see Chapter 11. The heat escaping the interior of a building tends to melt the snow in the middle of the roof. The melted snow refreezes as it approaches the overhanging eave, which does not receive any heat from the building's interior. The formation of an ice dam can make water back up under the shingles, Figure 1.3.

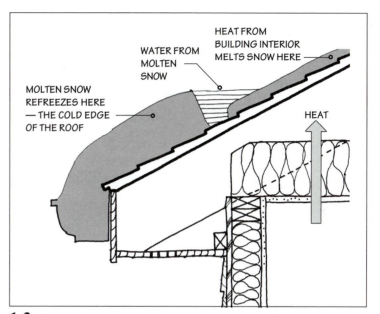

1.3 *Formation of an ice dam on an overhanging eave.*

1.2.3 Roof Deck

The deck, being a structural component of the roof, is its most important element. In a contemporary steep roof, the deck generally consists of plywood or oriented strandboard panels. A spaced deck, consisting of wood lath (typically 1 x 4 or 1 x 6 wood members spaced according to the length of shingles) may be used with some steep roof types, but its use is limited today.

1.2.4 Flashings

Flashings are additional waterproofing components used to create a watertight seal at terminations and transitions in the roof. Critical areas for flashings are valleys, eaves, chimneys, and other penetrations.

Flashings around roof penetrations, such as a chimney or a pipe, are particularly critical. The water is not only interrupted by a penetration but is redirected and compressed on a smaller area of the roof as it flows around a penetration. Consequently, the head pressure around a large penetration is considerably greater than in the field of the roof.

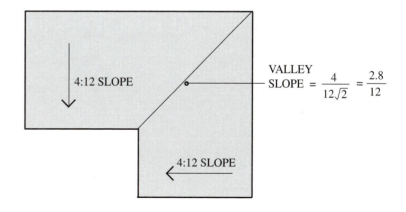

Table 1.1   Mean Service Life Spans of Commonly Used Steep Roofs

Roofing	Mean service life (years)
Natural slate	60
Clay tile	46
Asphalt glass fiber shingles	18
Asphalt organic shingles	18

1.2.5 Selection of a Steep Roof

Aesthetics is an important consideration in the selection of a steep roof because the roof is visible from the street level, which is not the case with a low-slope roof. Initial and long-term costs and the durability of the roof are other important considerations. Table 1.1 gives the mean service life spans of some of the commonly used steep roofs.[1.4]

However, it is important to realize that there are significant variations in life spans within each category shown in the table. For example, S-1 slates may last twice as long as S-3 slates (see Chapter 12), and some clay tile roofs can last 100 years or more. Local experience and expertise should, therefore, be relied on for more reliable data.

Once the type of steep roof has been selected, the method of installation and the associated construction details must conform with the manufacturer's recommendations and the roofing industry standards. Specifying untested details for the sake of so called "architectural creativity" can be a prescription for disaster. The manufacturer's warranty becomes void with details not recommended or approved by the manufacturer.

1.3 LOW-SLOPE ROOFS

The design and construction principles of a low-slope roof are far more intricate than those of a steep roof. The intricacy is not simply due to the more intricate nature of the water-resistive formulation of a low-slope roof. It is also due to an overwhelmingly large variety of alternatives available for the roof deck, roof membrane, and other components of the roof — a variety that is primarily due to the large size of the low-slope roof market. In the United States, there are nearly 100 low-slope roofing system manufacturers.

Another factor contributing to the intricacy is the multiplicity of issues that must be considered in the design and selection of a low-slope roof, such as roof drainage, wind uplift, water vapor transmission, hail impact, foot traffic, resistance to fire, and defense against chemical pollutants. Although these issues are important in the case of a steep roof, they are far more critical in a low-slope roof, because the low-slope roof is commonly used on high-rise and large industrial and commercial buildings.

Wind uplift is far greater on a high-rise roof than on a (low-rise) steep roof. Similarly, fire is far more critical for commercial and industrial roofs than for (residential-type) steep roofs. This is also true for chemical pollutants, which exist primarily on industrial roofs. The drainage design of a low-slope roof is much more involved than that of a steep roof. Because low-slope roofs are commonly used for high-budget commercial and industrial buildings, property insurance companies often insert additional design requirements, which add to roof design complexity.

1.3.1 Components of a Low-Slope Roof

In general, a low-slope roof has the following components, Figure 1.4:

- Roof membrane, including a protective cover or coating if needed
- Insulation
- Roof deck
- Flashings

In some roofs, particularly in high humidity environments, a vapor retarder may also be needed.

1.3.2 Roof Membrane

The roof membrane is the most important component of a roof, because it is the waterproofing layer. Roof membranes are divided under three general categories:

- Built-up roof membrane
- Modified bitumen roof membrane
- Single-ply roof membrane

A *built-up roof membrane* consists of three to five plies of fiberglass (or organic) felts with intervening moppings of bitumen (asphalt or coal tar). Fiberglass felts are more common with asphalt built-up roofs, while organic felts are more common with coal tar built-up roofs. Because both asphalt and coal tar are adversely affected by ultraviolet radiation, they are typically protected by a gravel cover. The gravel cover also increases their fire resistance. Of the two, asphalt built-up roofs are far more common than coal tar built-up roofs. Built-up roofs are covered in Chapter 2.

A *modified bitumen roof membrane* is similar to a built-up roof, because the modified bitumen membrane comprises two to three plies with intervening bitumen. In place of the felts, a modified bitumen roof uses polymer modified sheets that provide greater membrane flexibility. A protective gravel cover or a mineral granule surfaced top sheet is required.

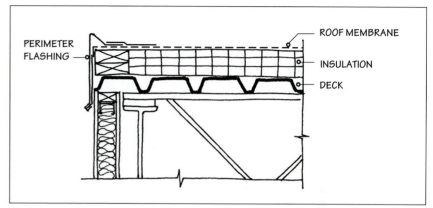

1.4 *Components of a low-slope roof.*

Commonly Used Low-Slope Roof Membranes

- Built-up roofs — asphalt and coal tar

- Modified bitumen roofs — SBS and APP

- Single-ply roofs
  - Ethylene propylene diene monomer (EPDM)
  - Polyvinyl chloride (PVC)
  - Chlorosulfonated polyethylene (CSPE)
  - Thermoplastic olefin (TPO)
  - Polyisobutylene (PIB)

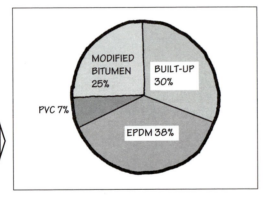

1.5 *Relative market shares of four more commonly used low-slope roof membranes (1999).*

A *single-ply roof membrane* consists of only one sheet of a synthetic polymer (plastic) and does not require any protective cover. Various types of single-ply roof membranes are currently used. Of these, EPDM has nearly 75% of the single-ply market share, followed by PVC. Other single-ply roof membranes have a relatively small market share. Thermoplastic olefine, TPO, is the latest addition to the single-ply family. Thus, its performance record is brief. Figure 1.5 shows the relative market shares of built-up, modified bitumen, EPDM, and PVC roofs.[1.5] Modified bitumen and single-ply roofs are covered in Chapter 3 of the text.

1.3.3 Roof Insulation

One of the major differences between a steep roof and a low-slope roof is the inclusion of insulation in a low-slope roof assembly. In a steep roof, the insulation is in the attic. In a typical low-slope roof, the insulation is sandwiched between the membrane and the deck.[2] Apart from reducing energy costs, insulation provides a suitable substrate for the roof membrane. In a steel roof deck, it also provides the necessary surface flatness.

Since there is occasional foot traffic on a low-slope roof, the insulation must be sufficiently rigid. Various types of low-slope roof insulations are used. Obviously, the insulation must be compatible with the deck as well as the membrane. For instance, phenolic foam insulation, once used extensively, is no longer used as it was discovered to corrode steel decks and steel fasteners. Similarly, some insulation varieties are chemically incompatible with some single-ply membranes, while others are unsuitable under a built-up roof. Low-slope roof insulations are covered in Chapter 4 of this text.

1.3.4 Roof Deck

Unlike a steep roof deck, which is primarily of wood or a wood-based material, a low-slope roof deck may be of steel, wood, cast-in-place concrete, precast concrete, gypsum concrete, or wood fiber-cement deck. Steel deck is commonly used for low-rise industrial buildings, while a concrete deck is popular in commercial structures. Low-slope roof decks are covered in Chapter 5.

---

[2] In a protected membrane roof, the insulation is above the membrane, see Section 4.10.

1.3.5 Roof Flashings

As with a low-slope roof, flashings are an integral part of a low-slope roof. However, flashings are more numerous and also more critical in a low-slope roof. Flashings are required at roof terminations, such as the free edges of a roof, at parapets, and roof expansion joints. Flashings are also required at penetrations, such as around interior roof drains, and around pipe or tubular supports for roof-top equipment.

Important low-slope roof flashing details are covered in Chapter 10. For a more comprehensive coverage, however, the reader is referred to the publications of the National Roofing Contractors Association (NRCA) and Sheet Metal and Air Conditioning Contractors National Association (SMACNA). These publications are suggested for inclusion in every architect's, roofing consultant's, and roofing contractor's library.

> *NRCA Roofing and Waterproofing Manual* by National Roofing Contractors Association, Rosemont Illinois, Volumes 1 and 2.
>
> *Architectural Sheet Metal Manual* by Sheet Metal and Air Conditioning Contractors National Association, SMACNA.

1.3.6 Selection of a Low-Slope Roof System

As stated previously, a low-slope roof design must account for several factors. Additionally, each roof component must not only serve its own function, but should also be compatible with other roof components. For instance, the insulation must not only give the required R-value, it must also provide a rigid substrate against hail and foot traffic. It should also have a long-term chemical compatibility with the deck and the membrane.

Similarly, the roof deck must not only provide the required structural support for the entire assembly and other loads, it must also be dimensionally stable to prevent the overstressing of the insulation and the membrane. It must provide a suitable base for the anchorage of insulation and the membrane and have adequate fire resistance.

With several factors that affect its performance and several components and subcomponents that constitute a low-slope roof, the roof design must take a system's approach. It should consider the interaction between roof components and the effects of external factors such as the external climate, solar radiation, wind, rain, hailstorm, fire, etc. The selection of all components of the system, including fasteners and adhesives, from the same manufacturer is, therefore, extremely important in the case of a low-slope roof.

Because a typical building will go through several cycles of reroofing, the durability of the roofing system should be an important consideration in its selection. Unfortunately, most of the published information on roof systems' performance is highly subjective, and roof performance varies significantly from region to region.

Table 1.2 Mean Life Spans of Commonly Used Low-Slope Roofs

Roofing	Mean service life (years)
Built-up roof — coal tar and organic felts	23
Built-up roof — asphalt and fiberglass felts	17
Built-up roof — asphalt and organic felts	15
Modified bitumen roof — SBS	16
Modified bitumen roof — APP	14
EPDM roof	14
PVC roof	14
CSPE roof	13
Metal panel roof	25

Further, there are wide variations in the performance of roof systems within the same category. For instance, a gravel-covered, 4-ply, fiberglass, built-up roof will far outlast a 3-ply, smooth surfaced, built-up roof. Similarly, a reinforced, fully-adhered, 60-mil-thick, EPDM roof will outperform a 45-mil, unreinforced, mechanically attached, EPDM roof. As another example, a standing seam copper roof may last more than 100 years in some areas, whereas a 26-gauge, corrugated galvanized steel roof may last less than 20 years in some climates.

As a rough guide, Table 1.2 gives the approximate mean service life spans of some of the important low-slope roof systems.[1.6] The manufacturer's warranty and on-site quality control should also be given due consideration.

1.4 OTHER ROOF TYPES

In addition to the roof types described earlier there are two other types that are used. These are:

- Sprayed-in-place polyurethane foam (SPF) roof
- Metal panel roof

In an SPF roof, liquid polyurethane foam is sprayed on the roof deck, which sets and hardens fairly quickly. Polyurethane foam is chemically similar to polyisocyanurate. Thus, it provides a jointless layer of insulation unlike that provided by the rigid board insulation in other low-slope roofs. The foam adheres to the deck and hence does not require any fasteners. A protective membrane coating is then applied to the foam, since the foam deteriorates under exposure to sunlight and other weathering elements. Because of its extremely small market share, SPF roof is not discussed in this text. Readers requiring detailed coverage of this subject are referred to other sources.[1.7,1.8]

Because of the short life spans of conventional low-slope roofs, metal panel roofs are becoming increasingly common. Metal panel roofs are more durable, but their initial cost is also higher. They may be used as low-slope or steep roofs, although they function better on steep slopes (slope greater than 3:12). A metal panel roof typically consists of 10- to 24-in.-wide panels with ribs or standing seams that are snapped together. Metal panel roofs are covered in Chapter 14.

1.5 ROOF DESIGN PROCESS

The roof design process is a multifaceted process. It includes selecting the roof system, i.e., the roof membrane, roof cover (if any), type of insulation, and deck. Apart from the long-term economics of the system, the selection process is a function of the code-mandated fire rating, wind uplift, and insulation requirements for the roof. The owner may also specify requirements based either on property insurance and/or roof warranty constraints. Roof warranties are discussed in Chapter 15.

Once the system has been selected, the roof's drainage design is worked out, and the flashing details are completed. The architect may either perform all of the functions in the above design process in-house or seek the help of a roofing consultant. For a large and complex building, it is usual for the architect to consult a roofing consultant. Roofing consultancy is a fast-developing specialty, which attracts both architects and engineers.

Even when a roofing consultant is involved, it is incumbent on the architect to coordinate and manage the entire design process. Various other functionaries may also be needed, such as a structural engineer, HVAC engineer, plumbing engineer, and specification writer.

REFERENCES

1.1   Herbert, R. D. *Roofing — Design, Criteria, Options, Selection* (Kingston, MA: R. S. Means and Company, 1989), p. 3.

1.2   Cash, C. G. "Selecting the Appropriate Roofing System," *Construction Specifier* (January 2000), p. 25.

1.3   Kane, K. "Another Strong Year for the Industry," *Professional Roofing* (April 1999), p. 14.

1.4   Cash, C. G. "Selecting the Appropriate Roofing System," p. 26.

1.5   Kane, K. "Another Strong Year for the Industry," p. 15.

1.6   Cash, C. G. "Selecting the Appropriate Roofing System," p. 26.

1.7   Griffin, C. W., and Fricklas, R. *Manual of Low-slope Roof Systems* (New York: McGraw Hill, 1995), pp. 405-432.

1.8   National Roofing Contractors Association. *NRCA Roofing and Waterproofing Manual* (Rosemont, IL: 1996), pp. 1425-1624.

2

BUILT-UP ROOF MEMBRANE

On a low-slope roof, the uppermost layer is the roof membrane.[1] It is this layer that functions as the waterproofing layer and is most directly subjected to the weathering elements. As stated in Chapter 1, the most commonly used roof membranes are:

- Built-up roof membrane

- Modified bitumen roof membrane

- Single-ply roof membrane

A built-up roof membrane consists of several individual layers laminated into one membrane. A single-ply membrane consists of a single layer. A modified bitumen membrane is between a built-up and a single-ply membrane and usually consists of two to three layers. A built-up roof is generally the most labor-intensive roof, followed by the modified bitumen roof and the single-ply roof. This chapter deals with built-up roof membranes; modified and single-ply membranes are covered in Chapter 3.

---

[1] In an inverted roof, the roof membrane is not the uppermost layer, see Section 4.10 in Chapter 4.

2.1 ANATOMY OF A BUILT-UP ROOF MEMBRANE

A built-up roof membrane consists of several layers of roofing felts adhered together by bitumen (asphalt or coal tar). In a typical built-up roof, a felt is laid over a mopping of bitumen, followed by a second mopping of bitumen, and then the second felt, and so on. Thus, a number of felt layers (called plies), separated by interply moppings of bitumen, are necessary to build a built-up roof membrane — hence, the name "built-up" roof.

A built-up roof normally consists of three to five plies. The greater the number of plies, the thicker and, hence, stronger and more durable the membrane. The last felt is typically covered with a surfacing material to protect the membrane from the effects of weather and external fire.

The most common surfacing material is gravel laid over a flood coat of bitumen. Because the quantity of bitumen for the flood coat is much greater than that required for interply mopping, it is poured over the roof, while the interply bitumen is simply mopped on. Figures 2.1 to 2.4 show a few stages in the laying of a typical built-up roof.

2.1(a) *With a bucket full of hot bitumen and a mop, a roofer begins to lay a built-up roof. Photo by Madan Mehta.*

BITUMEN DISPENSER

2.1(b) *Although the bitumen can be applied with mops, it is more convenient to use bitumen dispensers on large roofs. Photo by Madan Mehta.*

2.2(a) *The unrolling of felt over bitumen is followed by pressing the felt down with a squeegee. Photo by Madan Mehta.*

2.2(b) *Once all the felts have been laid, the roof is ready to receive the flood coat of bitumen and gravel surfacing. Photo by Madan Mehta.*

2.3(a) *Pouring of bitumen for the flood coat. Photo by Madan Mehta.*

2.3(b) *Covering the flood coat with gravel. Photo by Madan Mehta.*

2.4(a) *Although the bitumen for a flood coat can be poured with buckets, it is usually poured on large roofs using a bitumen dispenser as shown here. Photo by Madan Mehta.*

2.4(b) *On large roofs, it is more convenient to use gravel spreaders instead of shovels, see Figure 2.3(b). Photo by Madan Mehta.*

2.4(c) *Usually, the bitumen dispenser and aggregate spreader are used in tandem. Photo by Madan Mehta.*

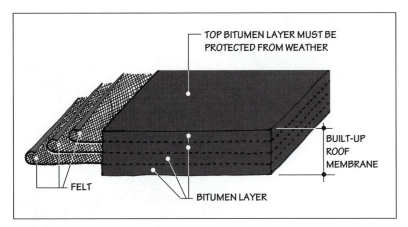

2.5 *The felts provide tensile strength to a built-up roof membrane, in which the bitumen is the waterproofing agent. The greater the number of felts, the stronger the roof membrane.*

In the alternate layers of felts and bitumen in a built-up roof, the bitumen is the waterproofing material. However, bitumen alone cannot be used, because it is a thermoplastic material. It becomes soft at high temperatures and begins to flow. At low temperatures, it becomes hard and brittle, and cracks. Thus, bitumen does not have the requisite tensile strength to withstand stresses imposed by the changes in temperature, deck movement, foot traffic, hail storm, etc.

The felts work as reinforcing material, giving the required tensile strength to a built-up roof membrane, Figure 2.5. Thus, the function of felts in a built-up roof membrane is similar to that of steel bars in a reinforced concrete member.

The felt also stabilizes the bitumen against flow, since the interwoven felt fibers form mini-receptacles within which the bitumen is held, preventing its flow, Figure 2.6. A heavy mopping of bitumen without the felt simply cracks in cold weather due to the lack of tensile strength and flows like a thick paste during hot weather, due to the lack of containment. In other words, the felts allow for a more significant build-up of bitumen, which increases the weatherproofing and waterproofing of the membrane.

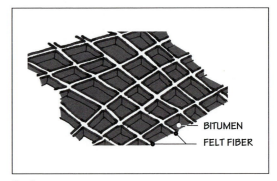

2.6 *Interwoven felt fibers form miniature containers to hold the bitumen, preventing its flow.*

A felt consists of fibers (or strands) pressed into a sheet. It may be either an *organic felt* or an *inorganic felt*, depending on whether the fibers are of organic or inorganic type. The organic felts are made from paper or wood fibers, or a combination of both. Inorganic felts are made from glass fibers. Asbestos fibers were once used but have been discontinued due to health concerns.

The manufacturing process for both organic and fiberglass felts is similar to paper making, in that a mass of fibers are pressed under rollers to give a thin, flat sheet. In fact, an untreated organic felt (without the bitumen treatment) is virtually indistinguishable from a thick hand-made paper. An untreated fiberglass felt looks like a woven mat. The weave in a fiberglass felt is so sparse that light and air can easily pass through it. By comparison, the organic felt is thick, nonporous, and opaque to light, Figure 2.7.

After the rolling process, the felts are treated with bitumen. Since both coal tar and asphalt are black in color, a treated felt is black in color. Treated felt is used in a built-up roof. Therefore, the term "felt" in our discussion generally implies a bitumen-treated felt. The treatment consists of simply covering the felt with bitumen.

There is a fine distinction between how the bitumen is held in a treated organic or fiberglass felt. An organic felt soaks the bitumen like a blotting paper. Therefore, an organic felt is considered to be *saturated* with bitumen. A fiberglass felt, on the other hand, is *impregnated* with bitumen.

The impregnation of bitumen in a fiberglass felt makes it more opaque, but despite the treatment, a fiberglass felt is highly porous. The treated organic felt is nonporous and, hence, water-resistant, Figure 2.8. Only an organic felt is specified as an underlayment for roof shingles and tiles or as a water-resistant layer over wall sheathing. Because of its porosity, a fiberglass felt cannot be used in such applications. However, as we shall see later, the porosity of fiberglass felts is an advantage in built-up roof applications.

2.2 BUILT-UP ROOF FELTS

2.7 *The partial visibility of the person holding an untreated fiberglass felt indicates its sparse weave. By comparison, an organic felt is opaque and nonporous.*

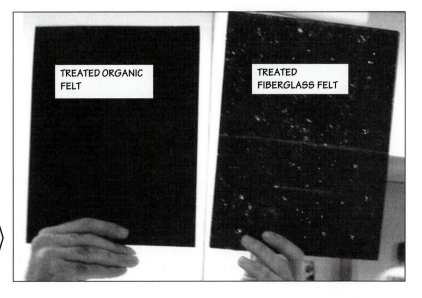

UNTREATED FIBERGLASS FELT · UNTREATED ORGANIC FELT

TREATED ORGANIC FELT · TREATED FIBERGLASS FELT

2.8 *Although less so than an untreated fiberglass felt, a treated fiberglass felt is fairly porous. A treated organic felt is nonporous and, hence, useful as a water-resistant underlayment. Photo by Madan Mehta.*

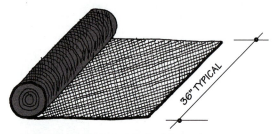

WIDTH OF A TYPICAL BUILT-UP ROOF FELT

Built-up roofing felts are typically manufactured in 36-in.-wide rolls, although metric (1-meter-wide) felts are also available from a few manufacturers. Since the bitumen is a highly tacky substance, the felts are surfaced with fine mineral sand or other release agent to prevent their adhesion inside the roll.

2.2.1 Fiberglass Felts versus Organic Felts

Fiberglass felts are, in general, stronger than organic felts. They are also equally strong in both the machine direction (the direction in which the rollers move) and the cross direction. The strength of an organic felt in the cross direction is only half its strength in the machine direction. That is why fiberglass felts are commonly used in built-up roofs. In fact, more than 90% of built-up roof felts in use today are fiberglass felts.

In addition to strength, porosity is another positive attribute of fiberglass felts. Since the asphalt at the time of application is at a high temperature (nearly 400ºF), any air trapped during mopping expands and forms blisters under the felt, if not allowed to escape.

If there is any moisture in the substrate, it turns into steam and forms blisters if unable to escape. Blisters obviously weaken the roof membrane, since they represent areas where the roof is unattached to the substrate. The pressure exerted on the membrane by water vapor and air inside the blister can exceed the tensile strength of the membrane, causing its rupture. The inherent porosity of fiberglass felt allows the escape of air and vapor.

Another reason not to use the organic felts is their propensity to absorb water. In extremely humid climates, organic felts, even during storage, can absorb moisture from the air. A humid felt obviously leads to blistering of the membrane. Organic felts, unlike fiberglass felts, are combustible — another reason against their use.

2.2.2 Types of Organic Felts

With several points disfavoring the organic felts, is there any use for them?

- *Asphalt-treated organic felts*: Asphalt-treated organic felts have limited applications in built-up roofs, but are used more as water-resistant underlayments for shingle or tile roofs and as water-resistant covers over walls. They are designated by a number, e.g., No. 15 or No. 30 felt. No. 15 felt implies that it weighs nearly 15 lb to cover one *roof square* — 100 sq ft. No. 30 asphalt saturated felt weighs nearly 30 lb per square.[2]

---

[2] As per the current ASTM standard D 226-97(a) "Standard Specifications for Asphalt-saturated Organic Felts Used in Roofing and Waterproofing," No. 15 asphalt saturated organic felt weighs 11.5 lb per 100 ft^2, not 15 lb. However, the designation No. 15 still continues — perhaps as a legacy of an earlier standard. Similarly, No. 30 asphalt saturated organic felt weighs 26 lb per 100 ft^2; No. 15 tar-saturated felt weighs 13 lb per 100 ft^2. Note that in roofing literature, a coverage of 100 ft^2 of roof is referred to as *roof square*, or simply a *square* (see the boxed section "Roof Square" later in this chapter).

• *Coal tar-treated organic felts*: Tar-treated organic felts are commonly used in tar built-up roofs. They are of one type only — No. 15. When used in built-up roofing, organic felts should preferably be of the perforated type. The perforations are typically 1/4 in. in diameter, spaced uniformly throughout the felt, with a minimum perforated area of 0.1%.

2.2.3 Types of Fiberglass Felts

• *Asphalt-treated fiberglass felts*: Asphalt-treated fiberglass felts are classified as Type III, IV, and VI, having a tensile (or tear) strength of 22 lb/in., 44 lb/in., and 60 lb/in. respectively, Figure 2.9. Types IV and VI are more commonly specified.

Type VI, the strongest and the most recently introduced felt, is recommended where the membrane is subjected to a high tensile stress. These stresses may be caused by a high diurnal or annual temperature differential that occurs in many regions, or by a relatively flexible deck, or by excessive impact on roof due to hailstorm and/or foot traffic.

In addition to using type VI felt, a thicker (4- to 5-ply) built-up roof membrane is recommended for the above situations, since a thicker membrane is stronger. Long-term roofing warranties by roofing manufacturers are usually contingent on the use of type VI felts. However, type IV felt is slightly easier to work with.

• *Coal tar-treated fiberglass felts*: Although somewhat used, tar-treated fiberglass felts are not recommended as built-up roof felts by some manufacturers. Due to the porosity of fiberglass felts and the cold flow property of tar, the tar filters through the felts so that the felts tend to sink to the bottom of the membrane, see Section 2.7.1. This separates the felts from the bitumen.

Tar-felt separation is exaggerated by the weight of gravel in gravel-covered roofs. The problem is more serious in warm climates in which the tar softens sufficiently on a hot afternoon. Lightweight aggregate surfacing, such as slag, may reduce the severity of the problem.[3]

2.9 *Tensile (or tear) strengths of types III, IV, and VI asphalt-treated fiberglass felts.*

---

[3] Mineral granule surfacing, although a light surfacing, is not acceptable. See Section 2.8.1 for additional details on slag surfacing.

Type VI fiberglass felt by one manufacturer. Photo by Madan Mehta.

TEAR STRENGTH 22 LB/IN.
TYPE III

TEAR STRENGTH 44 LB/IN.
TYPE IV

TEAR STRENGTH 60 LB/IN.
TYPE VI

2.3 LAYOUT OF BUILT-UP ROOF FELTS

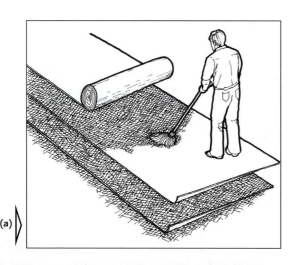

2.10 *(a) Successive built-up roof felts are generally laid in a shingle fashion, with the upper felt overlapping the lower felt by a constant dimension. (b) Installation of felts in shingled pattern. Photo courtesy of GAF Building Materials Corporation, Wayne, New Jersey.*

In a built-up roof, the felts are laid in shingle fashion,[4] the upper felt overlaps the lower felt by a constant dimension, Figure 2.10. In a 3-ply roof membrane, there must be at least 3 felts under any roof point. Similarly, a 4-ply roof must have 4 felts at every point.

The lap at the exposed end of a felt with respect to the lowest felt at that end, referred to as the *head lap*, is 2 in. (50 mm) — the industry standard, Figure 2.11. Under the head lap, there is one additional felt. Thus, there are 4 felts under a head lap in a 3-ply membrane. The dimension EXP is called the *exposure* of the felt. EXP is related to the number of plies by the following relationship:

$$\text{EXP} = \frac{\text{Felt width - Head lap}}{\text{Number of BUR plies}}$$

Thus, in a 2-ply membrane, EXP = 17 in. (432 mm), in a 3-ply roof, EXP = 11-1/3 in. (288 mm), and so on. Built-up roof felts are manufactured with 2-, 3- and 4-ply lines marked on them, as shown in Figure 2.12, to help roofers lay the felts correctly.

To provide the necessary number of felts at the starting edge of the roof (usually the roof's lowest edge), the first few felts are not the full width of 36 in. The width of the starter felts is obtained simply by dividing the full width by the number of built-up roof plies. Thus, in a 4-ply membrane, there are three partial-width felts at the starting edge — 9 in., 18 in., and 27 in. wide, Figure 2.13(a). In a 3-ply membrane, there are two partial width felts — 12 in. and 24 in. wide, Figure 2.13(b). In a 2-ply built-up roof membrane (not usually specified), there is only one partial width felt — 18 in. wide.

2.3.1 Advantages of Shingling

Shingling of felts results in completed sections of the roof at the end of each day. Thus, the membrane remains protected from interply moisture penetration during interruptions in roofing operations. If the felts were laid layer by layer on the entire roof, there is a possibility of moisture being trapped between felt layers, either from rain or overnight condensation.

---

[4] Where a base sheet is used as the first felt layer, such as on a nailable deck, that sheet is not shingled, but laid with a 2-in. overlap at the sides, see Figures 3.2 and 3.4 in Chapter 3.

Another advantage of shingling is that it provides better adhesion of plies compared to the phased application. This is due to a slower cooling of bitumen in a shingled membrane. In a shingled membrane, there are three to four layers of bitumen applied within a short time span. In a phased application, the previous layer of bitumen has virtually cooled off to the ambient temperature when the subsequent layer is applied.

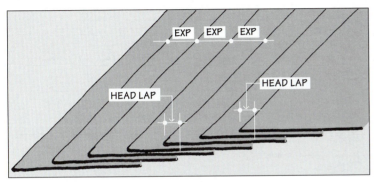

2.11 *Shingling of felts in a built-up roof, with terms "exposure" and "head lap" defined. The industry standard for head lap is 2 in.*

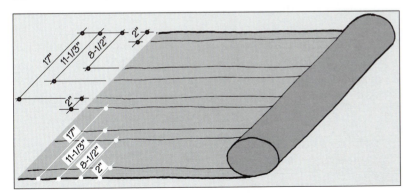

2.12 *Factory-applied lines on a built-up roof felt.*

2.13 *Partial width felts at the starting edge of (a) 4-ply membrane, and (b) 3-ply membrane.*

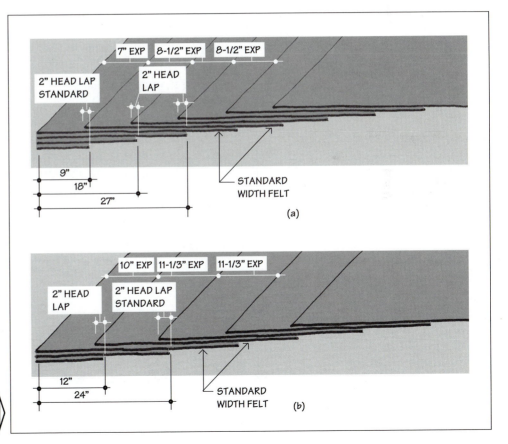

ROOF SQUARE

As stated previously, built-up roofing felts are generally made in 3-ft-wide rolls . Thus, a 36-ft-long roll has an area of 108 sq ft. However, it is generally assumed to cover a roof area of 100 sq ft. This assumption is based on the way the felts are laid under roof shingles or tiles. The felt underlayment provides a second line of defense against water penetration; the first line of defense are the shingles or tiles.

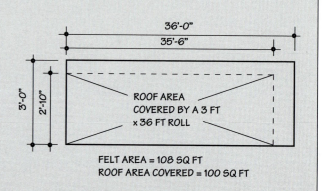

FELT AREA = 108 SQ FT
ROOF AREA COVERED = 100 SQ FT

The underlayment is generally laid with 2-in. laps at sides and 4-in. laps at the ends, so that one roll covers a roof area of 2 ft-10 in. by 35 ft - 8 in., which is equal to 101 sq ft, or approximately 100 sq ft. In the roofing industry, 108 sq ft is referred to as the *factory square* and the 100 sq ft as the *roof square*, or simply the *square*.

The fact that 108 sq ft of felt covers a 100-sq-ft roof area not only applies to felt underlayments, but also to felts laid in shingle fashion, as in a built-up roof. The figure below shows the shingling pattern of a 3-ply built-up roof. Observe that under a felt exposure of 11-1/3 in., there are three felts plus 1 in. of felt at the top and 1 in. of felt at the bottom of a head lap .

In other words, an 11-1/3-in.-wide roof area in a 3-ply roof requires (3 x 11-1/3 + 1 + 1), i.e., 36-in.-wide felt. With end laps of 4 in. in each felt, a 3-ft x 36-ft roll would cover a roof area of 11-1/3 in. x 35 ft 8 in., i.e., a roof area of 33.7 sq ft. Thus, three such rolls (an area of 324 sq ft) would be required to cover nearly 100 sq ft of roof. Similarly, in a 4-ply built-up roof, 432 sq ft of felt area is required to cover a roof area of 100 sq ft.

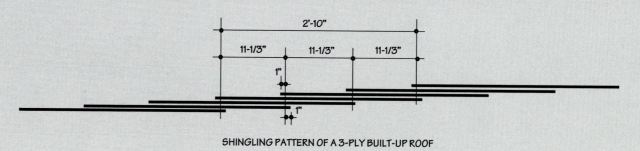

SHINGLING PATTERN OF A 3-PLY BUILT-UP ROOF

Treated felts described so far are called *ply felts*. Ply felts, placed alternately between bitumen moppings, make up a built-up roof membrane. In addition to ply felts, other types of felts, as described below, may be needed in a built-up roof.

2.4.1 Base Sheet

The first ply in some built-up roof membranes must be heavier than the normal ply felts. This is usually the case when the first ply must be nailed[5] to the deck, in which case it is referred to as the *base sheet*. The basic purpose of a base sheet is to provide a separation between the deck and the built-up roof.

For instance, built-up roof felts are not generally mopped directly on a lightweight insulating concrete fill, because of the moisture present in lightweight insulating concrete. In such cases, a nailed base sheet over the insulating concrete provides a dry moppable surface. Once the base sheet has been nailed, it is mopped with bitumen, which is then covered with a ply felt, then the bitumen mopping, and so on — as in a conventional built-up roof membrane, Figure 2.14.

A nailed base sheet is also used as a separation between the wood (or plywood) deck and the built-up roof membrane, where insulation is not available to separate the built-up roof membrane from the deck, see Section 5.4 in Chapter 5. This situation usually exists where the roof is either not insulated or the insulation is below the deck.

2.4 USE CLASSIFICATION OF BUILT-UP ROOF FELTS

Rolls of felt should be stored upright, not flat, as shown here. Photo by Madan Mehta.

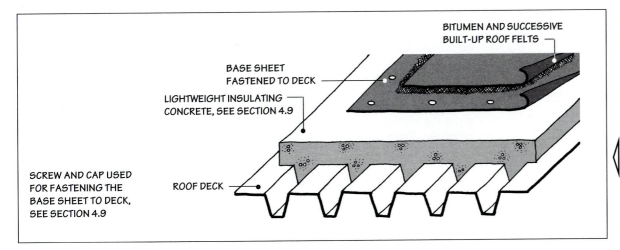

BITUMEN AND SUCCESSIVE
BUILT-UP ROOF FELTS

BASE SHEET
FASTENED TO DECK

LIGHTWEIGHT INSULATING
CONCRETE, SEE SECTION 4.9

SCREW AND CAP USED
FOR FASTENING THE
BASE SHEET TO DECK,
SEE SECTION 4.9

ROOF DECK

2.14 *The use of a base sheet below a built-up roof membrane. Note that the base sheet is not shingled with the rest of the roofing felts, but laid with 2-in. laps at the sides and 4-in. laps at the ends, see Figures 3.2 and 3.4 in Chapter 3.*

---

[5] Nails may be large head nails, but they are more commonly nails or screws with separate metal or plastic caps.

A base sheet must be thick enough to resist puncturing by nail caps. Thus, a base sheet is similar to a ply felt, except that it is coated with bitumen in addition to being saturated or impregnated with bitumen. The most commonly used based sheet is an asphalt coated and impregnated fiberglass felt. It comes in two types — types I and II; the latter is superior. Coated fiberglass felts are more impervious to water than the ply felts.

Asphalt-coated organic felts are suggested for use as base sheets by some roofing material manufacturers. However, they suffer from the same disadvantages as the organic ply felts.

2.4.2 Ventilation Sheet

A ventilation sheet is a special-purpose base sheet. It is a heavy-gauge felt, which is coated with bitumen and covered with granules on its underside. The roughness of the granulated surface lifts the membrane above the substrate, providing a continuous ventilation surface between the deck and the base sheet. In addition, the granule-covered surface is embossed with corrugations to provide continuous two-way ventilation channels, Figure 2.15.

A ventilation sheet is specified as a base sheet over substrates that have a potential of retaining moisture, such as lightweight insulating fill poured over an unslotted metal deck or a reinforced concrete roof slab. If a ventilation base sheet is not used in such a case, the moisture in the substrate will turn into water vapor under the effect of the sun's heat, creating large blisters and delaminating the roof membrane from the substrate.

The granules in the ventilation base sheet also protect the fiberglass scrim in the sheet from the alkalinity in the concrete deck. The alkalinity in portland cement degrades fiberglass. There are some foil-faced base sheets, which achieve the same protective effect.

A ventilation sheet is usually nailed to the substrate in the same way as a conventional base sheet. Spot mopping may be used in place of nailing, but it is important to verify that the system meets the wind uplift criterion, since spot mopping reduces the attachment. When a ventilation sheet is used over a damp substrate, there must be edge and field ventilation on the roof, see Section 10.7 in Chapter 10.

2.4.3 Cap Sheet

In some situations, a mineral granule covered sheet is used as the last roof ply, replacing the gravel-covered flood coat. Being the last sheet on the roof, it is referred to as the *cap sheet*. A cap sheet is similar to a base sheet, in that it is coated with bitumen, but the coating is generally heavier and covered with small

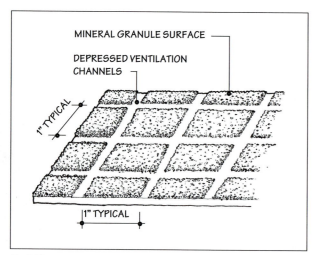

MINERAL GRANULE SURFACE

DEPRESSED VENTILATION CHANNELS

1" TYPICAL

1" TYPICAL

2.15 *Ventilation sheet (shown upside down).*

mineral granules on the top surface to provide protection from the weather. The other surface of the sheet is lightly dusted with fine sand to prevent adhesion in the roll.

Metal foil (aluminum, stainless steel, or copper) lamination bonded to bitumen in place of mineral granules is also used in a cap sheet. Smooth-surfaced cap sheets are also available. A modified bitumen cap sheet is also used over a built-up roof, but such a roof is generally referred to as a modified bitumen roof, see Section 2.8.3 and Chapter 3.

2.5 BITUMEN

As stated previously, two types of bitumen — *asphalt* and *coal tar* — are used in built-up roofing. Although both materials have the same appearance (both are black in color and highly viscous) and both are hydrocarbons, they are chemically different. Coal tar has a ring-like molecular structure, while the molecular structure of asphalt is chain-like, Figure 2.16.

It is nature's law that a material with a ring-like structure weathers more slowly (and thus is more durable) than the one with a chain-like structure. Thus, everything else being the same, a coal tar built-up roof is somewhat more durable than an asphalt built-up roof.[6]

Although both asphalt and tar are highly resistant to water, coal tar is slightly more so. Coal tar built-up roof manufacturers claim their roofs withstand ponded water, a claim not advanced by any other roofing membrane manufacturer.

However, asphalt built-up roofs are far more commonly specified than coal tar built-up roofs, although the former appeared on the scene much later. The primary reason is the significantly lower health risk to roofers from the use of asphalt than tar, see Section 2.7. The other benefits of asphalt are its greater availability and lower cost, compared to tar.

Yet another reason favoring the use of asphalt is tar's greater brittleness at low temperatures, since tar goes into the glass transition phase (solid brittle state) between 40 and 50°F (4.5 to 10°C). The corresponding temperature for (type III) asphalt is nearly 10°F (-12°C).

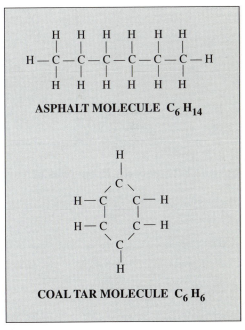

2.16 *Molecular structures of asphalt and coal tar.*

---

[6] Some roofing experts believe that the actual durability differences between tar and asphalt built-up roofs is marginal.

2.6 ROOFING ASPHALT

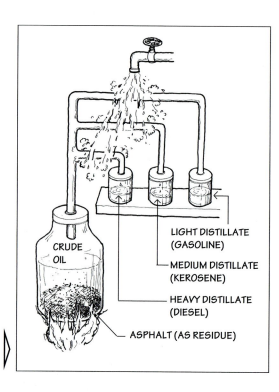

2.17 *Distillation of crude oil.*

Asphalt is the waste product (residue) obtained from the distillation of crude oil at petroleum refineries. In the distillation process, gasoline, kerosene, and diesel are given off in gaseous forms, which are condensed into liquid for final use. The residue in the distillation process is the asphalt, Figure 2.17. This asphalt, called the *straight-run asphalt*, is not fit to be used as roofing asphalt.

Straight-run asphalt is further refined by blowing hot air through it, yielding a product called *blown asphalt*. Blown asphalt is less susceptible to temperature fluctuations and is a harder, less sticky material. Blown asphalt is used in roofing. Blown asphalt is, however, not used in road applications.

2.6.1 Types of Roofing Asphalt

ASTM standard D 312 divides roofing asphalts into four types: type I — *dead level asphalt*, type II — *flat asphalt*, type III — *steep asphalt*, and type IV — *special steep asphalt*. The most important property that distinguishes one type from the other is the *softening point temperature* (SPT) of asphalt.

SPT is the temperature at which asphalt begins to flow. It is directly related to the weathering characteristics of asphalt. The lower the SPT, the more durable the asphalt, and the more easily the asphalt will heal any cracks caused by expansion or contraction in roof membrane. Figure 2.18 gives the SPT ranges of the four asphalt types.

Two other important properties of asphalt are its equiviscous temperature (EVT) and flash point (FP). EVT is defined as the temperature at which asphalt attains optimum viscosity for wetting the deck and fusing the plies together. The application temperature at the mopping surface must be equal to EVT plus/minus 25°F.

This, however, is not the temperature of the asphalt in the kettle, which must be a little higher than EVT to allow for the cooling of the asphalt that occurs during its transportation from the kettle to the point of application. As a guide to roofers, asphalt manufacturers usually provide the EVT of their product, the approximate values of which are given in Table 2.1.

FP is the temperature at which the gases given off during the heating of asphalt will ignite in the presence of an open flame. The heating of asphalt should be kept well below FP temperature, a value provided by the manufacturer.

Heating asphalt beyond the recommended maximum temperature not only involves fire hazard, but also adversely affects the asphalt's properties. For instance, it reduces the thickness of the mopped-on asphalt film, reducing felt adhesion.

Table 2.1 Important Properties of Various Asphalt Types

Type of asphalt	SPT (°F)	EVT or recommended application temperature (°F)	
		Mop applied	Mechanical spreader
Dead level (I)	135 - 150	350 ± 25	375 ± 25
Flat (II)	158 - 176	400 ± 25	425 ± 25
Steep (III)	185 - 205	425 ± 25	450 ± 25
Special steep (IV)	210 - 225	450 ± 25	475 ± 25

Source: Reference 2.1.

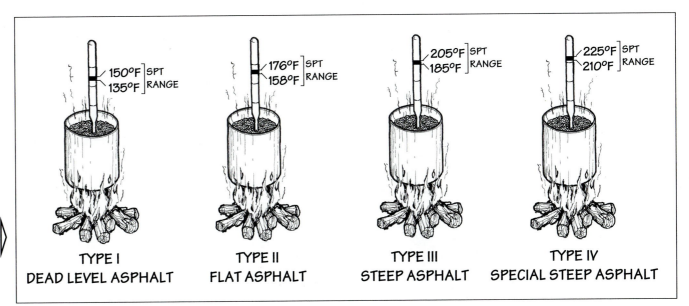

2.18 *Softening point temperature (SPT) ranges of various types of roofing asphalt. SPT is measured by ring-and-ball method as per ASTM Standard D 36-95.*

2.6.2 Type of Asphalt Required

Historically when organic felts were in use, type I (dead level) asphalt was recommended for low slopes — less than 0.5:12 (4%); type II (flat) asphalt for slopes less than 1.5:12 (12%); type III (steep slope) asphalt for slopes less than 3:12 (25%); and type IV (special steep) asphalt for slopes less than 6:12 (50%).

With the introduction of fiberglass felts, which have a greater slippage problem than organic felts, the most commonly used asphalt these days is one with a sufficiently high SPT — type III. Thus, type III asphalt is used as an interply adhesive and as an adhesive to bond insulation to deck or to bond two layers of insulation together. Because of its lower viscosity, type III (and also type IV) can be used to adhere bituminous flashings on vertical surfaces.

For these reasons, type III is often referred to as the general purpose roofing asphalt. In fact, nearly 85% of all asphalt used in roofing is type III asphalt.[2.2] It is easier to use (better workability) and can be heated to a higher temperature than types I and II. The higher temperature of mopped-on asphalt helps melt the asphalt already in the felts, providing better fusion between the felts.

Type IV asphalt performs better than type III, but its lower durability is a deterrent. However, type IV asphalt is sometimes used in hot climates in lieu of

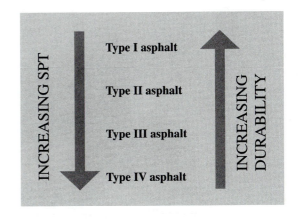

2.19 *Asphalt kegs at a construction site. Photo by Madan Mehta.*

type III. Type IV is also used with SBS-modified bitumen felts in which a higher asphalt temperature is an advantage, see Section 3.2 in Chapter 3. Both types III and IV asphalts do not bleed, unlike asphalt types I and II, and coal tar, which requires a felt envelope, see Section 10.5.2 in Chapter 10.

Type III asphalt is also specified for the flood coat for roofs in warm climates. However, in colder climates (and roof slope permitting), type I or type II asphalt should be considered for the flood coat due to its better weathering characteristics. A rough guideline for asphalt selection is given in Table 2.2.

Type III and IV asphalts are typically supplied at job sites in solid paper-wrapped kegs, Figure 2.19. Types I and II asphalts and coal tar are supplied in metal containers because of their lower SPT. The asphalt is generally melted in a roofing kettle on the ground and pumped up to the roof, Figure 2.20. Mops and buckets are used for mopping operations on the roof.

2.6.3 Amount of Asphalt Required

Approximately 25 lb of asphalt per roof square is recommended for interply moppings and 60 lb per roof square for the flood coat. The flood coat is poured on the roof, not mopped on, to provide the large asphalt quantity required for the flood coat.

Table 2.2 Recommended Asphalt Types for Various Conditions

Use condition	Recommended asphalt type
Interply moppings	Type III (25 lb/square)
Attaching two insulation layers	Type III (30 lb/square)
Flood coat	Type I to type IV (60 lb/square) depending on the climate and slope of roof deck, as follows: Type I: 0 - 1/4 in./ft (2%) Type II: 1/4 in./ft - 1 in./ft (2% - 8%) Type III: 1/4 in./ft - 3 in./ft (2% - 25%) Type IV: 1/4 in./ft - 6 in./ft (2% - 50%)

PIPE USED TO PUMP BITUMEN TO ROOF

KETTLE AND PUMP

2.20 *Bitumen heating kettle and pumping equipment. Photo by Madan Mehta.*

Coal tar (also called *tar* or *pitch*) is obtained from the distillation of coal. Although the distillate in this process is coal tar, the residue is coke, Figure 2.21. Coke is used in steel manufacturing industry, and coal tar is used in roofing, in the treatment of wood (as creosote), and in roads. The use of tar in roads is, however, prevalent only in countries with large coal deposits, e.g., Britain.

Coal tar is more expensive, and its fumes are more hazardous to roofers than asphalt. Irritation of eyes and nostrils are some of the common adverse effects resulting from the inhalation of tar fumes. Although tar's carcinogenic effect has not been fully established, tar containers carry warning labels to this effect. Roofers must take special precautions against tar fume inhalation.

2.7.1 Types of Coal Tar

Although coal tar is available in three types — types I, II, and III — types I and III are the roofing tars; type II is used in waterproofing applications. Type III, referred to as the *lower fuming tar*, was the more commonly used roofing tar until recently. It was specially developed with a lower fume hazard to replace Type I tar, referred to as *old-time pitch*.

However, lately there have been been numerous performance-related questions with respect to type III. Therefore, the most commonly used tar today is type I. Its SPT is between 126 to 140°F — a temperature range that is realized or exceeded on roofs in warm climates. Important data for type I tar is given in Table 2.3.

Type I coal tar has a lower SPT than type I roofing asphalt and, hence, is more self-healing. The self-healing property of coal tar roof is not simply the consequence of its lower SPT, but also because of its *cold flow* property. Coal tar starts to move (flow) at around 60°F — a temperature much lower than its SPT.

Because of its lower SPT and cold flow property, tar flow is a major problem, particularly in warm climates. In general, a tar roof should not be specified on a deck slope greater than 1/4 in. per ft. In any case, a felt envelope is required to overcome the flow and possible drippage of tar from the roof, see Section 10.5.2 in Chapter 10.

Because of its somewhat higher durability and greater water-resisting characteristics, a tar roof may be considered for reroofing an existing roof, where the roof slope is less than the currently mandated slope of 1/4 in. per ft and where incorporating the required minimum slope on the roof is not a possibility.

2.7 ROOFING COAL TAR

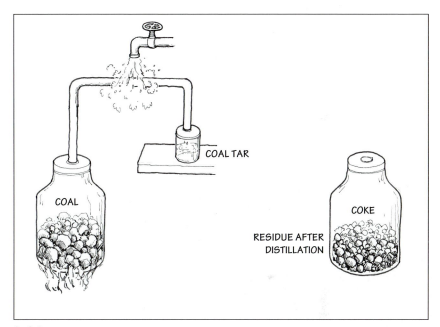

2.21 *Production of coal tar.*

Table 2.3 Important Properties of Coal Tar

Type of coal tar	SPT (°F)	Recommended application temperature (°F)
Type I	126 - 140	360 ± 25
Type III	133 - 147	375 ± 25

2.7.2 Felts Used in Coal Tar Roofs

As stated in Section 2.2.3, tar-felt separation is a problem in tar built-up roofs, in which impregnated fiberglass felts are used. Therefore, the commonly recommended felts are either organic felts or coated fiberglass felts.

2.7.3 Incompatibility of Tar and Asphalt

Tar and asphalt, being chemically different, are not compatible with each other. They should not be mixed together. However, it should be noted that asphalt flashing materials are commonly used with coal tar built-up roofs.

2.8 SURFACING ON A BUILT-UP ROOF

Both coal tar and asphalt degrade over a period of time, primarily due to their exposure to ultraviolet radiation. Therefore, the topmost layer in a built-up roof must be protected. Single-ply roof membranes do not require any protection, since they are chemically formulated to be relatively more resistant to ultraviolet radiation. Coal tar built-up roofs must be protected only with a flood coat of coal tar covered with aggregate. However, with asphalt built-up roofs, two options are available:

- Aggregate surfacing over a flood coat of asphalt

- Nonaggregate surfacing

2.8.1 Quality and Quantity of Aggregate Surfacing

Aggregate surface is by far the most commonly used. This surface is recommended on a built-up roof unless there are good reasons against its use. Apart from protecting the bitumen from ultraviolet radiation, an aggregate surface increases the fire resistance of the roof, protects the membrane from hail impact, and adds weight over the membrane, increasing its resistance to wind uplift.

Being a protective layer, the quality of aggregate is important. It must be hard enough to resist abrasion and round in shape so that it does not penetrate through the membrane under the weight of occasional foot traffic (traffic pads are needed on walking areas of the roof). It must also be opaque to sunlight and free of loose dirt so that it can bond with bitumen. Loose dirt provides no protective function since it settles into bitumen, reducing its adhesive property.

The aggregate must be a graded aggregate so that most particles sink into the bitumen. A small quantity of aggregate may nest in spaces between adhered particles. Average aggregate size recommended is 3/8 in. with a maximum aggregate size of 3/4 in. and a desired minimum of 3/16 in., although a small percentage of 3/32 in. aggregate is permitted by the relevant standard.[7] A minimum aggregate weight of 400 lb per square is recommended, Table 2.4.

Water-worn river gravel is ideal for the purpose, but crushed stone may be used if the traffic on the roof is minimal. Marble chips and blast furnace slag[8] also make good surfacing materials. Lightweight aggregates, which may get dislodged under high wind or rain storm, are generally discouraged. These will clog the drains and disintegrate under freeze-thaw action. However, because of particle shape, volcanic rock (which is lightweight) has good resistance to aggregate migration, which is why it is commonly used on sloped roofs.

Slag is an excellent surfacing material, since it is opaque and its pitted surface gives good adhesion with bitumen. For slag, the corresponding minimum weight is 300 lb per square, and 265 lb per square for volcanic rock. The weight of bitumen for a flood coat is nearly 60 lb per square for asphalt and 75 lb per square for tar.

The maximum slope for an aggregate surfaced roof is 3:12. However, for slopes in excess of 1/2:12, the use of volcanic rock is desirable, in addition to backnailing of felts, see Section 6.1.1 in Chapter 6. An aggregate surfaced (400 lb of aggregate per square) built-up roof on a slope not exceeding 3:12 meets Underwriters Laboratories' (UL) class A rating, see Section 7.3.4 in Chapter 7.

Table 2.4 Weights of Flood Coat Materials

Aggregate type	Recommended weight (lb per roof square)
Crushed stone or gravel	400
Slag	300
Volcanic rock	265
Bitumen flood coat	
Asphalt	60
Coal tar	75

2.8.2 Application of Aggregate Surfacing

If organic felts are used, the surfacing and flood coat must be applied as soon as possible after mopping the felts. Exposed organic felts pick up moisture from rain or overnight dew. The moisture causes blisters when the hot bitumen is poured. It is, therefore, advisable to apply flood coat and surfacing at the end of the same day as the rest of the felts.

If, for some reason, the flood coat and surfacing cannot be applied on the same day as the rest of the felts, the roof must be coated with a glaze coat of

---

[7] ASTM Standard D 1863, "Standard Specification for Mineral Aggregate Used on Built-up Roofs."

[8] Slag is a waste product from the blast furnace, used in the manufacture of iron from iron ore.

bitumen (nearly 15 lb per square). A reasonable delay between felt mopping and flood coat is, however, not an issue with fiberglass felts. However, if the delay is 30 days or longer, glaze coating the valleys and low areas may be beneficial. Long delays should be avoided.

2.8.3 Nonaggregate Surfacing — Cap Sheet

As stated in Section 2.3.2, the most commonly used nonaggregate surface is a mineral granule surfaced cap sheet, Figure 2.22. Metal foil surfaced cap sheets are also used. A foil-faced (modified bitumen) cap sheet may provide some benefit in energy saving, since a foil is a good radiant barrier, see Sections 3.2 in Chapter 3 and 4.4 in Chapter 4. However, foil-faced cap sheets are expensive and are generally less durable than mineral granule-surfaced cap sheets because they are more susceptible to mechanical damage.

Cap sheets are applied after the entire roof has been laid, not shingled with the rest of the felts. The laps between sheets are typically 2 in. on the sides and 6 in. on the ends. Being thick, a cap sheet is not very flexible and tends to curl up

2.22 *A roof with a mineral surfaced cap sheet. Photo by Madan Mehta.*

when unrolled. Therefore, it is usually cut to lengths of 12 to 18 ft, and each length is laid on the roof for some time before it is mopped so that the heat of the sun flattens the sheet, Figure 2.23.

Once the sheet has flattened, it is mopped with the mineral or foil side facing up. The first sheet is laid starting at the lowest point of the roof with a full mopping of bitumen. The remaining sheets are then laid using a "mop-and-flop" technique, in which the bitumen is mopped on the sheet's underside and the sheet turned over and laid on the roof. The bitumen must be adequately hot to ensure that it melts the coating already on the sheet. The amount of bitumen required is the same as for interply mopping.

Care should be taken in applying a cap sheet in cold weather, because the bitumen can chill during mopping and flopping operation and the rolls do not relax adequately. Built-up roofs with cap sheets can provide good performance, provided the cap sheet is counted as a sacrificial (additional) ply — a replacement for the flood coat.

As stated previously, nonaggregate surfacing (e.g., mineral granules or aluminum foil) should only be used when it is not possible to use flood-coated gravel surfacing. Mineral granules, being small in size, are gradually washed away by wind and rain, leaving the membrane unprotected from the weather. When that happens, the membrane deteriorates rapidly. Similarly, a foil corrodes, and some problems with delamination of the foil have been reported.

A few reasons for using a cap sheet in place of gravel covering on a built-up roof may be:

- Good quality aggregate is not available.

- The slope of roof is too steep for an aggregate surfaced roof. Foil surfacing is particularly attractive for steep and curved roofs, vaults, and domes.

- The roof is located in a high wind region and is not provided with a parapet, which can create a hazard due to windborne aggregate.

2.23 *Unrolling, cutting, and flattening of cap sheets before their installation. Photo by Madan Mehta.*

2.8.4 Nonaggregate Surfacing — Coatings

Built-up roofs can also be protected by coatings. The most commonly used coating is fibrated aluminum coating, which consists of extremely small aluminum flakes blended with cutback asphalt. Cutback asphalt is made from conventional asphalt and a petroleum-based solvent. The solvent dissolves the asphalt, so that the cutback asphalt does not need any heating to achieve application-grade viscosity.

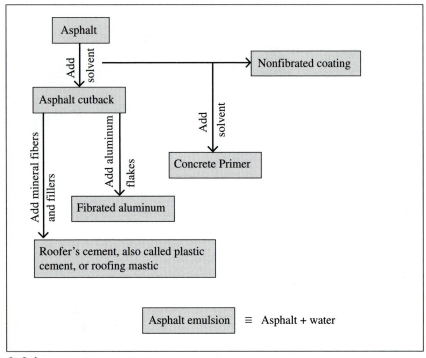

2.24 *Coatings and other roofing products made from asphalt.*

The solvent used in making cutback asphalt evaporates after a few days, leaving behind a hardened asphalt layer. The aluminum flakes used with the cutback are thoroughly intermingled with the asphalt, so that the coating consists of a bright surface. Fibrated aluminum coating is typically spray-applied. Such a coating is less forgiving of ponded water than is a gravel-covered built-up roof.

Another commonly used coating uses asphalt emulsion.[9] Asphalt can be dispersed in water by mixing hot asphalt, water, and an emulsifying agent and thoroughly mixing the ingredients. The resulting product is referred to as *asphalt emulsion.*

For roof coatings, the asphalt emulsion is blended with clay. Clay emulsions have very different properties than regular asphalt. The coating will not alligator and will provide some fire resistance. However, the surface on which the emulsion is applied must be relatively clean. Like the cutback coating, a clay emulsion coating is also less forgiving of ponded water than is a gravel-covered built-up roof. A list of coatings[2.3] and other products made from asphalt are listed in Figure 2.24.

REFERENCES

2.1 National Roofing Contractors Association. *NRCA Roofing and Waterproofing Manual* (Rosemont, IL: 1996), p. 213.

2.2 Roofing Industry Educational Institute. *Roofing Technology* (Englewood, CO: 1998) p. 2-A-29.

2.3 Roofing Industry Educational Institute. *Roofing Technology* (Englewood, CO: 1998) p. 2-C-3.

---

[9] An emulsion is a product resulting from the mixing of an otherwise immiscible liquid with another liquid so that the resulting product is reasonably homogenous, such as the mixing of vegetable oil or butter in water. Asphalt can be mixed with water using an emulsifying agent, such as bentonite clay. The resulting product is referred to as *asphalt emulsion.*

MODIFIED BITUMEN AND SINGLE-PLY ROOF MEMBRANES

Although coal tar and asphalt built-up roof membranes have been in use for nearly 150 years and 100 years respectively,[3.1] the other two membranes — modified bitumen and single-ply — are of more recent origins. Single-ply membranes were introduced in the 1950s in Europe and in the 1960s in the United States, but their widespread use had to wait until the oil crisis of 1973, when the price of crude oil quadrupled suddenly. This raised the cost of asphalt built-up roofs, making single-ply roofs cost effective.

The modified bitumen (also called *mod bit*) membranes were first used in Europe in the mid-1960s, but it took nearly a decade for their introduction in the United States. Currently, modified bitumen has approximately the same low-slope roof market share as the built-up roof. In this chapter, modified bitumen and single-ply roof membranes are discussed.

Membrane, Felt, and Sheet

As discussed in Chapter 2, the individual sheets between bitumen moppings in a built-up roof are referred to as felts, and the entire assembly of felts and bitumen moppings is referred to as a "membrane." When modified bitumen sheets were introduced, it was thought that only one modified bitumen sheet would perform as well as an assembly of felts and bitumen moppings in a built-up roof — the built-up roof membrane. Therefore, the modified bitumen sheets were referred to as "membranes" and were even included in the single-ply membrane family — a practice that continues to this day.

We now know that a single sheet of modified bitumen is inadequate, and that two or more sheets (plies) are generally needed to provide a reasonable roof. However, each such sheet is referred to as a membrane in some roofing literature, which is an incorrect use of the term "roof membrane." A membrane is the entire waterproofing layer on the roof. It may consist of one ply, as in a single-ply roof membrane; an assembly of several plies, as in a built-up roof; or two to three plies, as in a modified bitumen roof.

Similarly, the term "felt" in roofing vernacular is reserved for either an organic or fiberglass sheet, typically used in a built-up roof, which together with a bitumen mopping constitutes one built-up roof ply. Other roofing sheets are not referred to as felts. For instance, in a commonly used modified bitumen membrane assembly, consisting of two plies, the first ply is called the base sheet, and the second ply is called a cap sheet. The base sheet is usually a built-up roof felt,[1] and the cap sheet, a modified bitumen sheet.

---

[1] The base sheet can also be a smooth-surfaced modified bitumen sheet, see Section 3.2.

3.1 ANATOMY OF A MODIFIED BITUMEN SHEET

SBS-modified membrane	APP-modified membrane
• Greater flexibility • Greater resistance to cold environment	• Greater resistance to ultraviolet radiation

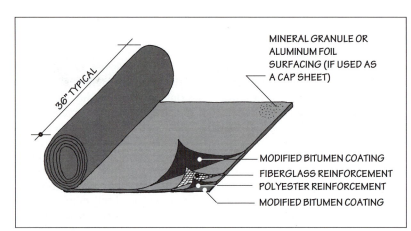

3.1 *Anatomy of a modified bitumen membrane with fiberglass and polyester scrims.*

A modified bitumen sheet is similar to a built-up roof membrane, because the waterproofing agent is the bitumen to which polymers have been added to modify the bitumen's properties. The polymer's addition to the bitumen improves its characteristics, so that the modified bitumen is more pliable and elastomeric as compared to the (unmodified) bitumen. The polymer also increases the ultraviolet radiation resistance of the bitumen. Modified bitumen is, therefore, more resistant to cold temperature and to ultraviolet radiation than the bitumen used in a built-up roof membrane.[2]

Out of the two modified bitumens — modified asphalt and modified coal tar — modified asphalt is far more commonly used. Coal tar modified bitumen sheets have been available since the mid-1990s, but their use is relatively uncommon.

Although some other modifiers are also used, the two most common asphalt modifiers are:

- Styrene butadiene styrene (SBS)

- Attactic polypropylene (APP)

The SBS modifier is a synthetic rubber. Therefore, SBS-modified asphalt has excellent elongation properties with reversibility. It remains flexible at temperatures below -10°F (-23°C). Therefore, an SBS sheet is more flexible and more resistant to cold temperature than an APP sheet.

The APP-modified asphalt has greater resistance to ultraviolet radiation, which gives an APP sheet a greater weatherability than an SBS sheet. Although less brittle than (regular) asphalt, APP-modified asphalt is less flexible than an SBS-modified asphalt. It has some flexibility at 30°F and above but is relatively brittle at temperatures below 20°F.[3.2]

A modified bitumen sheet consists of a reinforcing mat, called the *carrier*, which is impregnated and coated with modified bitumen on both sides. The carriers commonly used are polyester or fiberglass scrims, or both. A sheet that has both fiberglass and polyester reinforcements is referred to as a *dual carrier* sheet, Figure 3.1. The width of a modified bitumen sheet is generally 36 in., but 1-m-wide sheets are available from some manufacturers.

---

[2] Regular (unmodified) ashphalt and coal tar pitch become relatively brittle in a cold environment, see Section 2.5 in Chapter 2. However, this fact does not influence the performance of a built-up roof in cold climates as sometimes believed. For instance, the long-term performance of built-up roofs in Canada and the northern United States compares favorably with those of modified bitumen or single-ply roofs. Unless a built-up roof membrane is bent in cold weather due to excessive deck movement or some other cause, cold weather does not impact a built-up roof's long-term performance any more than it impacts a modified bitumen or a single-ply roof.

Polyester, which is itself a polymer, has high elongation and thus gives pliability to the sheet. It stretches 55% at room temperatures and is reasonably flexible at low temperatures. Polyester also adds puncture and tear resistance to the sheet, which is important in resisting rooftop traffic and damage caused by roofers' and repair persons' tools. Fiberglass has very little elongation (approximately 2%) but provides tensile strength and increases the sheet's fire resistance.

The thickness of a modified bitumen sheet varies from nearly 100 to 200 mil (2.5 mm to 5 mm).[3] Therefore, a modified bitumen sheet is much thicker than an asphalt felt, which is only 30 mil (0.75 mm) thick. It is also nonporous, unlike the asphalt-treated felt. A thicker modified bitumen sheet is selected where greater strength — to withstand greater impact and foot traffic — is required. Because of its greater thickness, a modified bitumen roof need only consist of two sheets to give almost the same performance as four to five plies of a built-up roof.

The top surface of a modified bitumen sheet may be smooth or surfaced with mineral granules or metal foil. A smooth-surfaced sheet is generally used as an intermediate ply or as a base sheet in a 2- or 3-ply modified bitumen membrane. A mineral granule or foil-faced sheet is used as a cap sheet in a modified bitumen roof or on a built-up roof, see Section 2.8.3 in Chapter 2. The commonly used metal foils are aluminum, copper, or stainless steel. A smooth-surfaced modified bitumen sheet may also be used as a cap sheet but must be protected by a bitumen flood coat and gravel, like a typical built-up roof.

3-PLY BUILT-UP ROOF MEMBRANE

150-MIL-THICK MODIFIED BITUMEN SHEET

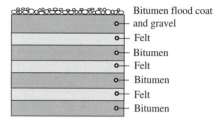
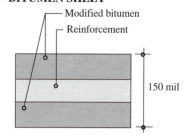

RELATIVE THICKNESS OF A 3-PLY BUILT-UP ROOF MEMBRANE AND A TYPICAL MODIFIED BITUMEN SHEET

An SBS sheet is typically mop applied, like a built-up roof felt, although a few manufacturers make torchable SBS sheets, see also Section 3.3.2. The low temperature flexibility (elastomeric nature) of an SBS sheet may provide some advantage in colder climates over a conventional built-up roof or an APP-modified bitumen roof.

Although the addition of SBS raises the softening point temperature of asphalt, the application temperature of SBS-modified asphalt (of nearly 350°F) is lower than that of roofing asphalts (400°F to 500°F, depending on the type of asphalt). That is why SBS-modified asphalt is not used for adhering an SBS sheet, since a temperature of 350°F is not high enough to melt the asphalt present in an SBS sheet. Therefore, SBS sheets are typically mopped with type IV roofing asphalt,

3.2 SBS-MODIFIED BITUMEN MEMBRANE

---

[3] A few modified bitumen manufacturers make sheets slightly thinner than 100 mil. For instance, one manufacturer makes 90-mil-thick sheets.

which has an application temperature of nearly 500°F. The amount of asphalt required is the same as for interply moppings in a built-up roof, i.e., nearly 25 lb per square.

A 2- or 3-ply SBS roof membrane gives good performance under most conditions. A 3-ply membrane may consist of an asphalt-coated base sheet, a smooth-surfaced SBS sheet, and then a granule-surfaced SBS cap sheet, Figure 3.2(a). A foil-faced SBS cap sheet may be substituted for a granule-surfaced cap sheet. A 2-ply SBS membrane typically consists of a base sheet (either an asphalt-coated base sheet or a smooth-surfaced modified bitumen sheet) followed by a mineral or foil-faced SBS cap sheet, Figure 3.2(b).

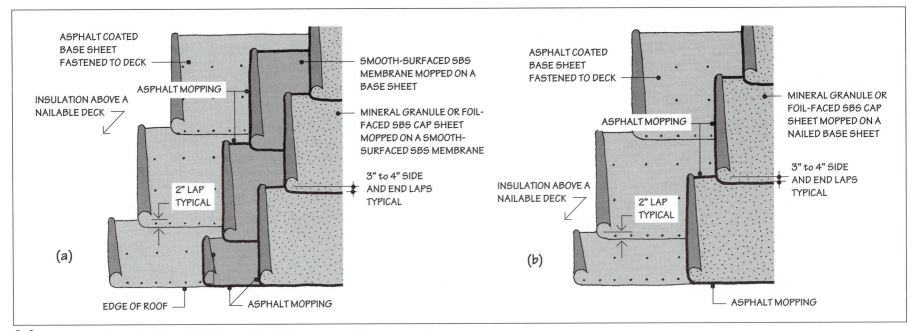

3.2 *(a) Granule- or foil-faced, SBS-modified bitumen cap sheet mopped to a smooth-surfaced SBS sheet, which is mopped over a nailed base sheet. (b) Granule- or foil-faced, SBS-modified bitumen cap sheet mopped over a nailed base sheet. Both these illustrations apply to a nailable deck. If the deck is a nonnailable deck, the base sheet is simply mopped over the deck or over the insulation, if the insulation is present over the deck. For the difference between a nailable and a nonnailable deck, refer to Section 5.1 in Chapter 5.*

3.2.1 Built-Up and SBS Hybrid Roof

An SBS-modified bitumen sheet can also be combined with a built-up roof membrane to give an SBS-built-up hybrid roof. Such a roof may consist of a 2- to 4-ply conventional built-up roof followed by a granule- or foil-faced SBS cap sheet. In place of an SBS cap sheet, a smooth-surfaced SBS sheet with asphalt flood coat and gravel surfacing may be used, as in a built-up roof, Figure 3.3.

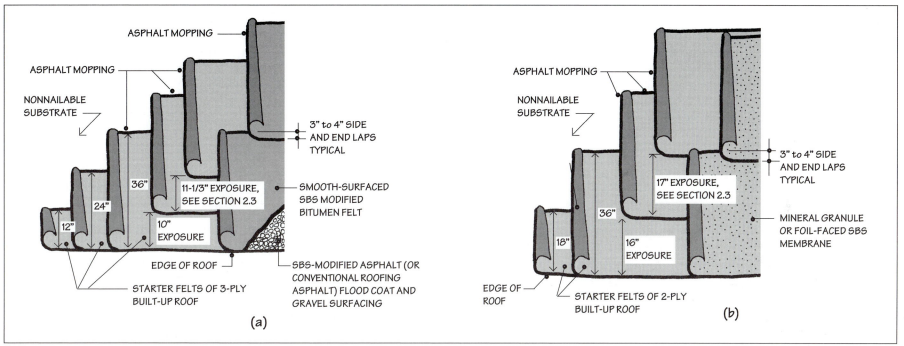

3.3 *(a) A smooth-surfaced SBS-modified bitumen sheet and gravel-covered flood coat over a 3-ply built-up roof. (b) Granule- or foil-faced SBS cap sheet over a 2-ply built-up roof.*

The asphalt for the flood coat is generally the regular (unmodified) roofing asphalt, although SBS-modified asphalt can also be used. SBS-modified asphalt is typically available in kegs, similar to the roofing asphalt. It is compatible with (regular) roofing asphalt and can be used with built-up roof felts or with SBS sheets.

On a nailable deck,[4] a hybrid SBS and built-up roof membrane typically consists of a base sheet followed by one, two, or three plies of a built-up roof and a granule-surfaced SBS cap sheet, Figure 3.4. Since the application of an SBS roof is similar to that of a built-up roof, a built-up roof crew can install it with little additional training.

3.4 *SBS-modified bitumen cap sheet over a 2-ply built-up roof plus a nailed base sheet.*

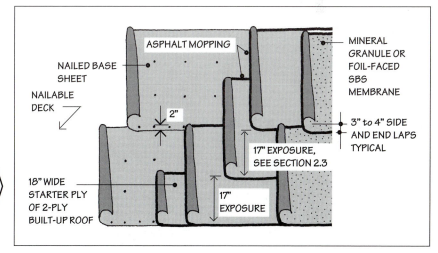

[4] Refer to Section 5.1 in Chapter 5 for a discussion of the difference between a nailable and a nonnailable deck.

3.2.2 Laps in SBS membranes

The side and end laps in SBS sheets, typically recommended by the manufacturers, are 3 to 4 in. (75 to 100 mm). Most roofing contractors use larger laps for a better seal. The laps must be carefully inspected during the laying operation, and the unsealed portions are sealed immediately with hot asphalt.

3.2.3 SBS Sheets as Base Flashings

Because of the elastomeric nature of an SBS sheet, it is commonly specified as a base flashing material with both SBS roof membranes as well as with built-up roof membranes. As explained in Chapter 10, the edge of the roof, particularly the junction between the roof and the parapet, referred to as the *base*, is subjected to a much greater dimensional change than the rest of the roof.

Built-up roof felts, made of fiberglass mats, are not as well suited for base flashing material because of their relative brittleness and relatively smaller thickness. In addition, fiberglass felts have memory, i.e., they have a tendency to straighten out, which makes their transition from the horizontal to the vertical surface problematic.

An SBS sheet, with its flexibility, greater thickness, and durability and its compatibility with the built-up roof membrane, makes it a suitable base flashing material with built-up as well as SBS roofs. The greater durability of an SBS base flashing as compared to built-up roof felts is not simply due to the former's greater thickness, but is also due to the polyester reinforcement. Mineral granule and foil surfacing available on SBS sheets also add to its durability. Therefore, mineral granule or foil-faced SBS sheets are used as flashings with built-up and SBS roofs. For a detailed discussion of flashings, refer to Chapter 10.

3.2.4 SBS Sheets and Built-Up Roof Felts with Cold Adhesives

SBS sheets and built-up roof felts can also be applied with a cold adhesive (which is similar in composition to roofer's cement, see Section 2.8.4 in Chapter 2). Cold-applied roofs are not as common as the hot-applied roofs. However, they are becoming increasingly popular, particularly with high-rise roofs, where hot asphalt cannot be pumped, and the liquid propane cylinders used with torchable sheets may be hazardous. The surfacing may consist of a variety of cold-applied coatings (see Section 2.8.4 in Chapter 2) or mineral granule-faced cap sheets.

A cold adhesive is made from *cutback asphalt*. Cutback asphalt is conventional roofing asphalt (generally Type I) that has been thinned (cutback) with a petroleum-based solvent. The solvent reduces the viscosity of asphalt to make it more easily spreadable. Cutback asphalt cures (hardens) as the solvent evaporates, leaving behind the original asphalt. Although fairly gluey in its original state, cutback asphalt develops the adhesive property further on curing.

However, this process takes more time than hot asphalt, which hardens fairly rapidly. Thus, foot traffic is generally restricted on a cold-applied roof for a few days. This delays those stages of roofing that follow the mopping of felts or sheets, such as the installation of flashings and drains and parapet or roof edge treatments. A roof's vulnerability to leakage until the cold adhesive cures is also a problem. A cold adhesive is generally applied with a brush or sprayed on the roof.

A major disadvantage of cold-applied SBS or built-up roof as compared to the hot-applied roof is the cold adhesive's lower (initial) adhesive power. A cold-applied roof is usually more expensive and also more sensitive to roofers' workmanship, which makes it less forgiving of any on-site quality control lapses, compared to a hot applied built-up or SBS roof. The amount of cold adhesive needed for interply moppings must be more exact than in a hot-applied roof.[3.3]

Another major disadvantage involves the memory of felts and modified bitumen sheets. They tend to return to their rolled state, unless flattened out, see Section 2.8.3 in Chapter 2. With the low adhesive power of cold adhesive, the roof membrane can develop wrinkles, which are potential leakage locations.

The temperature sensitivity of cold adhesives is also an issue. A cold adhesive needs to be warmed if the ambient temperature is below 50°F. A general lack of roofing contractors' familiarity with the cold-applied system is also a problem with cold-applied roofs. However, good cold adhesives are available from several manufacturers to provide a quality cold-applied roof.

A cold-applied roof can be topped with a mineral or foil-surfaced cap sheet or a site-applied surfacing. A commonly used site-applied coating is fibrated asphalt cutback, see Section 2.8.4 in Chapter 2. Although cold-applied built-up roofs are installed, it is far more common with an SBS roof.

3.3 APP-MODIFIED BITUMEN MEMBRANE

As mentioned in Section 3.1, an APP-modified bitumen sheet is made with APP (attactic polypropylene[5]) modified asphalt. Just as the addition of an SBS modifier raises the softening point temperature of asphalt, so does the addition of an APP modifier. In fact, the addition of an APP modifier raises the softening point

---

[5] The term "attactic" means amorphous — a substance that does not have a defined (crystalline) molecular structure. Liquids are amorphous, and solids are generally crystalline, with the exception of glass, which is an amorphous solid. Polypropylene is a type of polymer. Thus, attactic polypropylene implies an amorphous polymer.

3.5 *Granule-surfaced, APP-modified bitumen cap sheet being laid on a base sheet with the help of a propane torch. Photo by Madan Mehta.*

temperature of the APP-modified asphalt so much that an APP membrane cannot be hot mopped like the SBS sheet or a built-up roof felt. The application temperature of even type IV asphalt (nearly 500°F) is not high enough to melt the asphalt in an APP sheet for good adhesion.

The most common method of installing an APP sheet is through the open flame of a hand-held propane torch, Figure 3.5, which has a temperature of over 1,000°F. In this application, the flame is applied to the sheet roll from one end to the other. As the flame melts the modified asphalt on the underside of the sheet, the roll is unwound and pressed down. In this way, the sheet is fully adhered to the substrate.

The sheets are usually factory laminated with a thin polyethylene release sheet to prevent adhesion in the roll. The torch burns the polyethylene sheet. Some manufacturers use sand dusting in place of a polyethylene sheet.

An alternative to the hand-held torch is a *dragon wagon*, which consists of a series of propane torch heads mounted on a wheelable cart that also carries the APP sheet roll, Figure 3.6. A dragon wagon speeds up the installation of an APP sheet but should only be used on a large open roof with few penetrations.

3.3.1 Lap Seams in an APP Felt

In laying an APP sheet, a certain amount of molten bitumen flows out at the edges. The bitumen flow-out verifies that the bitumen in the sheet has melted sufficiently to ensure the sheet's adhesion to the substrate. If the APP sheet is a mineral-surfaced cap sheet, the flow-out bitumen must be protected with field-applied mineral surfacing, Figure 3.7. Most manufacturers recommend lap seams of 3 to 4 in. for APP sheets.

3.3.2 APP Roof's Suitability

Unless good job site quality control is maintained, the adhesion of a torched sheet with the substrate may not be as strong as that of a fully mopped sheet or felt. Therefore, a quality control mechanism to ensure complete adhesion of the sheet to the substrate, particularly at the lap seams, is fundamental to the success of an APP system.

An APP roof system has advantages in areas where the hot bitumen used in a conventional built-up roof (or with an SBS roof) cannot be pumped from the

3.6 *A dragon wagon with its multiple torches.*
Photo courtesy of Siplast, Irving, Texas.

ground to the roof, such as on the roof of a high-rise building. The torched system has similar advantage in cold climates, where keeping the asphalt hot enough between the kettle and the point of application is a problem.

In fact, the torch-adhered, SBS-modified bitumen roof may be preferred for a colder region for the preceding reasons and also because of the greater flexibility of an SBS roof as compared with an APP or a built-up roof.

However, the open torch used in laying a torchable membrane presents a fire hazard, which must be considered before specifying a torched membrane.[6] Fire extinguishers must be available on the roof for any emergency. Where possible, the use of wood cants should be avoided and substituted by perlite board cants, see Section 10.2.3 in Chapter 10.

Plastic foam insulation, if used, should be protected by overlaying a noncombustible board, such as perlite board, to shield the plastic foam from the heat of melted bitumen and accidental torching of the insulation. The work area should be carefully checked before workers leave the job site because smoldering insulation or wood nailers can burst into flames long after the roofers leave the roof. A fire watch for a specified time period after the completion of the day's work is required.

Although an APP sheet has a degree of ultraviolet resistance,[7] a surfacing over it gives additional protection. Mineral granule or foil surfacing on an APP cap sheet adds to its durability. Where practical, an APP roof should be flood coated and covered with gravel for greater durability and fire resistance.

3.7 *With a bucket full of mineral granules in one hand, a roofer sprinkles the granules to cover the bitumen flow-out at the seams of an APP cap sheet. Photo by Madan Mehta.*

3.3.3 APP and Built-Up Roof Hybrid

A two-layer APP roof — the first layer a smooth-surfaced APP sheet and the top layer a mineral-surfaced APP cap sheet — can provide adequate redundancy in most situations. Alternatively, an APP cap sheet may be used over two to three plies of built-up roof felts, giving an APP and built-up roof hybrid membrane. A minimum APP roof consists of an asphalt-coated base sheet followed by a mineral granule-surfaced APP cap sheet — see Figure 3.5 — recommended only where long-term performance is subordinate to initial cost.

---

[6] This is particularly important in reroofing applications, where the building owners may justifiably refuse the transportation of propane cylinders on building elevators.

[7] The greater ultraviolet resistance of an APP sheet must be viewed in the correct perspective. Although an APP sheet has a greater ultraviolet resistance than a built-up roof felt or an SBS sheet, a gravel-covered built-up roof gives a greater ultraviolet resistance than a smooth-surfaced, or even a mineral-granule-surfaced, APP membrane.

3.4 SINGLE-PLY ROOF

Although a built-up roof membrane (and to a smaller extent, a modified bitumen membrane) is constructed on the roof felt by felt, a single-ply roof has only a one-ply membrane and does not require the cumbersome use of hot bitumen. It is easier to lay because it has only one ply.

A single-ply membrane is made of a polymeric material. Since a polymer is a synthetic material, capable of great deal of chemical manipulation by minor changes in one or more of its constituents, a large number of polymers are used as roof membranes. However, single-ply membrane polymers can be divided into two broad categories:

COMMONLY SPECIFIED SINGLE-PLY ROOF MEMBRANES

HEAT WELDABLE

- PVC (polyvinyl chloride)
- CPE (chlorinated polyethylene)
- CSPE (chlorosulfonated polyethylene).
- TPO (thermoplastic olefin)

NONWELDABLE

- EPDM (ethylene propylene diene monomer)

- *Thermosetting polymer (unweldable plastic)* is a polymer that does not soften on heating once it is cured[8] into hardness, like a boiled egg. Therefore, the seams in a thermosetting membrane cannot be heat welded but must be adhered together by an adhesive or a double-sided seam tape. The most commonly used thermosetting membrane is EPDM, an acronym that stands for ethylene propylene diene terpolymer.[9]

- *Thermoplastic (heat weldable plastic)* is a polymer that softens on heating and hardens on cooling over and over again, like butter. Asphalt and coal tar behave like a thermoplastic. A thermoplastic material is heat weldable, which makes seaming operation relatively easier. However, thermoplastic polymer is not as stretchable as thermosetting polymer. Currently, the most commonly used thermoplastic roof membrane is PVC (polyvinyl chloride).

3.4.1 Advantages and Disadvantages of a Single-Ply Membrane

By virtue of the material of which it is made, a single-ply membrane is highly flexible and can withstand large elongation before failure. For example, a typical EPDM membrane will stretch 300% to 500% of its original length before tearing apart, as compared to 100% for an SBS-modified bitumen felt and 3% for a built-up roof felt.

---

[8] Curing (also referred to as vulcanization) is a process by which an otherwise thermoplastic material is converted to a thermosetting plastic by treating it with a curing agent (such as sulfur). The curing agent helps crosslink the polymer chains and converts a soft, tacky thermoplastic into a strong, elastic, and temperature-stable thermosetting material. Vulcanization was discovered simultaneously in 1846 by Charles Goodyear of the United States and Thomas Hancock of Britain.

[9] EPDM is incorrectly assumed to be an acronym for ethylene propylene diene monomer, since EPDM is not a monomer but a polymer. The mistake is perhaps due to the fact that the American Society for Testing and Materials (ASTM) classifies EPDM as an "M" class polymer.

For a variety of reasons,[10] a typical single-ply membrane comes in much wider and longer rolls than a built-up roof felt or a modified bitumen sheet, Figure 3.8. Although an advantage (since it reduces the number of lap splices, which reduces lap failure possibilities), a large roll size also means that roof penetrations are more difficult to work around. Therefore, single-ply membrane has an advantage on a large roof with few penetrations.

The relative flexibility and elongation characteristic of a single-ply membrane is useful in climates with a large annual or daily temperature variation. A single-ply membrane (particularly EPDM) retains its elastomeric character even in subzero (Fahrenheit scale) temperatures.

A major disadvantage of a single-ply roof membrane is the absence of second, third, or additional plies. This implies a lack of redundancy in a single-ply roof — a redundancy that is helpful in any waterproofing application. A single membrane puncture or split results in a roof leak in a single-ply roof. This is less likely to occur in a built-up roof because of its multiple plies.

By far the biggest disadvantage of a single-ply membrane is its lack of resistance to puncture and mechanical damage. There have also been problems with shrinkage on most single-ply membranes — EPDM and PVC.

Single-ply roofs became popular after the 1973 oil embargo when the cost of built-up roofs jumped dramatically. However, the single-ply roof's market share in the United States has remained virtually unchanged for a long time. This is partly due to the persistently depressed crude oil prices, which has made bituminous roof systems cost competitive — a situation that can change in future.

Each single-ply membrane type has some limitations of use. The limitation may be based on the cost of the installed membrane, but it is more likely to be based on the performance of the membrane under local weather and the roof environment. However, for a long time, the most commonly used single-ply roof membranes have been EPDM and PVC.

Currently, nearly 75% of single-ply roofs in North America are EPDM roofs, followed by 20% of PVC.[3.4] The remaining 5% of single-ply roof market share is held by other membrane types, Figure 3.9. Therefore, the following discussion is related primarily to EPDM and PVC roofs, although it is general enough to apply to other single-ply membranes also.

---

[10] The large roll size of a single-ply membrane is primarily a function of its weight, since heavier rolls are more difficult to handle on a roof. With a typical thickness of only 45 to 60 mil (1.1 to 1.5 mm), wider rolls of single-ply membrane can be handled, compared to modified bitumen rolls with their thickness of 100 to 200 mil (2.5 to 5 mm).

MEMBRANE IS FOLDED HERE IN THE ROLL

3.8 *Although this is a 30-ft-wide EPDM membrane (with a center fold so that the roll is only 15 ft wide), single-ply membrane rolls are available in much larger widths. Photo by Madan Mehta.*

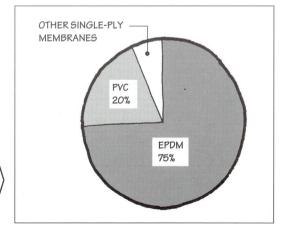

OTHER SINGLE-PLY MEMBRANES

PVC 20%

EPDM 75%

3.9 *Approximate market shares of various single-ply membranes.*

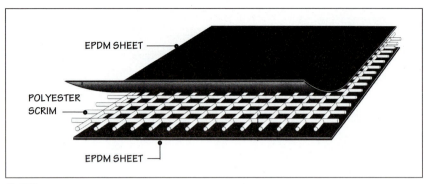

EPDM SHEET

POLYESTER SCRIM

EPDM SHEET

3.10 *Anatomy of a reinforced EPDM membrane. Sketch courtesy of Firestone Building Products, Carmel, Indiana.*

PROPERTY	EPDM MEMBRANE
Lap seam attachment	Adhesive or two-sided tape used to adhere laps
Resistance to UV	Good
Resistance to ozone	Good
Fire resistance	Fire-resistive EPDM available
Compatibility with insulating materials	Compatible with most insulating materials
Compatibility with fats and oils	Incompatible
Compatibility with asphalt and coal tar	Incompatible

3.4.2 EPDM Roof Membrane

Because EPDM is a synthetic rubber, it is essentially similar to the material used in automobile tires. Firestone is, therefore, one of the major EPDM membrane manufacturers. The typical thickness of an EPDM membrane is 45 to 60 mil (1.1 to 1.5 mm), although some manufacturers make a thicker membrane for use where a higher puncture and tear resistance is needed.

A higher puncture and tear resistance is also obtained with the use of a reinforced EPDM membrane, in which a polyester scrim is embedded between two layers of EPDM, Figure 3.10. Higher puncture and tear resistance is particularly important in a mechanically fastened membrane (see Section 3.5.2) since it is subjected to excessive stress and fatigue caused by membrane fluttering under high wind. An additional advantage of a reinforced membrane is its greater shrinkage resistance. Therefore, although unreinforced EPDM membranes are used, the trend is toward the use of reinforced membranes..

EPDM polymer is a relatively inert material. It is therefore chemically compatible with most deck and insulation materials. It is also inert to mild acids and bases. However, it reacts adversely with fats and oils. Fats and oils soften an EPDM membrane, leading to its gradual deterioration. Therefore, special detailing is required around kitchen exhausts on roofs with EPDM membranes.

Neoprene (polychloroprene), also a synthetic rubber like EPDM, is resistant to oils and fats, but because of weatherability and shrinkage concerns, its use as roof membrane is marginal.

EPDM membrane is also incompatible with asphalt and coal tar. Thus, if used for retrofit roofing over an existing built-up or modified bitumen roof, an EPDM membrane must be separated from asphalt or coal tar with a divorce layer. The incompatibility of EPDM with coal tar is greater than with asphalt.

The EPDM polymer does not have any inherent resistance to ultraviolet radiation. However, EPDM roof membrane manufacturers add carbon black to the polymer to increase its ultraviolet radiation resistance. Carbon black also increases the tensile and tear strength of the membrane. Thus, a white EPDM membrane, preferred for its energy saving potential, is less resistant to ultraviolet radiation. It is the black EPDM membrane that is commonly specified.

EPDM polymer also lacks inherent fire resistance, but fire-resistive EPDM membranes are available. However, with a ballasted EPDM roof, a non fire-resistive membrane may be specified, since the ballast will provide the fire resistance.

3.4.3 PVC Roof Membrane

PVC (polyvinyl chloride), the most versatile plastic, is available in two types. The rigid PVC is used for phonographic records, pipes, siding and window sashes. The soft and pliable type is used in shower curtains, raincoats, electrical wire insulation, and roof membranes. Softness and flexibility — properties that are necessary for a roofing membrane — are obtained through the addition of a plasticizer. However, despite the addition of a plasticizer, a PVC membrane, though flexible, is far less stretchable than an EPDM membrane.

Plasticizers used in earlier PVC membranes had the tendency to migrate out of the membrane. The loss of plasticizer made a PVC membrane become progressively more brittle, and caused it to shrink, resulting in its premature failure by fracturing. Premature failure of PVC membranes was so prevalent that it not only damaged the reputation of PVC membranes, but also virtually of all single-ply roof membranes.

The plasticizers used in the current PVC membranes are relatively more stable. The membranes are also polyester reinforced. Therefore, PVC membrane is gradually regaining acceptance as a roofing material. However, its market share is much smaller than that of EPDM membrane.

The primary advantage of a PVC membrane is that seams in the membrane can be heat fused. A simple tool, such as that shown in Figure 3.11, which supplies hot compressed air is all that is needed to fuse the seams. This makes roof installation much easier, compared to EPDM roofs, in which the seams must be joined together with an adhesive.

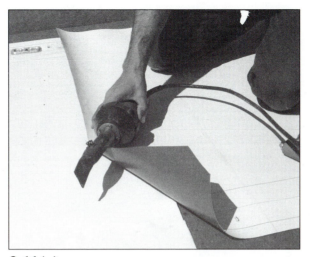

3.11(a) *Hand-held welding tool that supplies hot compressed air through a flat nozzle. Photo by Madan Mehta.*

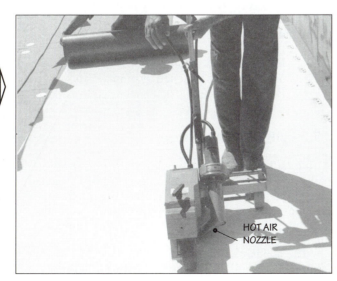

3.11(c) *Self-propelled hot air welding machine that welds and presses the seams — an alternative to the hand-held welding tool. The machine speeds the welding operation. Photo by Madan Mehta.*

HOT AIR NOZZLE

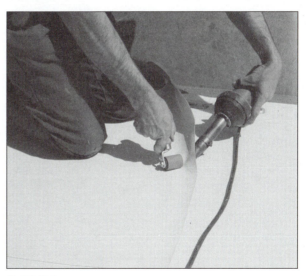

3.11(b) *A roofer welding the seams of a white PVC membrane and pressing down the fused seams. Photo by Madan Mehta.*

PROPERTY	PVC MEMBRANE
Lap seam attachment	Seams heat welded
Resistance to UV	Good
Resistance to ozone	Good
Fire resistance	Good
Compatibility with insulating materials	Incompatible with polystyrene foam insulation
Compatibility with fats and oils	Fair
Compatibility with asphalt and coal tar	Incompatible

Another advantage of PVC is the material's inherent fire resistance, which is provided by the chlorine atom in polyvinyl chloride. Therefore, even a white PVC membrane can provide an excellent fire resistance. -

PVC membranes are generally used in 45- to 80-mil (1.1- to 2.0-mm) thickness. They are available in several colors, although white and gray are more common. As a result of its fire resistance and color options, PVC membrane is often specified for domes and vaults, where the slope limits the fire rating of most other roofs.

Although resistant to mild acids, bases, oils and fats, a PVC membrane reacts adversely with asphalt and coal tar. In fact, PVC's incompatibility with asphalt and coal tar is much worse than that of EPDM. Thus, if PVC is to be used as retrofit roofing over an existing built-up or modified bitumen material, it is a good practice to completely remove the existing roof.

The use of a divorce layer (cover board, see Section 4.7.1 in Chapter 4) between the existing coal tar roof membrane and the new PVC membrane may not be adequate, since even the tar vapor permeating through the cover board can damage the PVC membrane. With an existing asphalt roof, a cover board may work, but it is not recommended by the authors. PVC also reacts adversely with polystyrene insulation. Polystyrene extracts plasticizers out of the membrane, embrittling the membrane.[3.5]

3.5 ATTACHMENT OF A SINGLE-PLY MEMBRANE TO SUBSTRATE

A single-ply roof membrane may be attached to the deck (over the insulation if present) in one the following three ways, although a fourth method, referred to as the partially adhered system, is sometimes used:

- Fully adhered system
- Mechanically fastened system
- Ballasted system

3.5.1 Fully Adhered System

A fully adhered, single-ply membrane does not require any gravel, granule, or ballast covering. The membrane is simply attached to the substrate — to the insulation, if present, which has already been fastened to the deck — by applying an adhesive to the underside of the entire membrane, Figure 3.12. Typically, the membrane is laid out flat on the roof according to a predetermined pattern and then folded back on itself, Figure 3.13.

The adhesive is now applied on the roof substrate by spray, brush, or roller. If sprayed, the adhesive is spread with a roller, Figure 3.14. The adhesive is also

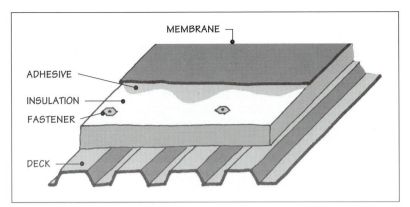

3.12 *A fully adhered membrane is attached to the substrate (usually an insulation that has been suitably fastened to the deck) by an adhesive over the entire interface between the substrate and the membrane.*

3.13 *A fully adhered membrane is first laid on the roof substrate according to a predetermined layout pattern. It is then folded over itself in preparation for the application of adhesive on the back of the membrane and on the substrate. Photo by Madan Mehta.*

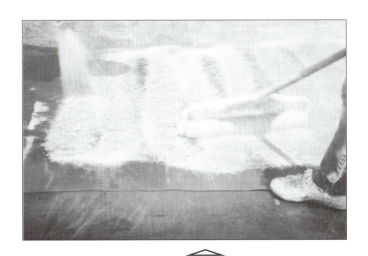

3.14 *The adhesive being sprayed on the substrate and spread by a roller. Photos by Madan Mehta.*

applied in the same way on the membrane, Figure 3.15. The adhesive should not be applied to lap seams. The membrane is now lifted over (unfolded) and returned to the substrate, Figure 3.16, and the same procedure repeated for the other half of the membrane. Finally, the entire membrane is pressed down with a squeegee, roller, or a broom.

After adhering the membrane, the laps are cleaned (primed) with manufacturer's primer,[11] and a double-sided tape is embedded in the lap, Figure 3.17. The tape not only gives a good seal but also makes the seam sealing process faster. Various stages of lap seam tape installation are shown in Figure 3.18.

3.15 *The adhesive being applied to the membrane. Photo by Madan Mehta.*

3.16 *After the adhesive has been applied to both the substrate and the back of the membrane, the membrane is lifted back and adhered to the substrate. Photo by Madan Mehta.*

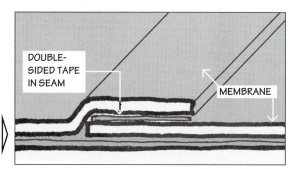

DOUBLE-SIDED TAPE IN SEAM

MEMBRANE

3.17 *Sealing of a lap joint between two single ply membranes.*

---

[11] The cleaning of lap seams is an important step — necessary to remove any dirt that might be present on the sheet. Some EPDM membrane manufacturers usually use talc or dust as a requirement of the vulcanization process and to prevent stickiness in the rolls.

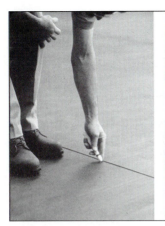

| GUIDE LINE IS DRAWN AT THE LOWER MEMBRANE OF THE LAP. | THE UPPER MEMBRANE IS FOLDED OVER AND THE LAP SURFACES CLEANED WITH THE MANUFACTURER'S PRIMER. | THE MANUFACTURER'S TWO-SIDED TAPE IS ADHERED ALIGNED WITH THE GUIDE LINE AND FIRMLY PRESSED DOWN. | THE UPPER MEMBRANE IS NOW ALLOWED TO FALL BACK AND THE RELEASE PAPER REMOVED FROM THE TAPE. | THE LAP SEAM IS NOW FIRMLY PRESSED DOWN TO ENSURE MAXIMUM BONDING. |

3.18 *Important steps in installing a double-sided tape in the lap seam of two EPDM membranes. Photos courtesy of Firestone Building Products, Carmel, Indiana.*

A fully adhered, single-ply membrane system is labor intensive compared to a mechanically fastened or a ballasted single-ply system. If the substrate (e.g., insulation) is properly fastened to the deck, the system works well for a high wind location. A fully adhered system is also particularly suited on a contoured roof, e.g., domes and vaults.

3.5.2 Mechanically Fastened System

In a mechanically fastened system, the membrane is laid over the insulation, which has already been anchored to the deck, Figure 3.19. The membrane is now anchored to the deck (generally through the insulation) using manufacturer's fasteners at required spacings, which are a function of the wind load on the roof.

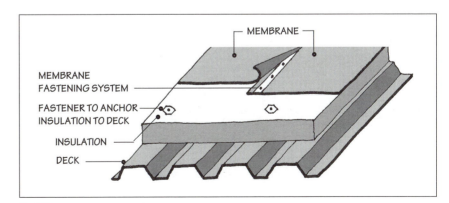

3.19 *Mechanically fastened, single-ply roof system.*

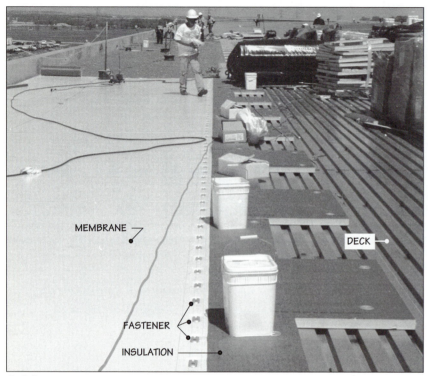

3.20 *Individual fasteners have been used to fasten this white PVC membrane to the deck. Photo by Madan Mehta.*

3.21 *Fastening of a single-ply membrane using batten bars. Photo courtesy of Firestone Building Products, Carmel, Indiana.*

The fastening system may consist of individual fasteners, each consisting of a cap and a screw, Figure 3.20. Alternatively, it may consist of screws and a continuous bar (referred to as a *batten bar* in the industry), through which the screws are applied, Figure 3.21. Most EPDM roofing manufacturers now use the batten bar system instead of the individual fastener system. Batten bars distribute the wind uplift load more evenly on the membrane than individual cap type fasteners do.

The batten bar, typically of metal or polymer, is covered over by the lap seam. The batten bars that are not under the seam are covered with an EPDM self-adhesive splice tape, Figure 3.22.

Under the effect of wind, a mechanically fastened system is subjected to concentrated loads at the fasteners. This is unlike a fully adhered system in which the loads are distributed over the entire membrane. Being dynamic in nature, the wind can make the membrane flutter, causing its premature failure at the fasteners.

Therefore, care should be taken in specifying a mechanically fastened system in a high-wind location. A properly designed mechanically fastened system with closely spaced fasteners can work well in a high-wind location. The use of an air barrier in the assembly can reduce flutter and increase the wind resistance of the assembly, see Section 8.5 in Chapter 8.

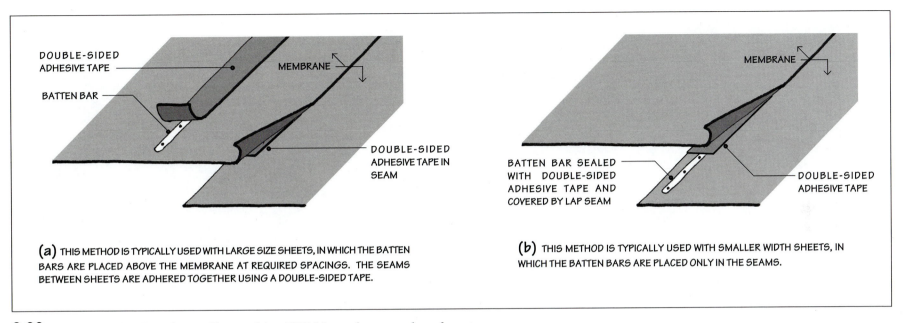

DOUBLE-SIDED
ADHESIVE TAPE

BATTEN BAR

MEMBRANE

DOUBLE-SIDED
ADHESIVE TAPE IN
SEAM

MEMBRANE

BATTEN BAR SEALED
WITH DOUBLE-SIDED
ADHESIVE TAPE AND
COVERED BY LAP SEAM

DOUBLE-SIDED
ADHESIVE TAPE

(a) THIS METHOD IS TYPICALLY USED WITH LARGE SIZE SHEETS, IN WHICH THE BATTEN BARS ARE PLACED ABOVE THE MEMBRANE AT REQUIRED SPACINGS. THE SEAMS BETWEEN SHEETS ARE ADHERED TOGETHER USING A DOUBLE-SIDED TAPE.

(b) THIS METHOD IS TYPICALLY USED WITH SMALLER WIDTH SHEETS, IN WHICH THE BATTEN BARS ARE PLACED ONLY IN THE SEAMS.

3.22 *Two methods of mechanically attaching EPDM membrane to the substrate.*

3.5.3 Loose-Laid Ballasted System

In a loose-laid ballasted system, the entire membrane is laid loose over the substrate, Figure 3.23. The lap seams are adhered together in the same way as a fully-adhered or a mechanically fastened system. The membrane is anchored to the deck only at the roof perimeter. The entire membrane is then covered with gravel, Figure 3.24. The weight of gravel required varies with the wind uplift on the membrane, see Section 8.6 in Chapter 8. Concrete pavers may also be used instead of gravel.

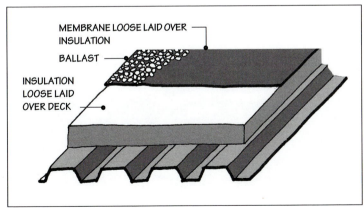

MEMBRANE LOOSE LAID OVER
INSULATION

BALLAST

INSULATION
LOOSE LAID
OVER DECK

3.23 *Ballasted single-ply roof system.*

3.24(b) *Ballast spreaders are used to spread the ballast on the roof. Photo courtesy of James Fell, Firestone Building Products, Carmel, Indiana.*

3.24(a) *Ballasted roof. (a) Ballast is usually brought on a large roof using either a conveyor belt or a crane, as in this case. Photo courtesy of James Fell, Firestone Building Products, Carmel, Indiana.*

The ballasted system is the most economical single-ply system, because it requires the least material and labor cost in anchoring the system. The ballast adds to fire resistance and weatherability. The system is an economical option for roofs of low-rise buildings in low-wind regions.

It is also suited for roof retrofits, since chemical compatibility between the existing and the new roof is less of a concern. A loose-laid cover board over the existing roof is basically all that is needed to separate the new roof from the old. However, the structural capacity of the existing deck to withstand the ballast load must be carefully verified.

A loose-laid ballasted system is not recommended for slopes greater than 2:12 (preferably not greater than 1:12). The dead load due to the ballast adds to the structural cost of the deck, particularly in long span buildings. A ballasted system meets no standard wind uplift criteria and is generally not specified in high-wind locations.

To reduce the puncture of the membrane due to occasional foot traffic on the roof, the ballast must be smooth and round, which is difficult to find at economical prices in most locations. The leaks are also difficult to locate due to the quantity of ballast.

A major weakness of the ballasted system is that due to thermal expansion and contraction of the membrane, all stresses are concentrated at the perimeter and penetrations, which can result in fastener failures at these locations. This is particularly true if the membrane shrinks with a decrease in ambient temperature.

3.6 ROOF MEMBRANE SELECTION

With so many different types of roof membranes available, which membrane is most appropriate for a project? Obviously, the selection of an appropriate membrane must be based on a large number of factors. The cost (both long-term and short-term) and the locally available roofing technology are indeed important in every project. However, another important factor includes the membrane's suitability to local weather conditions.

For instance, a built-up roof may be less prevalent in extremely cold climates, due to the membrane's increasing brittleness at lower temperatures. In addition, the application of most membranes in which bitumen or adhesive (e.g., fully adhered, single-ply membrane) is used requires several special precautions if the membrane is to be laid in cold weather, defined as the weather when the temperature is below 40°F. A mechanically fastened or loose-laid ballasted, single-ply membrane is easier to lay in such conditions.

The wind environment on the roof and roof profile are other important factors. Thus, a cap sheeted built-up roof, a mopped modified bitumen roof, or a fully adhered, single-ply membrane are preferred in high wind environments. Curved roofs and roofs with large slopes do not lend themselves to the application of hot bitumen. A fully adhered, single-ply membrane is generally selected for such projects.

The chemical environment on the roof must be examined to ensure the membrane's compatibility with the environment. Roofing manufacturers generally provide the required information. Their recommendations must be fully adhered to since a roof, being a system of integrated (and often interactive) components, must be compatible with each other. The roof warranty, an extremely important consideration in most major roofing projects, can become void if the manufacturer's recommendations are not followed, see Chapter 15.

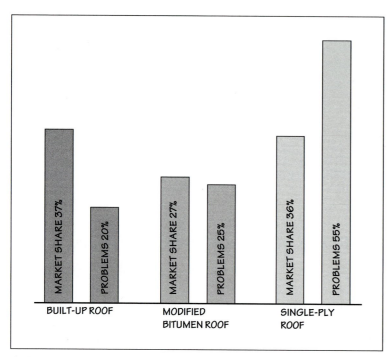

3.25 *Relative performance of built-up, modified bitumen, and single-ply membranes. Single-ply roofs include only EPDM and PVC roofs. Reference 3.6.*

3.6.1 Built-Up, Modified Bitumen, and Single-Ply Roofs Compared

The selection of a manufacturer and its system must be carefully evaluated by the design and construction professionals. The best test of any roof system's performance must come from several actual roofs. Unfortunately, it takes 10 years or longer to field-test a new product or system. Therefore, designers and specifiers must be careful in using a new and untested product.

This fact is endorsed by several ongoing studies by the National Roofing Contractors' Association (NRCA) which gives the performance statistics of various roofing alternatives, Figure 3.25. Note that the built-up roof, a system that is more than a century old, is least susceptible to major problems.

Thus, although the market shares of the built-up, modified bitumen, and single-ply membranes are approximately the same, only 20% of the built-up roofs experienced problems. By comparison, 55% of single-ply roofs experienced major problems. However, the reader should appreciate that roofing technology is highly dynamic and the relative performances of roof membranes can change with time. There is no substitute for keeping up to date with the latest information.

REFERENCES

3.1   Griffin, C. W., and Fricklas, R. *The Manual of Low-slope Roof Systems* (New York: McGraw Hill, 1995), pp. 194-95.

3.2   Blanchard, W. K. "Specifying a Roofing Hybrid — Modified Bitumen," *Roofing Technology* (Englewood, CO: Roofing Industry Educational Institute, 1998), pp. 3-18.

3.3   Hardy, S. *Roof Design* (New York, McGraw Hill: 1997), p. 77.

3.4   Private communication of the authors with Roofing Industry Educational Institute officials.

3.5   Scharff, R., and the Editors of Roofer Magazine. *Roofing Handbook* (New York, McGraw Hill: 1996), p. 112.

3.6   Cullen, William C., and Graham, Mark S. "Project Pinpoint Data Reveal Roof Systems' Strengths, Limitations," *Professional Roofing* (November 1996), p. 20.

4 ROOF INSULATION

Although insulation has long been used in buildings, the real thrust in its use was provided by the oil embargo of 1973, when oil prices quadrupled overnight. Prior to the embargo, the cost of energy use in buildings was relatively small. The embargo changed the situation abruptly, and the energy bills of buildings became their biggest recurring obligation.

Apart from raising the cost of energy use in buildings and in other sectors of an economy — e.g., manufacturing and transportation — the embargo also highlighted the depletability of earth's energy reserves. Consequently, most nations made energy conservation an important economic objective. Since nearly two-thirds of all energy consumed by an industrialized nation is in the construction and maintenance of buildings, energy conservation became an important building design criterion.

To achieve an energy conservative building requires a multifaceted strategy, which must take into account such factors as the macro and microclimatic conditions of the site, building shape, the type of heating, cooling, lighting, and other building service systems, as well as the design of the external envelope of the building.

Although all the above factors are important, the amount of energy that flows in and out of a building envelope plays an important role in the total energy consumed by a building. In general, the smaller this flow, the lower the energy consumption of a building. Since the energy flow through an insulating material is relatively slow, the exterior walls and the roofs of most contemporary buildings are insulated.

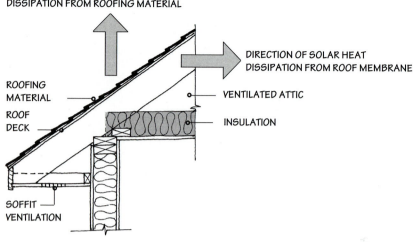

DIRECTION OF SOLAR HEAT
DISSIPATION FROM ROOFING MATERIAL

DIRECTION OF SOLAR HEAT
DISSIPATION FROM ROOF MEMBRANE

ROOFING
MATERIAL

ROOF
DECK

VENTILATED ATTIC

INSULATION

SOFFIT
VENTILATION

STEEP ROOF
TWO-WAY DISSIPATION OF
HEAT FROM ROOF MEMBRANE

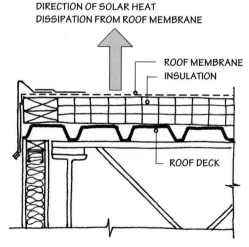

DIRECTION OF SOLAR HEAT
DISSIPATION FROM ROOF MEMBRANE

ROOF MEMBRANE
INSULATION

ROOF DECK

LOW-SLOPE ROOF
ONE-WAY DISSIPATION OF
HEAT FROM ROOF MEMBRANE

Location of Insulation in a Low-Slope Roof and a Steep Roof

In a roof, the insulation is typically provided in two different ways. In a pitched (steep-slope) roof, more commonly used in a residential type building, the insulation is placed in the attic space above the ceiling. The attic consists of a large ventilated air space between the roof deck and the insulation. In such a building, the solar heat absorbed by the roofing material is dissipated in both directions: (1) to the outside from above the roof, and (2) into the attic from underneath the roof deck. The heat entering the attic is carried to the outside by attic ventilation. The two-way dissipation of heat causes the roofing material's temperature to remain fairly close to the external air temperature.

In a flat or a low-slope roof, the insulation is typically sandwiched between the roof deck and the roof membrane. In this case, the solar heat absorbed by the membrane can only dissipate from above the roof membrane. The downward dissipation of heat is relatively small, since the insulation retards heat transfer into the building interior. Consequently, the roof membrane's temperature rises much above the external air temperature.

If a low-slope roof is not insulated, the heat absorbed by the membrane would also dissipate into the building interior, from where it would have to be removed by the building's cooling system. The provision of insulation reduces this mode of heat dissipation. Therefore, on a warm summer afternoon, the temperature of roof membrane on a low-slope roof can be up to 80°F greater than the corresponding air temperature.

Since higher temperatures lead to a faster deterioration of a roof membrane, the practice of insulating low-slope roofs has lowered the life spans of roof membranes on them. Some earlier roof membranes, installed directly over roof decks without any insulation, particularly over reinforced concrete decks, have survived for 30 years or longer. Today, with insulated decks, it is relatively rare for such roofs to last even 20 years.

Advantages of Insulating a Low-Slope Roof

Accelerated deterioration of the roof membrane is a major disadvantage of insulating a roof. Other disadvantages include increased cost, absorption of moisture by the insulation, and insulation movement — ridging and warping of insulation. Its advantages are, however, so numerous that roof insulation is generally the norm these days. Apart from the reduced energy use, some of the other advantages of insulating a roof are:

- Insulation reduces the expansion and contraction of a roof deck.
- Insulation can be used to provide the necessary slope in a roof, e.g., by using tapered insulation or lightweight insulating concrete poured to slope.

- On a metal deck, insulation provides an even substrate for the roof membrane. The same applies to precast concrete decks, such as the single-T and double-T prestressed concrete members.
- Insulation prevents or reduces the possibility of condensation of water vapor on the interior surface of a roof. Note, however, that insulation increases the possibility of condensation within the insulation.
- Insulation increases the comfort of building occupants by moderating the surface temperatures of interior surfaces.

Rigid versus Flexible Insulation

In this chapter, we shall deal with various aspects of insulating a low-slope roof. Although there are several similarities, the insulation used in a low-slope roof has one major difference from that used in a steep roof or in the walls of a building. The difference is between the rigidities of the two insulation types.

The insulation used in a steep roof or the walls of a building is typically in the form of soft and flexible batts or blankets. However, low-slope roof insulation must be able to withstand the impact of hail storm, occasional foot traffic, dropping of workers' tools, and the weight of snow or rainwater accumulation.

Additionally, low-slope roof insulation is required to span over metal deck flutes and discontinuities in a precast concrete deck. Therefore, low-slope roof insulation cannot be in the form of flexible batts or blankets, but must be fairly rigid. In addition to rigidity and the insulating property, there are several other requirements of a low-slope roof insulation that are discussed later in this chapter.

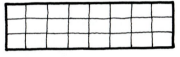

GRAPHIC NOTATION FOR RIGID INSULATION

GRAPHIC NOTATION FOR FLEXIBLE INSULATION — BATT OR BLANKET

From our daily experience, we observe that heat always flows from an object at a higher temperature to the other at a lower temperature, similar to the flow of water from a container at higher pressure to a container at lower pressure. The heat flow continues until the two objects become equal in their temperatures. There are three modes by which heat may flow from one object to the other:

- Conduction
- Convection
- Radiation

4.1 MODES OF HEAT TRANSFER

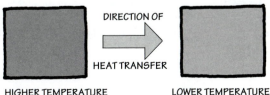

HIGHER TEMPERATURE OBJECT

DIRECTION OF HEAT TRANSFER

LOWER TEMPERATURE OBJECT

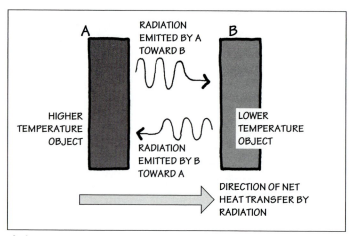

4.1 *Radiation exchange between two facing objects.*

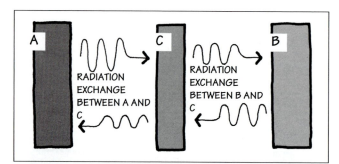

4.2 *Radiation exchange between two objects separated by an intervening object.*

Conduction is the only mode by which heat will travel from one part of a solid body to the other. In this mode, the particles of an object transmit heat to the adjacent particles by virtue of their physical contact with each other. When one end of a solid substance, such as a metal rod, is heated, we observe that the other end also becomes hot after a while. This occurs because the particles in the neighborhood of the heated end transmit the heat to the adjacent cooler molecules by conduction.

In conduction mode, the particles of the substance do not move from their respective locations. Heat transfer by *convection*, on the other hand, is characterized by the displacement of particles of the substance. Therefore, convection occurs only in liquids and gases.[1] When water in a container is heated on a stove, the water particles nearest the burner become warm and, hence, lighter. Being lighter, they rise up, giving way to heavier, cooler particles. These cooler particles are now heated and they also rise up. This process continues as long as the water is heated.

Radiation is unlike conduction and convection, since it does not require a medium. Heat transfer by radiation from one object to the other can occur even if there is no medium (solid, liquid, or gas) between them. That is how solar heat reaches the earth, since most of the space between the sun and the earth is a vacuum. Heat from a fireplace, burning candle, or an electric lamp reaches us by radiation.

Heat transfer by radiation occurs because every object produces electromagnetic waves by virtue of its temperature. These waves travel in space, much like the waves in an ocean. Since all objects produce radiation, there is a continuous radiation exchange between two objects facing each other. Each object emits heat to, and receives heat from, a facing object by radiation, Figure 4.1.

If the two facing objects are at the same temperature, the amount of heat emitted by each object is equal to the amount of heat received by it, resulting in a net heat transfer of zero between them. If one object is at a higher temperature than the other, it will emit a larger amount of heat but will receive less, resulting in a net radiant heat transfer from the warmer to the cooler object.

For radiation exchange between two objects to occur, they must be separated from each other, and there must be a direct line of sight between them. If the two objects, A and B, are intercepted by an intervening object, C, radiation exchange will not take place directly between A and B, since there is no direct line of sight between them. Instead, radiation exchange between them will occur through C. In other words, radiation exchange will take place between A and C, and between C and B, Figure 4.2.

---

[1] A small part of heat transfer in liquids is by conduction, since the particles of a liquid are in physical contact with each other. In gases, conduction mode of heat transfer is even smaller than in liquids.

During the process of heat transfer through an envelope component, all three modes usually come into play. Consider a cross-section through the brick cavity wall in Figure 4.3. Heat from the sun reaches the outer surface of the wall by radiation and is partly absorbed by the wall and partly reflected by it.

If the interior surface of the wall is cooler than the exterior surface, the absorbed heat will travel into the wall (from surface P to Q) by conduction, until it reaches the cavity space. Inside the cavity, two modes of heat transfer come into play simultaneously: convection through the air in the cavity, and radiation from surface Q to surface R. The subsequent mode is that of conduction through the inner leaf of the wall (from R to S). Finally, the heat is transferred from the interior surface of the wall (surface S) to interior air, furniture, and occupants by convection and radiation.

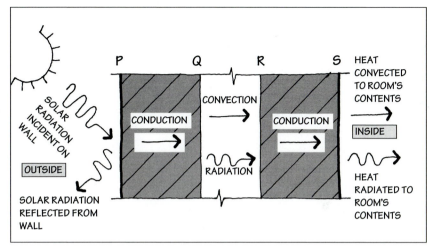

4.3 *Modes of heat transfer in a brick cavity wall, shown in cross-section.*

As indicated in Figure 4.3, all modes of heat transfer will usually contribute to heat flow through an envelope component. However, since an envelope component consists primarily of solid materials, the dominant mode of heat transfer through an envelope component is conduction. To understand the fundamentals of heat conduction, consider a homogeneous rectangular solid plate of thickness L, Figure 4.4.

Let the surface temperatures of the two opposite faces of the plate be t_1 and t_2, and let t_2 be greater than t_1. The amount of heat conducted through a unit area of the plate in unit time, i.e., the rate of heat conduction per unit area, q_c, can be shown experimentally to be given by:

$$q_c = \frac{k(t_2 - t_1)}{L} \qquad (4.1)$$

where $(t_2 - t_1)$ represents the temperature difference between the two opposite faces of the plate.

4.2 HEAT TRANSFER BY CONDUCTION

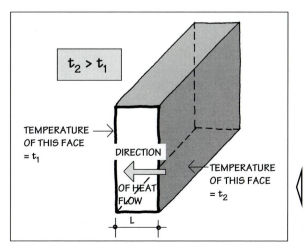

4.4 *Heat transfer by conduction through a plate of thickness L.*

Equation (4.1) shows that the rate of heat conduction through the plate is directly proportional to the difference between the surface temperatures of the opposite faces of the plate. If there is no difference between the surface temperatures, i.e., $(t_2 - t_1)$ is zero, no heat conduction will take place through the plate. Additionally, the rate of heat conduction is inversely proportional to the thickness of the plate, L. The greater the thickness, the smaller the heat transfer rate.

The term "k" in Equation (4.1) is called the *thermal conductivity* of the material. Being a material property, thermal conductivity is constant for a given material. If thermal conductivity is zero, then q_c is also zero, implying that heat conducted through such a component, regardless of its thickness, is zero. However, there is no real material for which k-value is zero. All materials have a finite k-value.

If a material's k-value is large, it is referred to as a *thermal conductor*. Metals, generally, have a high k-value, and hence they are good thermal conductors. Conversely, if the k-value is small, the material is referred to as a *thermal insulator*, or simply an *insulating material*.

4.2.1 Thermal Resistance — The R-Value

A property that relates more directly with the insulating value of a material is the reciprocal of thermal conductivity. It is referred to as thermal resistivity, or simply the *resistivity*, ρ. Thus, $\rho = 1/k$, or $k = 1/\rho$. If we replace k by $1/\rho$ in Equation(4.1), we obtain:

$$q_c = \frac{(t_2 - t_1)}{\rho L} \qquad (4.2)$$

The above equation can be rewritten as:

$$q_c = \frac{(t_2 - t_1)}{R} \qquad (4.3)$$

where we substituted $\rho L = R$

The term "R" in the above equation is called the *thermal resistance*, or more commonly the *R-value*. From Equation (4.3), we observe that the only property of the component that determines the rate of heat conduction through it is its R-value. The greater the R-value, the smaller the heat conducted through the component.

Thus, it is the R-value that is used in quoting the insulating effectiveness of a component. Most insulation manufacturers label their products with their R-values, Figure 4.5.

4.2.2 Units of ρ-Value and R-Value

From Equation 4.2, we see that if the units of q_c are Btu per square foot per hour (Btu/(ft^2·h), then the units of ρ are (ft^2·^{o}F·h)/(Btu·in.). Similarly, we can obtain the units of R from Equation (4.3) as (ft^2·^{o}F·h)/Btu.

The above units are in the customary U.S. system of units. In the SI system, q_c is expressed in Watts per square meter (W/m^2). Hence the units of ρ and R in the SI system are, respectively, (m·^{o}C)/W and (m^2·^{o}C)/W.

Since the units of ρ and R are rather complicated in both U.S. and SI systems, we usually omit their use in practice. However, since both units are currently used in the United States (although most other countries have long switched to the SI system), we must somehow identify the system of units being referenced. This is done by using the terms: ρ-value and ρSI-value; the latter refers to the same property in the SI system. The corresponding term for R-value is RSI-value.

4.2.3 Difference Between ρ-Value and R-Value

It is important to note the difference between ρ-value and R-value. Since R = ρL, the ρ-value and R-value are the same if L = 1. Thus, ρ-value = R-value for a 1-in.-thick component. It is the ρ-value that is used in comparing the insulating effectiveness of various materials. Thus, ρ-value may be looked at as the property of the material and the R-value as the property of the component of a given thickness. Table 4.1 gives the ρ-values of various commonly used building materials.

The relationship between ρ and R also indicates that if we know the ρ-value of a material, we can determine the R-value of any thickness of the same material. Thus, if the ρ-value of a material is 3.5, the R-value of a 1/2-in.-thick component of the same material is 1.75. For a 3-in.-thick component, the R-value is 10.5.

4.2.4 Effect of Density and Moisture Content on Insulating Value

Insulating materials are of low density, which is due to the air enclosed inside or between its solid constituents. It is the enclosed air that gives an insulating material its insulating property, since air has a high ρ-value compared with any

4.5 *Most insulation manufacturers label the R-value of their products. Photo by Madan Mehta.*

Quantity	U.S. units	SI units
Resistivity, ρ	$\dfrac{\text{ft}^2 \cdot {}^o\text{F} \cdot \text{h}}{\text{Btu} \cdot \text{in.}}$	$\dfrac{\text{m} \cdot {}^o\text{C} \cdot \text{h}}{\text{W}}$
Resistance, R	$\dfrac{\text{ft}^2 \cdot {}^o\text{F} \cdot \text{h}}{\text{Btu}}$	$\dfrac{\text{m}^2 \cdot {}^o\text{C} \cdot \text{h}}{\text{W}}$

Table 4.1 Thermal Resistivity — ρ-Value (i.e., R-Value for 1-in. Thickness) — of Commonly Used Building Materials

Material	Resistivity (ft²·°F·h)/(Btu·in.)	Material	Resistivity (ft²·°F·h)/(Btu·in.)
Metals (ρ-value for 1-in. thickness)		Expanded perlite (loose fill, density 5.0 pcf)	3.00
Steel	3.2×10^{-3}	Expanded perlite (loose fill, density 10.0 pcf)	2.40
Copper	3.2×10^{-4}	Expanded perlite board	2.80
Aluminum	3.2×10^{-3}	Perlite or vermiculite concrete	1.10
		Cellular (foamed) concete	1.30
Ceramic materials (R-value for 1- in. thickness)		Cellular (foamed) glass	2.90
Clay bricks	0.20		
Concrete — normal weight	0.15	Fiberglass or mineral (rock) wool — batt or blanket	4.00
Concrete — structural lightweight	0.30	Expanded polystyrene (EPS) board (bead board)	3.90
Concrete masonry — value depends on type of concrete and cell insulation		Extruded polystyrene (XEPS) board	5.00
Limestone	0.15	Polyisocyanurate board — impervious lamination on both faces	5.60
Sandstone	0.18	Polyurethane — spray applied	5.60
Glass	0.14		
Plaster	0.35	Gases — no convection currents (R-value for 1-in. thickness))	
Gypsum wallboard	0.60	Air	5.60
Portland cement plaster	0.30	Argon	8.90
		Carbon dioxide	9.90
Wood and coal (R-value for 1-in. thickness)		Chlorofluorocarbon (CFC) gas	16.50
Softwoods — solid lumber or plywood	0.90	Hydrochlorofluorocarbon (HCFC) gas	15.00
Wood charcoal	2.20		
Coal	0.85	Water (R-value for 1-in. thickness)	0.24
Roofing materials (R-value)			
Gravel-covered built-up roof (3/8-in. thickness typical)	0.30		
Asphalt shingles, or granule-covered built-up roof	0.20		
Single-ply roof membrane	0.10		
Wood shingles (1/2-in. thick typical)	0.90		
Slate or concrete roof tiles (1/2-in. thick typical)	0.05		
Insulating materials (R-value for 1-in. thickness)			
Granulated cork	3.00		
Wood fiber board	2.80		
Expanded vermiculite (loose fill)	2.10		

ρ-value = R-value of a 1-in. thick material.

To convert from ρ-value to ρSI-value	Multiply ρ-value by **6.93**
To convert from R-value to RSI-value	Multiply R-value by **0.176**

Values given in this table are representative rather than precise. Consult manufacturers' data for precise values.

solid material, see Table 4.1. In fact, "still" air is one of the best thermal insulators available.

Circulating air cannot be a good thermal insulator because it is the circulation of air that causes convection heat transfer. Thus, for a material to be a good thermal insulator, it must contain air in small pockets. In other words, a basic requirement of an insulating material is that its solid constituents must divide its volume into such tiny air spaces that air cannot circulate within them. With tiny air spaces, convection heat transfer is virtually eliminated. Most insulating materials are, therefore, fibrous, granular, or cellular in composition.

Apart from density, the amount of moisture content of the material affects its insulating value. Water has a low ρ-value, see Table 4.1. Consequently, the higher the moisture content, the lower the effectiveness of an insulator. Thus, an insulating material must be kept dry to retain its effectiveness. This is particularly important for a low-slope roof insulation, since by virtue of its location, it is vulnerable to rainwater absorption or condensation of moist interior air, see Section 9.4.2 in Chapter 9.

4.2.5 Entrapment of High Resistivity Gas Instead of Air

Although most insulating materials contain small volumes of air to provide high insulating value, some plastic foam insulations (or, simply, *foamed plastics*, discussed in Section 4.7) contain a gas with a higher resistivity than air. The gas commonly used these days[2] is hydrochlorofluorocarbon (HCFC) gas, which is nearly 2.5 times more effective than air in insulating effectiveness, see Table 4.1.

Foamed plastics that entrap HCFC are manufactured by using HCFC gas as a foaming agent in a liquid polymer. That is why they have the highest ρ-value, see Table 4.1. For instance, the ρ-value of bead board (a foamed plastic with air inside the beads) is 3.9, while that of polyisocyanurate board, which contains HCFC, is 5.6, Figure 4.6. Thus, a 1-in. thick polyisocyanurate board is almost as effective as a 1.8-in.-thick bead board.

Some of the HCFC gas trapped in cell cavities of plastic foams gradually finds its way into the atmosphere. Although the cellular structure of these foams consists generally of closed cells, it is not absolutely true. Therefore, air is able to permeate into the cell cavities of plastic foams driving some HCFC gas out, particularly from the edges and ends of a board.

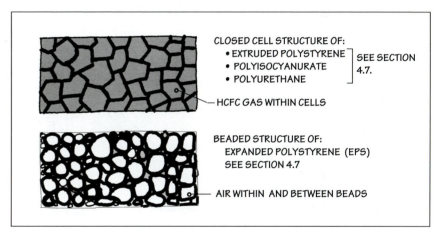

4.6 *Cellular structures of various plastic foam insulations.*

Plastic foam insulations foamed with HCFC gas:

- Extruded polystyrene
- Polyisocyanurate
- Polyurethane

---

[2] The gas used as foaming agent in plastic foams until a few years ago was chlorofluorocarbon (CFC) gas. However, it was found to deplete the protective ozone layer in the atmosphere. Being less destructive of the ozone layer, HCFC gas has replaced CFC gas. The insulating potential of HCFC is slightly lower than that of CFC, see Table 4.1.

The steady outward migration of HCFC gas means that the R-value of a plastic foam decreases with time. Therefore, in referring to the R-value of a plastic foam with HCFC gas, we generally quote its *stabilized* or *aged* R-value. The stabilized R-value is lower than the R-value immediately after the plastic foam's manufacture. In most cases, the R-value of such a material stabilizes after six months, after which the decrease in R-value is almost negligible.

4.3 R-VALUE OF A MULTILAYER COMPONENT

Usually a wall or roof assembly consists of two or more layers of different materials. For instance, a metal deck roof assembly consists of the metal deck, followed by layers of insulation, and finally the roof membrane. It can be shown theoretically that the total R-value of such an assembly is simply the sum of the individual R-values of each layer. Thus, if an assembly consists of various layers, whose individual R-values are R_1, R_2, R_3, R_4, etc., as shown in Figure 4.7, the total R-value of the assembly, R_t, is given by:

$$R_t = R_1 + R_2 + R_3 + R_4 + \cdots \qquad (4.4)$$

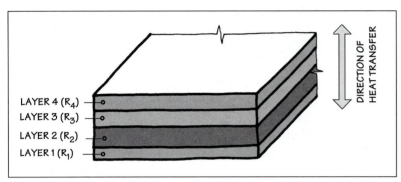

4.7 *A multilayer assembly.*

4.3.1 Surface Resistances

In addition to various layers of solid materials that comprise an envelope assembly, there are two invisible layers that contribute to the total R-value of an assembly. These layers are thin films of air of nearly zero velocity that cling to the surface of the assembly on each side, Figure 4.8. Since each air film has a certain thickness, it increases the total R-value of the assembly.

The R-value of each film is called the *film resistance*, or more commonly as the *surface resistance*. Thus, there is an internal surface resistance, R_{si}, and an external surface resistance, R_{so}, corresponding to the interior and exterior air films respectively. Since the surface resistances are always present, Equation (4.4) must be modified to the following format.

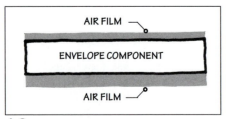

4.8 *Inside and outside air films.*

$$R_t = R_{si} + (R_1 + R_2 + R_3 + R_4 + \cdots) + R_{so} \qquad (4.5)$$

It is the total resistance obtained by including the two surface resistances that is responsible for *air-to-air heat transfer* through an envelope assembly. Since the inside air velocity is usually smaller than the outside air velocity, the inside film is thicker than the outside film. Hence, R_{si} is usually greater than R_{so}.

In fact, R_{si} and R_{so} do not depend on the air velocity alone but also on the texture of the surface and the direction of heat flow through the assembly. For instance, an increase in surface roughness increases the surface resistance. This is because a rougher surface creates a greater drag on air movement, reducing air velocity near the surface, and hence increasing the film thickness.

Although the values of R_{si} and R_{so} vary as stated, a good approximation of R_{si} is 0.7, and of R_{so} is 0.2 (in the U.S. system of units). Thus, $(R_{si} + R_{so})$ may be taken as approximately equal to 0.9, or say 1.0.

Since both surface resistances provide an R-value of only 1.0, they do not significantly add to the total R-value of a typical roof assembly, see calculations later in this chapter. They, however, contribute greatly to the R-value of a glazed window or a roof skylight, since a single sheet of glass has an extremely small — virtually zero — R-value. In fact, the total R-value of a window with a single sheet of glass is 1.0, which is provided almost entirely by the internal and external surface resistances.

$$R_{si} + R_{so} \approx 1.0$$

From Table 4.1, ρ-value of glass = 0.14

Hence, the R-value of a 3/8-in.-thick glass sheet = (3/8) 0.14 = 0.05

The total R-value of a skylight consisting of a 3/8-in.-thick glass = $R_{si} + R_{so} + 0.05 = 1.05$

Thus, the R-value of a single sheet of glass is virtually contributed by the film resistances.

In building envelopes, convection and radiation modes occur only in air cavities — wall cavities and attic spaces. Theoretically, the concept of R-value is applicable to solid components in which conduction is the only mode of heat transfer. However, the concept is extended to cavities also, and a cavity space is assigned an R-value just like a solid component.

The R-value of a cavity varies with the width of the cavity, its orientation (whether it is a horizontal or a vertical cavity), and the direction of heat flow. The change in the R-value of a cavity caused by a change in cavity width is a complex function of conduction, convection, and radiation heat transfers within the cavity space. For a vertical (wall) cavity, the R-value increases with cavity width up to 3/4 in. and then drops as the cavity width is increased.

The decrease in R-value with increasing width (beyond 3/4 in.) is so gradual that, for all practical purposes, the R-value of a wall cavity up to a width of 4 in. may be assumed to be 1.0. This takes into account the two film resistances within the cavity and both convection as well as radiation heat transfers.

4.4 HEAT TRANSFER BY CONVECTION AND RADIATION

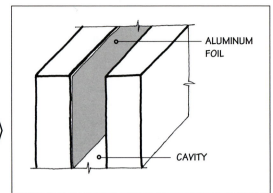

4.9 *Radiation heat transfer across a cavity space is reduced if one surface of the cavity is lined with aluminum foil.*

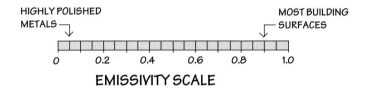

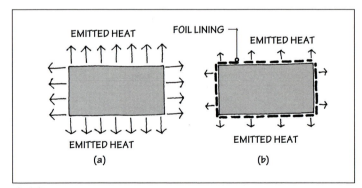

4.10 *Heat emitted by two identical objects that are at the same temperature. Object (b) is lined with aluminum foil. Therefore, it emits less heat.*

Note that radiation heat transfer is unaffected by the width of the cavity. As long as there is a space between the two opposite surfaces of a cavity, radiation heat transfer will occur between them. However, radiation heat transfer can be altered (reduced) by including a layer of aluminum foil within the cavity, Figure 4.9. This is generally achieved by laminating (also referred to as *lining the cavity* with) aluminum foil to one of the two surfaces of the cavity.

4.4.1 Effect of a Low Emissivity Material on Radiation Heat Transfer

The property by which aluminum foil reduces radiation heat transfer is due to the foil's low *emissivity*. Emissivity is a property of the surface of an object that refers to its potential to emit radiation. In fact, the magnitude of radiation emitted by an object is directly related to its emissivity and its temperature.[3] The effect of temperature on the radiation emitted by an object is well known. If an iron rod is placed inside a fire for a short while and then withdrawn, we can feel the heat emitted by the rod. If the same rod is placed in the fire for a long time and then withdrawn, we see that it emits more heat. The increase in radiated heat is due to a rise in the temperature of the rod.

The change in the magnitude of emitted heat caused by a change in the emissivity of the object is not observed as readily. However, if we were to take radiation measurements on a heated object, we will observe that it emits a certain amount of heat. If the same object is covered all around with an aluminum foil, we will observe that the heat emitted by it is much smaller,[4] Figure 4.10.

The emissivity of a material lies between zero and one. Most building materials (brick, concrete, wood, plaster, gypsum board, steel, etc.) have a high emissivity — approximately 0.9. Polished metals, on the other hand, have a low emissivity. A highly polished metal, such as stainless steel or aluminum, has an emissivity of only 0.05. This means that if an object made of brick, concrete, wood, etc., is covered with aluminum foil, the heat emitted by it will be (0.05/0.90) = 1/18th the heat emitted by the same object without the foil covering.

---

[3] The amount of heat emitted by an object is, in fact, proportional to the fourth power of temperature. Thus, if q_r represents the amount of heat emitted by an object per unit area, then:

$q_r = \beta e T^4$ where, e = emissivity of the object, T = temperature of the object in Kelvin, and β is a constant. For more details, refer to *The Principles of Building Construction* by Madan Mehta, Prentice Hall, 1997.

[4] Restaurants usually keep a baked potato covered with aluminum foil so that it emits less heat — to slow down its cooling. Aluminum foil also retains the moisture within the potato, being a good vapor retarder.

Note that emissivity is a property of the surface, not of the bulk of the material. Thus, changing the surface characteristic of an object will change its emissivity. For instance, plywood's emissivity is nearly 0.9, but if that plywood is laminated with aluminum foil, its emissivity will become only 0.05. Aluminum foil is the metal that is commonly used in building assemblies because of its low cost.

Lining a surface of the cavity with foil implies that the heat emitted by that surface is small, and hence the amount of heat transferred to the opposite surface is small. This increases the R-value of the cavity. Thus, the R-value of a typical foil-lined wall cavity is approximately 2.5, instead of 1.0 for an unlined cavity.

A fundamental fact related to emissivity is that *the emissivity of a surface is always equal to its absorptivity*. The absorptivity[5] refers to the potential of the surface to absorb radiation. Since most building materials have an emissivity of 0.9, their absorptivity is also 0.9, which means that they absorb 90% of radiation falling on them. A foil-lined surface, on the other hand absorbs only 5% of the radiation falling on it, since its absorptivity (or emissivity) is 0.05. Its reflectivity is therefore 0.95, i.e., it reflects 95% of the radiation falling on it. That is why a metal foil is also referred to as a *reflective insulation*, or a *radiant barrier*.

The implication of the above fact is that it is immaterial which side of the cavity is lined — warmer or the cooler side. Thus, if the warmer side of the cavity is lined, the radiation emitted by it is low because of its low emissivity. This radiation will fall on the opposite unlined surface, most of which (90%) is absorbed, Figure 4.11(a).

Now assume that the cooler side of the cavity is lined, Figure 4.11(b). Since the warmer side has an emissivity of 0.9, the radiation emitted by it is large. However, when this radiation falls on the opposite foil-lined surface, only 5% is absorbed, 95% is reflected back. Therefore, the amount of heat transferred to the opposite face is small — in fact, it is the same as that of the cavity of Figure 4.11(a).

4.4.2 R-Value of an Attic Space

The advantage of using an aluminum foil is more pronounced in an attic cavity than in a wall cavity. The reason is that radiation heat transfer is much more pronounced in an attic than in a wall cavity. Although the R-value of an attic varies from summer to winter, a typical unlined attic may be assumed to be of R-2.5. if the same attic is lined with aluminum foil, its R-value is approximately 6.5.

---

[5] Simply explained, radiation is classified under two types: (1) radiation from the sun, which is a high temperature source, and (2) radiation from terrestrial objects, such as the building surfaces, ground, etc., which are low temperature sources. While the absorptivity of a surface, with respect to low temperature radiation falling on it, is given by the surface's emissivity, it is the color of the surface that determines its absorptivity with respect to solar radiation.

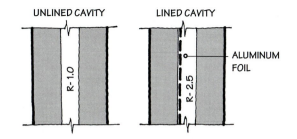

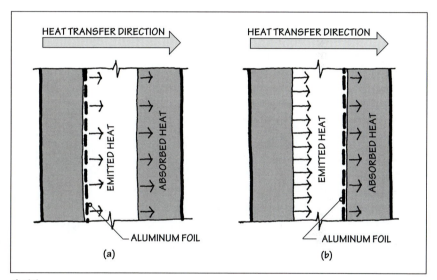

4.11 *Radiation heat transfer through a cavity is unaffected by the location of the foil lining in the cavity.*

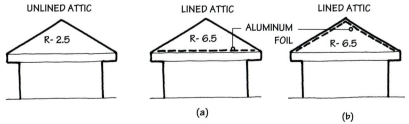

AS FAR AS R-VALUE IS CONCERNED, IT IS IMMATERIAL WHETHER THE FOIL IS PROVIDED (a) ABOVE THE CEILING OR (b) AT THE UNDERSIDE OF THE DECK

4.5 U-VALUE AND MINIMUM REQUIRED ROOF INSULATION

A property of an envelope component that relates more directly with heat transfer calculations is called the U-value. U-value is simply the reciprocal of the R-value. Thus:

$$U = 1/R_t$$

In other words, if the total R-value of an envelope assembly is 20.0, its U-value is $1/20 = 0.05$. A low U-value of the envelope implies a large amount of insulation present in the assembly, and vice versa.

To conserve the use of energy in buildings, energy codes mandate a minimum amount of insulation (R_{min}) in a building envelope. This is usually given in terms of U_{max} for wall and roof assemblies. The values of U_{max} for roof assemblies for several important U.S. locations are given in Appendix B.

CALCULATION OF THE U-VALUE OF AN ASSEMBLY

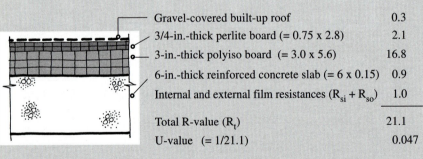

Gravel-covered built-up roof	0.3
3/4-in.-thick perlite board (= 0.75 x 2.8)	2.1
3-in.-thick polyiso board (= 3.0 x 5.6)	16.8
6-in.-thick reinforced concrete slab (= 6 x 0.15)	0.9
Internal and external film resistances ($R_{si} + R_{so}$)	1.0
Total R-value (R_t)	21.1
U-value (= 1/21.1)	0.047

Note: If there is a rigid board suspended ceiling below the roof, providing an air space between the roof and the ceiling, the R-value of this air space should be taken into account in calculating the U-value of roof assembly, see Section 4.4.2.

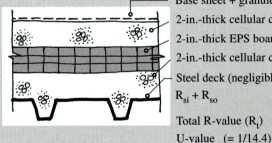

Base sheet + granule-covered mod. bit. roof	0.2
2-in.-thick cellular concrete fill (= 2 x 1.3)	2.6
2-in.-thick EPS board (= 2 x 4.0)	8.0
2-in.-thick cellular concrete fill (= 2 x 1.3)	2.6
Steel deck (negligible R-value)	0.0
$R_{si} + R_{so}$	1.0
Total R-value (R_t)	14.4
U-value (= 1/14.4)	0.069

Note: The concrete in the flutes of steel deck will increase the total R-value of the assembly, but only slightly; hence, it has been neglected.

Apart from the R-value or the U-value, there are several other properties that must be considered in the selection of a low-slope roof insulation. The more important such properties are discussed in this section.

4.6.1 Strength

The importance of compressive strength of a low-slope roof insulation has already been mentioned in the beginning of this chapter. Although there is no mandatory requirement, 20 psi is generally regarded as a desirable minimum compressive strength. Apart from the compressive strength, a sufficiently high cohesive strength (tensile strength perpendicular to the plane of the board) is also needed to resist wind uplift. Obviously, the greater the wind uplift on the roof, the greater the required cohesive strength.

4.6.2 Dimensional Stability

Expansion or contraction of insulation can cause stresses on the membrane, particularly if the membrane is fully adhered to the insulation. If both membrane and insulation expand and contract equally, there will be no stress. A large dimensional incompatibility between the membrane and the insulation can cause membrane failure at insulation joints, particularly of a fully adhered membrane.

Plastic foam insulations are generally more dimensionally unstable than other commonly used roof insulations. They have a higher coefficient of thermal expansion, Table 4.2. Aging and changes in environmental humidity also affect insulation dimensions.

For instance, plastic foam insulations containing HCFC gas show a long-term growth in size. This occurs as the smaller air (nitrogen, oxygen, carbon dioxide, and water vapor) molecules move into cell cavities at a faster rate than the outward diffusion of HCFC.[4.1] Consequently the gas pressure in cells increases, swelling the individual cells and thereby increasing the overall dimensions of the insulation, which can cause its curling, warping and buckling, Figure 4.12. The phenomenon is more pronounced in warm weather due to the added thermal expansion of gas in cells. The following strategies can be used to increase dimensional stability of insulation:

- Insulation that is anchored to the deck is less susceptible to dimensional changes. Loose-laid insulation will expand and contract freely. Therefore, roof membrane should not be fully adhered or anchored to loose-laid insulation.

4.6 OTHER IMPORTANT PROPERTIES OF ROOF INSULATION

Table 4.2 Coefficient of Thermal Expansion of Selected Insulating Materials

Insulation	Coefficient of thermal expansion ($^oF^{-1}$)
Plastic foams, including sprayed-in-place polyurethane	$30 - 40 \times 10^{-6}$
Perlite or wood fiberboard	10×10^{-6}
Lightweight insulating concrete	4×10^{-6}
Foamed glass	4×10^{-6}

Note: The values given in this table are approximate. For precise values, obtain manufacturer's data.

4.12 *Warping and curling of a plastic foam insulation under this fully adhered single-ply membrane. Photo by Stephen Patterson.*

- Using smaller insulation boards reduces the change in the width of joints between insulation boards. This reduces the stress on the membrane, since the expansion or contraction of a board is directly related to its linear dimension. Thus, using a 4-ft-long board will halve the change in joint width as compared to an 8-ft-long board. Note that a fully adhered membrane is subjected to maximum stresses at the insulation joints. A smaller change in joint width means a lower stress on the membrane.

- As far as possible, use insulation whose expansion and contraction is of the same order as the membrane, particularly the insulation layer that is directly below the membrane. Thus, if insulation is provided in two layers, the top layer should be as dimensionally compatible with the membrane as possible.

- Mechanically fastened membrane is better able to withstand dimensional instability of insulation than a fully adhered membrane.

FULLY ADHERED AND MECHANICALLY FASTENED ROOF MEMBRANES AND THEIR RELATIVE ABILITIES TO COPE WITH EXPANSION AND CONTRACTION OF SUBSTRATE

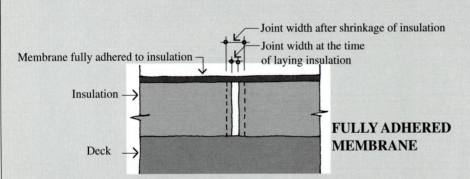

FULLY ADHERED MEMBRANE

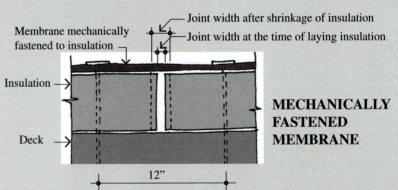

MECHANICALLY FASTENED MEMBRANE

Assume that the width of a joint between insulation boards at the time of laying the insulation is 0.1 in. If the insulation shrinks by 0.1 in. (due to change in thermal or moisture conditions), the joint width will now be 0.2 in. — a 100% dimensional change. Since the membrane is fully adhered to the insulation, this dimensional change is transferred to the membrane also. Most membranes are unable to withstand this (100%) change.

Assume once again the same width of joint — 0.1 in. before and 0.2 in. after the insulation shrinkage, except that the membrane is mechanically fastened to the deck at 12 in. on center. The dimensional change in the membrane in this case is 0.1 in. in 12 in., i.e., 0.8% — a much smaller change. Thus, a mechanically fastened membrane is better able to cope with the dimensional instability of substrate.

4.6.3 Combustibility and Resistance to High Temperature

Since a low-slope roof insulation is not exposed to the interior of the building, it need not be noncombustible. However, a noncombustible insulation will generally provide a higher rating for external fire exposure. If the membrane is torched-on directly to the insulation (without any underlying base sheet), it must be noncombustible and be able to withstand high temperatures.

4.6.4 Water Absorption and Chemical Compatibility

The wetting of insulation not only lowers its R-value, it also reduces its strength and accelerates its disintegration. A perlite board or wood fiberboard absorbs more water than a plastic foam insulation.

Insulation must also be compatible with the deck, the roof membrane and any adhesives used. Phenolic foam insulation was once used, but after it was discovered that it corrodes metal decks and fasteners, its use as roof insulation has been discontinued.

4.7 RIGID BOARD ROOF INSULATION TYPES

Low-slope roof insulations may be divided into rigid boards and poured-in-place lightweight insulating concrete fill. Rigid board insulations may be further subdivided into the combustible or noncombustible type:

- Combustible (i.e., organic) type, e.g., foamed plastics and wood fiberboard.

- Noncombustible (i.e., inorganic) type, e.g., perlite board, foamed glass, and fiberglass.

4.7.1 Foamed Plastics — Expanded and Extruded Polystyrene Boards

Foamed plastic insulations are made from two polymer groups: polystyrenes and polyurethanes. In the polystyrene group, there are two boards:

- Expanded polystyrene (EPS) board
- Extruded expanded polystyrene (XEPS) board

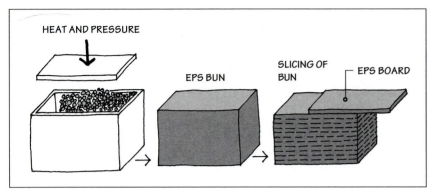

4.13 *Manufacture of EPS (bead) boards — a simplified version.*

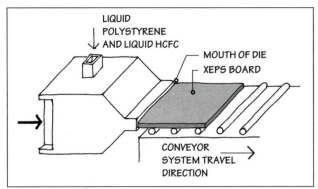

4.14 *Manufacture of extruded polystyrene (XEPS) boards — a simplified version.*

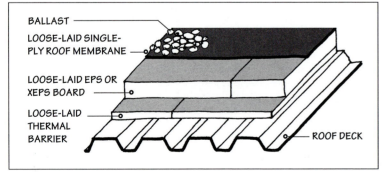

4.15 *EPS or XEPS boards are commonly used with loose-laid, ballasted, single-ply membranes.*

EPS boards (also referred to as bead boards) are made by packing the polystyrene beads in a mold and fusing them together under heat and pressure. The beads are tiny (nearly 1/8 in. diameter) hollow bubbles. The molded material is simply a large rectangular block, referred to as a "bun," which is sliced into boards of required thickness, Figure 4.13. EPS board is essentially of the same material as that used in picnic coolers.

Due to the relatively small capital investment needed in their production, there are a large number of EPS board manufacturers. By contrast, the extruded polystyrene board manufacturing requires a large capital outlay. Therefore, only a few manufacturers produce XEPS boards. XEPS boards are more expensive, stronger, and have a higher ρ-value than EPS boards.

XEPS boards are made by mixing a liquid polymer with liquid HCFC gas and forcing the mixture through a die, Figure 4.14. The version of HCFC gas used in XEPS manufacture works as a foaming agent since it vaporizes at a low temperature so that the polystyrene expands before it is extruded into shape through the die.

As indicated in Figure 4.6, the cellular structure of extruded polystyrene is one of interconnected cell walls to give closed cavities. This gives XEPS boards a much higher bending strength, compressive strength, and cohesive strength than the EPS boards, which consist of individual beads fused together. Because of their lower compressive strength, EPS boards are not generally recommended on roofs with frequent foot traffic or under roofer's buggies and carts with heavy loads.

Both EPS and XEPS boards are generally unsuitable for use directly over a metal deck, because in the event of an internal fire, they can disintegrate and release toxic fumes into the building interior through deck joints. A thermal barrier (typically a 5/8-in.-thick type "X" gypsum board) is required between the deck and EPS or XEPS boards.

Both EPS and XEPS boards cannot resist high temperatures. Their cellular structure begins to disintegrate at nearly 200°F. Therefore, they are not recommended as a substrate for built-up or modified bitumen roofs, unless covered with another layer of insulation that can withstand bitumen's high temperature — referred to as a *cover board*. Perlite board or wood fiberboard are commonly used as cover boards. Remember that the temperature of hot bitumen is nearly 450°F.

Another reason for using a cover board over EPS or XEPS boards is their low compressive strength. A stronger cover board increases the attachment to the deck and improves the resistance to localized crushing from deck traffic, hail storms, etc. That is why they are more commonly used with a loose-laid, ballasted, single-ply membrane, which does not need fasteners and, hence, obviates the need for a cover board, Figure 4.15. Both EPS and XEPS insulations are chemically incompatible with coal tar and PVC membrane. They are also damaged by solvents, such as splice cleaners, and some adhesives used in single-ply roof systems.

Because of its closed cell structure, XEPS board has excellent resistance to water absorption. EPS board, because of its beaded structure, is far more water permeable. That is why XEPS is an insulation of choice for a protected membrane roof, see Section 4.10.

4.7.2 Foamed Plastics — Polyurethane and Polyisocyanurate Insulation

The chemical difference between polyurethane and polyisocyanurate is extremely small. However, polyisocyanurate is more fire-resistive than polyurethane. Thus, polyisocyanurate board (also referred to as an *iso board*) is commonly used as low-slope roof insulation. Polyurethane, on the other hand, is more common as a foamed-in-place roof system, referred to as the *urethane roof*.

The version of HCFC gas used as a foaming agent in the manufacture of iso boards is different from that used with XEPS boards. It vaporizes at a higher temperature than the HCFC used in the production of XEPS boards. Therefore, the iso board requires facers on both faces to contain the foam until it fully solidifies, Figure 4.16.

The facers retard the migration of HCFC out of the iso board. That is why an iso board has a higher ρ-value than an XEPS board. The commonly used facers are glass fiber scrim and built-up roof felt. Perlite board and wood fiber board are also used, in which case the resulting board is referred to as a *composite board*. Aluminum foil-faced iso board is also available, but its use is generally limited to wall sheathing.

Although iso board can withstand the high temperature of hot asphalt, blister formation is a serious problem when built-up roof felt is mopped directly to the iso board. In addition, delamination of the top facer of iso board in such assemblies has been reported. Therefore, with a built-up roof membrane, it is advisable to use either wood fiber board or perlite board over the iso board. Blister formation is relatively small when built-up roof felts are mopped to perlite or wood fiber board. Perlite board is more commonly used because of its noncombustibility.

Although blister formation is problematic when built-up roof felts are mopped over the iso board, this is not so when perlite or wood fiber board is adhered to the iso board with a full mopping of asphalt, Figure 4.17(a). Similarly, iso board can be adhered to a concrete deck with a full mopping of bitumen, Figure 4.17(b).

4.7.3 Wood Fiber Board

Wood fiber board is made from wood or cane fibers and a binding agent. Like the plastic foams, it is combustible. However, unlike the plastic foams, it absorbs water and disintegrates, although asphalt coating on its faces decreases its water absorbency.

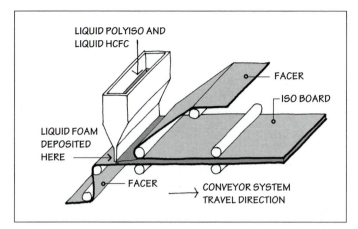

4.16 *Manufacture of iso boards — a simplified version.*

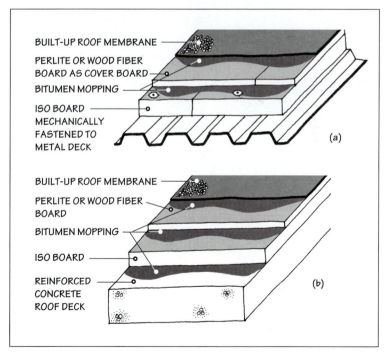

4.17 *Use of iso board insulation with built-up roof membrane over (a) metal deck, and (b) reinforced concrete deck.*

Because of its high density, wood fiberboard has a relatively high compressive strength. That is why it is commonly used in 4 ft x 8 ft size. Although thicker boards are available, the commonly used thickness is 1/2 in. Its low cost, compatibility with most roofing membranes, and high strength makes it a good cover board over plastic foams and a good recover board in reroofing applications.

Wood fiber board, used as a cover board over a plastic foam insulation, increases the compressive strength of the entire insulation assembly, since the typical strength of plastic foam insulation is low — nearly 20 psi. However, because of its relatively low ρ-value, wood fiber board is not used as primary insulation, see Table 4.1.

4.7.4 Perlite Board

Perlite is a glassy volcanic rock which is expanded into granular format by heat treatment. The expansion of perlite takes place because of a small amount of water in the crude perlite rock. When heated suddenly to a temperature of nearly 1,600°F, the water in the crushed perlite particles converts to steam. The pressure of steam expands perlite particles, creating small air-filled granules, Figure 4.18. The process of expanding perlite is similar to making popcorn.

Although the major ingredient in a perlite board is the expanded perlite granules and a binder, other materials such as cellulosic fibers (obtained from recycled paper or wood pulp) and synthetic fibers are added to increase the strength of the board. Asphalt is also added to provide water repellency and rot resistance. Thus, although a perlite board is largely noncombustible because of the perlite granules, it has combustible contents in it. Perlite boards with enhanced fire retardancy are available for use under torched-on roof systems.

Perlite board has excellent resistance to high temperature and is compatible with hot bitumen and most roof membranes. Blistering of hot bitumen mopped over perlite board is minimal. It has virtually the same coefficient of thermal expansion as a built-up roof membrane, which adds to its compatibility with built-up and modified bitumen roof membranes.

That is why perlite board in 3/4-in. or 1-in. thickness is commonly used as a cover board over foamed plastics, particularly with built-up roofs. Composite boards consisting of 1/2-in.- or 3/4-in.-thick perlite boards laminated to both sides of iso boards are also available. Some manufacturers make composite board with perlite board on one side and a roofing felt on the other side of an iso board.

The strength of a perlite board is relatively low. That is why it is commonly used in small sizes - 2 ft x 4 ft or 4 ft x 4 ft. It can be easily field cut to size.

CRUDE PERLITE ROCK   CRUSHED CRUDE PERLITE   EXPANDED PERLITE

4.18 *Stages in perlite production illustrate the great increase in volume that takes place on expansion.*

4.7.5 Foamed Glass and Fiberglass Boards

Foamed glass (also referred to as *cellular glass*) is made from foaming air through molten glass and letting the foamed liquid cool down. The cooled material is then cut into boards of required lengths and widths. It has a very high compressive strength. Hence, it is more commonly used as an insulation under a slab-on-grade and over plaza decks, which must withstand a great deal of traffic. It is uncommon as roof insulation because of its relatively low ρ-value, high cost, and its potential to tear roof membranes.

Fiberglass board, a material similar to fiberglass batt or blanket but in higher density format, was a popular low-slope roof insulation until a few years ago, but not today. Fiberglass boards used as roof insulation were laminated with a facer on one face of the board to yield a suitable substrate to mop on. However, the fiberglass board's low compressive strength, cost, and the delamination of the facer were among some of the reasons for its decline in usage as roof insulation.

4.7.6 Rigid Board Low-slope Roof Insulations Compared

Table 4.3 gives the relative usage of low-slope roof insulations. The data includes figures for all insulation types discussed in this section, i.e., perlite board, wood fiberboard, EPS, XEPS, iso board, cellular glass, and fiberglass.[4.2] Together, these seven insulation types have nearly 91% of the entire low-slope roof insulation market. Table 4.4 gives an overall view of the relative properties of these insulations.

Table 4.3 Rigid Board Low-Slope Roof Insulations — Market Shares

Insulation	Percentage market share
Perlite board	18
Wood fiberboard	16
EPS board	10
XEPS board	3
Iso board	44
Fiberglass and cellular glass	4
Others	9

Table 4.4 Rigid Board Low-Slope Roof Insulations — Comparison of Properties

Property	Insulating material					
	Perlite	Wood fiber	EPS	XEPS	Iso	Cellular glass
Compressive strength	High	High	Low	High*	High*	High
Compatibility with hot bitumen	Good	Good	Poor	Poor	Fair	Good
Blistering resistance with hot bitumen	Good	Good	Poor	Poor	Poor	Poor
Moisture resistance	Fair	Fair	Fair	Good	Good	Good
Coefficient of thermal expansion	Low	Low	High	High	High	Low
Thermal resistivity (R-value for 1 in. thick)	2.8	2.8	3.9	5.0	5.6	2.9

* XEPS and Iso board compressive strengths may be rated as "fair" to "high," depending on the density of the board.

4.8 PRIMARY AND SECONDARY ROOF INSULATIONS

Wherever thickness permits, it is desirable to use two (or more) layers of insulation in place of one layer. The first layer, as far as possible, should be mechanically fastened to the deck (above a thermal barrier where required), Figure 4.19. Mechanical fastening provides a more secure attachment against wind uplift. It is the preferred attachment method with most roof decks, except cast-in-place or precast concrete decks. With a reinforced concrete or a precast concrete deck, mechanical fastening is cumbersome. Therefore, hot bitumen is generally used to adhere the first insulation layer, see Figure 4.17(b). Cold adhesives, if specified, must be checked for their adhesive power.

The boards in the first insulation layer should be laid with continuous longitudinal joints and transverse joints staggered, Figure 4.20. Whether the first layer is fastened or mopped, the second layer should (when possible) be fully adhered to the first layer with hot bitumen, Figure 4.21. This recommendation is based on the fact that hot mopping of the second layer integrates the two layers, giving the insulation boards a higher bending strength.

4.19 *A two-person crew anchoring the insulation to the deck. One person lays the fasteners (screw and cap) in the correct locations, and the other person screws them down. Photos by Madan Mehta.*

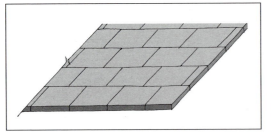

4.20 *Staggered layout pattern of rigid board insulation. Photo by Madan Mehta.*

If both layers are mechanically fastened, thermal bridging will occur at the fasteners. Similarly, if only one layer of insulation is used, thermal bridging will occur at the joints and the fasteners. An additional advantage of mopping the second layer is that it shortens the length of fasteners.

The longitudinal as well as the transverse joints in the second layer should be staggered from the first layer, in order to eliminate the leakage of heat through insulation joints.

The lower insulation layer is usually thicker than the upper layer. In such a case, the lower layer provides most of the R-value in the assembly, and the upper layer is usually a cover board — typically 1/2 in. to 1 in. thick. That is why the lower layer is referred to as the *primary insulation* and the upper layer as the *secondary insulation*. The secondary insulation is generally chosen for its compatibility with the roof membrane, and is therefore also referred to as *cover board*, see Section 4.7.1 in Chapter 4.

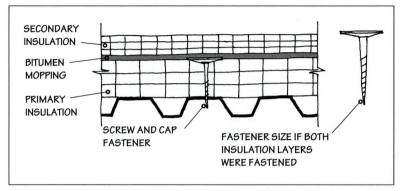

4.21 *Recommended detail of the anchorage of rigid board insulation to a nailable deck. On a nonnailable deck, both insulation layers are typically hot mopped.*

A low-slope roof insulation (other than the rigid boards) is lightweight insulating concrete fill. This is poured over the roof deck in wet format, in the same way as wet concrete is poured into forms. When the insulating fill hardens, it becomes monolithic with the deck. Therefore a deck with an insulating fill is also referred to as an *insulating roof deck*, see also Section 5.1.1 in Chapter 5.

The steel deck used with insulating concrete must be a galvanized steel deck. The galvanizing layer helps create a chemical bond between the insulating concrete and steel deck, increasing the adhesion between them. With rigid board insulation, a painted steel deck may be used. An insulating concrete fill may be of two types:

- Perlite or vermiculite concrete
- Cellular (foamed) concrete

4.9.1 Perlite or Vermiculite Concrete

Perlite or vermiculite concrete consists of portland cement and expanded perlite or expanded vermiculite in the ratio of 1 (portland cement): 4 to 8 (perlite or vermiculite). In this mix, portland cement-plus-water slurry is the binder, and perlite or vermiculite is the aggregate.

4.9 INSULATING CONCRETE FILL

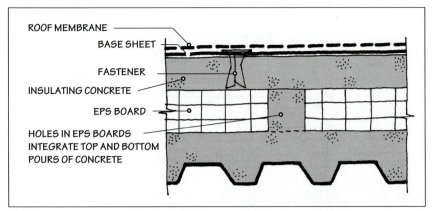

ROOF MEMBRANE

BASE SHEET

FASTENER

INSULATING CONCRETE

EPS BOARD

HOLES IN EPS BOARDS
INTEGRATE TOP AND BOTTOM
POURS OF CONCRETE

4.22 *Cross-section through an EPS-insulating fill sandwich.*

4.23 *Insulating concrete being poured over roof deck. Photo by Madan Mehta.*

4.24 *Holes in an EPS board. Photo by Madan Mehta.*

The process of producing expanded perlite has already been described. Expanded vermiculite is obtained by expanding mica, in the same way as perlite is expanded. Like perlite, vermiculite is also a mineral and is noncombustible. Thus, perlite and vermiculite concrete are noncombustible forms of insulation.

Since both perlite and vermiculite consist of small hollow granules, they tend to hold water within their voids. Thus, it takes a long time for water to evaporate out of perlite or vermiculite concrete — far longer than the evaporation of water from a structural concrete slab. Vermiculite granules hold more water than perlite granules, which is an advantage in hot dry climates, where a more rapid evaporation of water may tend to crack insulating concrete.

When laid on metal deck, manufacturers of perlite or vermiculite concrete recommend the use of a slotted deck. A slotted or perforated deck allows the moisture in the concrete to be gradually vented out from the underside of the deck by the building's heating and cooling system. Therefore, roof membrane can be installed when the concrete has become sufficiently hard to hold the fasteners but may not have fully dried.

Since below-the-deck venting cannot be provided in a reinforced concrete or a precast concrete deck, the use of vermiculite or perlite concrete on such decks requires that the insulating concrete be so dry that it does not create water vapor problems in the roofing membrane. Alternatively, topside venting should be provided vapor pressure relief, see Section 10.7 in Chapter 10.

Any water contained in the insulating concrete will convert to water vapor (steam) by the action of solar heat and, if not able to escape, will exert pressure on the membrane, delaminating it from the substrate. If the vapor pressure is excessive, tearing of the membrane may occur.

The insulating value of perlite or vermiculite concrete is much lower than most rigid board insulations, see Table 4.1. To increase its R-value, EPS boards are sandwiched between two pours of insulating concrete. Thus, the EPS-insulating concrete sandwich system consists of a layer of insulating concrete followed by a layer of rigid EPS boards, and finally a layer of insulating concrete, Figure 4.22. At the present time, only EPS boards are approved by the industry for use with insulating concrete.

The wet insulating concrete is pumped up to the roof from the ground, where the mix is prepared and poured over the deck — similar to the pumping and pouring of structural concrete, Figure 4. 23. To integrate the three layers of this sandwich into a monolithic whole, the EPS boards are provided with holes, Figure 4.24. Typically, six holes, each 3 in. in diameter, are provided in a 4 ft x 4 ft EPS board. To increase the fire rating of the roof, a layer of woven steel wire mesh is embedded just above the EPS boards and before the second concrete pour, Figure 4.25.

After the insulating concrete has hardened (typically after three to five days), a mineral-granule-faced base sheet is fastened to the concrete as a substrate for a built-up or modified bitumen roof. Special fasteners have been developed by the industry to fasten the base sheet, which can simply be driven into the lightweight concrete, Figure 4.26. The fasteners flare as they penetrate into the concrete, Figure 4.27. The wind uplift resistance provided by the fasteners is a function of the strength of concrete, the depth of concrete above EPS boards, and the center-to-center spacings of fasteners.

After the base sheet has been fastened, the built-up roof or modified bitumen membrane can be mopped to the base sheet. A single-ply membrane may also be installed over insulating concrete, but the insulating concrete manufacturers recommend consulting with single-ply membrane manufacturers for compatibility, etc.

4.25 *Woven steel wire mesh over EPS boards is laid on this roof before the second pour of insulating concrete. Photo by Madan Mehta.*

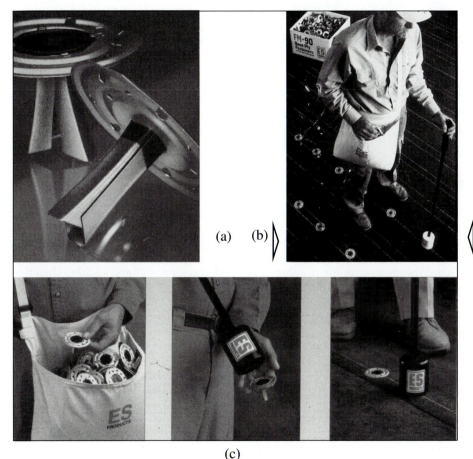

(a)   (b)

(c)

4.26 *(a) A type of fastener used for fastening the base sheet to insulating concrete. (b) Roofer fastening the base sheet. (c) Three-step procedure showing the use of a magnet-tipped fastening tool. Photos courtesy of ES Products Inc., Bristol, Rhode Island.*

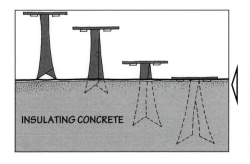

INSULATING CONCRETE

4.27 *The fastener flares as it is driven into the insulating fill. Sketch adapted from that of ES Products Inc., Bristol, Rhode Island.*

Advantages of Insulating Fill over Rigid Board Insulation

1.   Insulating fill has greater compressive strength than rigid board insulation, which provides a solid base for roof membrane.

2.   Insulating fill requires no fasteners. It bonds well with steel deck or concrete deck and has high internal cohesive strength. As a jointless insulation, it also works as an air barrier. It, therefore, provides a high wind uplift resistance.

3.   Insulating fill's noncombustibility adds to the roof's fire rating.

4.   Insulating fill requires no cutting of boards near the rooftop equipment and around the drains. This is a major advantage with a nonrectangular roof outline and/or with several types of rooftop equipment.

5.   Insulating fill can be used on dead-level decks, because the slope can be provided in the fill. If the same slope is provided by using tapered insulation, the system becomes expensive and complicated.

6.   Although insulating fill's R-value is lower than most rigid board insulations, it has higher heat storage (heat sink) capacity, which helps to moderate roof membrane's temperature.

Disadvantages of Insulating Fill over Rigid Board Insulation

1.   Although the membrane can be laid over rigid board insulation immediately, insulating fill must be left to dry (for nearly two to five days) before laying the membrane.

2.   Bottom side venting of insulation is generally required in insulating fill, which is not required with rigid board insulation.

3.   Special care must be taken to lay insulating fill in very cold or very hot climates, which is not a concern with rigid board insulation.

A major advantage of insulating concrete is that roof slope can easily be provided in the insulation, even if the roof deck is dead-level. This is done by using EPS boards of different thicknesses to create a stair-stepped pattern, Figure 4.28. Providing slope over a dead-level deck with tapered rigid board insulation is expensive and complicated, see Sections 6.3 and 6.4 in Chapter 6.

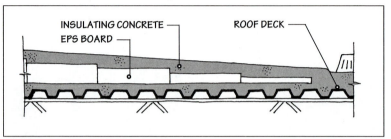

4.28 *Longitudinal cross-section through a roof showing stair-stepped EPS board pattern to achieve slope on a dead-level roof deck.*

4.9.2 Foamed Concrete

Foamed (also called "cellular") concrete is a nonaggregate concrete that consists of portland cement, water, and a liquid foaming concentrate. The foaming concentrate creates tiny air bubbles, so that when the mix hardens, it contains a matrix of air voids separated by pure portland cement walls. Because of the absence of aggregate, the ρ-value of foamed concrete is slightly higher than that of perlite or vermiculite concrete.

The absence of aggregate reduces the amount of water required to pump and place the foamed concrete compared to perlite or vermiculite concrete. Typically, foamed concrete requires only one-third the amount of water used in perlite or vermiculite concrete. Therefore, foamed concrete dries quicker.

Foamed concrete also does not need a slotted metal deck, although its use is preferred. The other details, such as the use of galvanized steel deck, EPS board sandwich, woven steel wire to provide a higher fire rating, fastening a base sheet, and stair-stepping EPS boards for roof slope, etc., are similar to those used with perlite or vermiculite concrete.

In a protected membrane roof, PMR, the insulation is laid loose over the roof membrane, which is installed straight on the deck, Figure 4.29. In the case of a steel deck, a cover board, typically a 1/2-in.- (13-mm) thick type "X" gypsum board, is used under the membrane to provide a flat surface. The type of membrane and its installation is similar to that in a conventional roof assembly. Any one of the various membranes (built-up roof, modified bitumen, or single-ply membrane) can be used in a PMR.

After the installation of the membrane and the associated flashings at roof perimeter and penetrations, the membrane is covered with insulation, which is then covered with ballast. The ballast may consist of river gravel, crushed stone or precast concrete pavers. Pavers make the entire roof surface walkable in addition to providing an easily maintainable roof. Pavers also make the roof look cleaner compared to gravel or crushed stone. Since the order of insulation and roof membrane is reversed in a PMR, it is also referred to as an *inverted roof*.[6]

With the protection provided to it by the insulation and the ballast cover, the roof membrane is shielded from weathering elements, such as ultraviolet radiation and hail and traffic impact. The membrane is also protected from thermal cycling — a major cause of a roof membrane's deterioration in a conventional roof assembly where the membrane is the uppermost layer.

In a PMR, the membrane is subjected to a much smaller thermal cycling because of the moderating effect of the overlying insulation. Consequently, PMR is an assembly of choice in extremely cold or hot climates, such as North Canada, Alaska, the deserts of Saudi Arabia, etc., where the membranes fail prematurely when used in a conventional way. In such climates, a conventional roof membrane can experience an annual temperature variation of up to 200°F year after year.

The performance of a PMR in moderate climates has also been reported to be quite good, particularly in terms of its durability. Note that a PMR with concrete pavers creates an assembly that is similar to a waterproofed plaza or usable terrace. It is, therefore, costlier than a conventional roof and also needs more regular maintenance, because clay, silt, and other fine particles deposited in insulation and paver joints can lead to bacterial and vegetation growth, which can accelerate the deterioration of the assembly.

---

[6] A patented proprietary version of PMR is called Inverted Roof Membrane Assembly (IRMA) by its manufacturer.

4.10 PROTECTED MEMBRANE ROOF

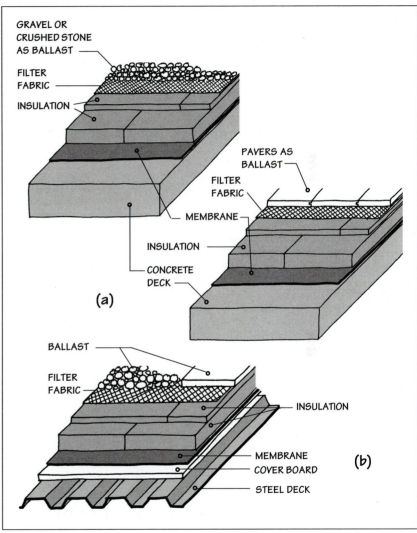

4.29 *A protected membrane roof assembly (PMR) over (a) concrete deck, and (b) steel deck.*

4.10.1 Insulation in a PMR

Since the temperature cycling and weathering elements are borne by the insulation in a PMR, insulation becomes a more critical component of the assembly. PMR insulation must be water impermeable, have high resistance to freeze-thaw cycles, high compressive strength, and a high dimensional stability.

Among the commonly used low-slope insulations, extruded polystyrene is the only insulation that meets these and the other requirements of a PMR. Therefore, at the present time, PMR roof assemblies are restricted to using extruded polystyrene boards only.

It is preferable to use two layers of insulation, particularly in severely cold climates, to reduce thermal bridging through insulation joints. Some PMR manufacturers integrate the upper layer of insulation and concrete paver into one board. Usually, such a paver-insulation combination is prefabricated by pouring latex-modified concrete over extruded polystyrene boards. The boards are generally tongued-and-grooved to provide interlocking mechanism between them. For greater wind uplift resistance, concrete pavers can be strapped together with steel straps.

4.10.2 Filter Fabric

Another important component in a PMR is a filter fabric, which consists of a porous plastic membrane laid over the insulation. Its purpose is to arrest silt and small debris flowing into insulation joints and restricting the insulation's expansion and contraction. The filter fabric also protects roof drains against blockage by such materials. For a more detailed discussion of PMR assemblies, the reader is referred to other sources[4.3] and manufacturers' literature.

REFERENCES

4.1   Griffin, C. W., and Fricklas, R. *The Manual of Low-slope Roof Systems* (New York: McGraw Hill, 1995), p. 77.

4.2   National Roofing Contractors Association. *Professional Roofing* (Rosemont, IL: April 1999), p. 17.

4.3   Griffin, C. W., and Fricklas, R. *The Manual of Low-slope Roof Systems* (New York: McGraw Hill, 1995), pp. 373-403.

5

ROOF DECK

As a component of a roof assembly on which the entire roof and the rooftop equipment rests, the roof deck is the most important part of a roof. The major function of a roof deck is to support the loads — dead load, live load, snow load. wind uplift, and the seismic load (in seismic areas). Therefore, the design of a roof deck is based primarily on structural considerations.

However, the architects and/or the roofing consultant must ensure that all loads to which the deck will be subjected have been accounted for in the structural design of the deck. For instance, roof slope and the drainage design of a roof — factors that typically fall within the work domain of an architect and/or a roofing consultant — can significantly affect the ponding load (due to rainwater) on a roof.

Similarly, roofing and reroofing operations often subject a roof to large concentrated loads due to the storage of felt rolls, stone ballast filled wheel carts, etc. These loads are generally heavier than the live load imposed on the roof at other times and must be duly considered in the design of the deck.

In addition to the structural concerns, there are several nonstructural requirements which must be satisfied if the deck is to perform as an appropriate base for the roof membrane. A deck that has not been designed to expand and contract, or a deck that has an uneven surface, cannot be a good substrate for the roof membrane.

These structural and nonstructural requirements of roof decks are discussed in this chapter. The chapter begins with a discussion of the various types of roof decks, followed by design and detailing strategies to accommodate the deck's expansion and contraction.

5.1 TYPES OF DECKS

A deck in a contemporary roof may be one of the following types:

- Steel
- Concrete
- Wood
- Cement fiber
- Gypsum concrete
- Lightweight insulating concrete

The deck types listed above are divided in two categories, based on the deck's resistance to fire exposure. Thus, a deck is categorized either as a *combustible* or a *noncombustible* deck. Combustible decks include (solid) wood, plywood, or oriented strandboard (OSB) decks. All other deck types are noncombustible decks.

Another classification is based on the deck's ability to accept fasteners for anchoring a base sheet or a roof membrane. Although different styles and shapes of fasteners are used with different decks, they are commonly thought of as nails. Therefore, a deck is classified either as a *nailable* or a *nonnailable* deck.

Nailable decks include those made of wood, plywood or OSB, gypsum concrete, cement fiber, and lightweight insulating concrete. Steel,[1] cast-in-place concrete, and precast concrete decks are nonnailable decks.

	Combustible deck	Noncombustible deck
Nailable deck	Wood plank, plywood, and OSB	Lightweight concrete, gypsum concrete, and cement fiber
Nonnailable deck		Steel, cast-in-place concrete, and precast concrete

5.1.1 Lightweight Insulating Concrete — An Insulation or a Deck?

A lightweight insulating concrete deck is not a true deck, since the insulating concrete is merely a wet fill poured over a steel deck. That is why lightweight insulating concrete was referred to as an insulating fill and covered as part of roof insulation in Chapter 4. The load-carrying component of such an assembly is the steel deck, although there is some composite structural action between the deck and the insulating concrete. The concrete adds to the assembly's stiffness. That is why the steel deck needed with insulating concrete is of a lighter gauge than that required with rigid board insulation.[2]

---

[1] A steel deck is not considered nailable because the insulation (and base sheet, or a mechanically fastened single-ply membrane) is screwed to it. On a cast-in-place concrete or a precast concrete deck, the insulation is typically attached by hot mopping. However, screw-type fasteners are available to fasten insulation, base sheet, or membrane to these decks. Screw-type fasteners are referred to as *mechanical fasteners* in roofing terminology.

[2] The steel deck used with lightweight concrete is typically 26 gauge, whereas a steel deck with rigid insulation is 22 gauge, see Section 5.2. The composite action between the insulating fill and the steel deck allows a thinner sheet metal to be used in an insulating concrete deck.

However, most roofing literature regards insulating concrete as a deck. Although the insulating concrete is commonly used with a steel deck, it may also be used to insulate concrete deck or a precast concrete deck, see Section 5.3.3.

5.2 STEEL DECK

Steel decks are among the most commonly used low-slope roof decks, particularly for industrial and low-rise commercial buildings. They are made by pressing sheet steel into the required shape — a process referred to as *cold forming*, since the steel is not heated in the process. Steel roof decks are commonly available in three profiles: *narrow rib*, *intermediate rib*, and *wide rib*, Figure 5.1.

Their depth is typically 1-1/2 in. (37 mm), although decks with greater depths are available[5.1] and are sometimes used. The deeper the deck or the wider the ribs, the greater the load-carrying capacity of the deck. Thus, for the same sheet thickness and deck depth, a wide rib deck has a greater load-carrying capacity than an intermediate rib deck, which in turn has a greater load-carrying capacity than a narrow rib deck.

Steel roof decks are commonly manufactured from 22-gauge to 16-gauge sheet steel. The minimum thickness mandated for a roof deck is 22 gauge.

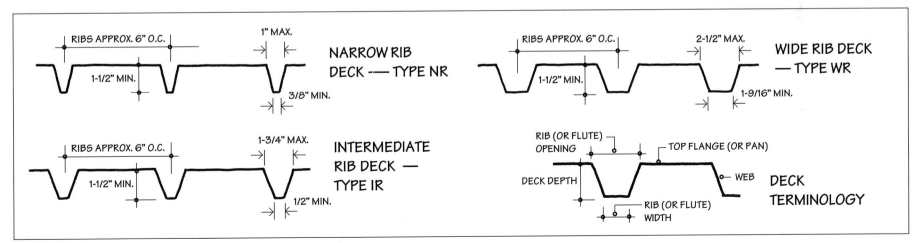

5.1 *Steel roof deck profiles.*

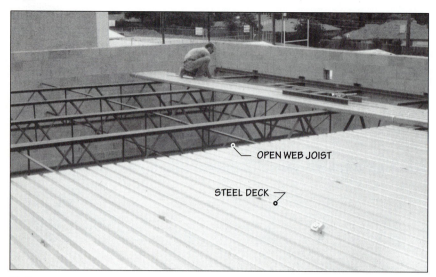

5.2 *Steel deck being laid over open web joists. Photo by Madan Mehta.*

5.3 *Welding of deck panels to supports. Photo by Madan Mehta.*

Virtually all Factory Mutual (FM) and Underwriters Laboratories (UL) requirements are based on a minimum 22-gauge deck thickness. The fastener (screw) retention of a deck increases significantly with an increase in deck thickness.

Roof decks are available with a paint finish, hot-dip galvanized, or simply prime painted. Priming of the deck only gives an impermanent protection and should not be specified. In corrosive or high-moisture environments, e.g., coastal areas, galvanized decks should be used. A G90 or better coating[3] is needed, depending on the environment. Galvanized decks (usually G90) are required with a lightweight insulating concrete fill, see Section 4.9 in Chapter 4. Painted decks cannot be used with an insulating concrete fill.

The width of a deck panel varies from 30 in. to 36 in., depending on the manufacturer. The length of the panel is usually not fixed, and the manufacturer will generally provide whatever length is specified. However, there are practical limitations on panel length, determined by transportation constraints and the ability of workers to handle long panels at the job site. Deck panels longer than 40 ft (12 m) are cumbersome to handle.

5.2.1 Steel Deck Support and Anchorage

Steel decks are typically supported on open web joists, Figure 5.2. Other supporting elements such as wide flange (I-section) beams may also be used in place of open web joists. Decks are usually anchored to supporting elements by puddle welding, Figure 5.3. A minimum weld diameter of 5/8 in. (15 mm) is required.[5.2] Weld areas should be field painted. As an alternative to welding, powder actuated fasteners or mechanical fasteners (Tek screws) may be used for deck anchorage.

The spacing of fasteners or welds is a function of wind uplift and whether the deck is designed to function as a horizontal diaphragm to resist lateral loads. The deck may also be required to provide lateral stability to the top flange of the supporting members (open web joists or beams).

---

[3] Corrosion resistance of a steel deck is directly proportional to the thickness of zinc coating. The thicker the coating, the greater the corrosion resistance. The amount of zinc coating (galvanizing) of steel sheets is specified as "Gxx," where "G" stands for galvanizing, and "xx" indicates average coating mass in ounces per square foot (oz/ft^2). Thus, a G60 coating means that the sheet is coated on both sides with an average of 0.60 oz/ft^2 of zinc, i.e., 0.30 oz/ft^2 on each surface of the sheet. A G90 coating implies 0.90 oz/ft^2 of zinc coating.

In the SI system, the same zinc coating is specified as "Zyy," where "yy" indicates average coating mass in grams per square meter (g/m^2). Since 1 oz/ft^2 = 305 g/m^2, a G60 coating is equal to Z180, and G90 coating is equal to Z275.

In other words, structural considerations govern the spacing of fasteners or welds. However, Factory Mutual loss prevention considerations may require closer fastener spacing — typically 12 in. on center in the field of the roof, as shown in Figure 5.4, and 6 in. on center in roof perimeter and corners.

Individual deck panels must be connected together at side laps, i.e., along the length of the panel. This prevents differential deflection between adjacent panels, which if allowed to occur will cause stresses on the insulation as well as the membrane. Depending on the design of the deck profile, side lap connection may be provided by screws, typically 36 in. (1.1 m) on center Figure 5.5(a), or welds. Alternatively, with interlocking panels, button punching of sheets may be used, Figure 5.5(b). At the ends, each deck panel must have a 2 in. (50 mm) minimum lap, which must occur at a support, Figure 5.6.

5.4 *Steel deck anchorage over supports.*

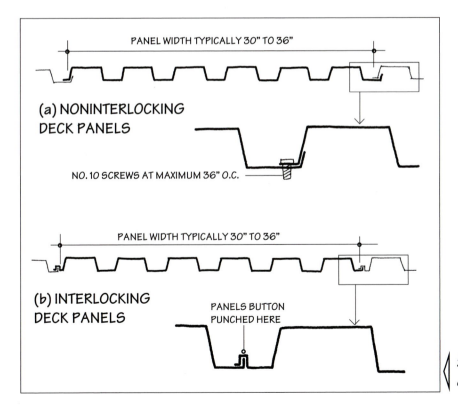

(a) NONINTERLOCKING DECK PANELS

PANEL WIDTH TYPICALLY 30" TO 36"

NO. 10 SCREWS AT MAXIMUM 36" O.C.

(b) INTERLOCKING DECK PANELS

PANEL WIDTH TYPICALLY 30" TO 36"

PANELS BUTTON PUNCHED HERE

5.5 *Side lap connection of individual deck panels.*

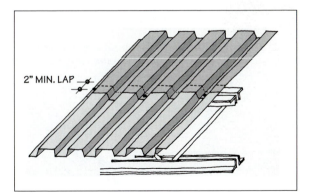

5.6 *End laps in deck panels.*

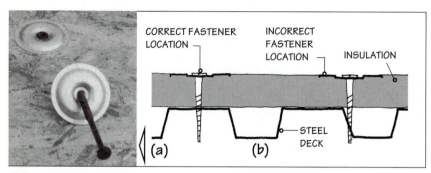

5.7 *(a) Typical screw-cap fastener to fasten insulation to steel deck. (b) Correct and incorrect fastener locations. Photo by Madan Mehta.*

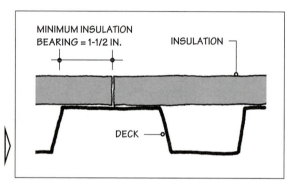

5.8 *Insulation should bear at least 1-1/2 in. over the top flange.*

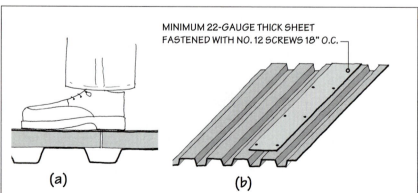

5.2.2 Steel Deck and Rigid Board Insulation

Because a steel deck has a negligible R-value and a negligible thermal capacity, a steel deck must be insulated. Additionally, because of the ribbed profile of a steel deck, a roof membrane cannot be directly attached to it. Rigid board insulation or lightweight insulating concrete fill is needed to provide a smooth surface for the roof membrane.

Rigid board insulation is attached to the deck through fasteners consisting of self-tapping screws and metal (or plastic) caps, Figure 5.7(a). The screws must be long enough to penetrate the deck by a minimum of 3/4 in. and should be engaged in the upper flange (pan) of the deck, not in the web or lower flange, Figure 5.7(b). The spacing of fasteners is a function of wind uplift intensity.

Joints between rigid board insulation must bear adequately over the top flange of the deck. A minimum of 1-1/2 in. (37 mm) bearing is recommended, Figure 5.8.

Insulation must not project over the rib opening, Figure 5.9(a). Projecting insulation can break or fracture under the roof live load destroying the vital substrate for the roof membrane. Field trimming of insulation boards is generally needed to prevent it from projecting into the rib opening. The trimming of insulation can be avoided by screwing a painted or galvanized steel sheet (minimum 22-gauge thick) over rib opening at the joint location.

As stated in Section 4.8 in Chapter 4, two layers of rigid board insulation is preferable to one layer, in which the first layer is mechanically fastened, and the second layer is adhered to the first layer with an adhesive, usually hot bitumen — an anchorage system called *fasten-one-mop-one*, see Figure 4.21. Insulation joints in each layer must be staggered, and the joints in the upper layer should be staggered from the joints in the lower layer. If the use of hot bitumen is ruled out, a two-layer staggered insulation system may be mechanically fastened by one set of fasteners.

The first layer of rigid board insulation must be thick enough to span over rib openings without being damaged by roof live load, e.g., foot traffic, wheel carts, etc. Insulation manufacturers provide minimum thickness of their product needed (flute spannability) for various deck types. As a rough guide, the thickness of the first layer of insulation should be at least 50% of the rib opening dimension, Figure 5.10. Typically, the second insulation layer is thinner than the first layer and works as a cover board.

5.9 *(a) Insulation projecting into rib opening is likely to be damaged by rooftop traffic. (b) The use of a steel sheet over rib openings obviates the need to trim insulation.*

5.2.3 Steel Deck and Roof Membrane

Over an insulation that has been mechanically fastened to a steel roof deck, there are several roof membrane alternatives. A built-up or modified bitumen roof membrane is applied by hot mopping over a compatible insulation, see Figure 4.17(a) in Chapter 4. A fully adhered single-ply membrane may also be used. However, the compatibility of adhesive or the membrane with the underlying insulation must be verified from the single-ply membrane manufacturer. Similarly, if the second layer of insulation has been attached using nail-one-mop-one system, the compatibility of the adhesive or the membrane with the bitumen must also be verified.

A mechanically fastened single-ply membrane may also be used. In this case, the insulation is first presecured to the deck with a nominal number of fasteners per board to hold the insulation in place until the membrane is installed. The membrane is now securely anchored to the deck through insulation, commensurate with the wind uplift.

In a loose-laid ballasted system, the insulation is generally laid loose on the deck, the membrane is then laid over the insulation, and it is finally covered with stone ballast, whose weight provides the wind uplift resistance. The membrane is anchored to the perimeter walls or to the curb. The membrane is not fastened in the field-of-roof. If the insulation must be nominally presecured to the deck, it should preferably be secured with self-locking plastic plates. Metal or nonlocking plates are generally not recommended, as fastener plates can damage the membrane, because the fasteners tend to backout under the weight of heavily loaded trolleys during ballasting operation.

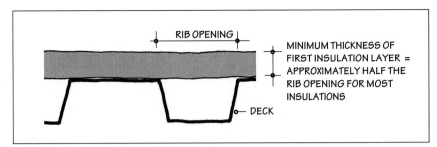

5.10 *The first layer of insulation must have a certain minimum thickness in order to span over the rib opening.*

5.3 STRUCTURAL CONCRETE DECK

Structural concrete decks are of two types:

- Sitecast (also called *poured-in-place* or *cast-in-place*)
- Precast

5.3.1 Sitecast Concrete Deck

Sitecast concrete decks are reinforced concrete slabs poured on a removable (plywood or steel) formwork. The formwork is removed after the concrete has attained sufficient strength. The 28-day strength of concrete is typically 4,000 psi, although a higher-strength concrete may be specified for greater durability or larger span capability.

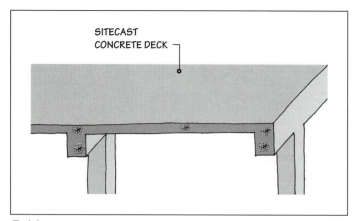

5.11 *A typical poured-in-place concrete structure.*

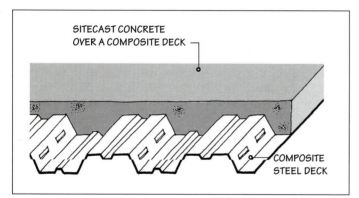

5.12 *Roof deck obtained from poured-in-place concrete over a composite steel deck.*

In high-rise buildings, sitecast concrete decks are often posttensioned.[4] Posttensioning increases the span capabilities of the deck for a given deck thickness. Typically, a sitecast concrete deck (posttensioned or not) is used with a reinforced concrete frame structure — reinforced concrete beams and columns. One of the several variations of such a deck is indicated in Figure 5.11.

In a steel frame building (with steel beams and columns), a steel roof deck, as described in the previous section, is commonly used. However, if such a building is to be expanded vertically in the future, the roof may be designed as a floor slab, which typically consists of concrete poured over a steel deck. In this case, the steel deck functions as a permanent (nonremovable) form for the concrete slab. That is why it is referred to as a *form deck*. Another advantage of a form deck for roofs is the additional sound insulation provided by the concrete.[5] This is important in sound-sensitive buildings in noisy areas, e.g., downtown and airports.

The form deck may be a *noncomposite deck* or a *composite deck*. A composite deck functions as positive (bending moment) reinforcement for the concrete. Therefore, with a composite deck, positive reinforcement for the slab is not needed. That is why a composite deck is usually of a heavier gauge and of a more complex profile to provide better interlocking with the concrete, Figure 5.12.

Apart from a more complex profile, the composite deck's surface is also embossed for an enhanced surface bonding so that both the concrete and the deck function as an integrated unit. A noncomposite form deck is similar to a conventional steel roof deck over which concrete is poured. Reinforcing bars are required, as in a standard concrete deck, obtained by pouring concrete in removable forms.

5.3.2 Precast Concrete Deck

Unlike poured-in-place concrete, in which the concrete is poured into the forms at construction site, precast concrete decks are made from individual concrete elements that are fabricated in a plant. The individual elements are simply

---

[4] Posttensioning is done with high strength cables (tendons) placed into the formwork before pouring the concrete. The tendons are enclosed within plastic sleeves or tubes, so that they are not bonded to concrete. Each tendon is anchored at one end to the concrete deck. After the concrete has gained sufficient strength, tendons are stretched to a predetermined level of tensile stress and then released. The unanchored end is provided with conical steel wedges, so that the tendons cannot relax after being released, which causes compression in concrete.

[5] Sound insulation of an element is primarily a function of its mass (weight). Thus, a normal weight concrete poured over a steel deck provides greater sound insulation than lightweight insulating concrete of the same thickness or rigid board insulation.

assembled at the site by stacking them side-by-side and connecting them at the joints to provide a continuous deck. The most common precast elements are *single T's*, *double T's,* and *hollow core slabs.*

Precast concrete elements are supported on beam and column frames or on loadbearing masonry walls. Single T's and double T's are typically prestressed[6] with high-strength steel cables, which increases their span rating. In fact, a single-T or double-T deck system is the only economical solution to obtain a concrete deck with large spans — 60 ft (18 m) and above — between the supporting beams or walls.

The joints in the precast elements give a deck surface that is uneven and irregular and hence unsuitable for direct application of the roofing membrane or the rigid board insulation. The unevenness may be exaggerated due to the upward camber present in deck elements created by prestressing. A level difference of 1 in. (25 mm) or more may be present between two adjacent precast elements across a joint.

If a roof membrane is either solidly adhered or spot bonded to a precast concrete deck, it will prematurely split at the joints in due course. Similarly, if rigid board insulation is bonded or fastened to such a deck, the deck's irregularities will simply be transferred to the insulation surface, unless the insulation is field tapered to smoothness — a cumbersome and costly process.

Roofing industry standards require differences in deck elevations to be grouted to create a smooth surface, but this is generally a poor solution. Ideally, the precast concrete deck elements should be fully covered over with sitecast concrete screed[7] or lightweight insulating concrete fill to yield a smooth unjointed surface, Figure 5.13.

Generally, a 2-in. (50-mm) fill is adequate, but the fill thickness should be determined after the deck elements have been installed and the degree of deck unevenness determined. With concrete screed, welded wire mesh reinforcement is generally needed to reduce shrinkage cracks.

5.3.3 Concrete Deck and Lightweight Insulating Concrete

Lightweight insulating concrete of sufficient thickness poured over a sitecast or precast concrete deck can provide the necessary insulation in addition to removing surface irregularities. In fact, in most situations, lightweight insulating concrete may be a preferred method of insulating a sitecast or a precast concrete deck.

---

[6] The process of prestressing is similar to posttensioning except that prestressing of tendons is done before pouring the concrete into the forms. Prestressing is applicable only to precast concrete elements, and posttensioning to sitecast concrete.

[7] Concrete screed is like concrete, which may be normal weight screed (weighing nearly 145 lb/ft³) or a lightweight screed (weighing nearly 120 lb/ft³). Lightweight screed should not be confused with lightweight insulating concrete, which weighs only 20 to 40 lb/ft³.

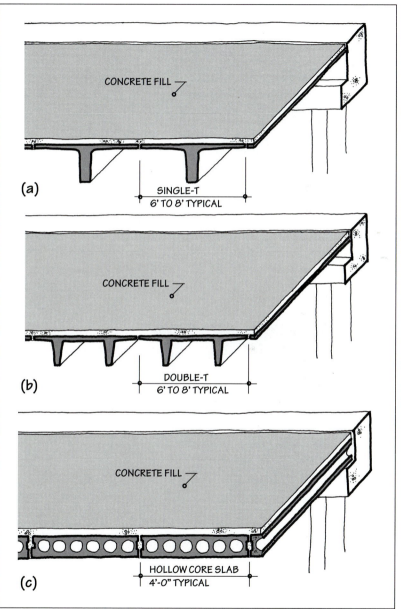

5.13 *Three most commonly used precast concrete roof decks — (a) single-T, (b) double-T, and (c) hollow core slab.*

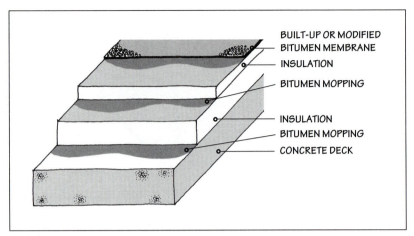

5.14 *Attachment of insulation and roof membrane over a dry sitecast concrete deck.*

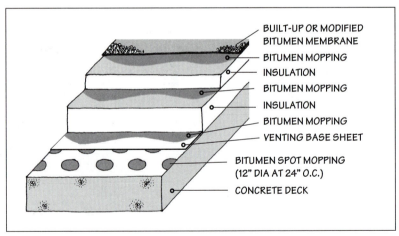

5.15 *Attachment of insulation and roof membrane to a concrete deck with a small amount of residual moisture.*

Because it is usually difficult to dry a lightweight insulating concrete fill completely, a venting base sheet should be mechanically fastened to the fill before applying a built-up or modified bitumen membrane. Another reason for using a venting base sheet is the alkalinity of lightweight insulating concrete which reacts adversely with the fiberglass felts in a built-up or a modified bitumen roof. Provisions must also be made for topside ventilating in such a roof assembly, see Section 10.7 in Chapter 10.

5.3.4 Concrete Deck and Rigid Board Insulation

As stated in Section 4.8 in Chapter 4, although mechanical fasteners (screws) have recently been developed that can be used to attach rigid board insulation to a concrete deck, they are cumbersome to use. Concrete screws are similar to self-tapping screws used with metal decks and do not require any expansion plugs or sleeves, but do require predrilling of holes in concrete.

Mechanical fastening should not be used with a prestressed or a posttensioned concrete deck. The fasteners can damage prestressing or posttensioning cables, reducing the level of stress in them, which may be hazardous to the structural integrity of the structure.

The most commonly used method[8] of attaching insulation to a concrete deck is through solid mopping of hot asphalt, Figure 5.14. However, before asphalt is applied, the deck must be thoroughly cleaned of any loose dirt and scales and subsequently primed with solvent-based asphalt primer. Priming helps to absorb the dust and scale that cannot be removed by sweeping, blowing, or other method of preparation.

Concrete primers must be sufficiently thin to penetrate the concrete. Thick primer may need field thinning with the help of the manufacturer's solvent. Primer must dry completely before the asphalt is applied, which usually takes a few hours.

It is important that the concrete deck surface (including the fill) must be sufficiently dry before the application of primer or asphalt. Any residual moisture in the deck will cause blistering in hot asphalt, weakening its adhesive power. Smaller insulation boards adhere better than larger boards, since they conform better to surface irregularities.

If there is a concern about residual moisture in the deck, a venting base sheet should be spot mopped to the deck. Insulation (preferably in two layers) can then be fully mopped over the base sheet and a built-up or modified bitumen membrane applied over the insulation in the conventional manner, Figure 5.15. Suitable ventilation of roof assembly is required in such a case, see Section 10.7 in Chapter 10.

---

[8] In addition to hot bitumen, there are a variety of cold adhesives available for attaching insulation to a concrete deck, but their adhesive power may not be as strong as that of hot bitumen.

Curing agents (e.g., sprayed-on polyethylene film) are sometimes used with sitecast or precast concrete decks. It is important to ensure that they are compatible with roofing components — bitumen and the roof membrane. In case of doubt, concrete curing agents should not be used.

5.3.5 Roof Membrane and a Concrete Deck

Where roof insulation is not required, a roof membrane can be installed directly over a (smooth-surfaced) cast-in-place concrete deck. A built-up or a modified bitumen membrane is installed in the conventional way by first priming the deck and subsequently hot mopping various layers.

In the case of residual moisture being present in the deck, a venting base sheet should be spot mopped to the deck first. A built-up or modified bitumen membrane can then be solidly mopped to the base sheet, similar to that shown in Figure 5.15. Ventilation of roof assembly is required.

A fully adhered single-ply membrane may also be used. However, the membrane manufacturer must be consulted for the membrane's compatibility with the insulation and also with the bitumen used in adhering the insulation to the deck.

A loose-laid, ballasted, single-ply membrane with underlying (loose-laid) rigid board insulation can be an economical solution with a concrete deck. This is particularly true because a concrete deck is usually stiff and has a high load-carrying capacity to take the weight of the ballast. Two layers of insulation, with staggered joints between layers, is preferable to a single layer.

With a loose-laid ballasted system, leveling screed or concrete fill may be avoided if the deck joints are caulked with an elastomeric sealant and the deck's surface irregularities feathered with a portland cement grout, Figure 5.16.

5.16 *A loose-laid, ballasted, single-ply membrane is a good roofing system in most situations over a precast concrete deck, see also Section 3.5.3 in Chapter 3.*

TESTING A CONCRETE DECK FOR DRYNESS

Pour a small amount of hot asphalt (at nearly 400°F) over the deck. If the asphalt does not foam or bubble excessively, the deck is sufficiently dry. Try to peel the asphalt layer with your fingers after it has cooled to the ambient temperature. If the asphalt layer peels off, the deck is too wet for bitumen application.

Another method, which works on a sunny day, is to lay a small sheet of glass over the deck and tape all its edges securely. If after a few hours, there is no visible condensation under the glass, the deck is dry enough to receive hot asphalt.

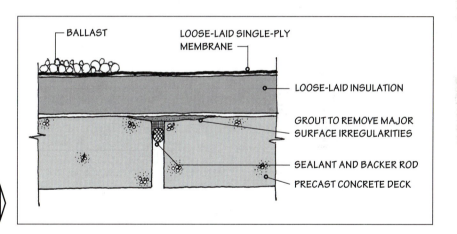

BALLAST — LOOSE-LAID SINGLE-PLY MEMBRANE — LOOSE-LAID INSULATION — GROUT TO REMOVE MAJOR SURFACE IRREGULARITIES — SEALANT AND BACKER ROD — PRECAST CONCRETE DECK

5.4 WOOD DECK

Wood decks can be of two types:

- Wood plank
- Wood panel — plywood or oriented strandboard (OSB)

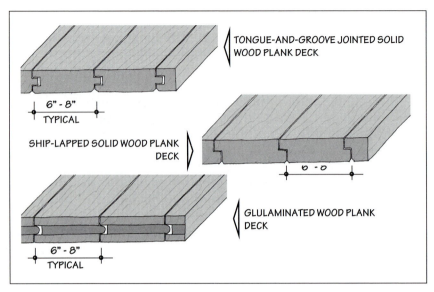

5.17 *Commonly used wood plank deck profiles.*

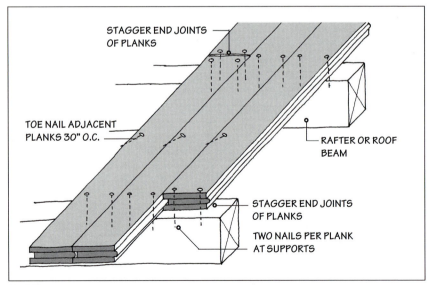

5.18 *Layout and anchorage of wood planks.*

5.4.1 Wood Plank Deck

A wood plank deck generally consists of solid sawn lumber planks, supported on rafters or roof beams. The thickness of planks depends on the distance between the supports, but it must be at least 1 in. (25 mm) nominal, i.e., 3/4 in. (19 mm) actual. The width of each plank should preferably be less than 8 in. (200 mm).

The planks should be tongued-and-grooved or ship-lapped at sides, which integrates adjacent planks and prevents differential deflection between them, Figure 5.17. Although the earlier plank decks were of solid sawn lumber, glulaminated lumber decks are more common these days, particularly for thicker planks.

The end joints of wood planks should be staggered, Figure 5.18. To reduce problems caused by shrinkage, wood plank decks should be constructed of kiln dried lumber and protected from moisture during roofing operations and storage.

5.4.2 Wood Plank Deck, Insulation, and Roof Membrane

Insulation can be installed directly over a plank deck with the help of screws and metal (or plastic) caps, similar to those used for fastening insulation to a steel deck. Because a two-layer insulation is preferable to a single layer, the second layer should be mopped with hot bitumen to the first layer. The mopping of the second layer of insulation is particularly important with wood decks, since it protects the membrane against any fastener backout due to expansion and contraction in wood. Built-up or modified bitumen roof may now be mopped over the insulation in the conventional manner.

In order to ensure that bitumen does not drip through the joints in the first layer of insulation, and from there through the joints in the planks, red rosin paper[9] is placed between the insulation and the deck, Figure 5.19.

The plank deck can also be insulated by first nailing a coated base sheet to the deck (with large head nails) and subsequently mopping the insulation over the base sheet. A built-up or modified bitumen membrane can now be mopped over the insulation, Figure 5.20(a). Rosin paper is needed under the base sheet to prevent bitumen from dripping through the laps in the base sheet.

---

[9] Rosin paper is a heavy nonbituminous paper, typically red brown in color and manufactured in 36-in. rolls. It is recommended over a wood plank deck because of several closely spaced joints in such a deck. It helps prevent bitumen seeping through the joints of overlying insulation or through the laps of base sheet and then dripping through deck joints. It is simply nailed to the deck to hold it in place until the insulation or base sheet has been fastened to the deck. Rosin paper is not required with a wood panel deck, because it has much fewer joints.

In other words, bitumen mopping or adhesive should not be used directly over a wood plank deck. The use of nails is recommended with the first layer — insulation or base sheet. Thus, if a built-up or modified bitumen roof is to be applied directly over a plank deck, a coated base sheet must be nailed first, with a rosin paper underlayment, Figure 5.20(b).

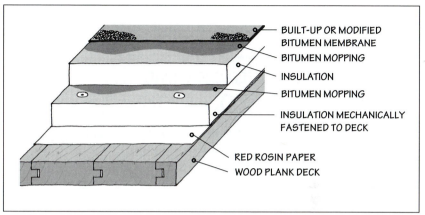

5.19 *Built-up roof over a wood plank deck.*

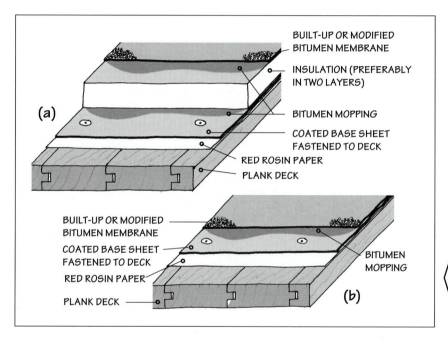

5.20 *(a) Attachment of insulation and roof membrane over a plank deck. (b) Attachment of roof membrane directly over a plank deck (without roof insulation).*

5.4.3 Wood Panel Decks

With the exception of churches, specialty ski lodges, and motels, etc., wood plank decks are relatively uncommon in new construction these days, since they have largely been replaced by structural wood panels. Wood plank decks are, however, encountered in reroofing situations. Wood panels, used as roof decks, are of the following three types:

- Plywood — also referred to as a *veneered panel*
- Oriented strandboard (OSB) — also referred to as a *nonveneered panel*
- Composite panel — consisting of an oriented wood strand core sandwiched between wood veneers on both faces of the panel

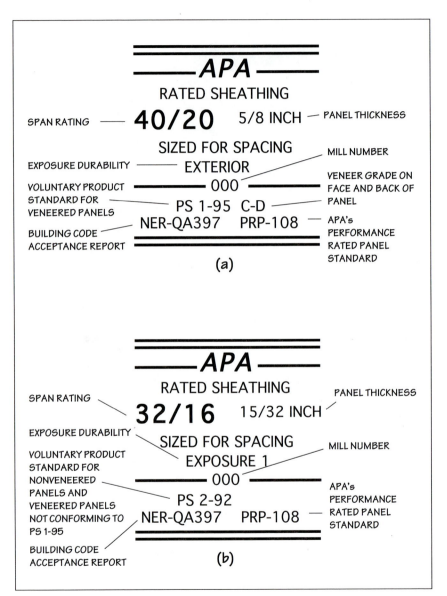

SPAN RATING

EXPOSURE DURABILITY

VOLUNTARY PRODUCT
STANDARD FOR
VENEERED PANELS

BUILDING CODE
ACCEPTANCE REPORT

PANEL THICKNESS

MILL NUMBER

VENEER GRADE ON
FACE AND BACK OF
PANEL

APA's
PERFORMANCE
RATED PANEL
STANDARD

APA
RATED SHEATHING
40/20   5/8 INCH
SIZED FOR SPACING
EXTERIOR
000
PS 1-95   C-D
NER-QA397   PRP-108

(a)

SPAN RATING

EXPOSURE DURABILITY

VOLUNTARY PRODUCT
STANDARD FOR
NONVENEERED
PANELS AND
VENEERED PANELS
NOT CONFORMING TO
PS 1-95

BUILDING CODE
ACCEPTANCE REPORT

PANEL THICKNESS

MILL NUMBER

APA's
PERFORMANCE
RATED PANEL
STANDARD

APA
RATED SHEATHING
32/16   15/32 INCH
SIZED FOR SPACING
EXPOSURE 1
000
PS 2-92
NER-QA397   PRP-108

(b)

5.21 *(a) A typical APA grade stamp on a veneered (plywood) panel. (b) A typical grade stamp on a nonveneered (OSB) panel.*

The first two types — plywood and OSB — are more commonly used than the composite panels. Most structural wood panel manufacturers have their panels rated by the American Plywood Association (APA)[10] according to voluntary standards established by U.S. Department of Commerce and the panel manufacturing industry. Note that these standards are voluntary and need not be followed by every manufacturer.

The APA rating, which is stamped on each panel, provides much useful information to the designer and builder. Two typical rating (grade) stamps — one related to a plywood panel, and the other to OSB panel — are shown in Figure 5.21.

The two most important information items on a grade stamp are the durability classification and the span rating of the panel. The panel's durability[11] is either rated as "exposure 1" or "exterior." An exposure 1 rated panel is used in situations where it will eventually be covered, such as a roof deck. However, an exposure 1 panel can withstand external climate (rain and sunshine) due to long construction delays.

An exterior rated panel is meant for permanent exposure to the weather. Both exterior and exposure 1 panels have the same waterproof glue. The difference between their durability classification is due to the quality of veneers and other factors that affect panel performance. Thus, OSB panels cannot be manufactured to "exterior" rating due to the problem of edge swelling in them.

The span rating of a panel is indicated by two numbers. For instance in Figure 5.21(a), 40/20 indicates that the panel can be used as roof deck if the supporting rafters are spaced a maximum of 40 in. on center. If the same panel is used as a floor deck, the floor joists should not be spaced more than 20 in. on center. Similarly, a span rating of 20/0 means that the maximum spacing of rafters is 20 in. and the panel cannot be used as a floor deck.

Note that the span ratings, as interpreted above, refer mainly to residential-type structures. Low-slope commercial decks are generally subjected to heavier loads than are residential roofs. Therefore, the above interpretation is not applicable to low-slope roofs. APA publishes information about the maximum span ratings[5.3] for their panels for low-slope commercial roofs, Table 5.1.

The information in Table 5.1 is contingent on (1) the long edges of the panel being perpendicular to rafters, (2) long edges of panels being continuous over two or more rafters, and (3) the long edges of adjacent panels are joined together

---

[10] APA is a trade association consisting of nearly 75% of mills that manufacture veneered and nonveneered structural wood panels in the United States.

[11] The product standard has provisions for "interior" rated panels also, which do not require a waterproof glue, but only exterior and exposure 1 rated panels are currently made by manufacturers.

with metal clips, Figure 5.22. As an alternative to clips, the long edges of the panels may be blocked by wood members between rafters — a more cumbersome alternative.

In addition to the structural requirements, adjacent panels are required to have at least a 1/8-in. (3-mm) gap between them on all sides. The design of metal clips is such that they not only interconnect adjacent panels to stiffen the deck, but also produce the required gap between them, as shown in Figure 5.23.

Table 5.1 Recommended Maximum Spans for APA-Rated Panel Spanning Over Two or More Supports in Low-Slope Roofs

Panel thickness (in.)	Span rating	Maximum span (in.)	Number of clips between each support
15/32, 1/2	32/16	24	1
19/32, 5/8	40/20	32	1
23/32, 3/4	48/24	48	2
7/8	60/32	60	2

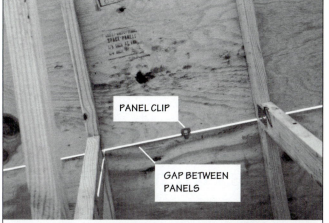

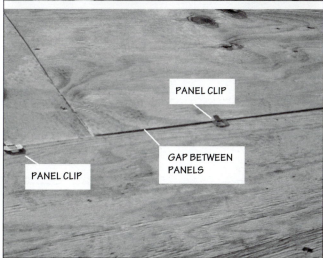

(a)

(b)

5.23 *(a) A 1/8-in. gap between adjacent wood panels and panel clips as seen from below the deck. (b) Same as (a) but seen from above the deck. Photos by Madan Mehta.*

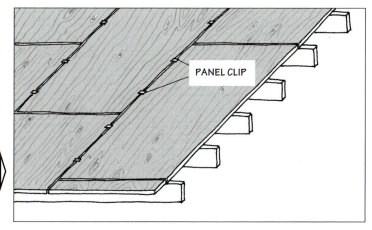

5.22 *Wood deck panel layout and panel clips.*

5.4.4 Wood Panel Decks, Insulation, and Roof Membrane

The attachment of insulation and/or roof membrane over a wood panel deck is similar to that on a wood plank deck, except that with a wood panel deck, rosin paper is not needed because it has fewer joints.

5.5 GYPSUM CONCRETE DECK

Gypsum concrete decks, which were popular during the 1950s and 1960s, are relatively uncommon today. They can be of two types: poured gypsum deck and precast gypsum deck. Precast gypsum decks are no longer used,[5.4] but several exist in service and are encountered in reroofing situations. Therefore, the following discussion is limited to poured gypsum decks only.

The most common construction for poured gypsum decks consists of bulb T's, which are structural steel elements spanning between open web steel joists, Figure 5.24. The bulb T's support a form board, a gypsum product similar in appearance to gypsum wallboard. Gypsum concrete is poured over the form board, embedding a steel wire fabric reinforcement.

Gypsum concrete sets quickly, within about an hour, and is ready for roofing operations thereafter. Some roofing material manufacturers may, however, require a day or two between pouring of gypsum and subsequent roofing operations so that the deck attains sufficient strength. Since the chemical reaction between water and gypsum is rapid and creates sufficient heat, gypsum decks can be poured in cold weather, unlike concrete or lightweight insulating concrete.

Since gypsum is water soluble, it should not be left exposed to weather for long periods. For the same reason, leakage of roof can substantially damage a gypsum deck. Reroofing gypsum decks, which have deteriorated due to roof leakage, can be highly dangerous. The deck may have deteriorated sufficiently to give in to the weight of a roofer. Thus, gypsum decks should not be used in highly moist environments, e.g., swimming pools or manufacturing facilities that release a great deal of moist air.

Gypsum decks must be ventilated to an interior space.[5.5] That is why the form board used with gypsum decks must be vapor permeable. This allows the moisture present in the deck, or that absorbed by it during its use and service, to dry from the deck's underside — a construction similar to slotted metal deck used with lightweight insulating concrete, see Section 4.9 in Chapter 4.

Most roofing material manufacturers recommend fastening a coated base sheet to a gypsum deck with mechanical fasteners. Note that a gypsum deck is a

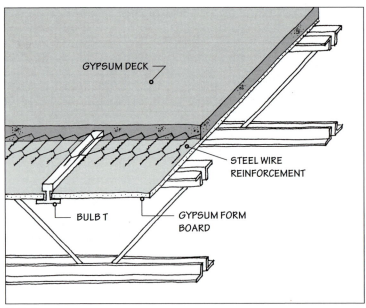

GYPSUM DECK

STEEL WIRE REINFORCEMENT

BULB T

GYPSUM FORM BOARD

5.24 *Typical poured gypsum deck construction.*

nailable deck. Insulation can then be mopped to the base sheet, over which a built-up or modified bitumen membrane can be applied in the conventional manner. If no roof insulation is needed, the membrane is applied directly over the base sheet. For a single-ply membrane used directly over a gypsum deck, the single-ply membrane manufacturer should be consulted.

A cement fiber deck consists of wood fibers that are pressed and bonded together with an inorganic cement and molded into panels. The panels provide a structural deck, whose underside is sound absorbing. Because of its sound-absorbing property, a cement fiber deck is commonly used in noisy interiors, e.g., gymnasiums, entrance foyers, etc., or where a relative quiet is needed, e.g., libraries and conference halls. The random wood fiber arrangement in panels provides an aesthetically interesting interior surface, Figure 5.25(a).

Because of its fibrous composition, a cement fiber deck also provides some thermal resistance. However, additional above-deck insulation is generally needed, which may be provided by rigid board insulation nailed to the deck with insulation joints offset from deck panel joints. Additional insulation also provides a smoother surface for membrane application, since a cement fiber deck surface is generally rough, particularly at the joints. Smoothing can also be achieved with a nailed base sheet to which additional insulation or roof membrane can be mopped. Note that a cement fiber deck is a nailable deck surface, providing a reasonably high nail withdrawal resistance.

Manufacturers also provide a composite panel in which a plastic foam insulation is sandwiched between a cement fiber panel and a wood fiberboard, or a plywood (or OSB) panel, Figure 5.25(b). In such a panel, foam insulation provides most of the R-value of the deck, and the wood fiberboard (or plywood or OSB) provides a surface on which the roof membrane can be installed.

5.6 CEMENT FIBER DECK

(a)

(b)

CEMENT FIBER BOARD

ISO BOARD

ORIENTED STRAND-BOARD

5.25 *(a) Random fiber arrangement in a cement fiberboard deck. (b) A composite board consisting of cement fiberboard, polyisocyanurate insulation, and a wood fiberboard. In this composite board, the cement fiberboard is exposed to the interior of the building. The wood fiberboard provides a surface that is compatible with most roofing membranes. Photos by Madan Mehta.*

5.26 *Composite cement fiber deck panels (see Figure 5.25(b)) being installed on a steel supporting frame. Photo by Madan Mehta.*

5.27 *Two typical roof membrane details on a cement fiber deck. For other conditions, consult cement fiber deck manufacturer, e.g., Tectum.*

The panels are generally made in tongue-and-groove profile and can be screw-fastened directly to steel joists, Figure 5.26, or to wood beams. Panels of various thickness are available for various span ratings and roof loads. Where a greater sound insulation is needed, normal weight concrete or lightweight insulating concrete fill may be poured over deck panels.

Roof membrane is applied over cement fiber deck in the same way as on a gypsum or lightweight concrete deck. In other words, a coated base sheet is generally recommended if a built-up or modified bitumen membrane is applied directly to the deck, Figure 5.27. Deck manufacturers will usually provide details and specifications for various conditions.

Cement fiber decks cannot withstand high humidity environments. The manufacturer must be consulted if the product is to be used in roofs over swimming pools or other humid environments. For the same reason, cement fiber decks must be installed in dry weather, and temporary protection from moisture must be provided until the application of roof membrane.

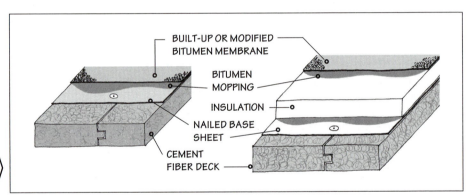

BUILT-UP OR MODIFIED BITUMEN MEMBRANE

BITUMEN MOPPING

INSULATION

NAILED BASE SHEET

CEMENT FIBER DECK

5.7 LIGHTWEIGHT INSULATING CONCRETE DECK

Lightweight insulating concrete deck has been covered in Section 4.9 in Chapter 4 as part of the above-deck insulation. Since lightweight insulating concrete provides adequate insulation, additional rigid board insulation over insulating concrete is generally avoided. The moisture in lightweight insulating concrete may be trapped by the overlying insulation, damaging the insulation as well as the roof membrane, unless arrangements are made to provide sufficient ventilation in the roof assembly.

Loose-laid rigid board insulation over lightweight insulating concrete with a slotted metal deck may be acceptable. However, lightweight insulating concrete manufacturers must be consulted for details.

A roof is subjected to much greater thermal stress than other envelope elements, since it receives solar radiation throughout the day and is not protected by adjacent buildings. A wall, on the other hand, receives solar radiation only for a part of the day and is usually shaded by neighboring buildings, trees, etc. Thus, in most buildings, a roof undergoes substantial thermal expansion and contraction.

The design response to these dimensional changes is to provide expansion joints in a building. Without expansion joints, the roof membrane will be severely stressed, leading to its failure. An expansion joint, also referred to as a *building separation joint*, is generally 1-1/2-in. (38-mm) wide.[12] It divides a large and geometrically complex building into smaller individual buildings. The idea is to make these smaller buildings expand and contract independent of each other. The separation not only responds to thermal expansion and contraction, but also to any other movement in building, e.g., foundation settlement.

An expansion joint goes through a building all the way up to the roof. At an expansion joint, each floor is separated from the adjacent floor at the same story and a roof is separated from the adjacent roof. In other words, two sets of beams and two sets of columns, separated by nearly 1-1/2 in. space are needed at an expansion joint, Figure 5.28.

5.8 EXPANSION AND CONTRACTION IN A ROOF DECK

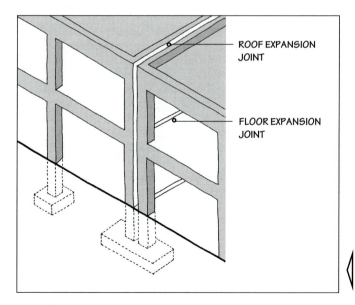

ROOF EXPANSION JOINT

FLOOR EXPANSION JOINT

5.28 *Typical arrangement of columns and beams on both sides of an expansion joint*

---

[12] In a seismic zone, the width of building separation joint (expansion joint) can be much larger.

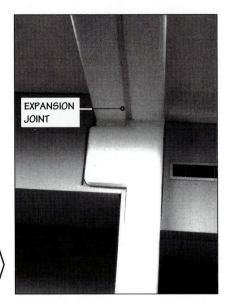

5.29 *A building expansion joint with a double beam, but a single column. Photo by Madan Mehta.*

Ideally, the adjoining foundations should also be separated. However, this is typically not done, and a common foundation is generally provided for the two separated parts of the building. The duplication of columns at the joint is sometimes avoided by incorporating a corbel in the column, Figure 5.29.

Expansion joints should generally be provided every 200 ft (60 m) in a simple rectangular building. They may be spaced more closely if the building geometry is complex. For example, it is wise to provide an expansion joint where the building changes direction, e.g., at an L-junction or a T-junction. For the same reason, an expansion joint should be provided where there is an abrupt change in building height, Figure 5.30.

5.8.1 Detailing a Roof Expansion Joint

An expansion joint must be detailed to ensure that the separated parts of the building can move independent of each other in both a vertical as well as horizontal direction. A flexible joint cover at the roof, which ensures a watertight seal along with insulation and condensation control at the joint, must be provided. Treated wood curbs are generally needed to provide vertical drainage barriers on both sides of the joint against ponded water or driving rain. A minimum of an 8-in. (200-mm) high barrier above the roof surface is generally recommended.

Two commonly used details of roof expansion joint are shown in Figures 5.31 and 5.32. Figure 5.31 shows a flexible sheet metal joint cover wrapped over a sheet metal cleat. The sheet metal commonly used is galvanized steel (G90 or better coating). Stainless steel or copper may be specified for greater durability. Figure 5.32 shows a joint cover made of an elastomeric bellow (typically neoprene) fused to sheet metal flanges on both sides.

If there is a parapet wall on the roof, the expansion joint must go through the parapet wall. The junction between the roof expansion joint and the parapet wall must be carefully detailed to ensure a watertight, but flexible, seal.[5.6]

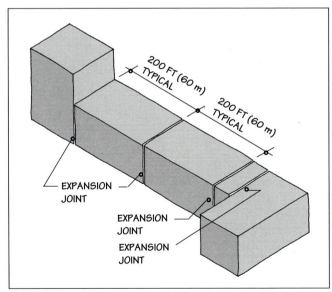

5.30 *Arrangement of expansion joints in a building.*

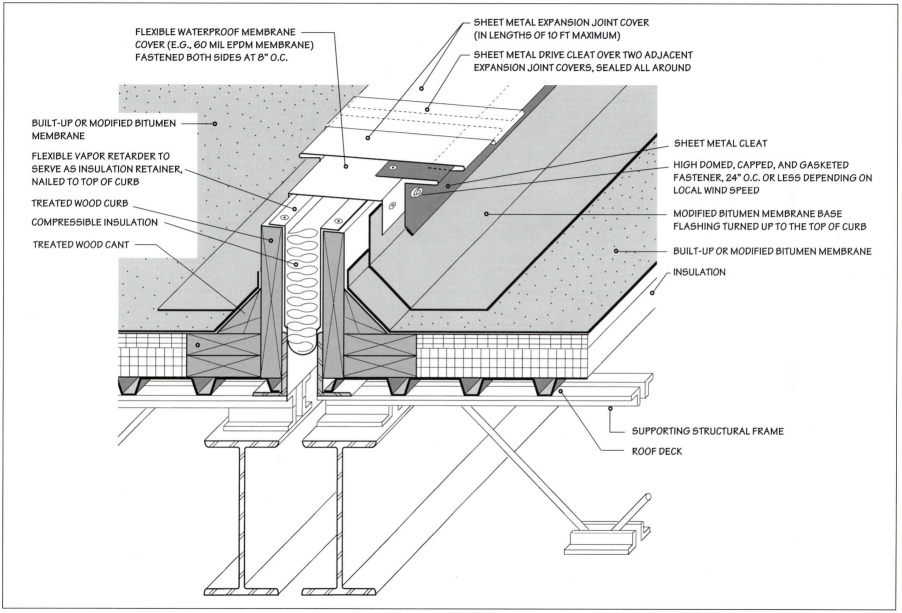

FLEXIBLE WATERPROOF MEMBRANE
COVER (E.G., 60 MIL EPDM MEMBRANE)
FASTENED BOTH SIDES AT 8" O.C.

SHEET METAL EXPANSION JOINT COVER
(IN LENGTHS OF 10 FT MAXIMUM)

SHEET METAL DRIVE CLEAT OVER TWO ADJACENT
EXPANSION JOINT COVERS, SEALED ALL AROUND

BUILT-UP OR MODIFIED BITUMEN
MEMBRANE

FLEXIBLE VAPOR RETARDER TO
SERVE AS INSULATION RETAINER,
NAILED TO TOP OF CURB

TREATED WOOD CURB

COMPRESSIBLE INSULATION

TREATED WOOD CANT

SHEET METAL CLEAT

HIGH DOMED, CAPPED, AND GASKETED
FASTENER, 24" O.C. OR LESS DEPENDING ON
LOCAL WIND SPEED

MODIFIED BITUMEN MEMBRANE BASE
FLASHING TURNED UP TO THE TOP OF CURB

BUILT-UP OR MODIFIED BITUMEN MEMBRANE

INSULATION

SUPPORTING STRUCTURAL FRAME

ROOF DECK

5.31(a) *A typical roof expansion joint cover detail. See also Figures 5.31(b) and 5.32.*

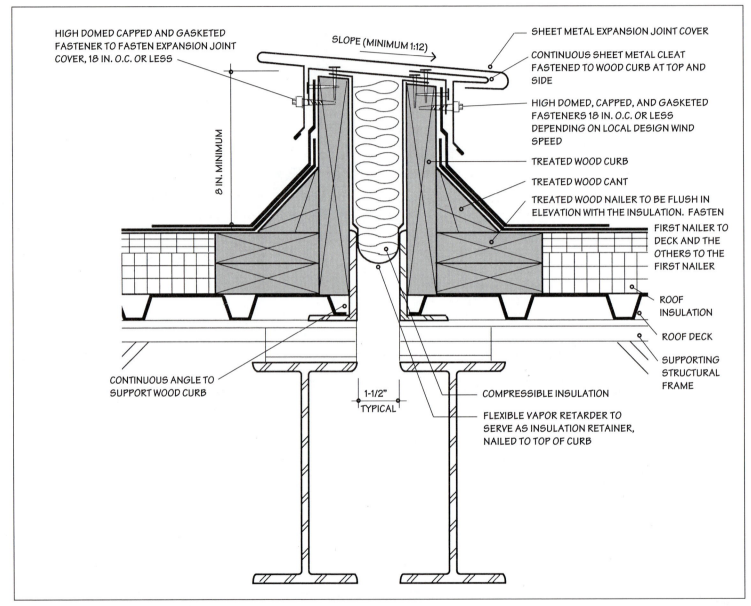

HIGH DOMED CAPPED AND GASKETED
FASTENER TO FASTEN EXPANSION JOINT
COVER, 18 IN. O.C. OR LESS

SLOPE (MINIMUM 1:12)

SHEET METAL EXPANSION JOINT COVER

CONTINUOUS SHEET METAL CLEAT
FASTENED TO WOOD CURB AT TOP AND
SIDE

HIGH DOMED, CAPPED, AND GASKETED
FASTENERS 18 IN. O.C. OR LESS
DEPENDING ON LOCAL DESIGN WIND
SPEED

TREATED WOOD CURB

TREATED WOOD CANT

TREATED WOOD NAILER TO BE FLUSH IN
ELEVATION WITH THE INSULATION. FASTEN

FIRST NAILER TO
DECK AND THE
OTHERS TO THE
FIRST NAILER

ROOF
INSULATION

ROOF DECK

SUPPORTING
STRUCTURAL
FRAME

8 IN. MINIMUM

CONTINUOUS ANGLE TO
SUPPORT WOOD CURB

1-1/2"
TYPICAL

COMPRESSIBLE INSULATION

FLEXIBLE VAPOR RETARDER TO
SERVE AS INSULATION RETAINER,
NAILED TO TOP OF CURB

5.31(b) *A typical roof expansion joint cover detail, drawn in section. See Figure 5.31(a) for a three-dimensional version.*

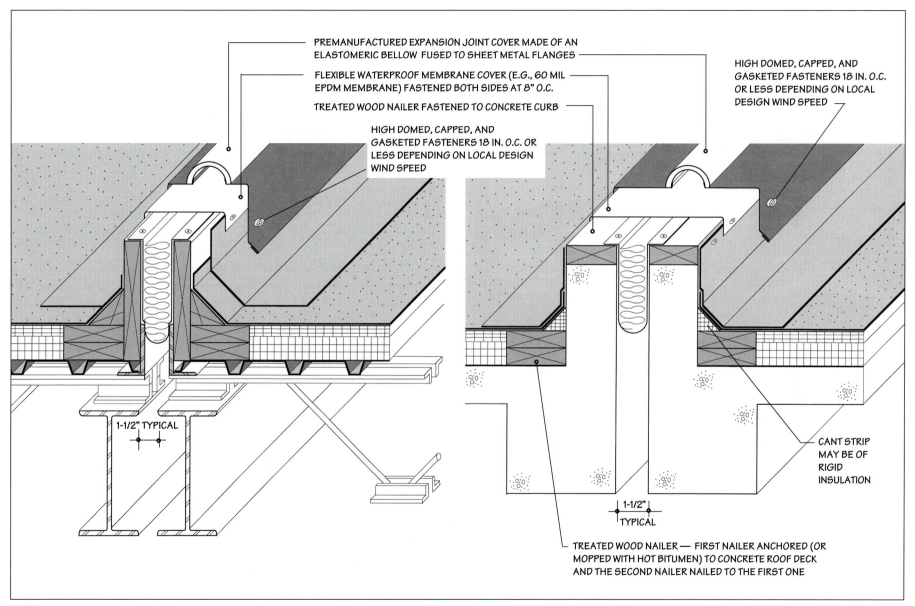

PREMANUFACTURED EXPANSION JOINT COVER MADE OF AN ELASTOMERIC BELLOW FUSED TO SHEET METAL FLANGES

FLEXIBLE WATERPROOF MEMBRANE COVER (E.G., 60 MIL EPDM MEMBRANE) FASTENED BOTH SIDES AT 8" O.C.

TREATED WOOD NAILER FASTENED TO CONCRETE CURB

HIGH DOMED, CAPPED, AND GASKETED FASTENERS 18 IN. O.C. OR LESS DEPENDING ON LOCAL DESIGN WIND SPEED

HIGH DOMED, CAPPED, AND GASKETED FASTENERS 18 IN. O.C. OR LESS DEPENDING ON LOCAL DESIGN WIND SPEED

1-1/2" TYPICAL

1-1/2" TYPICAL

CANT STRIP MAY BE OF RIGID INSULATION

TREATED WOOD NAILER — FIRST NAILER ANCHORED (OR MOPPED WITH HOT BITUMEN) TO CONCRETE ROOF DECK AND THE SECOND NAILER NAILED TO THE FIRST ONE

5.32 *Roof expansion joint cover detail. This detail is similar to that of Figure 5.31, except that it has an elastomeric bellow joint cover in place of a sheet metal joint cover. For items not identified in these drawings, see Figure 5.31(b).*

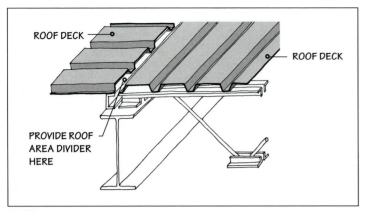

ROOF DECK

ROOF DECK

PROVIDE ROOF AREA DIVIDER HERE

5.33 *Change in the roof deck's span directions and the location of a roof area divider.*

5.8.1 Roof Area Divider

Where an expansion joint cannot be justified, a roof area divider is generally provided. For instance, if there is a change in the direction of the spans of two adjacent roof areas and the building length does not justify an expansion joint there, a roof area divider is provided at that location, Figure 5.33. Similarly, a roof area divider is needed where one side of the roof may be of sitecast concrete and the other side of a different material (e.g., steel) or a different structural system (e.g., precast concrete units).

A roof area divider is not a true joint in the roof, but a divider that separates two adjacent areas of the roof. It is detailed like an expansion joint, so that the drainage in divided roof areas are independent of each other. In other words, water from one area of the roof should not go to the other area through a roof area divider.

A roof area divider is also needed where an expansion joint should have been designed but has not been provided due to a design lapse or some other reason. Thus, unless there are reasons for a closer spacing, such as a change in roof deck span directions or a change in deck material, roof area dividers should be spaced nearly 200 ft (60 m) apart, like the expansion joints.

A typical roof area divider consists of a double wood curb fastened to a wood base plate, which is anchored to the deck. Both sides of the roof are flashed, Figure 5.34.

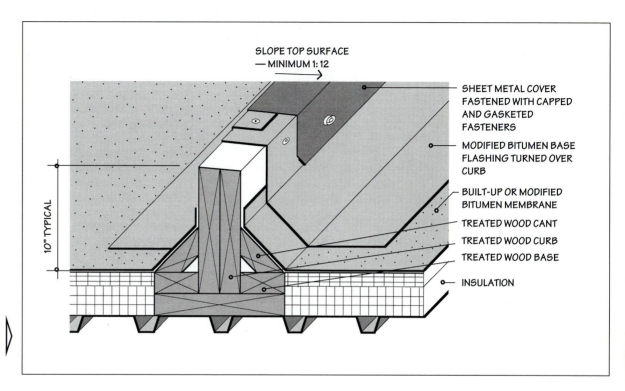

SLOPE TOP SURFACE
— MINIMUM 1:12

SHEET METAL COVER
FASTENED WITH CAPPED
AND GASKETED
FASTENERS

MODIFIED BITUMEN BASE
FLASHING TURNED OVER
CURB

BUILT-UP OR MODIFIED
BITUMEN MEMBRANE

TREATED WOOD CANT

TREATED WOOD CURB

TREATED WOOD BASE

INSULATION

10" TYPICAL

5.34 *Typical roof area divider detail.*

REFERENCES

5.1   Steel Deck Institute. "Design Manual for Composite Decks, Form Decks, Roof Decks and Cellular Deck Floor Systems with Electrical Distribution," Steel Deck Institute Publication No. 29 (Fox River Grove, IL: 1995), p. 37.

5.2   Ibid.

5.3   American Plywood Association. *Residential and Commercial Design/Construction Guide* (Tacoma, WA: 1998), p. 53.

5.4   National Roofing Contractors Association. *Handbook of Accepted Roofing Knowledge* (Chicago, IL: 1996), p. 34.

5.5   Ibid.

5.6   Sheet Metal and Air Conditioning Contractors National Association, Inc. *Architectural Sheet Metal Manual* (Chantilly, VA: 1993) p. 5.2.

6 DESIGN FOR DRAINAGE

A well-drained roof is not only more water resistive, but it is also more durable and structurally safer. A roof on which the water ponds for long periods deteriorates more rapidly than a roof that does not pond, or does so briefly. Roofing bitumens have certain compounds that dissolve under the sustained pressure of standing water, reducing the membrane's life. The adhesives used in single-ply membranes also deteriorate under similar conditions.[6.1] That is why most roofing manufacturers exclude the repair of leaks in areas where the water does not drain freely.

With a density of 62.5 lb/ft^3 (1,000 kg/m^3), water is a fairly heavy substance. A 1-in. (25-mm) depth of water adds a weight of 5.2 lb/ft^2 (250 Pa) on the roof. The typical roof design live load is only 20 lb/ft^2, and the building codes allow a reduction in the above figure for structural elements with large tributary areas.

In fact for economic reasons, the live load reduction is often invoked in the structural design of a roof deck assembly, particularly in the design of a long span roof. Thus, it is not unusual to find a roof structure designed for an average live load of only 12 to 16 lb/ft^2. This figure is exceeded by the weight of a mere 3 in. (75 mm) of ponded water. A poorly drained roof can accumulate this much water fairly quickly under heavy downpours with disastrous results. The primary cause of most roof collapses is excessive water ponding.

In addition to structural and durability benefits, a well-drained roof does not allow the deposition of windborne clay or silt on the roof. Clay and silt deposits can lead to vegetation growth, producing punctures and leaks in the roof membrane. Clay and silt deposits can also make roof repairs more complicated. Fungal growth on the membrane can also occur on poorly drained roofs.

Although permanently ponded roofs were, at one time,[1] advocated by some enthusiasts for their energy-saving potential, blockage of ultraviolet radiation, and stabilization of roof temperature, the waterproofing problems associated with such roofs are too numerous to consider their use, except in special situations. The plumbing assembly needed to maintain a constant water level on such a roof is another problem. Good drainage is, therefore, a major requirement of a low-slope roof.

Two important aspects of roof drainage design are roof slope and the roof's drainage system. These and other related aspects such as crickets, flashings, and detailing around the drains are discussed in this chapter.

---

[1] Water has a much a higher specific heat than any building material. It can, therefore, provide a large heat storage capacity, which helps to stabilize roof temperature and thereby cut heating and cooling costs. This effect is similar to the effect of a large water body on environmental temperature, such as that of an ocean or a large lake. Because of the large heat storage capacity of water, a location close to the ocean or a large lake has mild year-round temperatures compared to an inland location.

6.1 ROOF SLOPE

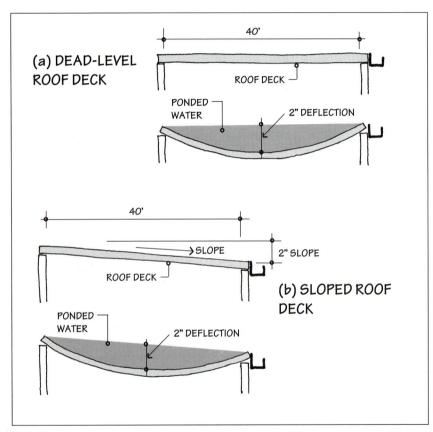

6.1 *(a) Ponding of water on a dead-level roof deck due to deck deflection. (b) Ponding of water on a sloped deck where the roof slope is equal to deck deflection. The illustrations are not to scale; the vertical scale has been exaggerated for the sake of clarity.*

Obviously, a fundamental drainage requirement is the slope of the roof. Theoretically, if the roof is perfectly flat, it will drain — albeit slowly — since there is no place for the water to stand. However, construction tolerances and workmanship lapses are such that high and low spots are bound to occur on a roof deck. These (unintentional) surface irregularities on an otherwise dead-level deck will produce ponded water, which can only clear through evaporation.

Apart from the unintentional surface irregularities, a major cause of ponding on a roof is the deflection of the deck. Initially on a dead-level roof, the weight of a thin sheet of running water causes the deck to deflect a little. As the deck deflects, it is able to hold more water, causing additional deflection, which increases the depth of water further, which in turn causes additional deflection, and so on. If the deck lacks stiffness, the progressive increase in ponding may exceed the structural capacity of the deck, leading to its failure. Several roof collapses have occurred as a result of this phenomenon.

A roof deck is typically designed for a maximum permissible deflection of span/240 under the roof live load. Thus, if the span of a roof joist or beam is 40 ft, the permissible maximum deflection under the full live load is (40x12)/240 = 2.0 in., which will create a 2-in. depth of water at its center, Figure 6.1(a). If such a deck slopes 2 in. in 40 ft (i.e., 1:240 slope) or less, its drainage potential improves only marginally, Figure 6.1(b). Thus, from the drainage perspective, a slope of 1:240 in such a roof is virtually equivalent to a dead-level roof, since under deck deflection it will almost pond the same amount as a dead-level roof. In other words, for a positive slope, the above roof deck must slope more than 1:240.

Although several roofs have been built with inadequate or no slope in the past, the minimum roof slope mandated by present-day building codes is 1/4 in. to 1 ft (i.e., 1/4:12, or 1:48, or say 2%). Although a 1/4:12 slope is required, a steeper slope is not necessarily better. A steeper slope will no doubt improve roof drainage (thereby increasing the roof's durability), but it creates several other problems.

For instance, the fire resistance of a roof decreases with increasing slope, see Section 7.3 in Chapter 7. That is why a gravel-covered built-up roof is usually limited to a 3:12 (33%) slope, beyond which it does not carry any fire rating. For the same reason, a granule-surfaced built-up roof is typically limited to a slope of 1/2:12 (4%). Increasing roof slope also increases the roof's cost — another disadvantage associated with an increasing roof slope.

6.1.1 Slippage of Built-Up Roof Felts and Modified Bitumen Sheets

In addition to the problems stated earlier, there is a problem of slippage of built-up roof felts and modified bitumen sheets with increasing roof slope. The slippage of felts and sheets becomes critical if the roof slope exceeds 1:12. In general, roofing material manufacturers require that built-up roofing felts with gravel covering be nailed to wood nailers if the roof slope exceeds 1/2:12. The nailing of felts or sheets to control their slippage is referred to as *back nailing*. The maximum slopes typically used for a mineral-granule-surfaced and a smooth-surfaced built-up roof are 1:12 and 2:12 respectively, beyond which backnailing is required.

Modified bitumen sheets, being heavier, have a greater slippage problem than built-up roof felts. Therefore, slope requirements are more stringent with modified bitumen roofs. Typically, modified bitumen sheets require back nailing for roof slopes greater than 1:25 (0.5 in. to 1 ft).

Backnailed roofs require 2 x 4 (nominal) pressure treated wood nailers between insulation boards, spaced as per roofing membrane manufacturer's recommendation. The spacing of nailers varies between 10 to 25 ft, depending on roof slope, the manufacturer and the type of roof. The greater the slope, the smaller the spacing. The nailers are aligned perpendicular to roof slope, Figure 6.2.

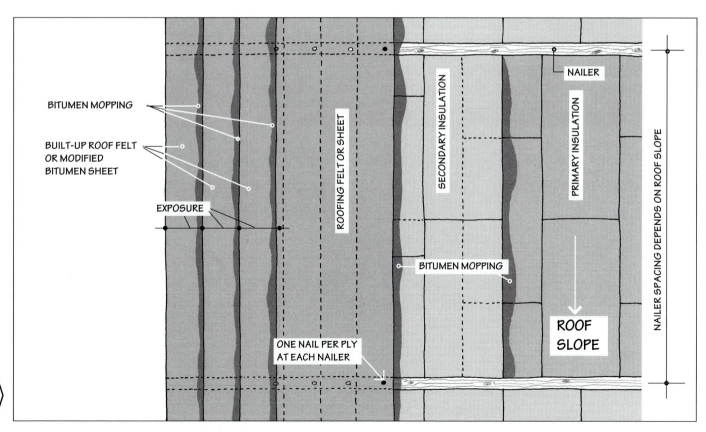

6.2 *Backnailing of roofing felts or sheets.*

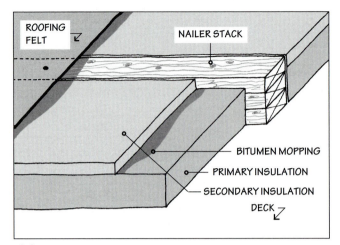

6.3 *The top surface of nailers must be flush with the top surface of insulation.*

Roof felts or sheets are laid with their long dimension parallel to the direction of the slope, i.e., perpendicular to the nailers. Each felt or sheet is nailed to each nailer by one nail, approximately 1 in. (25 mm) from the felt's leading edge. Nails must have at least 1 in. diameter caps, either integral with the nail or as a separate cap.

Cap sheets are nailed similarly. However, the termination of the length of a cap sheet must occur at a nailer. At its terminal end, a cap sheet requires at least five nails, which are covered over by the lap of the succeeding cap sheet

On a nailable deck, the nailers must be securely fastened with mechanical fasteners. On a nonnailable deck, the nailers should be adhered with hot bitumen. Multiple nailer stack is required so that the height of nailer stack is equal to the thickness of insulation, Figure 6.3.

6.2 EXTERNAL AND INTERNAL DRAINAGE SYSTEMS

The drainage system of a low-slope roof can be of two basic types:

- External drainage system
- Internal drainage system

An *external drainage system* consists of either a gutter and downspout assembly, as shown in Figure 6.4, or scuppers. A gutter-downspout assembly is only applicable to a roof that slopes toward the external edges of the building. Thus, the drainage may be provided from one, two, or four external edges, Figure 6.5.

A scupper is simply a hole in the parapet wall, Figure 6.6. Being the simplest way to drain a flat roof, scuppers have been in use for centuries. Several historical buildings still retain their highly decorative scuppers, referred to as *gargoyles*. Although the modern architecture's trend toward formal clarity and directness led to the ornamental gargoyle being transformed to a simple rectangular element, several architects, chiefly Le Corbusier, used large projecting concrete scuppers in buildings, Figure 6.7.

6.4 *External drainage — a gutter-downspout assembly in a low-slope roof. Photos by Madan Mehta.*

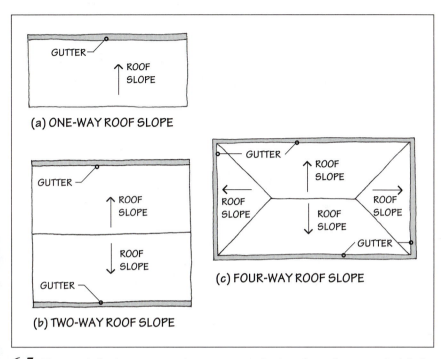

6.5 *External drainage — various ways to drain a low-slope roof with the help of gutters.*

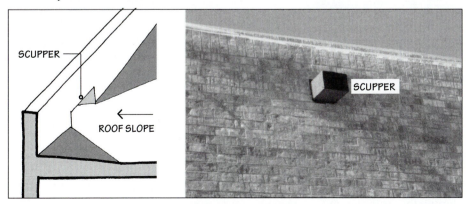

6.6 *External drainage through a typical scupper. Photo by Madan Mehta.*

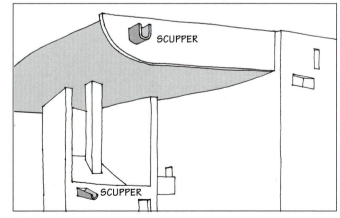

6.7 *The Chapel at Ronchamp by Le Corbusier.*

6.8 *A roof drain with strainer. Photo by Madan Mehta.*

An *internal drainage system* consists of an assembly of roof drains and pipes. A roof drain is basically a hole in a roof deck, Figure 6.8. One or more drains are connected to a horizontal pipe, which is hung below the deck, Figure 6.9. Each horizontal pipe terminates into a vertical pipe (called a *leader*), which is also placed inside the building. The leaders connect to an underground stormwater drainage system. If there is no underground drainage system, the leaders discharge the water on a paved ground that slopes away from the building.

An internal roof drainage system is aesthetically less obtrusive. However, its main advantage is that it is protected from the weather and thereby provides a more reliable drainage system in colder climates. An external system, such as a gutter, can get clogged by snow in freezing weather and by debris, leaves, and other waste materials. However, an external system with a roof overhang will get the water away from the roof more quickly, providing more efficient drainage.

6.9 *Plumbing associated with an internal roof drainage system. Photo by Madan Mehta.*

6.3 PROVIDING ROOF SLOPE

Two means are commonly employed to provide slope in the roof. These are:

*   Sloping the roof deck structure
*   Using tapered insulation

The required slope for a roof structural assembly is commonly achieved by sloping the structure toward one side (for narrow buildings) or toward both sides of a central ridge line for wider buildings. This implies using column lines of different terminal elevations, so that the tops of beams are placed at different heights. This is explained in Figure 6.10, which shows part of the structural framing plan for a 120-ft-wide building.

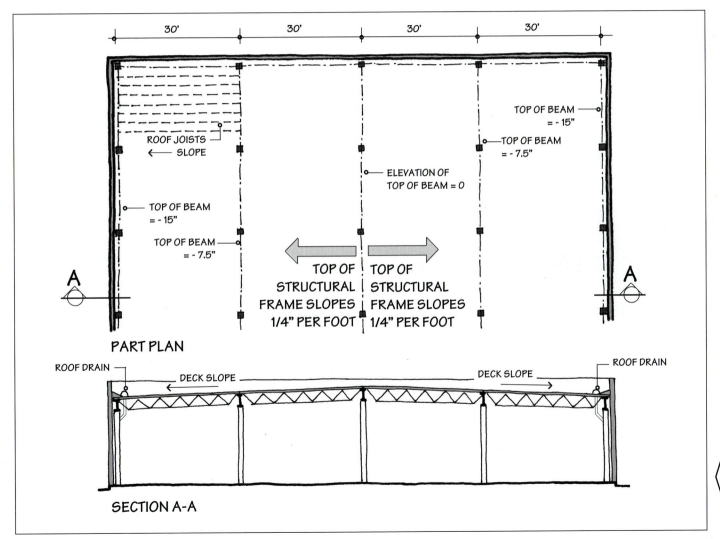

6.10 *Framing plan and section of a roof structure that slopes 1/4 in. per ft in both directions of a central ridge line.*

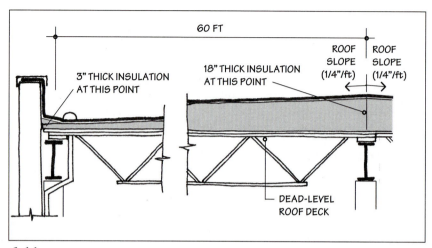

6.11 *Creating roof slope by using tapered insulation on a flat deck of the building of Figure 6.10.*

6.12 *A typical tapered rigid insulation board. Photo by Madan Mehta.*

Because the roof slopes 1/4:12, the total change in roof height from the central ridge line is 60/4 = 15 in. With two structural bays on either side of the center of the building, the top of the beams are placed at 7.5 in. and 15 in. below the top of the central (ridge) beam, assumed to be at zero height.

6.3.1 Tapered Insulation

An alternative to sloping the structural frame is to use a flat deck and achieve the roof slope by using tapered rigid insulation. This alternative is, however, costlier than the first alternative — incorporating the slope in the structural frame. The reason is that the old insulation must be completely discarded and replaced by new insulation at the time of reroofing. Since the life span of even a good roof assembly seldom exceeds 20 years, reroofing adds a large recurring insulation expense for roofs in which the slope has been provided by the use of tapered insulation.

Additionally, the thickness of insulation at high points of a flat deck can be extremely large. Because insulation is expensive, this adds to the cost of the roof. As an example, consider once again the 120-ft-wide building shown in Figure 6.10. If the required slope is the same (1/4:12) and the structural frame of this building is absolutely flat (i.e., all members are at the same terminal height), the total required roof slope will be 15 in. in either direction.

Thus, if the minimum insulation needed at any point on this roof is 3 in., the thickness of insulation at the ridge must be 18 in., Figure 6.11, which is extremely large. The cost of the insulation is not merely in the material but also in its installation on the deck. A thicker insulation requires longer and heavier fasteners, compared to a thinner insulation.

Tapered insulation boards are generally manufactured in 4 ft x 4 ft size. To provide different roof slopes, tapered boards with different tapers are available — 1/8 in. per ft, 1/4 in. per ft, 3/8 in. per ft, and 1/2 in. per ft. The most commonly used taper is 1/4 in. per ft, which gives 1-in. taper in a 4-ft-long board. Thus, the thickness of such a board differs by 1 in. at its two opposite edges. A typical tapered board is shown in Figure 6.12.

To build the slope on a deck, the insulation assembly generally consists of both tapered boards as well as boards of uniform thickness (called *fillers*). Several different tapered board profiles may be required. Thus, to provide a 1/4 in. per ft roof slope with 4 ft x 4 ft boards, three different tapered board profiles — A, B, and C — and 3-in.-thick fillers are required, Figure 6.13. To provide 1/2 in. per ft slope, only one tapered board profile with a 2-in.-thick filler is required, Figure 6.14.

The average thickness of insulation in the roof of Figure 6.11 can be cut into half by sloping the insulation toward the interior. The roof drains are now located in two interior valleys, Figure 6.15. The same roof profile can be obtained by

6.13 *Layout of tapered rigid insulation boards to provide 1/4 in. per ft slope. Three types of tapered boards and 3-in. fillers have been used in this case. Tapered board type A has a thickness of 0.5 in. at one edge and 1.5 in. at the other edge. The thickness of type B varies from 1.5 in. to 2.5 in., and that of type C varies from 2.5 in. to 3.5 in. If 2-in.-thick fillers are used, only types A and B are required.*

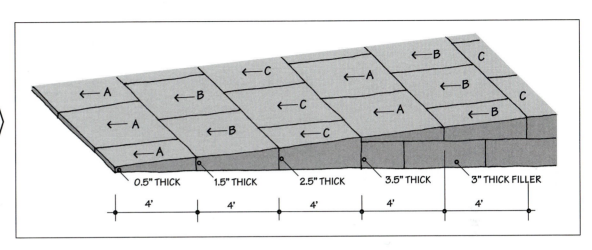

0.5" THICK   1.5" THICK   2.5" THICK   3.5" THICK   3" THICK FILLER

4'   4'   4'   4'   4'

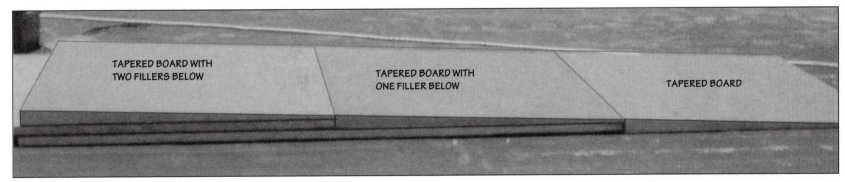

TAPERED BOARD WITH
TWO FILLERS BELOW

TAPERED BOARD WITH
ONE FILLER BELOW

TAPERED BOARD

6.14 *Tapered boards, each 4 ft x 4 ft with 1/2 in. per ft taper in one direction, and 2-in.-thick fillers. Photo by Madan Mehta.*

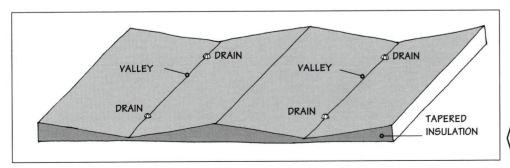

VALLEY   DRAIN
DRAIN
VALLEY   DRAIN
DRAIN
TAPERED
INSULATION

6.15 *Use of tapered insulation on a flat deck to create valleys for drainage.*

sloping the structural frame, Figure 6.16. Note that in either case, the entire valley line is at constant elevation — no slope.

To provide a more efficient drainage within a valley, crickets are needed. In fact, crickets are particularly required for the roof of Figure 6.16, since the structural configuration prevents the drains to be installed in the valley itself. The drains must be placed at some distance (2 to 3 ft) from the valley line, Figure 6.17. This ponds the entire valley line with water, unless the valley is flattened with tapered insulation. However, for better drainage, crickets should be installed in the valley, as explained in the following section.

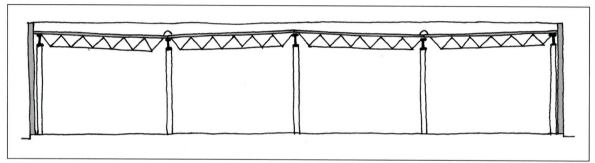

6.16 *Valleys formed in the roof by sloping the structural members.*

6.17 *If the valleys are formed by sloping the structural members, roof drains cannot be located exactly on the valley line.*

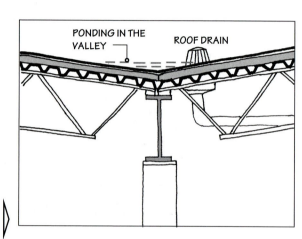

6.4 ROOF CRICKETS

A cricket is a pyramidical formation on the roof, generally made from tapered insulation boards. It alters the roof slope between the drains to provide a more efficient drainage.

Several types of crickets may be needed on a roof. The simplest type uses (full) *diamond crickets*. They are required where the roof slopes from both sides into a valley, Figure 6.18. Where structural configuration does not permit the placement of drains exactly on the valley line (see Figure 6.17), sumps may be formed at the tip of crickets and the drains located within the sumps, Figure 6.19. An actual installation of crickets on a roof is illustrated in Figure 6.20.

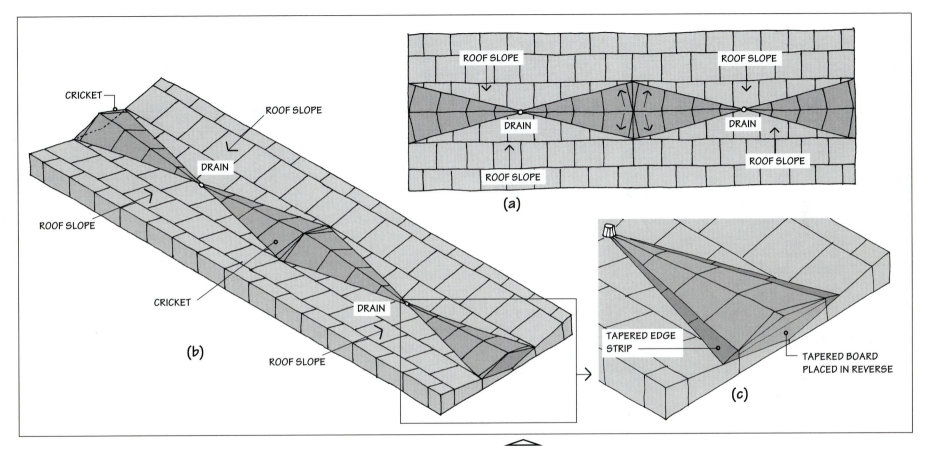

CRICKET

ROOF SLOPE

DRAIN

ROOF SLOPE

CRICKET

DRAIN

ROOF SLOPE

(b)

ROOF SLOPE

ROOF SLOPE

DRAIN

ROOF SLOPE

DRAIN

ROOF SLOPE

(a)

TAPERED EDGE STRIP

TAPERED BOARD PLACED IN REVERSE

(c)

6.18 *Layout of 4 ft x 4 ft tapered boards on a flat deck to produce a two-way roof slope, creating a valley. The valley is covered with crickets shown in (a) plan view and (b) isometric view. (c) Detail of a cricket.*

A cricket is generally made from tapered boards. Because the tapered boards slope down to a finite thickness (typically 0.5 in.), tapered edge strips (which slope to zero thickness at one edge) are needed to provide a smooth transition. Tapered edge strips are generally made from a more rigid material, such as wood fiberboard or perlite board.

6.19 *The use of a sump around the drain, when the drain cannot be located between the tips of crickets.*

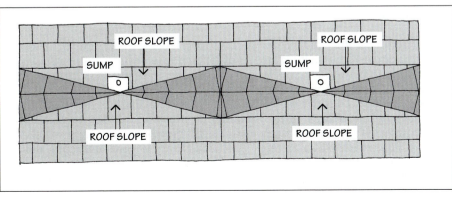

ROOF SLOPE

ROOF SLOPE

SUMP

SUMP

ROOF SLOPE

ROOF SLOPE

6.20 *Creating crickets on a roof. Photos courtesy of Roofing Systems Group, Johns Manville, Denver, Colorado.*

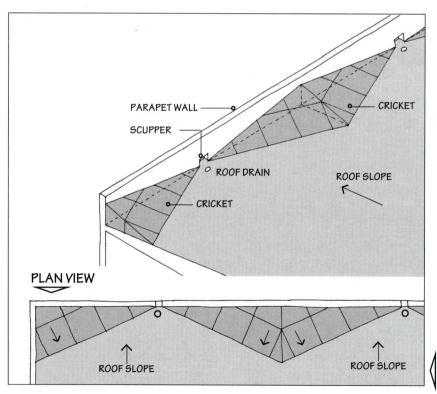

PLAN VIEW

6.21 *Crickets on a roof that slope toward a parapet wall and is drained by a through-the-wall scupper or a roof drain placed near the wall.*

The other more commonly used cricket type is a half diamond cricket. Half diamond crickets are required where the roof slopes toward one or two opposite edges and is drained by the use of scuppers or drains placed near the edges of the roof, Figure 6.21.

The use of crickets may be completely (or almost) avoided in a roof, where two-way valleys are created by the use of tapered insulation, Figure 6.22. This solution is particularly attractive where the drains must be located at a considerable distance from the roof's edge. However, it involves an excessive use of tapered insulation, which can be expensive.

Tapered insulation or crickets are not needed with lightweight insulating concrete, as the required slope can be created through concrete fill, see Section 4.9 in Chapter 4.

6.4.1 Warped Roof Deck

A roof profile similar (but not identical) to a two-way valley profile, discussed earlier, can be created without the use of tapered insulation. This is achieved by sloping the structural frame in two directions. The resultant deck has a two-way curvature and is therefore referred to as a *warped deck*.

For instance, consider once again the framing plan of Figure 6.10. If the alternate interior columns in this building terminate at a lower height than the other columns, the deck that such a structural frame supports is a warped deck. Thus, in Figure 6.23, if columns P, Q, R, and S are of a smaller height, the roof

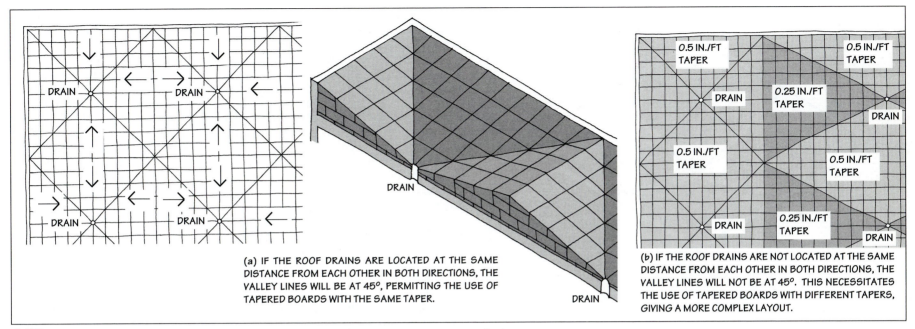

(a) IF THE ROOF DRAINS ARE LOCATED AT THE SAME DISTANCE FROM EACH OTHER IN BOTH DIRECTIONS, THE VALLEY LINES WILL BE AT 45°, PERMITTING THE USE OF TAPERED BOARDS WITH THE SAME TAPER.

(b) IF THE ROOF DRAINS ARE NOT LOCATED AT THE SAME DISTANCE FROM EACH OTHER IN BOTH DIRECTIONS, THE VALLEY LINES WILL NOT BE AT 45°. THIS NECESSITATES THE USE OF TAPERED BOARDS WITH DIFFERENT TAPERS, GIVING A MORE COMPLEX LAYOUT.

6.22 *The use of tapered boards to create two-way valley lines terminating into a drain.*

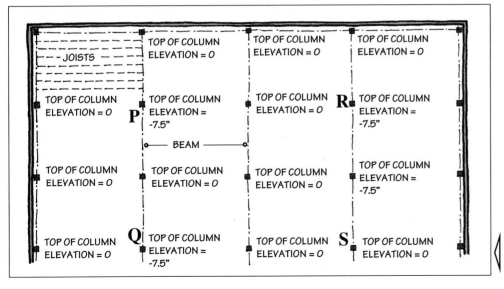

6.23 *Relative elevations of the top of columns to produce a warped deck.*

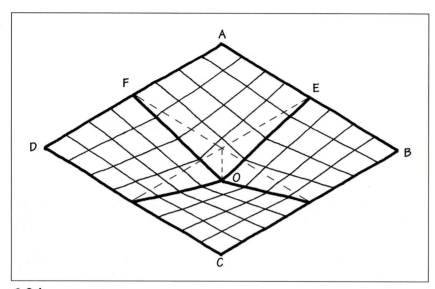

6.24 *Construction of a warped surface (hyperbolic paraboloid) with straight wires.*

surface created by the joists spanning between beams and the deck spanning between the joists has a double curvature. From a geometrical viewpoint, this roof surface is a hyperbolic paraboloid surface.

To comprehend a hyperbolic paraboloid surface, construct a wire frame, ABCD, that is square in shape, Figure 6.24   Now take a point, O, which is vertically below the center of the frame, and connect the midpoint of each side of the frame with point O. This divides the wire frame into four smaller frames.

Now consider one of these four smaller frames, say the frame AEOF. Divide the opposite edges of this frame — edges AF and EO — in equal parts and join the corresponding points on the opposite edges by wires. Repeat the same construction with edges AE and FO. The surface created by this matrix of wires is a hyperbolic paraboloid surface. It is so called because a vertical section through the surface, along AO, is a hyperbola and a vertical section through FE is a parabola.

Hyperbolic paraboloid concrete shell structures were very popular during the 1960s and the 1970s. Their popularity lay in their structural efficiency and because their formwork could be made from straight linear elements. Thus, wood planks could be used to create the formwork.

Note that a warped deck is normally used with a metal deck roof, since a metal deck roof assembly is constructed of linear elements — beams, joists, and the deck panels. That is why warped metal decks are becoming increasingly popular. Although a wood deck can also be warped, its use is relatively rare. The roof drains in a warped deck are placed at its lowest point. Thus, in Figure 6.24, the drain is located near the point O.

It is important to appreciate that, in a warped deck, there is virtually always a column directly below the lowest point so that the drain cannot be placed at the lowest point on the roof. A sump is, therefore, required to prevent standing water around a drain.

6.5 PRIMARY AND SECONDARY DRAINAGE SYSTEMS

Because an excessive ponding of water on a roof caused by the failure of the roof's drainage system can lead to structural collapse, an important drainage design requirement is redundancy. *Redundancy* refers to providing a second line of defense in the event of the failure of the first line. Thus, roof drainage redundancy means incorporating a *secondary drainage system* to cater to that (supposedly rare) situation when the *primary drainage system* gets blocked or fails in some other manner. The secondary system is also referred to as the *overflow system*.

The provision of a secondary drainage system is not required if the roof is drained by roof edge gutters and downspouts since the ponding of water on such a roof cannot occur, see Figure 6.4. However, if internal drains or scuppers are used in conjunction with parapet walls, the possibility of roof ponding exists, and hence the secondary drainage is mandated. A secondary drainage system is required regardless of whether the primary drainage consists of roof drains or scuppers.

6.5.1 Primary and Secondary Roof Drains

Two alternatives are used to satisfy the secondary drainage requirement. The first alternative — the preferred one — is to duplicate every drain, in which a set of two drains located close to each other are used. One of these is a primary drain, and the other a secondary drain. Both primary and secondary drainage systems must be completely independent of each other, i.e., they must have their own horizontal and vertical plumbing lines, Figure 6.25.

The secondary drains should not become operative unless the primary system is blocked. Therefore, the elevation of a secondary drain's inlet should be above the head of water that will exist above the primary drain's inlet under the maximum rainfall intensity. Elevating the secondary drains also tends to prevent debris from blocking the drainage of the overflow system.

Generally, the difference in elevation between a secondary drain and the adjacent primary drain is kept at 2 in. However, as a good design practice, this elevational difference should be calculated as shown in Appendix D (Example D.3).

Because the triggering of the secondary drainage is a serious warning, the water from the secondary system should not be discharged into the underground stormwater line. Instead, it should be discharged in an obvious external location so that the seriousness of the situation is noticed immediately. Most designers provide the secondary system discharge just below the second floor level, Figure 6.26.

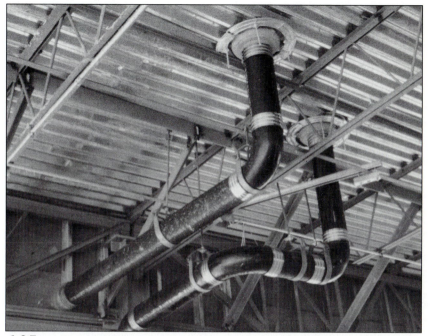

6.25 *Primary and secondary drains with their independent pipe lines. Photo by Madan Mehta.*

6.26 *Suggested discharge location for secondary roof drain.*

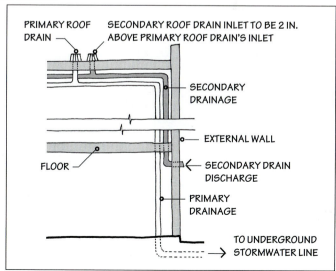

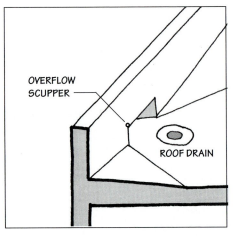
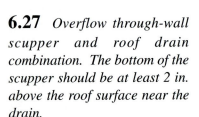

OVERFLOW SCUPPER

ROOF DRAIN

6.27 *Overflow through-wall scupper and roof drain combination. The bottom of the scupper should be at least 2 in. above the roof surface near the drain.*

6.5.2 Through-Wall Scupper as a Secondary Drainage Element

The second alternative, which works only if the roof drains are placed near the parapet wall, is to use through-wall scupper and roof drain combinations, Figure 6.27. In this combination, the roof drains are part of the primary drainage system and the scuppers are overflow elements. The bottom of each scupper inlet is between 2 in. to 4 in. above the level of the corresponding roof drain inlet.

6.5.3 Rain Load due to the Blockage of Primary Drains

Because the secondary drainage system (roof drains or overflow scuppers) are raised above the inlet level of primary drains, the blockage of primary drains will cause ponding of water on the roof. The architect or the roofing consultant must work out the depth of water build-up on the roof caused by the failure of the primary drainage system and advise the structural engineer accordingly. This is discussed further in Appendix D.

6.6 SIZING ROOF DRAINS AND ASSOCIATED PIPES

Roof drainage design must conform to the local plumbing code. The most important factor that determines the size of roof drains and the associated pipes is the maximum anticipated rainfall at the location. The International Plumbing Code[6.2] requires that the rainfall received in a one-hour period during the worst storm with a 100-year return period be used as the *design rainfall intensity* (for the primary drainage system). The design rainfall intensity — maximum 1-hour, 100-year rainfall — for major U.S. cities is given in Appendix C. For instance, the design rainfall intensity for Fort Worth, Texas, is 4.0 in.

6.6.1 Number and Size of Roof Drains for Primary Drainage

A roof drain is generally made of cast iron, and its size is expressed by the diameter of its inlet, Figure 6.28. It is typically available in 3-, 4-, 5-, 6- and 8-in. diameters, although some manufacturers make 2- and 2.5-in. drains also. A drain with a diameter of 3 in. or less is generally not specified, except for a small roof area, such as a balcony or entrance porch. The 4-in. and 5-in. drains are the most commonly used. Note that a smaller drain is more easily blocked.

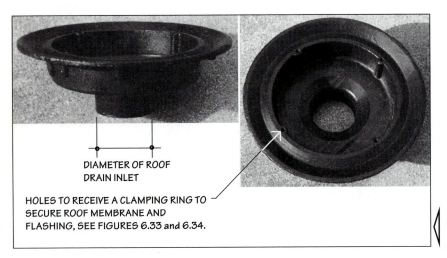

DIAMETER OF ROOF DRAIN INLET

HOLES TO RECEIVE A CLAMPING RING TO SECURE ROOF MEMBRANE AND FLASHING, SEE FIGURES 6.33 and 6.34.

6.28 *A typical roof drain. Photos by Madan Mehta.*

The number and the size of drains required for a roof is a function of the design rainfall intensity and the area of the roof. The roof area used in this computation is the projected roof area, i.e., the plan area of the roof. Thus, the slope of the roof is irrelevant in this computation. Plumbing codes provide the maximum projected roof area that a drain of given size can handle, Table 6.1.

Several drains are connected to a horizontal pipe that runs below the roof, see Figure 6.9. In most buildings, the drains and the horizontal pipes are concealed by the ceiling below the roof. To prevent condensation caused by cold rainwater flowing through horizontal pipes, the bottom of roof drains should be insulated.

The horizontal pipes are sloped. Typical slopes are 1/8 in. per ft, 1/4 in. per ft, or 1/2 in. per ft. The required sizes of the horizontal pipes are obtained from Table 6.2.

Each horizontal pipe terminates into a vertical pipe (referred to as a *leader*). The leaders should be placed inside the building, and preferably insulated all around. The roof area that a leader can handle is the same as that of the roof drain, i.e., as given in Table 6.1.

Notes:

1. If the rainfall is different from 1 in., simply divide the values in this table by that rainfall value. For example, if the rainfall at a location is 3 in., divide the values by 3.

2. The values given in this table can be approximated by the following formula.

$$A \approx 455 \, (d)^{8/3}$$

where A = maximum projected roof area in ft^2, and d = diameter of the drain in inches.

3. To convert area in ft^2 to area in m^2, multiply values by 0.092. To convert drain diameter in in. to drain diameter in mm, multiply the diameter by 25.4.

4. Values in this table are to be used for preliminary sizing. Local plumbing code should be consulted for more authoritative information.

Table 6.1   Drainage Capacity of Roof Drains and Leaders, If the 1-Hour, 100-Year Rainfall = 1 in.

Diameter of drain (in.)	Maximum projected roof area (sq ft)
2	2,880
3	8,800
4	18,400
5	34,600
6	54,000
8	116,000

Table 6.2 Drainage Capacity of Horizontal Drainage Pipes, If the 1-Hour, 100-Year Rainfall = 1 in.

Diameter of horizontal pipe (in.)	Maximum projected roof area (sq ft)		
	Pipe slope — 1/8 in. per ft	Pipe slope — 1/4 in. per ft	Pipe slope — 1/2 in. per ft
3	3,288	4,640	6,576
4	7,520	10,600	15,040
5	13,360	18,880	26,720
6	21,400	30,200	42,800
8	46,000	65,200	92,000
10	82,800	116,800	171,600
12	133,200	188,000	266,400

Notes:

1. If the rainfall is different from 1 in., simply divide the values in this table by that rainfall value. For example, if the rainfall at a location is 3 in., divide the values by 3.

2. The values given in this table can be approximated by the following formula:

$$A \approx 1775 \, (d)^{8/3}(s)^{1/2}$$

where A = maximum projected roof area in ft^2, d = diameter of the drain in in., and s = horizontal pipe slope. For instance, if the pipe slope is 1/4 in. per ft, s = 1/48 = 0.0208.

3. To convert area in ft^2 to area in m^2, multiply values by 0.092. To convert drain diameter in in. to drain diameter in mm, multiply the diameter by 25.4.

4. Values in this table are to be used for preliminary sizing. Local plumbing code should be consulted for more authoritative information.

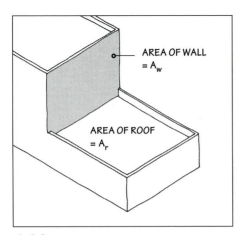

AREA OF WALL = A_w

AREA OF ROOF = A_r

6.29 *The area of the roof to be considered in designing its drainage system is not A_r, but $(A_r + 0.5A_w)$.*

6.6.2 Number and Size of Roof Drains for Secondary Drainage

Because the plumbing codes require that the secondary drainage system (roof drains and the associated horizontal and vertical pipes) be completely separate from, and of the same capacity[2] as, the primary drainage system, the design of the secondary system does not need any additional calculations. Thus, in practice, we simply duplicate the primary drains and the associated pipes, which constitutes the secondary system.

6.6.3 Effect of an Adjoining Wall on Roof Drainage

Because wind can deflect rain to the vertical surface, a wall abutting a roof can increase the amount of water on a roof. The code, therefore, requires that one-half the area of the wall that may direct water on the roof should be added to the roof area in sizing the primary or secondary drains, pipes, and leaders, Figure 6.29.

6.6.4 Minimum Number of Roof Drains

The minimum number of roof drains (either primary or secondary drains) on a roof are specified by the plumbing code. On a roof with an area of less than 10,000 ft^2, a minimum of two drains are generally mandated. If the roof area is greater than 10,000 ft^2, a minimum of four drains are required.

---

[2] For a while, some plumbing codes (Reference 6.2) required that the design of the secondary roof drainage system be based on twice the rainfall intensity used for the design of the primary system. Thus, if the design (hourly) rainfall intensity for the primary drainage system was 4 in., the design of the secondary drainage system was to be based on an (hourly) rainfall intensity of 8 in. This meant that the capacity of the secondary drainage system (roof drains and the horizontal and vertical pipes) was to be twice that of the primary drainage system — a highly conservative approach.

Statistically, doubling the maximum 1-hour, 100-year rainfall intensity corresponds to the maximum 15-minute, 100-year (hourly) rainfall intensity. Thus, doubling the capacity of the secondary drainage system is tantamount to designing it for the worst 15-minute (hourly) rainfall in a 100-year period.

Primary and Secondary Drainage Design Using Roof Drains

Example 6.1: Determine the size and number of roof drains and the diameters of associated horizontal and vertical pipes for a low-slope roof measuring 150 ft x 200 ft in plan. Location: Fort Worth, Texas.

Solution for the primary system: From Appendix C, design rainfall intensity for Fort Worth, Texas = 4.0 in. Try 4 in. drains. From Table 6.1, the drainage capacity of a 4-in. drain for 1-in. rainfall is 18,400 ft². With a rainfall of 4.0 in., its drainage capacity = 18,400/4.0 = 4,600 ft².

Total roof area = 150 x 200 = 30,000 ft². Hence, the number of 4-in. drains needed = 30,000/4,600 = 6.52. Since the layout of drains is to be symmetrical, we will use 8 drains, so that each drain will serve a roof area of 30,000/8 = 3,750 ft². The layout of drains is shown in Figure 1.

We shall connect all 4 drains (on one side of the roof) to one horizontal pipe line at a slope of 1/4 in. per ft, which in turn is connected to one leader. The capacity of a 5-in. horizontal pipe from Table 6.2 is 18,800 ft² for a rainfall intensity of 1 in. per hour. With a rainfall intensity of 4 in. per hour, its capacity is 18,800/4.0 = 4,700 ft². Since the first drain serves a roof area of 3,750 ft², the initial horizontal line is 5 in. in diameter. The second line receives water from 7,500 ft². We now need a 6-in. line, since the capacity of a 6-in. line = 30,200/4.0 = 7,550 ft², which is greater than the required 7,500 ft². The layout of horizontal pipes is shown in Figure 2.

The size of the vertical leader is determined from Table 6.1. The total roof area to be drained by one leader = 75 x 200 = 15,000 ft². From Table 6.1, an 8-in. leader is needed, with a capacity of 116,000/4.0 = 29,000 ft². Note that a 6-in. leader with its capacity of 54,000/4 = 13,500 ft² is inadequate.

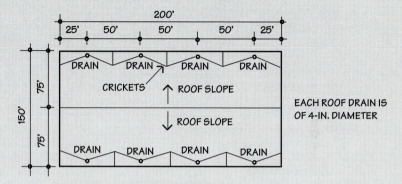

Figure 1. Layout of roof drains.

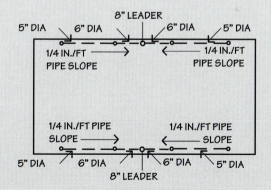

Figure 2. Layout of horizontal pipes and leaders (vertical pipes) for the primary system.

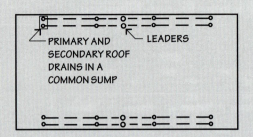

Figure 3. Layout of primary and secondary drainage systems for the roof in Example 6.1.

Solution for the secondary system: As stated in Section 6.6.2, the secondary drainage system's capacity is generally required by plumbing codes to be identical to that of the primary system. In other words, we simply duplicate the primary system, as shown in Figure 3.

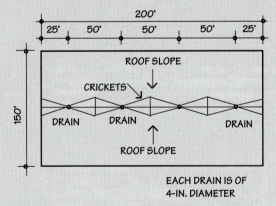

EACH DRAIN IS OF
4-IN. DIAMETER

Figure 4. Layout of roof drains of Example 6.2.

Example 6.2: Design the drainage system for a low-slope roof if the design (1-hour, 100-year) rainfall at a location is 2.0 in.

Solution: From Table 6.1, a 4-in. drain will serve an area of $18,400/2 = 9,200$ ft^2. With a total roof area of 30,000 ft^2, we need $(30,000/9,200) = 3.3$ drains. Thus, provide 4 roof drains. The layout of the drains is shown in Figure 4.

The design of horizontal pipe lines and the design of the secondary system is similar to that of Example 6.1.

Secondary drains' inlet level: The difference in elevation between the inlets of the primary and secondary drains must be established based on the head of water that accumulates under the rainfall intensity used for primary drainage design. This is discussed in Appendix D.

On a metal deck, the roof drains are placed by field-cutting a hole in the deck. Since this torch-cut hole is not precise, a drain receiver — a flat plate with a precise round hole to receive the drain — is placed over the field-cut hole, Figure 6.30. The drain is now placed on the receiver, Figure 6.31.

6.7 DETAILING A ROOF DRAIN

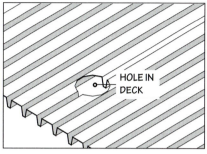

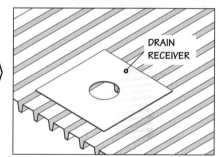

6.30 *Roughness of a field-cut hole in a metal deck and, hence, the need of a drain receiver. Photo by Madan Mehta.*

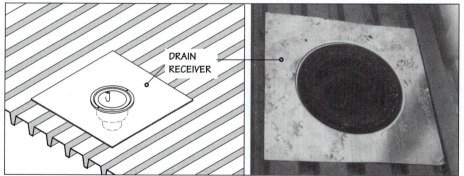

6.31 *The drain is installed on the drain receiver. Photo by Madan Mehta.*

The insulation is now laid on the deck and field-tapered to the drain, Figure 6.32(a). Where a large thickness of insulation is required in the vicinity of a drain, a drain extension is bolted to the drain, Figure 6.32(b) and the insulation tapered up to the drain extension.

Roof membrane and flashing is then brought up to the drain and secured in place by a clamping ring that is bolted to the drain. The clamping ring also functions as a receiver for the strainer.

Flashing, as explained in Chapter 10, is additional layers of waterproofing around terminations or penetrations in a roof. In a built-up roof, the flashing around a drain generally consists of a lead or copper sheet, which is embedded under two sheets of bitumen felt (referred to as *stripping plies*), or one sheet of modified bitumen, Figures 6.33 and 6.34(a). With a single-ply roof membrane, the stripping plies and lead (or copper) sheet flashing are not required, Figure 6.34(b).

INSULATION TAPERED TO DRAIN

ROOF DRAIN

DRAIN EXTENSION

ROOF DRAIN

(a)   (b)

6.32 *(a) Insulation is field-tapered to the drain. (b) A drain extension is used where required. Photo by Madan Mehta.*

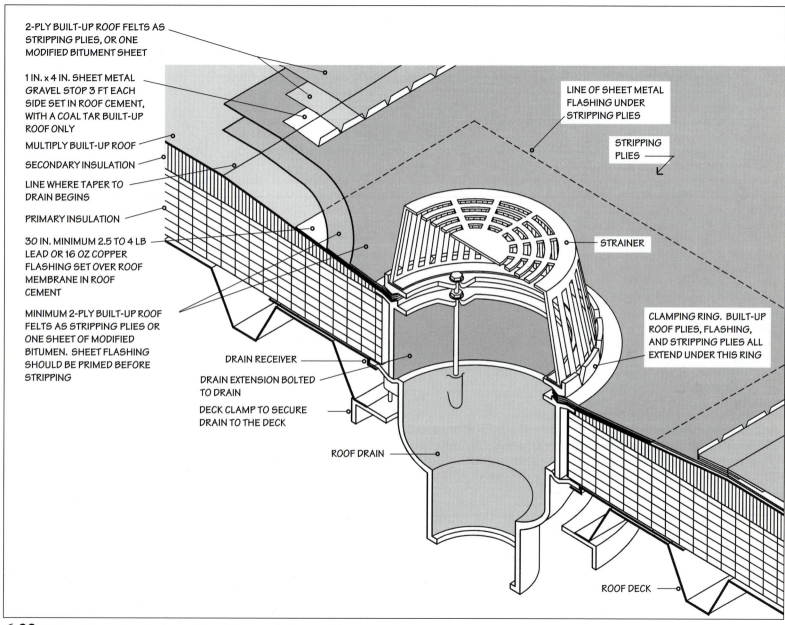

2-PLY BUILT-UP ROOF FELTS AS STRIPPING PLIES, OR ONE MODIFIED BITUMENT SHEET

1 IN. x 4 IN. SHEET METAL GRAVEL STOP 3 FT EACH SIDE SET IN ROOF CEMENT, WITH A COAL TAR BUILT-UP ROOF ONLY

MULTIPLY BUILT-UP ROOF

SECONDARY INSULATION

LINE WHERE TAPER TO DRAIN BEGINS

PRIMARY INSULATION

30 IN. MINIMUM 2.5 TO 4 LB LEAD OR 16 OZ COPPER FLASHING SET OVER ROOF MEMBRANE IN ROOF CEMENT

MINIMUM 2-PLY BUILT-UP ROOF FELTS AS STRIPPING PLIES OR ONE SHEET OF MODIFIED BITUMEN. SHEET FLASHING SHOULD BE PRIMED BEFORE STRIPPING

LINE OF SHEET METAL FLASHING UNDER STRIPPING PLIES

STRIPPING PLIES

STRAINER

CLAMPING RING. BUILT-UP ROOF PLIES, FLASHING, AND STRIPPING PLIES ALL EXTEND UNDER THIS RING

DRAIN RECEIVER

DRAIN EXTENSION BOLTED TO DRAIN

DECK CLAMP TO SECURE DRAIN TO THE DECK

ROOF DRAIN

ROOF DECK

6.33 *Three-dimensional view of detailing around a roof drain.*

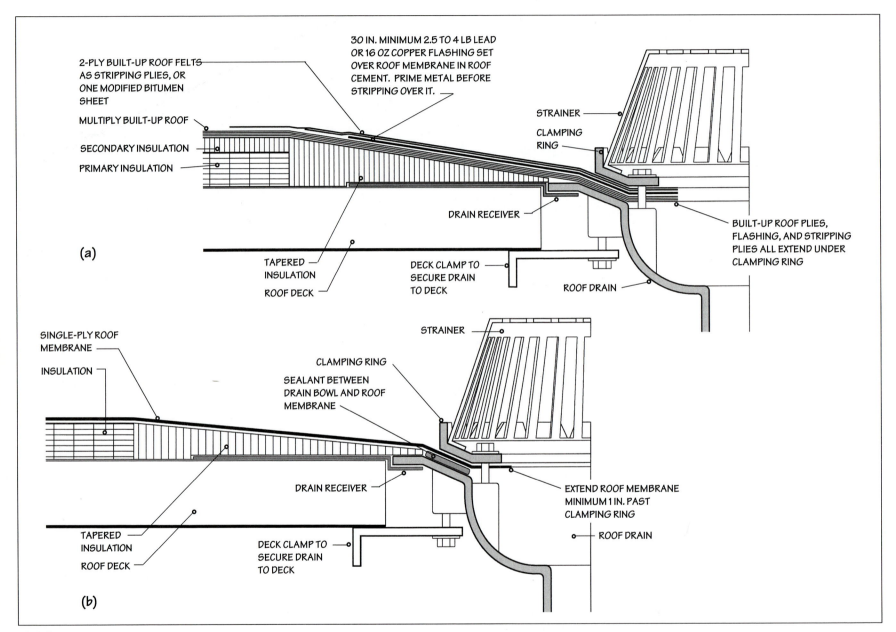

2-PLY BUILT-UP ROOF FELTS AS STRIPPING PLIES, OR ONE MODIFIED BITUMEN SHEET

MULTIPLY BUILT-UP ROOF

SECONDARY INSULATION

PRIMARY INSULATION

30 IN. MINIMUM 2.5 TO 4 LB LEAD OR 16 OZ COPPER FLASHING SET OVER ROOF MEMBRANE IN ROOF CEMENT. PRIME METAL BEFORE STRIPPING OVER IT.

STRAINER

CLAMPING RING

DRAIN RECEIVER

BUILT-UP ROOF PLIES, FLASHING, AND STRIPPING PLIES ALL EXTEND UNDER CLAMPING RING

(a)

TAPERED INSULATION

ROOF DECK

DECK CLAMP TO SECURE DRAIN TO DECK

ROOF DRAIN

SINGLE-PLY ROOF MEMBRANE

INSULATION

STRAINER

CLAMPING RING

SEALANT BETWEEN DRAIN BOWL AND ROOF MEMBRANE

DRAIN RECEIVER

EXTEND ROOF MEMBRANE MINIMUM 1 IN. PAST CLAMPING RING

ROOF DRAIN

TAPERED INSULATION

ROOF DECK

DECK CLAMP TO SECURE DRAIN TO DECK

(b)

6.34 *Detailing around a roof drain with (a) built-up roof membrane, (b) single-ply roof membrane.*

6.7.1 Strengthening a Metal Deck Around a Drain

It is important that the metal deck be structurally strengthened with additional framing around the drain, Figure 6.35. On a reinforced concrete deck, such additional framing is unnecessary, and the installation of the drain is relatively simple, since a precise hole can be left in the roof deck while casting it, Figure 6.36.

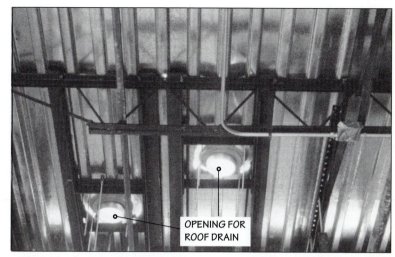

6.35 *Strengthening of the structural frame by additional framing members around a drain on a metal deck. Photo by Madan Mehta.*

6.36 *Installation of a roof drain over a reinforced concrete deck. Photo by Madan Mehta.*

6.8 SCUPPER AS A DRAINAGE ELEMENT

A through-wall scupper or an open-top scupper, Figure 6.37, although used in place of roof drains, are poor drainage elements. A scupper is easily blocked and prone to leakage. A bottle or tin can, leaves, plastic bags, paper, etc., can easily block a scupper opening. A roof drain, with its strainer, can function despite the blockage caused by such objects, since the water can go through the top of the strainer and find its way into the drain, Figure 6.38.

The International Plumbing Code[6.2] recognizes a scupper only as a secondary drainage element — for overflow purposes. Although, it does not specifically disallow the use of a scupper as a primary drainage element, it does not give any guidelines for its design.

As an overflow element, the minimum required opening area of a scupper (as given by the International Plumbing Code) is three times the cross-sectional area of a primary roof drain, with a minimum height of 4 in. Thus, if the primary roof drain is of 4-in. diameter (area = 12.6 sq in.), the minimum overflow scupper opening area is 37.8 sq in. A 5 in. x 8 in. scupper will be adequate in this case.

In the authors' opinion, the International Plumbing Code criterion is arbitrary and may result in an undersized scupper. It is suggested that the design of an overflow scupper be based on a rational analysis as given in Appendix D. Additionally, the depth of water accumulated on the roof must be calculated and the structural engineer informed.

Since the cost of providing a scupper is small, an oversized scupper is a good design practice. If a scupper is used as a primary drainage element, the authors recommend that it should be sized as a secondary drainage element, based on the analysis of Appendix D. However, note that a separate secondary drainage system is still required, which could also consist of scuppers.

6.37 *Through-wall and open-top scuppers.*
Photo by Madan Mehta.

6.38 *Relative performance of a scupper and a roof drain under conditions of blockage.*

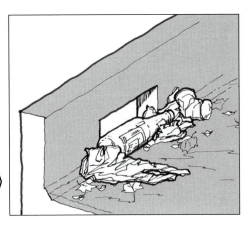

6.8.1 Anatomy of a Scupper

A typical through-wall scupper consists of two sheet metal elements: a throat and a flange, Figure 6.39. The sheet metal typically used is galvanized steel, although aluminum, copper, and stainless steel are also used. The throat and flange are joined together. If made of galvanized steel, the throat and flange are soldered together. The aluminum throat and flange are welded together.

After the roof membrane has been installed, the throat-flange assembly is inserted in the wall opening, Figure 6.40(a). Using roofer's cement, the scupper interior and its surroundings are flashed with flashing material (modified bitumen sheet for built-up or modified bitumen roofs, or single-ply sheet with a single-ply roof), Figures 6.40(b) and (c). Finally, the base flashing (see Chapter 10) covers the scupper surrounds, Figure 6.40(d).

FLANGE TOWARD THE OUTSIDE SURFACE OF WALL FOR A NONPROJECTING SCUPPER

THROAT

FLANGE

WALL ASSEMBLY

SEAL AND BACKING

SCUPPER FLANGE

SCUPPER THROAT

WALL ASSEMBLY

ROOF LINE

OVERFLOW SCUPPER DETAIL IN SECTION
ROOF MEMBRANE, FLASHING ETC. NOT SHOWN

6.39 *Anatomy of a through-wall sheet metal scupper.*

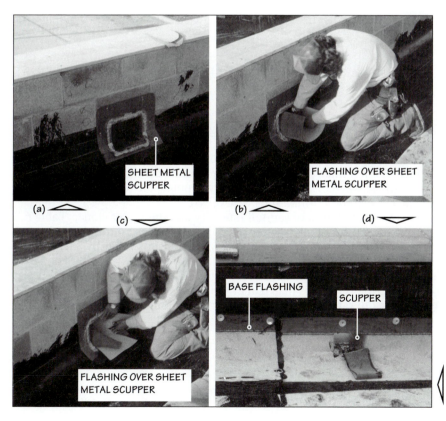

SHEET METAL SCUPPER

FLASHING OVER SHEET METAL SCUPPER

(a)

(b)

(c)

(d)

FLASHING OVER SHEET METAL SCUPPER

BASE FLASHING

SCUPPER

6.40 *Installation of, and flashing around, a through-wall sheet metal scupper. Photos by Madan Mehta.*

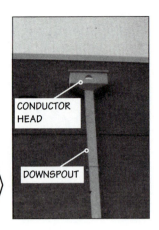

6.41 *A through-wall scupper that discharges into a conductor head and into a downspout. Photo by Madan Mehta.*

If used as an overflow element, the scupper is made to project out of the parapet wall by a few inches and allowed to discharge water directly on the ground. If used as primary drainage element, a downspout with a conductor head is typically used with every scupper, Figure 6.41. The conductor head prevents the water from splashing and diverts the water into the downspout.

6.9 EDGE GUTTER AS A DRAINAGE ELEMENT

Gutters may be either semicircular or rectangular in profile. Figure 6.42 shows a rectangular gutter and the flashing needed to waterproof the edge of the roof. Gutters require expansion joints along their length and must discharge water into downspouts. For a semicircular gutter profile and the details of expansion joints and connection between the gutter and the downspouts, the reader should consult *Architectural Sheet Metal Manual* by SMACNA.[6.3]

Gutter size is a function of rainfall intensity and the gutter slope. Table 6.3 gives the size of a semicircular gutter if 1-hour, 100-year rainfall intensity is 1 in. For other rainfall intensity, divide the values in this table by that rainfall intensity.

Table 6.3 can also be used to size a rectangular gutter, provided the rectangular gutter cross-section is not less than that of the corresponding semicircular gutter. The depth-to-width ratio of the rectangular gutter should not be less than 0.75.

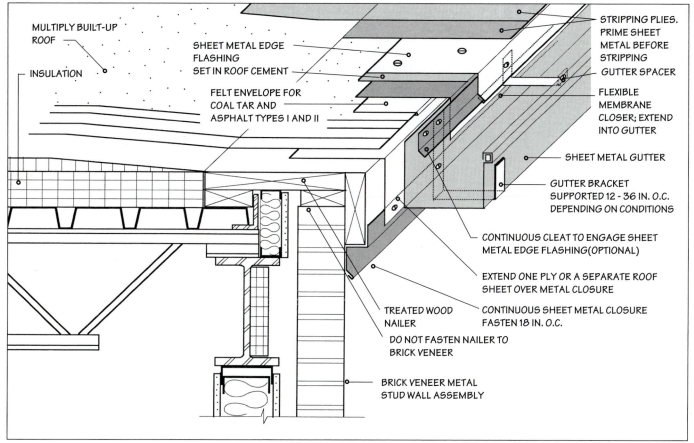

MULTIPLY BUILT-UP ROOF

INSULATION

SHEET METAL EDGE FLASHING
SET IN ROOF CEMENT

FELT ENVELOPE FOR COAL TAR AND ASPHALT TYPES I AND II

STRIPPING PLIES. PRIME SHEET METAL BEFORE STRIPPING

GUTTER SPACER

FLEXIBLE MEMBRANE CLOSER; EXTEND INTO GUTTER

SHEET METAL GUTTER

GUTTER BRACKET SUPPORTED 12 - 36 IN. O.C. DEPENDING ON CONDITIONS

CONTINUOUS CLEAT TO ENGAGE SHEET METAL EDGE FLASHING (OPTIONAL)

EXTEND ONE PLY OR A SEPARATE ROOF SHEET OVER METAL CLOSURE

TREATED WOOD NAILER

CONTINUOUS SHEET METAL CLOSURE FASTEN 18 IN. O.C.

DO NOT FASTEN NAILER TO BRICK VENEER

BRICK VENEER METAL STUD WALL ASSEMBLY

6.42 *Detail of a typical roof edge gutter. Adapted from Reference 6.3; consult this reference for additional details.*

Table 6.3 Size of Semicircular Roof Gutters

Diameter of gutter (in.) — gutter slope 1/16 in. per ft	Maximum projected roof area (sq ft)
3	680
4	1,440
5	2,500
6	3,840
7	5,520
8	7,960
10	14,400

Notes:

1. If the rainfall is different from 1 in., simply divide the values in this table by that rainfall value. For example, if the rainfall at a location is 3 in., divide the values by 3.

2. Multiply above values by $\sqrt{2}$, if the slope of gutter is 1/8 in. per ft; multiply by 2, if the slope of gutter is 1/4 in. per ft; multiply by $2\sqrt{2}$, if the slope of gutter is 1/2 in. per ft.

3. To convert area in ft^2 to area in m^2, multiply values by 0.092. To convert gutter diameter in in. to gutter diameter in mm, multiply its diameter by 25.4.

4. Values in this table are to be used for preliminary sizing. Local plumbing code should be consulted for more authoritative information.

REFERENCES

6.1   Griffin, C. W., and Fricklas, R. *The Manual of Low-slope Roof Systems* (New York: McGraw Hill, 1995), pp. 30-33.

6.2   International Code Council. *International Plumbing Code* (Falls Church, VA: 1997).

6.3   Sheet Metal and Air Conditioning Contractors National Association, Inc. *Architectural Sheet Metal Manual* (Chantilly, VA: 1993), Chapter 1.

7

DESIGN FOR FIRE

Roof assemblies contain a large amount of combustibles. Roofing bitumens, single-ply membranes, membrane adhesives, plastic foam insulations, vapor retarders, etc., are all combustible materials. In addition, the deck may also be combustible. Therefore, a typical roof assembly presents a high degree of fire hazard.

A roof is also an important structural component because a roof deck must carry all gravity loads imposed on the roof. In most structures, a roof deck is also required to function as a horizontal diaphragm, which connects the vertical components (walls or column-beam frames) of the building together, providing stability to the entire building against lateral loads.

If the roof deck fails, due to a burn-out, a wind blow-off, or any other cause, the structure can collapse. In fact, roof blow-offs due to wind storms and hurricanes are so common that it costs the U.S. economy millions of dollars annually.

Fire and wind are, therefore, considered to be the two major hazards that a low-slope roof assembly has to withstand. Other hazards are hailstorm and foot traffic. This chapter deals with the factors that influence the design of roof assemblies to withstand fire. Wind and hailstorm issues are discussed in the following chapter.

7.1 LIFE SAFETY AND INSURANCE CONCERNS IN ROOF DESIGN

The adequacy of a roof assembly against fire and wind is judged from two basic perspectives:

- *Life safety perspective*: The level of safety provided by the assembly to the occupants of the building in the event of a fire or high-speed winds

- *Property loss perspective*: The level of protection provided by the assembly to the building and its contents to prevent or reduce loss caused by fire and wind

It is obvious that both perspectives are interrelated, since an increased life safety generally increases property protection, and vice versa. However, life safety issues are more critical and are highly regulated by building codes. Property protection issues, on the other hand, are not merely the concern of the building codes, but also of the insurance companies that insure the property against fire and wind-induced losses. Generally, the insurance companies' requirements for property protection are more stringent than the building code's requirements. Generally, the insurance premiums are lower if the roof assembly (and the building as a whole) meets the insurance companies' requirements.

7.1.1 Underwriters Laboratories and Factory Mutual

Two independent nonprofit organizations, recognized for establishing standards for fire and wind resistance of assemblies in the United States, are the Factory Mutual (FM) Research Corporation and the Underwriters Laboratories (UL).[1] In addition to establishing standards, both organizations maintain laboratories to test roofing assemblies and other building products. Several insurance companies use UL- or FM-tested assemblies as the basis on which they develop their requirements for granting insurance coverage for a building. UL and FM standards are also the basis of several building code provisions on roofs.

Both UL and FM have their origins in loss insurance. UL was established in 1894 by insurance companies to test newly introduced electrical devices that were known to cause fires in buildings, resulting in large claims by the insured. Over the years, UL has diversified and now evaluates and certifies the safety of a large variety of products.

In fact, a UL label on a product is a mark of rigorous testing to ensure a high level of safety to consumers. In the realm of building construction, a major contribution of UL has been in testing building assemblies for their performance against fire and wind, see Section 7.4.

---

[1] Factory Mutual Research Corporation is based in Norwood, Massachusetts. The head office of Underwriters Laboratories is in Northbrook, Illinois.

Similarly, FM was established in 1835 by a group of textile mill owners in response to the exorbitant premiums being charged by the insurance companies to insure their mills against fire losses. Originally called the Manufacturers Mutual Fire Insurance Company, its purpose was to self-insure properties, thereby spreading the risk among member manufacturers. To minimize the risk, fire-resistive standards of building construction were established with mandatory compliance by mill owners before they could obtain insurance coverage.

Today, FM is a major insurance organization that maintains its own independent research and testing establishment, called the Factory Mutual Research Corporation (FMRC). Like UL, FMRC maintains its own testing laboratories to test roofing and other products.

A fire in a building may originate from a source located inside the building — an interior fire — or from a source located outside the building — an exterior fire. From the roofing standpoint, these two types of fires are also referred to as *below-deck* and *above-deck* fires, respectively. Two indices are used to evaluate the safety of a roof assembly against an internal fire:

- Fire resistance rating
- Below-deck heat and fire spread rating

7.2.1 Fire Resistance Rating

One of the important design strategies employed to increase fire safety in buildings is to subdivide it into compartments so that the fire is limited to the compartment of its origin. The strategy is based on the fact that the fire will either extinguish itself after a while due to lack of oxygen in the compartment or take some time to spread to other compartments. During this period, occupants can exit the building or relocate to a place of safety.

The concept of compartmentation, as shown in Figure 7.1, assumes that the barriers (walls, floor, and roof) bounding the compartment will be constructed so that a burn-out of the fuel in the compartment will not seriously affect the adjacent compartments. A fire barrier must, therefore, meet the following criteria:

7.2 INTERIOR FIRE EXPOSURE

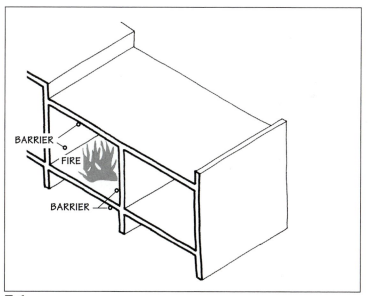

7.1 *Strategy of compartmentation to reduce damage by an interior fire.*

- *Structural integrity*: The barrier should be able to perform its intended structural function, i.e., it should be able to carry the loads for which it is designed.
- *Fire tightness*: The barrier should develop no cracks, since a crack will allow flammable gases and flames to spread to the adjacent compartments.
- *Temperature of the unexposed surface*: The temperature of the unexposed side of the barrier should remain so low that the combustibles in the adjacent compartment will not ignite by the heat radiated or conducted from the exposed side.

When exposed to a fire for a sufficient length of time, all barriers, regardless of their construction, eventually crack, disintegrate, and collapse. Thus, a barrier can satisfy the above requirements for a limited duration only. The ability of a component to endure fire for the duration during which it satisfies the above requirements is called the *fire resistance rating* (or simply, the fire rating) of the component.

In other words, fire rating is the property of a barrier to confine the fire to the compartment of its origin for a particular duration. Accordingly, the fire rating of an assembly is measured in hours or minutes. A two-hour fire rating implies that the assembly can withstand fire for two hours. Note that by virtue of its definition, fire rating is the property of the assembly, not of the material. The fire rating of a material, such as concrete or wood, is meaningless.

The test that is used to evaluate the fire resistance rating of an assembly is ASTM E 119, "Standard Test Methods for Fire Tests of Building Construction and Materials." This test requires that building assemblies be tested in a standard furnace which attempts to simulate conditions in an actual fire. For a more detailed discussion of fire resistance, refer to a book on building construction.[2]

When referring to the fire rating of a roof, we typically include the ceiling also so that the roof assembly (as far as its fire rating is concerned) consists of roof-ceiling assembly. A roof-ceiling assembly includes all components between the interior ceiling, and the exterior roof membrane — ceiling, air conditioning ducts, light fixtures, electrical conduits, roof deck, insulation, roof covering, etc. Thus, if a roof-ceiling assembly has a fire rating of 1 hour, it means that it will withstand (standard test) fire for 1 hour, after which the fire will likely escape through the roof to the adjacent room.

The most comprehensive listing of the fire ratings of assemblies is that by the Underwriters Laboratories published annually as "Fire Resistance – with Hourly Ratings for Beams, Columns, Floors, Roofs, Through-Penetration Firestop Systems, Walls and Partitions." This publication lists fire ratings of various manufacturers' assemblies, tested as per ASTM E 119 Standard, which is equivalent to UL Standard 263.

---

[2] Madan Mehta. *Principles of Building Construction* (Upper Saddle River, NJ: Prentice Hall, 1997).

7.2.2 Interior Fire Spread Rating

Another important index of a roof's performance with respect to internal fire is the speed at which a fire spreads on the underside of the roof deck. The impetus to include below-deck fire spread as a fire safety index came after the disastrous fire in the General Motors plant in Livonia, Michigan, in 1953. In this fire, nearly 1.5 million square feet of building was destroyed in little more than one hour. The prime cause of the large magnitude of this disaster was the speed at which the flames traveled on the underside of the roof deck.

The roof assembly of the GM plant, nearly 20 ft in height, was typical of industrial roof assemblies at the time. It consisted of a metal deck on which a 2-ply built-up roof was hot-mopped directly to the deck, followed by a layer of wood fiberboard insulation, and finally a multi-ply built-up roof with gravel cover, Figure 7.2. The first 2-ply built-up roof functioned as a vapor retarder.

At about 3:50 P.M., a welder's spark accidentally ignited the residue in a nearby drip pan. Because the drip pan was nearly 11 ft high, it was not readily accessible.[7.1] Before the fire in the drip pan could be extinguished, it had buckled, spilling the burning oil on the floor. By 4:00 P.M., molten bitumen from the roof started to drip down through the joints in the roof deck, which further fueled the fire.

At nearly 4:15 P.M., the roof and the walls of the building started to collapse. The observers of the accident reported that the roof bitumen was dripping nearly 100 ft in advance of the flames. In this 1800-ft-long building, the fire advanced through the building in about one hour — at the rate of 30 ft per minute. Eventually, the entire structure collapsed.

After the GM plant fire, UL and FM jointly built a 100-ft-long, 20-ft-wide, and 10-ft-high test structure (referred to as the *White House*), in which several metal deck roof assemblies were tested. Based on these tests, it was concluded that there should be no combustibles between the metal deck and the insulation. Therefore, mechanical fastening of the insulation to metal deck, instead of hot mopping the insulation, is the only acceptable method now. However, the second layer of insulation can be hot-mopped to the first layer of insulation. Similarly, a built-up roof ply can also be mopped over the mechanically fastened insulation.

Based on the White House tests, both FM and UL developed smaller-scale tests to test roof assemblies for below-deck fire and heat spread, Figure 7.3. Unfortunately, in developing the small-scale tests, FM and UL adopted different

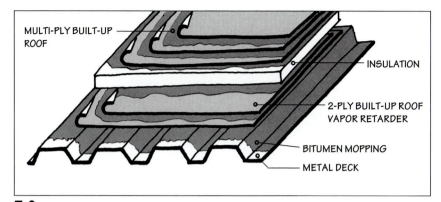

7.2 *Roof assembly of GM Plant at Livonia, Michigan, showing direct mopping of built-up roof plies to steel deck.*

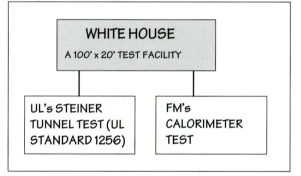

7.3 *White House test results were used by UL and FM to develop smaller-scale tests to assess a roof assembly's performance during a below-deck fire.*

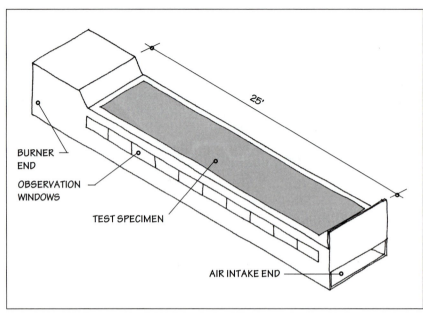

7.4 *Steiner tunnel.*

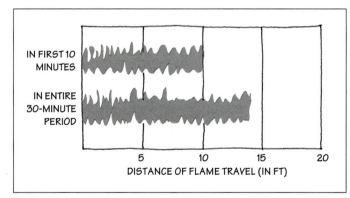

7.5 *Maximum permissible flame spread of a roof assembly to pass the Steiner tunnel test (UL Standard 1256).*

approaches. The UL test (promulgated as UL 1256) is a pass or fail test. It measures the spread of a below-deck fire in the Steiner tunnel,[3] Figure 7.4.

The roof assembly to be tested is placed in the standard size opening at the top of the tunnel furnace (nearly 25 ft long), and the burners are lit from one end of the tunnel. The spread of flames is observed through observation holes. If the flames do not advance beyond 10 ft in the first 10 minutes or beyond 14 ft in the entire 30-minute test period, the assembly passes; otherwise, it fails the test, Figure 7.5. A roof assembly passing the test is called "fire classified" by UL.

The FM test for interior fire hazard measures the total heat released by the entire roof assembly when exposed to fire from below the deck. Referred to as the *calorimeter test*, it exposes the roof assembly test specimen to fire in a standard fire chamber, Figure 7.6. If the assembly gives off no more than 410 $Btu/ft^2/$min, it is classified as a Class 1 Roof assembly; otherwise, it is a Class 2 assembly. A Class 2 assembly has no upper limit on heat release. Thus, like the UL Steiner tunnel test, the FM calorimeter test is also a pass-fail test.

Insurance companies (particularly the FM group of insurance companies) charge lower premiums to insure buildings with a Class 1 roof assembly. For some occupancies, a Class 2 assembly may qualify for the same insurance coverage if the building is sprinklered with an approved automatic sprinkler system. On the other hand, an insurance company may require automatic sprinklers even with a Class 1 roof assembly if the occupancy has a large fire hazard.

As described in Section 7.4, FM's Class 1 rating for a roof assembly is not simply based on the calorimeter test. It is a comprehensive rating based on a battery of tests, which includes testing for external fire exposure, wind uplift, and hailstorm resistance.

Roof assemblies with noncombustible decks such as cast-in-place concrete, precast concrete, cement fiber, and gypsum decks (with a minimum thickness of 2 in.) do not require a calorimeter test, regardless of the type of insulation or the

---

[3] The Steiner tunnel is also used to determine the flame spread and smoke density ratings of construction assemblies, as per ASTM Standard E 84 (also promulgated as UL Standard 723). UL 1256 and UL 723 Standards are similar but with one important difference. UL 723 measures how quickly the flame spreads on the surface of a material and the degree of visibility through the smoke developed during the test. Test Standard UL 1256 measures the burning properties of the entire (roof) assembly, not just one material. A deck with a low flame spread rating and smoke density (as determined by the UL 723 test) may completely fail when tested under the UL 1256 test.

The UL 1256 Standard was revised in 1998. In the revised standard, a roof assembly may either comply with the Steiner tunnel test, as described here, with the White House test (in a 100-ft x 20-ft x 10-ft chamber), or with a new test performed in an intermediate size chamber measuring 12 ft x 8 ft x 8 ft. The White House test apparatus is designated as Part I, the Steiner tunnel as Part II, and the intermediate test chamber as Part III.

type of roof membrane used. However, to receive an FM Class 1 rating, they must be subjected to other tests: external fire exposure, wind uplift, and hailstorm damage.

For the calorimeter test, a steel deck assembly does not qualify as a noncombustible deck assembly (although a steel deck is noncombustible) because of the possibility of fuel from the top of the roof penetrating the building through deck joints. Similarly, a lightweight insulating concrete deck does not qualify as a noncombustible deck unless it has at least 2-in.-thick concrete above the top surface of the deck. In other words, the embedded polystyrene insulation must have at least 2-in.-thick insulating concrete below it for the lightweight concrete deck to be classified as a noncombustible deck.

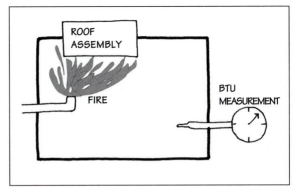

7.6 *Setup for FM's calorimeter test. Roof assemblies on noncombustible decks are exempt from this test.*

A roof assembly must also be evaluated for performance with respect to an external fire. An external fire exposure to a roof can occur either from an internal fire escaping through windows and other wall openings, Figure 7.7, or from an external fire source. The external fire source may be due to burning brands (see Section 7.3.3) from a nearby roof of an adjacent building or an adjacent part of the same building.

The standard test[7.2] for evaluating a roof assembly against external fire is ASTM E 108,"Test Methods for Fire Resistance of Roof Covering Materials" (also promulgated as UL 790). FM follows ASTM E 108. Thus, UL and FM tests on external fire exposure are almost identical. This test, which consists of three component tests, evaluates two important properties of a roof:

- The rate at which the roof-covering material flames. The test that evaluates this property is called the *spread of flame test*.

- The penetration of external fire into the interior of the building, i.e., the degree of protection that the roof cover provides to the deck. Two tests are used to evaluate this property: *intermittent flame test* and *burning brand test*. Since the degree of protection provided by a roof cover to a deck is not relevant with noncombustible decks (cast-in-place concrete, precast concrete, gypsum, and steel decks), these two tests are not required for noncombustible decks. Only roof assemblies with combustible decks[4] (wood and plywood decks) are subjected to these tests.

7.3 EXTERIOR FIRE EXPOSURE

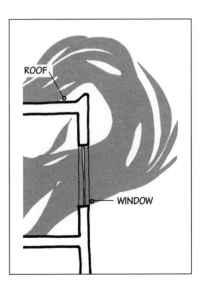

7.7 *Exterior surface of a roof attacked by an internal fire.*

---

[4] The above-deck roof assembly is tested for exterior fire exposure.

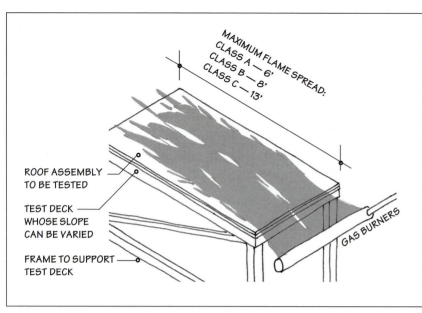

MAXIMUM FLAME SPREAD:
CLASS A — 6'
CLASS B — 8'
CLASS C — 13'

ROOF ASSEMBLY
TO BE TESTED

TEST DECK
WHOSE SLOPE
CAN BE VARIED

FRAME TO SUPPORT
TEST DECK

GAS BURNERS

7.8 *Setup for spread of flame test (ASTM E 108 OR UL 790).*

Based on the previous three tests, a roof cover assembly (roof membrane plus insulation, if any) is rated as Class A, B, or C. A Class A roof is more fire-resistant than a Class B roof, which, in turn, is more fire-resistant than a Class C roof.

7.3.1 Spread of Flame (SOF) Test

In this test, the roof cover assembly is placed on a test deck, made of wood boards and measuring nearly 3 ft x 13 ft. One end of the deck contains gas burners with an air blower behind the burners that directs the flames over the roof covering, Figure 7.8. For Class A and B evaluations, the flame is on continuously for 10 minutes; for Class C evaluation, the flame is on for 4 minutes. Failure occurs if the flame spreads beyond 6 ft in the direction of air flow for Class A rating, 8 ft for Class B rating, and 13 ft for Class C rating. Additionally, there should be (1) no significant lateral spread of fire, (2) no glowing embers emitted from the roof assembly, and (3) no portion of top surface of deck visible during the test.

Since the spread of flame increases with roof slope, the test deck is set on a slope specified by the roof covering manufacturer. Thus, for a particular roof assembly, there is a maximum slope beyond which its rating will be lowered.

7.3.2 Intermittent Flame (IF) Test

The intermittent flame test uses the same apparatus as the spread of flame test and measures the penetration of fire into the deck by a pulsating source. The flames are, therefore, applied in on-off cycles. During the off period, the assembly is cooled rapidly. For Class A and B ratings, the flame temperature is maintained at 1400°F with 15 and 8 on-off cycles, respectively. For a Class C rating, the flame temperature is maintained at 1300°F with 3 on-off cycles.

During the test, the underside of the test deck is observed for its charring and cracking. Failure is assumed if there is substantial charring of the test deck.

7.3.3 Burning Brand (BB) Test

This test measures the performance of the assembly to burning *brands* (a stack of wood) that may land on the roof from a nearby fire source. The fire is produced by placing a brand on top of the assembly and igniting it. The burning brand is fanned and the assembly observed for charring of the deck. For a Class A rating, the brand consists of 12-in.-long wood strips, the entire brand measures 12 in. x 12 in. x 2-1/4 in. and weighs 4.4 lb. For Class B and C ratings, the brand sizes and weights are smaller, Figure 7.9.

The test is continued until all of the brand has been consumed or until failure occurs. Failure is assumed if the underside of deck chars or cracks substantially, as in the IF test.

7.3.4 Exterior Fire Exposure and Built-Up Roofs

Although the actual classification of a particular roof assembly must be obtained from the manufacturer (or from the UL or FM publication), built-up roof assemblies, in general, achieve the following exterior fire exposure ratings when tested as per ASTM E 108 Standard.

- A built-up roof (3 plies or more) with fiberglass felts achieves a Class A rating, provided the deck incline is no greater than 3 in 12 and the roof is surfaced with gravel, crushed stone, or slag over a flood coat, as specified in Figure 7.10(a).
- A 3-ply built-up roof plus a mineral granule cap sheet receives the same rating over a noncombustible deck, if the deck incline is not greater than 1 in 12, Figure 7.10(b).
- A 3-ply built-up roof with a mineral granule cap sheet (over a combustible or noncombustible deck) receives a Class B rating with a maximum incline of 0.75 to 12, Figure 7.10(c).

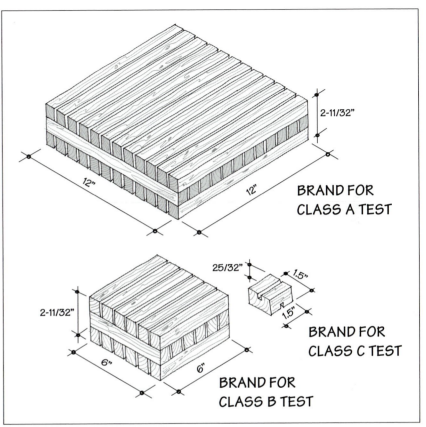

7.9 *Wood brands for Class A, B, and C tests.*

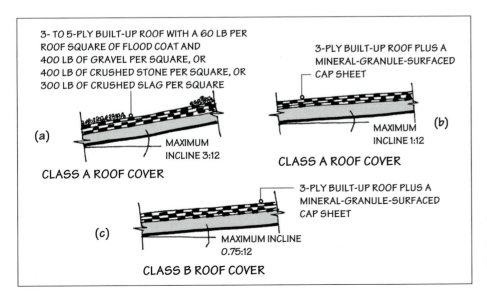

7.10 *Built-up roof generic classifications under ASTM E 108 test. Individual manufacturers' assembly ratings must be obtained for a precise rating.*

7.4 FM AND UL TEST DATA

Table 7.1 Summary of Fire Tests of Roof Assemblies

Interior Fire Exposure	Exterior Fire Exposure
1. Fire resistance rating (ASTM E 119 or UL 263). Rating specified in hours and minutes. 2. Interior fire spread — a pass/fail rating. Test required only with combustible decks. • UL Steiner tunnel test (UL 1256) • FM calorimeter test	ASTM E 108 (UL 790) Roof assemblies rated as Class A, B, or C.

Table 7.2 FM and UL Roofing Test Data Publications

FM	UL
Approval Guide — Building Materials: A Guide to Equipment, Materials and Services Approved by Factory Mutual Research Corporation	*Roofing Materials and Systems Directory*

Tests and standards required to classify a roof assembly for its fire performance, discussed in earlier sections, are summarized in Table 7.1. Note that UL and FM test requirements are identical for exterior fire exposure. For interior fire resistance ratings of roof assemblies, FM does not have a requirement. For interior fire spread, FM uses the calorimeter test, whereas UL uses the Steiner tunnel test.

Both UL and FM routinely test manufacturers' roof assemblies and classify (rate) them. Tested assemblies that meet respective UL and FM standards are listed in UL and FM publications, Table 7.2. Although there is some similarity between UL and FM tests (as evident from Table 7.1), there is one fundamental difference between the UL and FM approaches to roof classifications.[5]

FM classification is a comprehensive classification based on all of the following tests: calorimeter test, ASTM E 108 test, hail storm damage test, and wind uplift test. FM does not perform individual tests on assemblies. It must perform all tests when requested by a manufacturer to test its assembly. UL, on the other hand, will perform individual tests on assemblies as requested by the manufacturer.

This difference in approach is reflected in their publications. In the FM publication, various components of the assembly are listed, followed by its ratings under all tests. For instance, an assembly may carry the following three FM ratings:

Class 1-A, Class 1-60, and Class 1-SH.

Number "1" in all of the above ratings indicates that the assembly has passed the calorimeter test. Assemblies with noncombustible decks are exempt from the calorimeter test, see Section 7.2.2.

Assemblies that pass the calorimeter test (or noncombustible deck assemblies) are considered as "approved" assemblies. Only approved assemblies are included in the FM publication and are referred to as *Class 1 assemblies*. The "A" refers to the assembly's classification under ASTM E 108 test; "60" refers to the assembly's wind uplift rating, i.e., it withstood 60 psf of uplift force under the wind uplift test; "SH" refers to the assembly's ability to withstand severe hailstorm, see Section 8.7 in Chapter 8.

In the UL publication, the assembly is described, and its rating for a particular test is stated. Thus, if the same assembly has been tested for UL 709 (equivalent to ASTM E 108) and for UL 580 (wind uplift), it is listed in two different places with the respective ratings.

FM and UL publications are extremely useful to architects, roofing consultants, and roofing material manufacturers, as they are the only organizations

---

[5] Although both UL and FM rate assemblies for fire and wind uplift resistance, construction specifications typically refer to UL standards for fire resistance and to FM standards for wind uplift resistance.

that provide important test data for roofs. Whether a building is insured against damage or not, a roof must meet building code requirements for fire, wind uplift, and hail resistance. Thus, in designing a roof assembly, reference to a UL or FM publication is almost always required.

Building codes prescribe a minimum fire resistance rating of building components, including roof-ceiling assemblies. In fact, the *type of construction* of a building is based on the fire ratings of its major components: structural frame, exterior and interior walls, floors, and roofs. The higher the fire resistance rating of building components, the better the type of construction.

The most fire-resistive construction is Type I, followed by Types II, III, IV, and V, Table 7.3. Type V is the least fire-resistive construction. Except for Type IV (which is *heavy timber* classification), other types of construction are subdivided into subtypes A and B. Thus, there are Type IA and Type IB; the latter is less fire-resistive than the former.

The maximum built-up area and the maximum height of a given building as permitted by a building code is a function of the type of construction and its occupancy. The occupancy refers to the building use, whether it is an assembly building, business building, industrial, residential, etc.

Buildings that house a large number of people in one room, such as auditoriums, assembly halls, classrooms, large restaurants, etc., are assembly occupancies. They require a higher fire rating for its components, i.e., a better type of construction. Residential occupancies such as single-family dwellings generally have no code requirement for fire ratings and are typically constructed of Type VB construction. Thus, code-permitted maximum built-up area and height is largest if the building is of Type IA construction, followed by other types. For additional details about the permissible built-up area, refer to the local building code.[6]

---

[6] The United States now has one model building code (in place of the earlier three model codes). This new code is referred to as the *International Building Code* and is published by the International Code Council. Local building codes, which may be based on this model code, govern requirements.

7.5 BUILDING CODE REQUIREMENTS FOR A ROOF'S FIRE PERFORMANCE

Table 7.3 Fire Resistance Ratings (in Hours) and Type of Construction

Building component	Type I		Type II		Type III		Type IV	Type V	
	A	B	A	B	A	B		A	B
Structural frame — columns, girders, trusses	3	2	1	0	1	0	HT	1	0
Bearing walls Exterior	3	2	1	0	2	2	2	1	0
Interior	3	2	1	0	1	0	1	1	0
Nonbearing walls Exterior Interior	Varies with occupancy and separation distance from property line								
Floor construction including supporting beams and joists	2	2	1	0	1	0	HT	1	0
Roof construction including supporting beams and joists	1.5	1	1	0	1	0	HT	1	0

Source: Adapted from the *2000 International Building Code*, copyright © 2000, International Code Council, Inc., Falls Church, Virginia. All rights reserved. Reprinted with permission of author.

154

Table 7.4 Minimum Roof Cover Class and Type of Construction

Type of construction	IA	IB	IIA	IIB	IIIA	IIIB	IV(HT)	VA	VB
Roof cover class	B	B	B	C	B	C	B	C	C

Source: Adapted from the *2000 International Building Code*, copyright © 2000, International Code Council, Inc., Falls Church, Virginia. All rights reserved. Reprinted with permission of author.

Building codes also regulate the fire classification of roof coverings (based on ASTM E 108 tests) for a given construction type, Table 7.4. Thus, construction Types IA, IB, and IIA require a minimum of a Class B roof cover. Note that building code requirements are minimum requirements.

Thus, although building codes do not require a Class A roof cover for any construction type, generally Class A roof cover is specified for most commercial buildings, regardless of the type of construction. Also, note that while there is a large difference between the ASTM E 108 test requirements for Classes B and C, the difference between Class A and B requirements is much smaller. In other words, Class B roof cover is closer in performance to Class A roof cover than to Class C roof cover.

REFERENCES

7.1 Laaly, H. O. *The Science and Technology of Traditional and Modern Roofing Systems* (Los Angeles, CA: 1992), p. 53-22.

7.2 American Society of Testing and Materials. "Standard Test Methods for Fire Tests of Roof Coverings," ASTM E 108-90 (Philadelphia).

DESIGN FOR WIND AND HAIL

As stated in Chapter 7, wind-caused roof damage in the United States represents a major recurring loss. To prevent this damage, the most important requirement is that the roof deck be securely anchored to the supporting structural framework. In addition to the anchorage of the deck to the structural frame of the building, the above-deck assembly must be anchored to the deck. This chapter deals with the latter issue, i.e., the design of the anchorage system of the above-deck assembly with the roof deck.

It is obvious that the strength of a roof's anchorage to the deck is a function of the wind uplift on the roof. The greater the uplift, the stronger the required anchorage. Designing a roof that is safe and secure against wind uplift consists of two parts:

• Determining the maximum wind uplift pressure to which the roof assembly may be subjected.

• Determining the assembly's anchorage system whose holding power equals or exceeds the wind uplift pressure. The anchorage system implies the type of fasteners and their center-to-center spacing or the type of adhesives if the assembly is fully (or partially) adhered.

This chapter dwells at length with the first part, i.e., calculating the wind uplift pressure on the roof. The second part is simply a selection process in which the roof assemblies that can withstand the calculated wind pressure are selected from the Factory Mutual's (FM)[1] or Underwriters Laboratories (UL)[2] publication. FM and UL publications list the roof assemblies and the uplift pressure they can withstand — a list that is based on actual measured responses of roof assemblies' uplift resistance.

Unfortunately, there is no generic procedure by which the anchorage system can be designed because the holding power of a fastened or adhered system is a complex function of various components of the assembly, and not merely of the anchorage system. The type of deck, its gauge or thickness, type and thickness of insulation, type and thickness of roof membrane, etc., also affect the holding power of the anchorage system.

Therefore, the FM (or UL) wind uplift rating applies to the entire roof assembly. No change can be made to any component of the assembly if its wind uplift rating is to be maintained.

---

[1] Factory Mutual Research Corporation. *Approval Guide — Building Materials: A Guide to Equipment, Materials & Services Approved by Factory Mutual Research Corporation for Property Conservation.*

[2] Underwriters Laboratories. *Roofing Materials and Systems Directory.*

8.1 WIND UPLIFT RATINGS OF FM-APPROVED ROOF ASSEMBLIES

Table 8.1 FM-Approved Roof Assembly Class and Field-of-Roof* Wind Uplift Pressure

Calculated field of roof wind uplift pressure	Recommended FM-approved roof class
< 30 psf (1.4 kPa)	Class 1-60
> 30 psf (1.4 kPa) ≤ 37.5 psf (1.8 kPa)	Class 1-75
> 37.5 psf (1.8 kPa) ≤ 45 psf (2.2 kPa)	Class 1-90
> 45 psf (2.2 kPa) ≤ 52.5 psf (2.5 kPa)	Class 1-105
> 52.5 psf (2.5 kPa) ≤ 60 psf (2.9 kPa)	Class 1-120
This table continues in steps of 15 psf with no upper limit.	

* See Sections 8.2.7 and 8.3 for the explanation of the term "field-of-roof."

As stated in Section 7.4 in Chapter 7, FM classification of roof assemblies is a comprehensive classification, which gives an assembly's wind uplift rating in addition to fire and hail ratings. At the end of this chapter are FM listings of two major U.S. roofing material manufacturers, which illustrate the format in which information of a typical FM-approved roofing assembly is available.

In terms of its wind uplift rating, a roof assembly belongs to one of the following FM classes:

- Class 1-60
- Class 1-75
- Class 1-90
- Class 1-105
- Class 1-120, etc., increasing by 15 without any prescribed upper limit

A rating of 1-60 means that the assembly has been tested to withstand an uplift pressure of 60 pounds per square foot (psf). Similarly, an assembly with Class 1-75 rating has a test capacity of 75 psf uplift pressure.

"Class 1" preceding a wind uplift rating implies that it is an FM Class 1 roof assembly, which as stated in Section 7.4, means that the assembly has passed a variety of tests including the calorimeter test or uses a noncombustible deck (cast-in-place concrete, precast concrete, gypsum, or cement-fiber deck, see Section 7.2.2 in Chapter 7. An FM Class 1 assembly is also called an "FM-approved assembly."

A safety factor of 2.0 is used in determining an assembly's suitability to withstand a given wind uplift. Thus, a Class 1-60 roof assembly can be used in a situation where the calculated wind uplift pressure is less than or equal to 30 psf. Similarly, a 1-75 assembly is recommended where the assembly may experience a wind uplift of 37.5 psf or less. More appropriately, a Class 1-75 assembly is specified where the actual wind uplift lies between 30 and 37.5 psf, Table 8.1.

Note that the wind uplift pressures listed in Table 8.1 refer to the "field-of-roof" pressures. The uplift pressures at the edges and corners of a roof are greater than those in the field of the roof, see Section 8.2.7.

The maximum uplift rating of an FM-approved assembly to date is 1-990, which can be used where the calculated field-of-roof uplift pressure is 495 psf. This figure may be exceeded as more manufacturers seek to develop assemblies with higher uplift capacity.

Determining wind loads on buildings is fairly complex. A comprehensive coverage of the subject is beyond the scope of this text. Therefore, only those aspects of wind load will be discussed that are relevant to roof design. A reader interested in a detailed discussion of the subject should refer to the American Society of Civil Engineers' publication ASCE 7, entitled *Minimum Design Loads for Buildings and Other Structures.*[8.1] Another source is *Loss Prevention Data: Wind Loads to Roof Systems and Roof Deck Securement*[8.2] — FM publication 1-28.

The ASCE publication is a comprehensive publication and must be used to determine wind loads (as well as other loads) on the structural frame of the building and building components — walls, roofs, windows, etc. The FM publication focuses on roofs only. However, due to the differences in their basic approaches, the calculated wind uplift pressures obtained from the ASCE and the FM methods are not always identical.

The ASCE publication is generally referenced by building codes; therefore, it is the one discussed here. Before entering into a detailed discussion of the ASCE procedure, a few general concepts related to wind loads on roofs are presented.

Note, however, that for a nonstandard building type or height, such as a complex building shape, wind tunnel testing may be required to determine wind load on roofs.

8.2.1 Induced Pressure and Suction

Like all other fluids, air has a mass. In fact, air has a density of nearly 1.2 kg/m^3. In other words, a 1 m x 1 m x 1 m (3.3 ft x 3.3 ft x 3.3 ft) volume of air weighs nearly 1.2 kg, i.e., 2.6 lb. Because of its mass, moving air possesses kinetic energy, which is converted to pressure when it meets an obstruction. Generally, positive pressure is exerted on the windward wall of a rectilinear building and negative pressure (suction) on other walls, Figure 8.1(a). Wind tunnel tests have shown that on the windward wall, wind pressure increases with height. On the leeward wall, however, there is no appreciable change in suction pressure with respect to height, Figure 8.1(b).

Turbulence effects caused by ground roughness may, however, cause pressure reversal on a given surface. Thus, a building surface may be subjected to positive pressure at one moment and suction at the following moment. Usually for a given surface, there is a dominance of either positive pressure or suction.

Assuming turbulence-free air movement, a roof comes under suction when the wind is parallel to the ridge, Figure 8.2(a). For wind blowing perpendicular to the ridge, the leeward slope is subjected to suction, Figure 8.2(b). The windward slope, on the other hand, comes under suction if the slope is less than nearly 30° — a slope of 7:12.

8.2 WIND LOAD FUNDAMENTALS

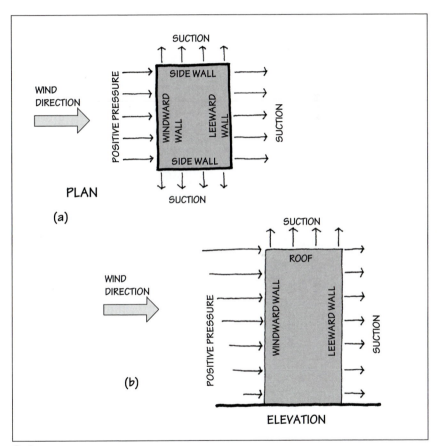

8.1 *Induced pressure and suction on a building relative to wind direction.*

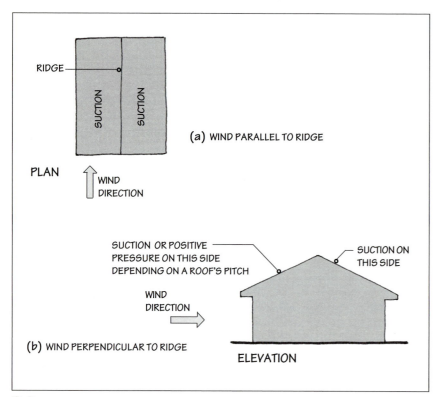

RIDGE

SUCTION

SUCTION

(a) WIND PARALLEL TO RIDGE

PLAN

WIND
DIRECTION

SUCTION OR POSITIVE
PRESSURE ON THIS SIDE
DEPENDING ON A ROOF'S PITCH

SUCTION ON
THIS SIDE

WIND
DIRECTION

(b) WIND PERPENDICULAR TO RIDGE

ELEVATION

8.2 *Wind pressures on a sloping roof.*

At nearly 30° slope, the pressure on the windward side of the roof is nearly zero under turbulence-free conditions. As the slope is increased beyond 30°, the pressure on the windward side of roof is positive pressure, which increases with increasing slope. In general, suction (uplift pressure) governs the wind design of a roof, particularly that of a low-slope roof. This is so even under extreme turbulence obtained during peak winds.

8.2.2 Design Wind Speed

Fundamental to determining wind loads on buildings is the wind speed. Obviously, buildings must be designed for the maximum probable wind speed at a location. The highest wind speeds are usually contained in a tornado. After tornadoes, hurricanes represent the second most severe wind storms. Known as typhoons or tropical cyclones in Asia, hurricanes pose a greater life safety and economic hazard to buildings than tornadoes.

Despite the generally greater wind speeds in tornadoes, tornado wind speeds are usually not considered in determining wind loads on buildings. The reason is that a typical tornado strikes a small area of the ground, seldom exceeding 1500 ft (460 m) end to end. Thus, the probability of a tornado, particularly a severe one, striking a building is extremely small. It is not uncommon to see a building badly damaged by a tornado, while the adjacent buildings have either not been damaged at all or have suffered only minor damage.

A hurricane, on the other hand, covers a much larger area than a tornado, sometimes up to 600 miles (950 km) in diameter. A hurricane also has a much longer life span, typically a week or longer, as compared to a typical tornado, which lasts only a few minutes.

Thus, the peak wind speed at a location in the United States, which is also the location's design wind speed, is governed by hurricanes and other storms instead of tornadoes. Records of peak wind speeds are continuously being recorded at various locations all over the world. By international agreement, wind speeds are recorded at 33 ft (10 m) above ground.

Because wind is turbulent, its speed varies rapidly with time, particularly in a storm. Therefore, peak wind speed is measured by averaging it over a certain time period. If the averaging time is large, the measured peak wind speed is small, and vice versa. Thus, the peak wind speed of a given storm can be described variously, depending on the averaging period.

In the United States, wind speeds are recorded by averaging over successive 3-second durations, referred to as 3-second gust speeds. The ASCE 7 document uses the peak 3-second gust speed at a location, with a 50-year recurrence interval, as the design wind speed. A 3-second gust speed map of the United States is given in Figure 8.3. The 50-year recurrence interval means that it is the maximum wind speed recorded in the preceding 50 years.

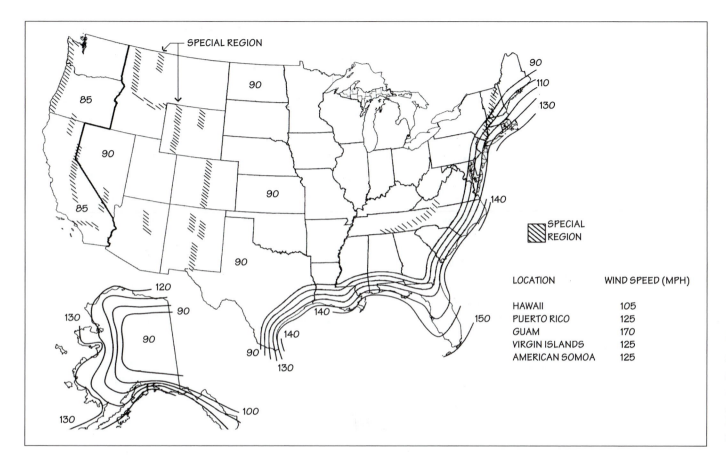

8.3 *Three-second peak wind speed map of the United States in mph. Multiply values by 1.61 to convert to km/h.*

Source: Reference 8.1 with permission. For more accurate values, consult this reference.

LOCATION	WIND SPEED (MPH)
HAWAII	105
PUERTO RICO	125
GUAM	170
VIRGIN ISLANDS	125
AMERICAN SOMOA	125

8.2.3 Wind Pressure and Wind Speed

As wind speed increases, so does the pressure exerted by wind on building surfaces. In fact, wind pressure is directly proportional to the square of wind speed. Thus, if the wind speed increases by a factor of 2, the wind pressure increases by a factor of 4.

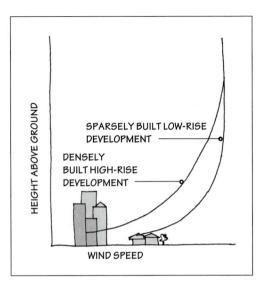

8.4 *Increase of wind speed with respect to height above ground.*

Table 8.2 Ground Roughness (Exposure) Categories

Category A refers to a large city center in which at least 50% of buildings are more than 70 ft (21.3 m) high and the building under consideration is surrounded by such obstructions on all sides for at least 0.5 mile or 10 times the height of the building, whichever is greater.

Category B refers to an urban, suburban, or a wooded area with several closely spaced obstructions of roughly the size of single-family dwellings or larger, and the building under consideration is surrounded by such obstructions on all sides for at least 1500 ft (460 m) or 10 times the height of the building, whichever is greater.

Category C refers to an open terrain with scattered obstructions whose height is generally less than 30 ft (9.5 m). This category includes flat open country and grasslands.

Category D refers to a flat unobstructed ground facing a large body of water (a lake or sea) that extends for a distance of at least one mile (1.6 km) from the building under consideration. Category D is assumed to continue inland from such a body of water for a distance of up to 1500 ft or 10 times the height of the building, whichever is greater.

8.2.4 Wind Speed Variation with Terrain and Height Above Ground

Through our daily experience, we know that wind speed increases with height above ground. An open window on a higher floor feels more breezy than one on a lower floor. The increase of wind speed with height is not the same at all locations but varies with the local terrain.

If the local terrain has a dense grouping of several tall buildings, such as in a city center, the wind speed increases gradually with height. On the other hand, if the local terrain is sparsely built-up with low-rise residential buildings, the increase in wind speed with height is relatively steeper, Figure 8.4. The steepest increase of wind speed with height occurs in a large open stretch of land or water.

The local terrain is classified into four ground roughness categories — Categories A, B, C, and D. Ground roughness is more commonly referred to as *exposure category*. Exposure Category A refers to a large city center; exposure Category B refers to an urban/suburban area or a highly wooded area; exposure Category C refers to an open terrain with scattered obstructions; and exposure Category D refers to a location facing a large stretch of water such as a large lake or an ocean. More precise definitions of these categories are given in Table 8.2.

8.2.5 Ballooning Effect in a Partially Enclosed Building

Building envelopes are not perfectly airtight. Even a fully enclosed building, with fixed glazing, is subjected to infiltration and exfiltration of air through cracks in the perimeter, e.g., around doors and windows. The infiltration or exfiltration is greater with open areas in walls, such as open or broken windows. Because of air infiltration or open areas in walls, the interior of a building is always subjected to some internal pressure in addition to the pressure on the exterior surfaces of the building.

Internal wind pressure is critical in buildings that have large openings in one wall or two adjacent walls of a building, such as an aircraft hangar, or a dock area with roll-up doors. These openings tend to "cup" the wind, creating a ballooning effect on a building's interior, Figure 8.5(a). Buildings with such openings are referred to as *partially enclosed buildings*. As far as the roof is concerned, if the walls of the floor immediately below the roof have a concentration of openings in one or two adjacent walls, the roof is subjected to a significant internal pressure due to the ballooning effect. This internal pressure adds to the uplift pressure that acts on the external surface of the roof, Figure 8.5(b).

The precise definition of a partially enclosed building, with reference to wind loads on a roof, is given in Table 8.3. If all the walls of the floor immediately below the roof are virtually open, there is no internal pressure on the roof. Such a building is referred to as an *open building*. A building not complying with either the requirements of a partially enclosed building or an open building is referred to as an *enclosed building*. In an enclosed building, the internal pressure is much smaller than in a partially enclosed building.

8.2.6 Definition of an Opening

In determining wind loads on buildings, an opening is an aperture or a hole in the building envelope through which air can flow. This definition implies that a window, or glazing, which fails structurally under peak (design) wind loads must be considered as an opening in determining wind loads. If a window or glazing is not assumed as an opening, it must be designed to withstand the design wind pressure.

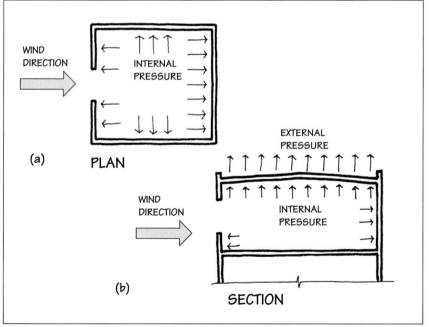

8.5 *Internal pressure (ballooning effect) in a partially enclosed building.*

Table 8.3   Definitions of a Partially Enclosed Building, an Open Building, and an Enclosed Building

Partially Enclosed Building
From a roof's perspective, a building is considered to be "partially enclosed" if it satisfies all of the following three conditions:

In the floor immediately below the roof, the total area of openings in one wall (A_o) exceeds the sum of areas of all openings in other walls (A_{oi}) by 10% or more. In other words, if
$A_o > 1.10 A_{oi}$, condition 1 is satisfied.

In the floor immediately below the roof, the total area of openings in the wall with the largest opening area is greater than 4 ft^2 (0.37 m^2) or 1% of the area of that wall (A_g), whichever is smaller. In other words, if
$A_o > 4$ ft^2, or if
$A_o > 0.01 A_g$, condition 2 is satisfied.

In the floor immediately below the roof, the percentage of openings in the balance of the building envelope (excluding the wall with largest opening area) is less than 20% of the sum of roof area as well as the total remaining wall area. In other words, if
$A_{oi} \leq 0.2 A_{gi}$, condition 3 is satisfied.
A_{gi} = roof area + total wall area (excluding the wall with the largest opening area).

Open Building
From a roof's perspective, a building is considered to be "open" if all of the walls immediately below the roof are at least 80% open.

Enclosed Building
From a roof's perspective, a building that does not comply with the requirements of either a partially enclosed building or an open building is considered to be "enclosed."

However, if a building complies with the definitions of both the "open" and "partially enclosed" categories, it is considered to be "open."

Symbols
The symbols used in this table are summarized below.
A_o = Total area of openings in the wall with largest area of openings.
A_{oi} = Sum of areas of openings in other walls.
A_g = Area of wall with largest area of openings.
A_{gi} = Roof area + total wall area (excluding the wall with largest area of openings).

Table 8.4 Definition of a Windborne Debris Region

A windborne debris region is one that is located in a hurricane-prone region satisfying either of the following two conditions:

1. It is located within one mile of the coastal mean high water line where the basic wind speed is ≥ 110 mph and in Hawaii.

2. It is located in an area where the basic wind speed is ≥ 120 mph.

In the United States and its territories, the hurricane-prone regions are the Atlantic Ocean and Gulf of Mexico coasts, where the basic wind speed > 90 mph, and Hawaii, Puerto Rico, Guam, Virgin Islands, and American Samoa.

Source: Adapted from Reference 8.1, with permission.

In addition to being structurally adequate to withstand design wind pressure, a window or glazing should be able to withstand the impact of windborne debris. This is particularly important in a windborne debris region, where windborne debris can shatter the glass. ASCE 7 Standard requires that all glazing up to 60 ft above ground in a building located in a windborne debris region must be debris impact resistant (in addition to being wind pressure resistant) if the glazing is not to be considered as an opening. Buildings in Category I (Table 8.8), which include minor storage facilities, agricultural buildings, etc., are exempt from this requirement. The definition of a windborne debris region is given in Table 8.4.

8.2.7 Field-of-Roof, Perimeters, and Corners

Wind uplift on a wall or a roof is far from uniform, even at the same height above ground. Wind loads are larger at building discontinuities than in the middle of a wall or a roof. Thus on a roof, the highest wind loads occur at roof corners, followed by roof perimeter (edges). The wind load is minimum in the middle of the roof — referred to as the *field-of-roof*. Therefore, increased membrane anchorage is required at the perimeter and corners of the building. Precise definitions of perimeter, corners, and field-of-roof are given in Section 8.3.

8.3 ASCE METHOD OF DETERMINING WIND UPLIFT ON A LOW-SLOPE ROOF

The ASCE method of determining wind uplift pressures on a low-slope roof[3] divides buildings in two categories depending on the mean roof height:

•   Buildings whose mean roof height, h ≤ 60 ft (18.3 m)

•   Buildings whose mean roof height, h > 60 ft (18.3 m)

Mean roof height is the average of the eave height and the height of the roof's ridge. However, for a low-slope roof (roof pitch ≤ 2:12), mean roof height may be taken as the eave height. For both categories, wind uplift pressure is given by the following equation:

---

[3] ASCE Standard defines a low-slope roof as one whose slope is ≤ 2:12. According to the National Roofing Contractors Association (NRCA), a low-slope roof has a slope of ≤ 3:12.

$$p = q_h [(GC_p) - (GC_{pi})] \qquad (8.1)$$

Where, GC_p = external pressure constant. It is the product of gust factor, G, and pressure coefficient C_p. As a simplification, the ASCE Standard gives comprehensive values of GC_p, rather than giving separate values for G and C_p, Table 8.5.

GC_{pi} = internal pressure constant. It reflects the ballooning effect. Once again, the ASCE standard gives comprehensive values of GC_{pi}, Table 8.6.

q_h = velocity pressure (in psf) at mean roof height, as given below:

$$q_h = 0.00256(K_h)(K_{zt})(K_d)(V^2)(I) \qquad (8.2)$$

In Equation (8.2), K_h = velocity pressure exposure coefficient. It varies with mean roof height and the terrain's exposure category. Values of K_h are given in Table 8.7.

K_{zt} = wind speed-up factor that occurs if the building is located on an escarpment, which can cause the wind speed to increase (see Appendix E). Where wind-speed-up effects are absent, as is generally the case, $K_{zt} = 1.0$.

K_d is called the wind directionality factor with a value = 0.85. The reason for including K_d is to account for the extremely low probability that the maximum wind velocity will occur in the direction that produces the maximum wind load on the building and its components.

In the previous versions of the ASCE Standard (prior to the 1998 version), the wind directionality factor was embedded in safety provisions. In the 1998 version, the safety provisions were altered, and this factor had to be brought to the load side of wind design. Because the safety provisions of a roof's wind

See Table 8.3 for the definitions of "open," "partially enclosed," and "enclosed" buildings. *Windborne debris region* is defined in Table 8.4.

Source: Adapted from Reference 8.1, with permission.

Table 8.5 Values of External Pressure Coefficient (GC$_p$)

Mean roof height ≤ 60 ft (18.3 m)		Mean roof height > 60 ft (18.3 m)	
Zone	(GC$_p$)	Zone	(GC$_p$)
1 (field)	-1.0	1 (field)	-1.4
2 (perimeter)	-1.8	2 (perimeter)	-2.3
3 (corner)	-2.8	3 (corner)	-3.2

PLAN OF ROOF   PLAN OF ROOF

a = 10% of least horizontal dimension of building, or 0.4 h, whichever is smaller, but not less than 3 ft.
Effect of a parapet: If a parapet ≥ 3 ft is provided around the entire roof, zone 3 may be considered as zone 2.
h = mean roof height of building.
"field" stands for "field-of-roof."
Negative values of (GC$_p$) indicate uplift pressure.

Source: Adapted from Reference 8.1, with permission.

Table 8.6 Values of Internal Pressure Coefficients (GC$_{pi}$) for a Building of Any Mean Roof Height

Enclosure classification	(GC$_{pi}$)
Open buildings	0.00
Partially enclosed buildings	0.55
Enclosed buildings	0.18

Table 8.7 Values of Velocity Pressure Coefficient (K_h)

Mean roof height, ft (m)	Exposure category				Mean roof height, ft (m)	Exposure category			
	A	B	C	D		A	B	C	D
0 - 15 (0-4.6)	0.68	0.70	0.85	1.03	120 (36.6)	0.73	1.04	1.31	1.48
20 (6.1)	0.68	0.70	0.90	1.08	140 (42.7)	0.78	1.09	1.36	1.52
25 (7.6)	0.68	0.70	0.94	1.12	160 (48.8)	0.82	1.13	1.39	1.55
30 (9.1)	0.68	0.70	0.98	1.16	180 (54.9)	0.86	1.17	1.43	1.58
40 (12.2)	0.68	0.76	1.04	1.22	200 (61.0)	0.90	1.20	1.46	1.61
50 (15.2)	0.68	0.81	1.09	1.27	250 (76.2)	0.98	1.28	1.53	1.68
60 (18.0)	0.68	0.85	1.13	1.31	300 (91.4)	1.05	1.35	1.59	1.73
70 (21.3)	0.68	0.89	1.17	1.34	350 (106.7)	1.12	1.41	1.64	1.78
80 (24.4)	0.68	0.93	1.21	1.38	400 (121.9)	1.18	1.47	1.69	1.82
90(27.4)	0.68	0.96	1.24	1.40	450 (137.2)	1.24	1.52	1.73	1.86
100 (30.5)	0.68	0.99	1.26	1.43	500 (152.4)	1.29	1.56	1.77	1.89

For values of K_h, where h > 500 ft (152.4 m), see Reference 8.1.

design are not governed by the ASCE Standard but by FM or UL provisions (see Section 8.1), we suggest its exclusion. If K_d is included in calculations, the wind loads will be 15% lower than those calculated without its use.

V = design wind speed as obtained from Figure 8.3.

I = importance factor, as obtained from Table 8.8. Factor "I" refers to the relative importance of building, and its value ranges from 0.77 to 1.15.

8.3.1 Effect of a Parapet

For a low-slope roof with a parapet all around its perimeter, 3 ft (0.9 m) or greater in height, the corners are subjected to reduced pressure (see Table 8.5). This provision is based on the assumption that the parapet is able to maintain its structural integrity during a peak windstorm. In other words, the protective effect of the parapet should be considered only when it has been designed to withstand peak wind loads.

Table 8.8 Values of Importance Factor (I)

Nature of occupancy	Category	Importance factor, I	Nature of occupancy	Category	Importance factor, I
Buildings and other structures that represent a low hazard to human life in the event of failure including, but not limited to: • Agricultural facilities • Certain temporary facilities • Minor storage facilities	I	0.87*	In hurricane-prone regions, buildings and other structures that contain toxic, explosive, or other hazardous substances and do not qualify as Category IV structures shall be eligible for classification as Category II structures for wind loads if these structures are operated in accordance with mandatory procedures that are acceptable to the authority having jurisdiction and which effectively diminish the effects of wind on critical structural elements or which alternatively protect against harmful releases during and after hurricanes.		
All buildings and other structures except those listed in categories I, III, and IV	II	1.00			
Buildings and other structures that represent a substantial hazard to human life in the event of failure including, but not limited to: • Buildings and other structures where more than 300 people congregate in one area • Buildings and other structures with elementary school, secondary school, or day-care facilities with a capacity greater than 150 • Buildings and other structures with a capacity greater than 500 for colleges or adult education facilities • Health-care facilities with a capacity of 50 or more resident patients but not having surgery or emergency treatment facilities • Jails and detention facilities • Power-generating stations and other public utility facilities not included in Category IV Buildings and other structures containing sufficient quantities of toxic, explosive, or other hazardous substances to be dangerous to the public if released, including but not limited to: • Petrochemical facilities • Fuel storage facilities • Manufacturing or storage facilities for hazardous chemicals • Manufacturing or storage facilities for explosives Buildings and other structures that are equipped with secondary containment of toxic, explosive, or other hazardous substances (including, but not limited to, double wall tanks, dikes of sufficient size to contain a spill, or other means to contain a spill or a blast within the property boundary of the facility and prevent release of harmful quantities of contaminants to the air, soil, ground water, or surface water) or atmosphere (where appropriate) shall be eligible for classification as a Category II structure.	III	1.15	Buildings and other structures designed as essential facilities including, but not limited to: • Hospitals and other health-care facilities having surgery or emergency treatment facilities • Fire, rescue, and police stations and emergency vehicle garages • Designated earthquake, hurricane, and other emergency shelters • Communications centers and other facilities required for emergency response • Power-generating stations and other public utility facilities required in an emergency • Ancilliary structures (including, but not limited to, communication towers, fuel storage tanks, cooling towers, electrical substation structures, fire water storage tanks, or other structures housing or supporting water or other fire suppression material or equipment) required for operation of Category IV structures during an emergency • Aviation control towers, air traffic control centers, and emergency aircraft hangars • Water storage facilities and pump structures required to maintain water pressure for fire suppression • Buildings and other structures having critical national defense functions	IV	1.15

* This may be reduced to 0.77 for a hurricane-prone region with design wind speed > 100 mph. See Table 8.4 for the definition of *hurricane-prone region*.

Source: Adapted from Reference 8.1, with permission.

Examples of Wind Uplift Calculations on Low-Slope Roofs

Example 1: Using the ASCE procedure, determine the wind uplift pressures (field-of-roof, perimeters, and corners) on the roof of a two-story office building in Houston, Texas, which measures 80 ft x 80 ft in plan. The roof is a low-slope roof (roof pitch ≤ 2:12), and the roof height is 25 ft above ground. The building is located in exposure Category B. The windows at the second floor level (floor immediately below the roof) are as shown in the accompanying sketch. Windows are wind pressure and missile impact resistant. Assume no wind speed-up effect, i.e., $K_{zt} = 1.0$.

Solution: From Figure 8.3, design wind speed for Houston, Texas, V = 120 mph. From Table 8.7 , K_h = 0.70. From Table 8.8, the building belongs to Category II. Hence I = 1.0. From Equation 8.2,

$q_h = 0.00256 (k_h)(K_{zt}) (V^2)(I) = 0.00256(0.70)(1.0)(120)^2(1.0) = 25.8$ psf

From Table 8.5, $GC_p = -1.0$

From Table, 8.6, $GC_{pi} = 0.18$. Because the windows are pressure and missile impact resistant, they do not classify as openings. Hence, it is an "enclosed" building, not a "partially enclosed" building or an "open" building, see Table 8.3. From Equation (8.1), the field-of-roof uplift pressure is:

$p_{field} = q_h[(GC_p) - (GC_{pi})] = 25.8[-1.0 - 0.18] = -30.4$ psf

Similarly, uplift pressure on perimeters and corners are:

$p_{per} = 25.8[-1.8 - 0.18] = -51.1$ psf

$p_{cor} = 25.8[-2.8 - 0.18] = -76.9$ psf

These values are listed in the accompanying table.

Example 2: Determine the wind uplift pressures on the roof of the building in Example 1 if the windows are wind pressure resistant, but not missile impact resistant. All other data is the same as in Example 1.

Solution: $q_h = 25.8$ psf (the same as in Example 1)

From Table 8.4, Houston lies in a windborne debris region. Because the windows are not missile impact resistant, they are considered as openings. Determine from Table 8.3 whether the building qualifies as a "partially enclosed" building.

The total area of openings in the west wall (the wall with the largest area of openings) = A_o = 100 ft². The total area of openings in other walls = A_{oi} = 15 + 55 + 15 = 85 ft². Since $A_o > 1.10 A_{oi}$,

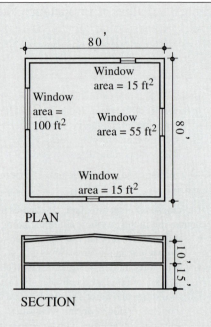

PLAN

SECTION

Roof Uplift Pressures for the Building in Example 1

Location	Roof uplift (psf)
Field-of-roof	30.4
Perimeter	51.1
Corner	76.9

condition 1 in Table 8.3 is met. Condition 2 is also met since 100 ft² > 4 ft² and > 0.01 A_g, where A_g = area of west wall = 80 x 10 = 800 ft². Check condition 3. Roof area = 80 x 80 = 6,400 ft². Total wall area (excluding west wall) = 3(80 x 10) = 2,400 ft². Thus, the total envelope area (excluding the west wall) at the floor below the roof = A_{gi} = 8,800 ft². Since A_{oi} < 0.2 A_{gi}, condition 3 is also met.

Thus, all three conditions in Table 8.3 are met. In other words, the floor immediately below the roof is classified as "partially enclosed." From Table, 8.6, GC_{pi} = 0.55. The values of GC_p are the same as in Example 1. From Equation (8.1),

$p_{field} = q_h[(GC_p) - (GC_{pi})] = 25.8[-1.0 - 0.55] = -40.0$ psf

Similarly, uplift pressures on perimeters and corners are:

$p_{per} = 25.8[-1.8 - 0.55] = -60.6$ psf

$p_{cor} = 25.8[-2.8 - 0.55] = -86.4$ psf

The uplift pressures are listed in the accompanying table.

Example 3: Determine the uplift pressures on the roof of the building in Example 2 if the building is located in Oklahoma City. Assume exposure Category B, and K_{zt} = 1.0.

Solution: Oklahoma City is not in a windborne debris region. Hence, missile impact resistance is not required of windows. Since the windows are wind pressure resistant, they are not considered as openings. The building will be classified as an "enclosed building."

From Figure 8.3, design wind speed for Oklahoma City, V = 90 mph. As in Example 1, K_h = 0.70, I = 1.0, and K_{zt} = 1.0. From Equation 8.2,

$q_h = 0.00256 (k_h)(K_{zt}) (V^2)(I) = 0.00256(0.70)(1.0)(90)^2(1.0) = 20.7$ psf

From Table 8.5, GC_p = -1.0

From Table, 8.6, GC_{pi} = 0.18

$p_{field} = q_h[(GC_p) - (GC_{pi})] = 20.7[-1.0 - 0.18] = -24.4$ psf

Similarly, uplift pressure on perimeters and corners are:

$p_{per} = 20.7[-1.8 - 0.18] = -41.0$ psf

$p_{cor} = 20.7[-2.8 - 0.18] = -61.7$ psf

The uplift pressures are listed in the accompanying table.

Wind Uplift Pressures for the Building in Example 2

Location	Roof uplift (psf)
Field-of-roof	40.0
Perimeter	60.6
Corner	86.4

Wind Uplift Pressures for the Building in Example 3

Location	Roof uplift (psf)
Field-of-roof	24.4
Perimeter	41.0
Corner	61.7

8.4 SELECTING A ROOF ASSEMBLY TO WITHSTAND CALCULATED WIND UPLIFT AND DETAILING ITS ANCHORAGE

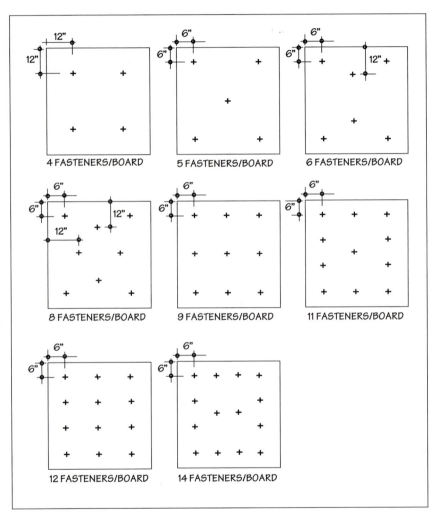

8.6 *Recommended fastener layout patterns for 4 ft x 4 ft insulation boards.*
Source: Reference 8.4, with permission. See this reference for fastener patterns with 2 ft x 4 ft, 3 ft x 4 ft, and 4 ft x 8 ft insulation boards.

After determining the uplift pressures, we can specify an FM-approved roof assembly that can withstand the preceding pressures. This is accomplished by the following six-step procedure:

- *Step 1:* Determine the FM roofing class (Class 1-60, 1-75, 1-90, etc.) based on the highest calculated uplift pressure, which will typically occur at the corners of the roof. For instance, if the calculated uplift pressure at corners is 77 psf, the assembly must be rated to withstand (77 x 2 =) 154 psf. Since FM wind uplift classification increases in steps of 15 psf (see Table 8.1), an FM 1-165 roof assembly will be needed for the corners.

- *Step 2:* Select a suitable roof assembly from the listings given in FM's *Approval Guide*[8.3] that belongs to the same (or a higher) class — the class determined from Step 1. Thus, in the preceding case, a roof assembly that has a rating of 1-165 or higher will be selected.

The anchorage system listed in the *Approval Guide* for the selected assembly can be one of various types, depending on the type of roof assembly. Some of these anchorage systems are described below:

(a) *Insulation mechanically fastened to deck and roof membrane fully adhered to insulation, or a built-up roof (or a modified bitumen roof) applied over insulation:* In this case, the *Approval Guide* gives the maximum contributory area for one fastener. For instance, if the maximum contributory area for one fastener for a Class 1-90 assembly is 2.25 ft^2, the number of fasteners required for a 4 ft x 4 ft insulation board are 16/2.25 = 7.1. This must be rounded off to the next higher integer, i.e., 8. Thus, this assembly needs 8 manufacturer-specified fasteners per 4 ft x 4 ft board. The fasteners are to be evenly distributed on each board and should conform to the FM recommended layout pattern, Figure 8.6.

(b) *Base sheet mechanically fastened to deck over loose-laid or nominally[4] presecured insulation, and built-up roof (or modified bitumen membrane) applied to base sheet:* In this case, the *Approval Guide* gives the center-to-center spacing of fasteners in the side, end laps, and field of the base sheet. For instance, a base sheet may be required to be fastened to the deck through the insulation at 9 in. o.c. in the side laps and 18 in. o.c. staggered in two intermediate rows spaced 12 in. apart. The membrane is then fully adhered to the base sheet.

---

[4] Nominal presecurement of insulation is to keep the insulation in place until the membrane is anchored to the deck. In practice, it generally implies the use of four fasteners for a 4 ft x 4 ft board and five fasteners for a 4 ft x 8 ft board.

(c) *Single-ply membrane fastened to deck over loose-laid or nominally presecured insulation:* In this case, the *Approval Guide* gives the center-to-center spacing of fasteners (typically in conjunction with batten bars (see Section 3.5.2 in Chapter 3) to fasten the roof membrane to the deck through the insulation. For instance, a reinforced EPDM membrane may be required to be fastened to the deck through the insulation at 6 in. o.c. over batten bars spaced 6 ft o.c.

- *Step 3:* Determine the areas occupied by the corners of the roof from Table 8.5 and specify the roof assembly obtained in Steps 1 and 2. This completes the assembly specification for the corners of the roof.

- *Step 4:* Repeat Steps 1 to 3 for the perimeter of the roof. Let the calculated uplift pressure for perimeter be 51 psf. In other words, the perimeter must withstand a pressure of 102 psf, requiring a 1-105 assembly. Therefore, select a fastening pattern from the FM *Approval Guide* for the same assembly (selected earlier for the corners) that is rated as 1-105 or higher.

- *Step 5:* Now repeat Step 4 for the field of the roof. If the field-of-roof uplift pressure is 30 psf, select a fastening pattern rated as 1-60 or higher.

8.4.1 Manufacturers' Submittals

As an alternative to FM's *Approval Guide*, the architect, engineer, or roofing consultant may request submittals from selected roofing material manufacturers about their roofing assemblies that meet the requirements of wind uplift in field roof, perimeters, and corners. The submittals should provide all of the components of a roofing assembly and the details of the manufacturer's fastening system. These submittals must include independent testing to verify uplift resistance.

8.5 WIND UPLIFT RESISTANCE AND AIR PERMEABILITY OF ROOF COMPONENTS

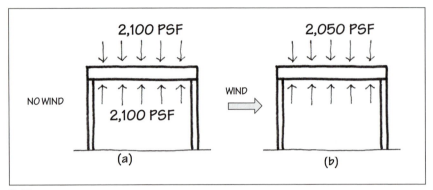

8.7 *Air pressure on the exterior and interior surfaces of a roof: (a) no wind; (b) wind movement that results in an uplift pressure of 50 psf on the roof.*

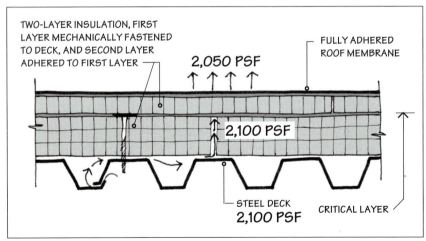

8.8 *If this roof assembly is subjected to a wind uplift of 50 psf, it means that the air pressure on top of roof membrane = 2,050 psf, and the air pressure at the bottom of the second layer of insulation = 2,100 psf.*

So far, we have discussed wind uplift issues without considering the air permeability of roof components. Although a roof membrane must be completely air impermeable for waterproofing reasons, other components of the assembly, such as the insulation and the deck, need not be. For instance, a steel deck is air permeable since the air can pass through deck joints. The same is true of rigid board insulation, particularly a single-layer insulation, which allows the air to permeate through insulation joints. A cast-in-place concrete deck, on the other hand, is air impermeable because of its monolithicity.

The air permeability of below-membrane roof components affects the uplift resistance of a roof assembly. To appreciate this fact, let us review the fundamentals of wind loads. When there is no wind (zero wind speed), the air pressure on the inside and outside surfaces of a component are the same — equal to the atmospheric pressure, Figure 8.7(a). Since the atmospheric pressure works on both sides of an assembly, the assembly is in perfect equilibrium and no wind load is imposed on it. Incidentally, the atmospheric pressure is nearly 2,100 psf (101 kPa) — an enormous pressure indeed! This pressure works on a component in all directions.

Wind disturbs this equilibrium. Wind movement changes the pressure on the outside surface of the assembly, while the pressure on the inside surface remains the same — 2,100 psf. Thus, when we say that the wind uplift on a roof is 50 psf, what we are really saying is that the pressure on the top surface of the roof is 2,050 psf and the pressure on the bottom surface is 2,100 psf — the atmospheric pressure, Figure 8.7(b).

Assume now that the above-roof assembly consists of a metal deck with two layers of insulation. The first insulation layer is mechanically fastened to the deck, and the second insulation layer is mopped to the first layer of insulation. A built-up roof membrane covers the insulation, Figure 8.8. In this case, the air pressure on top of the roof membrane is 2,050 psf, and the pressure at the underside of the metal deck is the atmospheric pressure — 2,100 psf.

8.5.1 Critical Layer

To equalize inside and outside air pressures, the inside air will tend to move upward. It can pass through the joints in the metal deck and through the first insulation layer, but not through the adhesive between the first and second insulation layers. Therefore, the adhesive interface between the two insulation layers is at the same pressure as the inside air pressure — atmospheric pressure of 2,100 psf.

In other words, the wind pressure differential between the inside and outside of the roof occurs at the adhesive interface. We call this layer the *critical layer*. Thus, a critical layer against wind uplift is the lowest air impermeable layer in the assembly — the lowest layer in the assembly with atmospheric pressure at its underside. If failure due to wind uplift is to occur in the assembly, it will initiate at the critical layer.

Let us now examine a roof assembly that consists of a steel deck and a loose-laid (or nominally presecured) single layer of insulation topped with mechanically fastened single-ply membrane, Figure 8.9. Since the deck and insulation are both air permeable, the critical layer in this assembly is the membrane — being the lowest air impermeable layer. The pressure on top of the membrane is 2,050 psf, and the pressure at its bottom is the atmospheric pressure of 2,100 psf.

Because a single-ply membrane is a flexible sheet, abrupt changes in external air pressure will cause it to flutter. The intensity of fluttering depends on the air permeability of insulation and deck joints. If the insulation boards are tight fitting, the intensity of flutter is smaller, and vice versa. Fluttering causes membrane fatigue at the locations of fasteners, accelerating membrane failure.

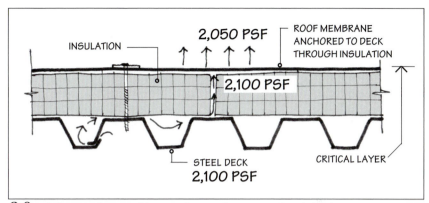

8.9 *If this roof assembly is subjected to a wind uplift of 50 psf, it means that the air pressure on top of the roof membrane = 2,050 psf, and the air pressure at the bottom of the membrane = 2,100 psf.*

8.5.2 Use of Air Barriers in Roof Assemblies

The fluttering of the membrane in the assembly of Figure 8.9 can be reduced by introducing an air barrier. The air barrier, typically a thick plastic sheet with all joints securely taped, is placed immediately over the steel deck. With the air barrier in place, the insulation and the membrane act compositely to resist wind load, which reduces membrane fatigue at fastener locations.

8.5.3 Concrete Deck with Fully Adhered Insulation and Membrane

Now examine a roof assembly that consists of a cast-in-place concrete deck, with solidly mopped insulation, and a fully adhered roof membrane, Figure 8.10. In this assembly, the first air impermeable layer is the concrete deck; hence, it is the critical layer. Since the insulation and membrane are fully adhered to the deck, the entire assembly — the deck, insulation and the membrane – resists wind uplift as a composite. However, it is important that the air infiltration at the perimeter of a concrete deck is eliminated to retain its air barrier effect.

Since a cast-in-place concrete deck is heavy, its weight adds to the wind uplift resistance. That is why most roof assemblies approved by FM to withstand high wind loads consist of concrete decks with fully adhered insulation and membrane.

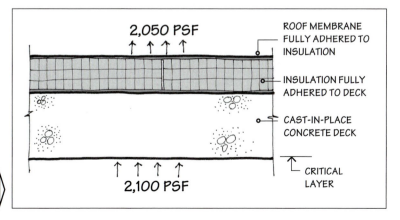

8.10 *The critical layer against wind uplift in this assembly is the concrete deck.*

8.6 LOOSE-LAID, BALLASTED, SINGLE-PLY MEMBRANE

Unlike other assemblies, loose-laid, ballasted, single-ply roof membrane assemblies are not FM-approved (at the present time), although FM gives recommendations for wind uplift design of a loose-laid ballasted system.[8.5] The most referenced standard for wind uplift design of loose-laid ballasted systems, however, is that by SPRI,[5] also published as an ANSI standard.[8.6] ANSI/SPRI design procedure is discussed here briefly. For detailed information, the reader should consult this reference.

Although the ANSI/SPRI Standard allows the use of a loose-laid ballasted roof on buildings up to 150 ft high, extreme caution is advised in specifying such a roof that is greater than 60 ft in height. The same caution is recommended for buildings with a roof slope $\geq$ 2:12 or on buildings in high wind regions. High winds also exaggerate wind scouring, which refers to ballast congregation, leading to an uneven coverage of the roof.

8.6.1 ANSI/SPRI Procedure for Loose-Laid Ballasted Roof Design

ANSI/SPRI design procedure consists of the following three steps:

- *Step 1*: Select the design wind speed for the location from Figure 8.3.

- *Step 2*: Determine the minimum ballasting system (System 1, 2, or 3) from the appropriate table — Table 8.9 (a to f). For instance, if wind speed = 100 mph, terrain exposure category is B, parapet height = 26 in., and roof height = 50 ft, then from Table 8.9(e), the minimum ballasting system is System 1.

- *Step 3*: Now specify the details of the ballasting system outlined in the following section.

8.6.2 Ballasting System Details

The ANSI/SPRI Standard recognizes three ballasting systems: System 1, System 2, and System 3. System 1 has the least, and System 3 has the highest wind uplift resistance.

- *System 1:* This system may consist of one of the following three alternatives: (1) # 4 smooth river rounded ballast at the rate of at least

Table 8.9(a) Maximum Permissible Wind Speed (mph) — Roof Parapet (Gravel Stop) < 6 In. High

Building height (ft)	System 1 Exposure A&C	System 1 Exposure B	System 2 Exposure A&C	System 2 Exposure B	System 3 Exposure A&C	System 3 Exposure B
0-15	90	105	120	120	140	140
> 15-30	90	105	120	120	130	140
> 30-45	85	90	110	120	130	140
> 45-60	NO	NO	110	120	130	140
> 60-75	NO	NO	110	110	120	120
> 75-90	NO	NO	NO	NO	NO	NO
> 90-105	NO	NO	NO	NO	NO	NO
> 105-120	NO	NO	NO	NO	NO	NO
> 120-135	NO	NO	NO	NO	NO	NO
> 135-150	NO	NO	NO	NO	NO	NO

---

[5] SPRI was an acronym for the Single Ply Roofing Institute, whose title has recently been changed to "Sheet Membrane and Component Suppliers to the Roofing Industry."

10 psf; (2) standard concrete pavers weighing not less than 18 psf; (3) approved interlocking concrete pavers weighing not less than 10 psf. The same amount of ballast or pavers may be used in perimeter and corners, as in the field-of-roof. The particle size gradation of # 4 ballast is given in Table 8.10.

- *System 2:* This system consists of one of the following ballast types and weights:

Field-of-roof: Same specification as for System 1.

Corners and perimeter: # 2 ballast at the minimum rate of 13 psf, concrete pavers weighing not less than 22 psf, or approved interlocking pavers weighing not less than 10 psf. The particle size gradation of # 2 ballast is given in Table 8.10.

Table 8.9(b) Maximum Permissible Wind Speed (mph) — Roof Parapet 6 In. to Less Than 12 In. High

Building height (ft)	System 1		System 2		System 3	
	Exposure A&C	B	Exposure A&C	B	Exposure A&C	B
0-15	90	105	120	120	140	140
> 15-30	90	105	120	120	140	140
> 30-45	85	90	120	120	140	140
> 45-60	NO	NO	110	120	130	140
> 60-75	NO	NO	110	110	130	130
> 75-90	NO	NO	NO	NO	NO	NO
> 90-105	NO	NO	NO	NO	NO	NO
> 105-120	NO	NO	NO	NO	NO	NO
> 120-135	NO	NO	NO	NO	NO	NO
> 135-150	NO	NO	NO	NO	NO	NO

Table 8.9(c) Maximum Permissible Wind Speed (mph) — Roof Parapet 12 In. to Less Than 18 In. High

Building height (ft)	System 1		System 2		System 3	
	Exposure A&C	B	Exposure A&C	B	Exposure A&C	B
0-15	105	110	120	120	140	140
> 15-30	90	105	120	120	140	140
> 30-45	85	105	120	120	140	140
> 45-60	85	90	110	120	130	140
> 60-75	85	85	110	110	130	130
> 75-90	85	85	110	110	120	120
> 90-105	NO	NO	95	95	110	110
> 105-120	NO	NO	95	95	110	110
> 120-135	NO	NO	95	95	110	110
> 135-150	NO	NO	95	95	110	110

Table 8.9(d) Maximum Permissible Wind Speed (mph) — Roof Parapet 18 In. to Less Than 24 In. High

Building height (ft)	System 1		System 2		System 3	
	Exposure A&C	B	Exposure A&C	B	Exposure A&C	B
0-15	110	110	120	120	140	140
> 15-30	110	110	120	120	140	140
> 30-45	95	110	120	120	140	140
> 45-60	85	95	120	120	140	140
> 60-75	85	85	110	110	140	140
> 75-90	85	85	110	110	120	130
> 90-105	NO	NO	95	95	110	120
> 105-120	NO	NO	95	95	110	110
> 120-135	NO	NO	95	95	110	110
> 135-150	NO	NO	95	95	110	110

Table 8.9(e) Maximum Permissible Wind Speed (mph) — Roof Parapet 24 In. to Less Than 36 In. High

Building height (ft)	System 1 Exposure A&C	B	System 2 Exposure A&C	B	System 3 Exposure A&C	B
0-15	110	110	120	120	140	140
> 15-30	110	110	120	120	140	140
> 30-45	95	110	120	120	140	140
> 45-60	85	110	120	120	140	140
> 60-75	85	85	120	120	140	140
> 75-90	85	85	110	110	140	140
> 90-105	NO	NO	110	110	140	140
> 105-120	NO	NO	110	110	140	140
> 120-135	NO	NO	110	110	140	140
> 135-150	NO	NO	95	95	140	140

Table 8.9(f) Maximum Permissible Wind Speed (mph) — Roof Parapet 36 In. to Less Than 72 In. High

Building height (ft)	System 1 Exposure A&C	B	System 2 Exposure A&C	B	System 3 Exposure A&C	B
0-15	110	110	120	120	140	140
> 15-30	110	110	120	120	140	140
> 30-45	95	110	120	120	140	140
> 45-60	95	110	120	120	140	140
> 60-75	85	85	120	120	140	140
> 75-90	85	85	110	110	140	140
> 90-105	85	85	110	110	140	140
> 105-120	85	85	110	110	140	140
> 120-135	85	85	110	110	140	140
> 135-150	NO	85	110	110	140	140

Source for Tables 8.9(a to e): Reference 8.6 with permission.

- *System 3:* This system consists of the following ballast type and weight:

  Field-of-roof: Same specification as for the corners and perimeter of System 2.

  Perimeter: Specify a fully adhered or mechanically fastened single-ply membrane capable of resisting calculated wind uplift in the perimeter, with no loose-laid ballast in the perimeter.

  Corners: Specify a fully adhered or mechanically fastened single-ply membrane capable of resisting calculated wind uplift in the corners, with no loose-laid ballast on the corners.

8.6.3 Definitions of Perimeter and Corners

The perimeter and corner areas for a loose-laid ballasted system are defined as follows and illustrated in Figure 8.11.

- *Corners*: The dimension of a corner is 40% of the building height, but not less than 8.5 ft.

- *Perimeter*: The perimeter is a rectangular section parallel to the roof edge and connecting the corners. The width of the perimeter is the smaller of: 10% of the smaller dimension of the roof in plan and 40% of the building height, but not less than 8.5 ft.

8.6.4 Maintenance of Loose-Laid Ballasted Roof

Loose-laid ballasted roof must be periodically checked against wind scouring. If the scour is less than 50 ft^2, the ballast should be replaced. However, if the scour is greater than 50 ft^2, the ballast should be upgraded to the next higher system.

Table 8.10 Particle Size Gradation of No. 2 and No. 4 Ballast

Ballast or aggregate number	Nominal size	Amounts finer than each laboratory sieve, weight percent							
		3 in.	2.5 in.	2 in.	1.5 in.	1.0 in.	0.75 in.	0.5 in.	0.375 in.
# 2	2.5 to 1.5 in.	100	90 -1 00	35 - 70	0 - 15	....	0 - 5	....	....
# 4	1.5 to 0.75 in.	....	....	100	90 - 100	20 - 55	5 - 15	....	0 - 5

Crushed stone may be substituted for ballast. In that case, a protective layer is required between the membrane and crushed stone.
Source: ASTM Standard D 448.

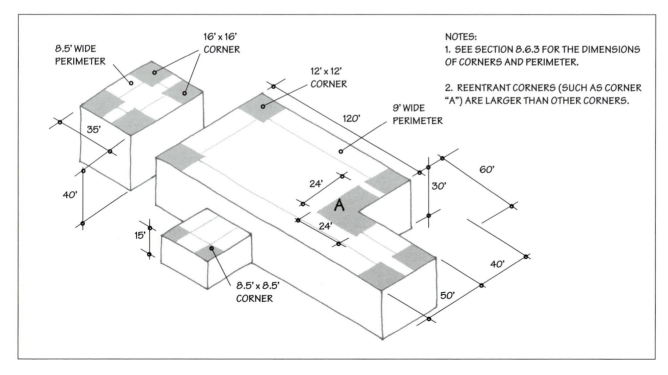

8.11 *Corners and perimeters of a loose-laid ballasted roof.*

8.7 HAIL RESISTANCE

FM divides approved roof assemblies under two categories of hail resistance:

- Severe hail (SH)
- Moderate hail (MH)

All FM-approved assemblies meet the SH criteria, unless listed as MH in FM's *Approval Guide*.[8.7]

Based on FM's hail impact tests, hail resistance of a built-up roof is greatly improved by a gravel or a slag cover over a flood coat of bitumen, which also provides greater fire resistance and durability. When a smooth-surfaced built-up roof must be used, a minimum of four plies (with fiberglass felts) are recommended by FM.

Because of the absence of a covering on a single-ply membrane, the type of insulation under the membrane has an impact on the roof's hail resistance. Therefore, it is important that only FM-approved insulation be used with single-ply membranes.

Because of wind scouring on built-up roofs, it is necessary to examine ballasted roofs periodically and to redistribute ballast on areas that have been bared by wind.

Hail resistance can vary significantly with temperature and aging. Some catastrophic failures have occurred on aged roof membranes as a result of hail impact.

Examples of Listings from FMRC Approval Guide

GenFlex Roofing Systems, 1722 Indian Wood Circle, Suite A, Maumee, OH 43537

Roof Cover:	GenFlex RM, RM-C
Deck:	Steel, Concrete, Wood, Cementitious Wood Fiber, Gypsum
Laps:	4.5 in. (114 mm) wide side laps sealed with a 2 in. (51 mm) wide heat weld
Application:	Mechanically attached or fully adhered
Hail Rating:	Class 1-SH
ASTM E 108:	Class A noncombustible deck at 1 in 12 slope
	Class B combustible deck at 1 in 12 slope as follows:

1) New construction with 1 in. (25 mm) thick wood fiberboard or perlite or isocyanurate insulation listed below and min 0.25 in. (6.4 mm) thick Dense Deck separating the insulation and deck.
2) Reroof construction with GenFlex RM, RM-C applied directly over existing BUR.

Construction # 1: Min 1.3 in. (33 mm) thick ACFoam-II, Hy-Tec, E"NRG"Y-2, PSI-25, GenFlex Iso 1, GenFlex Iso HC1, UltraGuard, Hy-Therm AP, ISO-95 + GL, Pyrox, Millox, Multi-Max FA, Ultra/M-II AEF, or min 1.0 in. (25 mm) thick Esgard, Celotex Fiberboard, GAFTEMP Fiberboard, Huebert Fiberboard, or Owens-Corning Specialty & Foam Products Insulation System (see Owens -Corning Specialty & Foam Products) is presecured to the deck. GenFlex RM, RM-C secured to the deck as follows:

Construction # 1a: Steel, Concrete. GenFlex II RM Seam Discs (Steel or Plastic) or Rawl Lap Plates used with Olympic Heavy Duty screws spaced 12 in. (305 mm) o.c. with laps spaced 48 in. (1.2 m) o.c. Meets Class 1-90.

Construction # 1b: Steel, Concrete. GenFlex RM Seam Disc, DekFast 2 in. Metal Plates or GenFlex Bar Anchors and fasteners placed within laps which are spaced max 70.5 in. (1.8 m) o.c. Fastener spacing within the laps is 12 in. (305 mm) o.c. for Class 1-60 or 6 in. (152 mm) o.c. for Class 1-90.
Fasteners, Steel: GenFlex #14 HD, Olympic Standard, Olympic Heavy Duty; #12, GenFast #14, #14-10 Roofgrip; #12, #14, #15 DekFast; #12-11 InsulFixx, #14-10 InsulFixx; TruFast HD.
Fasteners, Concrete: GenFlex #14 HD, Olympic Heavy Duty, GenFast #14, #14-10 Roofgrip; #14, #15 Dekfast, HD InsulFixx; TruFast HD.

Construction # 1c: Steel. SFS IF2-10 Screws and IG/IG-C metal plates placed within laps which are spaced max 70.5 in. (1.8 m) o.c. Fastener spacing within the laps is 6 in. (152 mm) o.c. Meets Class 1-90.

Construction # 1d: Cementitious Wood Fiber, Gypsum. Olympic NTB Magnum spaced 12 in. (305 mm) o.c. within laps spaced 48 in. (1.2 m) o.c. Meets Class 1-90.

Authors' Comments

GenFlex RM, RM-C are polyester reinforced PVC sheet white, grey, or tan top, 0.045 to 0.60 in. thick

These are various roof insulations. For example, ACFoam-II is a poly-iso board by Atlas Roofing Corp., Atlanta, GA; E"NRG"Y-2 is a poly-iso board by Johns Manville Corp. Portland, ME.

Source: Adapted from Reference 8.3, with permission.

Elastizell Corp of America, Box 1462, Ann Arbor, MI 48106

Roof covers:	Asphaltic BUR, Modified Bitumen or Single-Ply
Deck:	Range II Elastizell Lightweight Insulating Concrete
Base Sheet:	See below

Construction # 1: Steel Form Deck Construction - A slurry of Range II Elastizell Lightweight Insulating Concrete is placed on the form deck filling the corrugations plus a min of 1/8 in. (3 mm) thickness above the top flange, immediately followed by min 1 in. (26 mm) to a max 12 in. (305 mm) thickness of Approved Polystyrene Insulation for a 1-60 wind classification and a min 2 in. (50 mm) to a max 12 in. (305 mm) thickness of Polystyrene Insulation for a 1-90 wind classification. The deck is either Wheeling Corrugating Company Type BW fluted (vented or nonvented unless specified) galvanized (G60) steel form deck which is 22 ga. [0.036 in. (0.91 mm)], 1-1/2 in. (38 mm) deep and 36 in. (0.91 m) wide or Wheeling Corrugating Company vented or nonvented Tensilform 75 which is 26 ga. [0.018 in (0.46 mm)], 15/16 in. (24 mm) deep, and 30 in. (0.76 m) wide. A min of 2 in. (51 mm) thick Range II Elastizell Lightweight Insulating Concrete is immediately placed over the Polystyrene Insulation.

   Within 48 to 72 hours an Approved base sheet is mechanically fastened as described below. The base sheet is covered with a roof covering consisting of a FMRC Approved 3-ply organic or glass felt BUR or min. 2-ply torched or hot asphalt applied modified bitumen roof cover. An alternate construction is to install a hot asphalt applied Approved insulation over the base sheet followed by either the prescribed BUR or modified bitumen roof cover. An alternate construction is to install ACFoam-II, Pyrox or Multi-Max FA placed with all joints staggered and adhered with hot asphalt applied at a nominal rate of 20-25 lb/sq (1.0-1.2 kg/m^2) in single or multiple layers — See insulation listings. An approved Seaman single-ply roof cover is applied per roof cover listings.

   As an alternate, Sarnafill G410 Felt Back roof cover is adhered over the surface of the Range II Elastizell Lightweight Insulating Concrete. Sarnacol 2121 Adhesive squeegee applied in one coat at a nominal rate of 2.25 gal/sq (0.92 L/m^2) or Sarnacol 2170 Adhesive roller applied at a rate of 0.8 to 1.0 gal/sq ((0.33 to 0.41 L/m^2) as a primer and allowed to dry. This is followed by a second coat of Sarnacol 2170 roller applied at the same rate. The roof cover is immediately rolled into the adhesive with a weighted roller and the seams sealed with a min. 1.5 in. wide heat welded seam.

REFERENCES

8.1   Structural Engineering Institute of the American Society of Civil Engineers. *Minimum Design Loads for Buildings and Other Structures, ASCE 7-98* (Reston, VA: 1998).

8.2   Factory Mutual Engineering Corporation. *Loss Prevention Data: Wind Loads to Roof Systems and Roof Deck Securement, 1-28* (Norwood, MA: 1996).

8.3   Factory Mutual Engineering Corporation. *Approval Guide, 1999: A Guide to Equipment, Materials and Services Approved by Factory Mutual Research Corporation for Property Conservation* (Norwood, MA: 1999).

8.4   Factory Mutual Engineering Corporation. *Loss Prevention Data: Above-Deck Roof Components, 1-29* (Norwood, MA: 1996).

8.5   Ibid.

8.6   SPRI — Sheet Membrane and Component Suppliers to the Commercial Roofing Industry. *Wind Design Standard for Ballasted Single-ply Roofing Systems ANSI/SPRI RP-4-1997* (Needham, MA: 1997).

8.7   Factory Mutual Engineering Corporation. *Approval Guide, 1999.*

DESIGN FOR WATER VAPOR CONTROL

Air is a mixture of several gases and water vapor. Water vapor can permeate through a roof assembly and condense therein, causing metal corrosion, wood decay, and insulation wetting. The wetting of insulation lowers its R-value, and prolonged wetting can eventually disintegrate it.

Excessive condensation can appear as drippage of water from the roof assembly. Therefore, flow of water vapor into a roof assembly must be controlled. This chapter examines the principles of water vapor flow and their application to roof assemblies.

179

9.1 WATER VAPOR IN AIR

Air is never absolutely dry, because all air contains a certain amount of water in the form of water vapor.[1] Like air, water vapor is a gas. Consequently, it exerts pressure on the surfaces of the enclosure containing it. However, although air and water vapor are thoroughly mixed together, the pressure exerted by water vapor is independent of that exerted by air.[2] In other words, air pressure and vapor pressure are not added together but are considered separately.

Vapor pressure is directly related to the amount of water vapor present in air. The air cannot contain an unlimited amount of water vapor. When the air contains the maximum amount of water vapor it can possibly hold, it is referred to as *saturated air*, and the corresponding vapor pressure is referred to as the *saturation vapor pressure*.

The amount of water (in the form of water vapor) in saturated air is a function of the air temperature. In fact, the amount of water vapor in saturated air increases exponentially with air temperature, Figure 9.1. For instance, the amount of water in saturated air at 0°F is nearly 5.5 grains per lb of dry air; (1 lb = 7,000 grains, abbreviated as "gr"). At 20°F, the amount of water is approximately 15.0 grains per lb of dry air; at 40°F, the corresponding amount of water is 36.4 grains; at 60°F, it is 77.3 grains, and so on.

Because the vapor pressure is directly related to the amount of water in air, the saturation vapor pressure also increases exponentially with air temperature, as shown in Figure 9.1.

9.1.1 Relative Humidity of Air

The occurrence of saturated air is relatively uncommon. Outside air is saturated with water vapor only during or immediately after a rain shower. Inside air is seldom saturated. In other words, the inside air at a given temperature contains less water vapor than the saturated air (at that temperature).

The amount of water vapor in air is usually not given in terms of its "absolute" value, but as a "relative" amount of water vapor, which is referred to as the *relative humidity*, RH, of air. The relative humidity of air, which is expressed in percentage form, is given by:

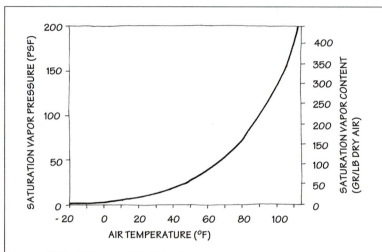

Temperature (°F)	Saturation vapor content (gr/lb of dry air)	Saturation vapor pressure (psf)
-20	2.0	1.0
-10	3.0	1.5
0	5.5	2.5
10	9.0	4.5
20	15.0	7.5
30	24.0	11.5
40	36.5	17.5
50	53.5	25.5
60	77.5	37.0
70	110.0	52.5
80	155.5	73.0
90	217.5	100.5
100	301.0	137.0
110	414.0	184.0

$$RH = \frac{\text{Weight of water vapor held in air}}{\text{Weight of water vapor in saturated air}} \times 100 \qquad (9.1)$$

9.1 *Saturation water vapor content and saturation vapor pressure as functions of air temperature.*

---

[1] Vaporization of water occurs at all temperatures. If we leave some water in a saucer, we see that it eventually disappears. In fact, this water converts into water vapor and mixes with air. Steam is simply the vaporization of water at its boiling point.

[2] This fact is based on Dalton's Law of Partial Pressures.

Because the amount of water vapor in air and the vapor pressure of air are directly related, the relative humidity is also defined by the ratios of vapor pressures:

$$RH = \frac{\text{Vapor pressure of air}}{\text{Vapor pressure of saturated air}} \times 100 \qquad (9.2)$$

From Equation (9.1), we see that saturated air has an RH = 100%. Similarly, a 50% RH means that the air contains 50% of the amount of water present in saturated air. More specifically, 1 lb of air at 50% RH and at 70°F contains (0.5)110 = 55 gr of water as water vapor. From Equation 9.2, this mass of air will exert (0.5)52.5 = 26.3 psf of vapor pressure. A 0% RH means that the air is absolutely dry. The vapor pressure exerted by such air is obviously zero.

The use of relative humidity of air (in place of absolute humidity) is based on human sensation to water vapor content in air. Air feels drier or damper depending on its relative humidity, not on its absolute humidity. Thus, air at 20% RH feels drier than air at 50% RH, even though the former may contain more water vapor. For instance, air at 20% RH and 100°F, containing nearly 60 gr of water vapor, feels drier than air at 50% RH and 70°F, which contains only 55 gr of water vapor, Figure 9.2.

Air with a low relative humidity dries human skin, produces static electricity in carpeted interiors, causes respiratory health problems, and is generally uncomfortable. Similarly, air with a high relative humidity feels moist, promotes fungal growth, and is also uncomfortable and unhealthy. Generally, the relative humidity of mechanically conditioned air in offices is kept at nearly 40%.

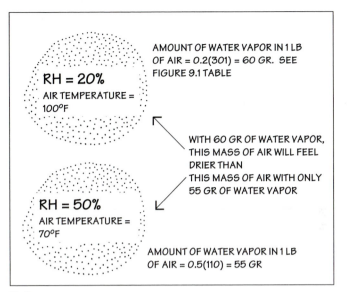

9.2 *Human sensation of the dryness or dampness of air depends mainly on its relative humidity.*

Consider air at a certain temperature and relative humidity. If no moisture is added or subtracted from this air and its temperature is increased, its relative humidity will decrease. For example, if the air at 50% RH and at 70°F is sealed inside a container and the temperature of the air is increased to 90°F, the relative humidity of the air decreases to nearly 25%, Figure 9.3.

9.3 *An increase in the temperature of air without changing its water content reduces the air's relative humidity.*

9.2 CONDENSATION OF WATER VAPOR

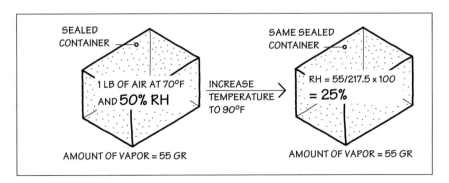

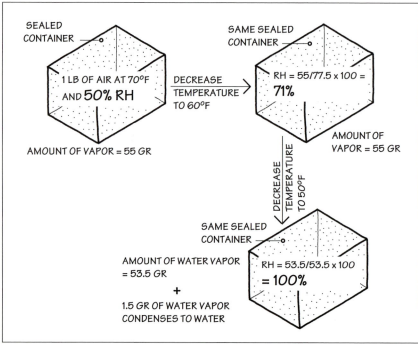

SEALED CONTAINER

1 LB OF AIR AT 70°F AND **50% RH**

AMOUNT OF VAPOR = 55 GR

DECREASE TEMPERATURE TO 60°F

SAME SEALED CONTAINER

RH = 55/77.5 x 100 = **71%**

AMOUNT OF VAPOR = 55 GR

DECREASE TEMPERATURE TO 50°F

SAME SEALED CONTAINER

AMOUNT OF WATER VAPOR = 53.5 GR

+

1.5 GR OF WATER VAPOR CONDENSES TO WATER

RH = 53.5/53.5 x 100 = **100%**

9.4 *A decrease in the temperature of air without changing its water content increases the air's relative humidity. When RH equals 100%, air condenses.*

Similarly, if the same container is cooled to 60°F, we see that the relative humidity of air increases to nearly 71%, Figure 9.4. A further decrease in temperature further increases the air's relative humidity until the relative humidity reaches 100%, beyond which any additional decrease in the temperature of air will lead to the conversion of water vapor into water — a phenomenon referred to as *condensation*.

The temperature at which the air becomes saturated (i.e., its RH reaches 100%) is called its *dew point temperature*, or simply the *dew point* of air. Thus, from Figure 9.4 we observe that the dew point of air (at 70°F and 50% RH) is slightly above 50°F, because at 50°F, the air can only hold 53.5 gr of water vapor, see Figure 9.1 table. Since the air (at 70°F and 50% RH) contains 55 gr of vapor, 1.5 gr of vapor must convert to water if the air's temperature is lowered to 50°F.

Values of the dew point of air at different temperatures and relative humidities are given in Table 9.1. At or below the dew point, the water vapor condenses into water.

Condensation occurs commonly in nature. The surface of a cup containing ice or cold water becomes wet because the warm and humid ambient air in contact with the surface of the cup cools to below its dew point. At this temperature, the air sheds excess water vapor by converting it into water, which deposits on the surface of the cup. In building interiors, condensation is observed during the winter on window glass. Such condensation is more pronounced in interiors with greater amounts of moisture such as indoor swimming pools, aerobic centers and gymnasiums, hotel kitchens, etc.

9.2.1 Interstitial and Surface Condensation

Apart from condensing on the surfaces of a window glass or any other cold surface, warm interior air can also condense within a wall or roof assembly. If the water vapor can permeate into an envelope assembly, it will condense where the temperature of the assembly is at or below the dew point of permeating vapor. When water vapor condenses inside a wall or roof assembly, it is referred to as *interstitial condensation*, as opposed to *surface condensation* that occurs on a surface such as a window glass.

Although both surface and interstitial condensation are undesirable, the latter is more so. Interstitial condensation wets the assembly, which accelerates the corrosion of metals and the decay of wood, decreases the R-value of insulation, and generally reduces the strength of assembly components. It is important to appreciate here that water vapor by itself is not damaging to a building assembly. It becomes damaging when it converts into water.

Because the inside and outside air are generally at different temperatures, there is a gradual change of temperature with an assembly. The rate of change of temperature is directly related to the R-value of the component within the assembly. The change of temperature is small within a component with a small R-value; the change is large within a component with a high R-value.

The consequence of this is that, in an insulated assembly, the dew point occurs within the insulation (see the box entitled "Temperature Gradient" at the end of this chapter). Therefore, a convenient solution to preventing (or reducing) interstitial condensation is to prevent or reduce the flow of water vapor into the insulation. This is accomplished by using a vapor retarder in the assembly.

Table 9.1 Dew Point of Air as a Function of Air Temperatures and Relative Humidity

RH (%)	Air temperature ($^{\circ}$F)								
	30	40	50	60	70	80	90	100	110
100	30	40	50	60	70	80	90	100	110
90	28	37	47	57	67	77	87	97	107
80	25	34	44	54	64	73	83	93	103
70	22	31	40	50	60	69	79	88	98
60	19	28	36	46	55	65	74	83	93
50	15	24	33	41	50	60	69	78	88
40	11	18	27	35	45	53	62	71	81
30	5	14	21	29	37	46	54	62	72
20	3	8	13	20	28	35	43	52	62
10	1	5	6	9	13	20	27	34	43
0				This air will not condense.					

The flow of water vapor through a building envelope can take place by one or both of the following modes:

- Leakage of air
- Water vapor diffusion

9.3.1 Leakage of Air

Because air and water vapor are thoroughly mixed, any leakage of air through the envelope is also accompanied by the leakage of water vapor. The leakage of air takes place at cracks, penetrations, and unsealed joints between the assembly members. Thus, most leakage of air occurs through doors, windows, and skylights, since the joints between the glass and its frame or between a door and door frame, etc., cannot be fully sealed against air penetration.

9.3 MODES OF WATER VAPOR FLOW

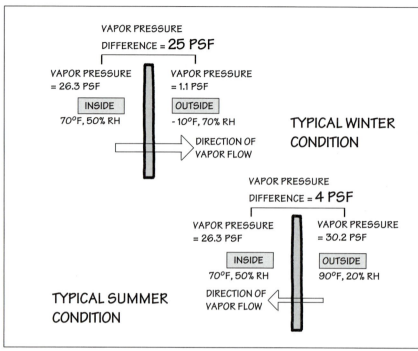

VAPOR PRESSURE
DIFFERENCE = **25 PSF**

VAPOR PRESSURE = 26.3 PSF

VAPOR PRESSURE = 1.1 PSF

INSIDE
70°F, 50% RH

OUTSIDE
-10°F, 70% RH

TYPICAL WINTER CONDITION

DIRECTION OF VAPOR FLOW

VAPOR PRESSURE
DIFFERENCE = **4 PSF**

VAPOR PRESSURE = 26.3 PSF

VAPOR PRESSURE = 30.2 PSF

INSIDE
70°F, 50% RH

OUTSIDE
90°F, 20% RH

TYPICAL SUMMER CONDITION

DIRECTION OF VAPOR FLOW

9.5 *Vapor pressure differentials between the inside and outside air during typical winter and summer conditions in most of North America.*

Units of Vapor Permeance

U.S. System of Units
1 perm = One grain of water vapor permeating through 1 square foot of a component per hour under a vapor pressure difference of 1 inch of mercury. In other words:

SI System of Units
1 perm = One nanogram of water vapor permeating through 1 square meter of a component per second under a vapor pressure difference of 1 Pascal. In other words:

$$1 \text{ perm } = 1 \frac{gr}{(h)(ft^2)(in. \text{ of } Hg)}$$

$$1 \text{ perm } = 1 \frac{ng}{(s)(m^2)(Pa)}$$

1 (U.S.) perm = 57.2 (SI) perm

To qualify as a vapor retarder for use in a roof, the perm rating of a component should not exceed 0.1 perm, or 5.7 (SI) perm.

9.3.2 Vapor Diffusion and the Use of Vapor Retarder

The second mode of vapor flow — vapor diffusion — takes place independently of the air flow. It occurs due to the vapor pressure differential between the inside and the outside air. Vapor flows (diffuses) from a region of higher vapor pressure to that of a lower vapor pressure.[3]

Generally, warm air has higher vapor pressure than cold air. Thus, vapor flows from the inside to the outside during the winter. In summer, the direction of vapor flow may be reversed (from outside to the inside), particularly in warm coastal regions. However, in most of North America, the vapor flow from the inside to the outside is more critical. This is due to the generally higher inside-to-outside vapor pressure differential that occurs during the winter as compared with summer differentials, Figure 9.5.

The rate at which water vapor flows (diffuses) through a building component is measured by its vapor permeability. The unit of vapor permeability is called the *permeance,* or simply the *perm.* A material with a higher perm value (or rating) is more vapor permeable. If the perm rating is zero, the material is vapor impermeable. Such a material is a perfect vapor retarder — in fact, a vapor barrier — provided it is free of holes, cracks, and unsealed joints.

Apart from being a property of the material, perm rating is also a function of the component's thickness. A larger thickness of the same material has a lower perm rating. Perm ratings of selected materials are given in Table 9.2. For instance, the perm rating of a 4-mil-thick polyethylene sheet is 0.08 (in the U.S. system); a 6-mil-thick polyethylene sheet's perm rating is 0.06.

To qualify as a vapor retarder, the perm rating of the material must be 0.1 perm (in the U.S. system). Glass and metals (even a thin metal foil, such as aluminum foil) have a zero perm rating. Roof membranes — built-up roof, modified bitumen, and single-ply membranes — are excellent vapor retarders.

---

[3] According to Dalton's Law of Partial Pressures, vapor diffusion is independent of air pressure. Thus, vapor flows from a higher vapor pressure region to a lower vapor pressure region, even though the lower vapor pressure region may have a higher air pressure.

Table 9.2 Perm Ratings of Selected Materials

Component	Perm rating (perm)	Component	Perm rating (perm)
Aluminum foil (unpunctured)	0.0	Brick masonry, 4 in. thick	0.8
Aluminum foil on gypsum board	0.1	Concrete block masonry, 8 in. thick	2.4
Built-up roofing, 3 to 5 ply	0.0	Plaster on metal lath	15.0
15 lb asphalt felt	4.0	Building paper, grade A	0.25
PVC (plasticized), 4mil thick	1.2	Building paper, grade B	0.38
Polyethylene sheet, 4 mil thick	0.08	Interior primer plus 1 coat flat oil	
Polyethylene sheet, 6 mil thick	0.06	paint on plaster	1.6 - 3.0
Polyethylene sheet, 8 mil thick	0.03	Exterior oil paint, 3 coats on wood	0.3 - 1.0

Because the vapor pressure is generally higher in warmer air, the conventional wisdom is to install a vapor retarder on the warm side of the assembly. Thus in most parts of North America, a vapor retarder is installed toward the inside of the envelope assembly.

9.4.1 Vapor Retarder in a Steep Roof Assembly

In a steep roof assembly, a vapor retarder (generally a 6-mil or thicker polyethylene sheet) is typically installed in the ceiling — between the interior gypsum board and the insulation above, Figure 9.6.

In addition to using a vapor retarder, it is also important to ventilate the envelope assembly between the vapor retarder and the outside. The idea is that if any vapor escapes through the vapor retarder, it should be able to mix with the (infinite mass of) outside air to prevent its condensation within the assembly. That is why a typical attic must be ventilated.[4] Without adequate attic ventilation, the vapor will be trapped in the attic, where it can condense.

Since the dew point generally occurs within the insulation, attic insulation must be vapor permeable. That is why the most commonly used attic insulation is fiberglass batt or blanket insulation.

---

[4] In extremely cold climates, subjected to frequent blowing snow and rain, some builders and designers prefer to use an unventilated (airtight) attic in order to prevent cold drafts in the attic. Such a design requires a vapor retarder with nearly zero perm rating, see Reference 9.1.

9.4 VAPOR RETARDER IN A ROOF ASSEMBLY

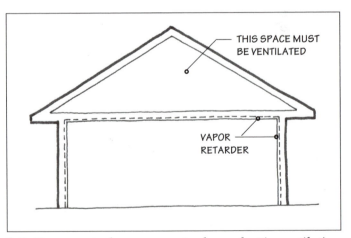

9.6 *Vapor control — vapor retarder and attic ventilation — in a steep roof.*

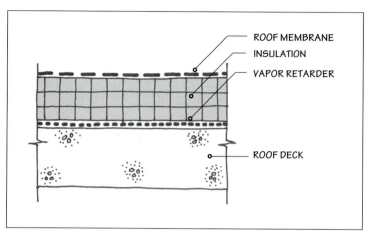

ROOF MEMBRANE
INSULATION
VAPOR RETARDER
ROOF DECK

9.7 *Location of a vapor retarder in a low-slope roof assembly (see also Figure 9.10).*

9.4.2 Vapor Retarder in a Low-Slope Roof Assembly

Because a vapor retarder should be placed on the warm side of an assembly, its correct location in a low-slope roof is between the insulation and the roof deck, Figure 9.7. However, since the roof membrane is also a good vapor retarder, the insulation is sandwiched between two vapor retarders. With no possibility of ventilation in a low-slope roof assembly, this arrangement traps any vapor, escaping through the vapor retarder, within the insulation.

Several low-slope roofs with the above arrangement have experienced premature disintegration of insulation. Thus, although the earlier roofing industry practice suggested the use of a vapor retarder whenever there was a question as to its need, the current recommendation suggests otherwise: *do not use a vapor retarder in a low-slope roof assembly unless it is really required.*

In any case, the use of a vapor retarder in a contemporary low-slope roof assembly does not make much sense since the commonly used insulation — polyisocyanurate board — is itself a good vapor retarder. With its closed cell structure and staggered joints between primary and secondary insulation layers, the flow of vapor into the insulation is sufficiently retarded.

However, the current recommendation is based on a detailed study[9.2] which has been summarized into vapor drive contours for the United States. These contours, Figure 9.8, give the minimum interior relative humidity (for an interior temperature of 68°F/20°C) that must exist before a vapor retarder in a low-slope roof assembly is specified.

From Figure 9.8, we observe that since the interior relative humidity in most commercial interiors is nearly 40%, a vapor retarder is not required in a low-slope roof except in the cold, northern parts of the United States. A vapor retarder may also be required in certain manufacturing facilities that have a high interior relative humidity.

The contours of Figure 9.8 are based on an interior temperature of 68°F/20°C. If the interior temperature is different from 68°F, the corresponding equivalent RH, which corresponds to the same vapor pressures as given by the contours of Figure 9.8, may be obtained from Figure 9.9.

For example, from Figure 9.8, the minimum interior RH required for the use of a vapor retarder in New York City is 50%. This assumes an interior air temperature of 68°F. If the interior air temperature in a building in New York City is maintained at 60°F, the corresponding minimum RH (as read from Figure 9.9) is nearly 67%. In other words, at an interior temperature of 60°F in a building in New York City, the interior relative humidity should exceed 67% before a vapor retarder in a low-slope roof assembly is specified.

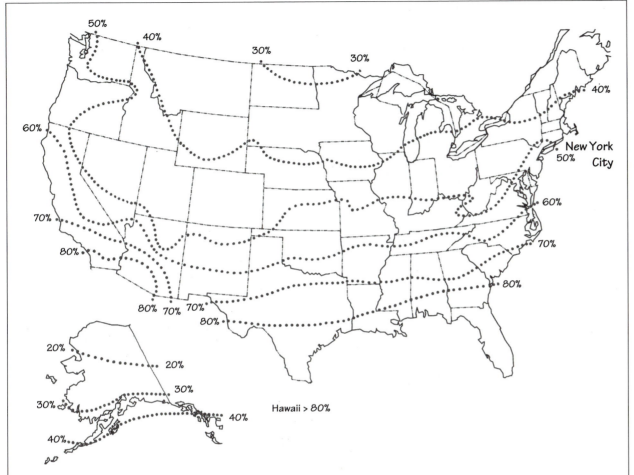

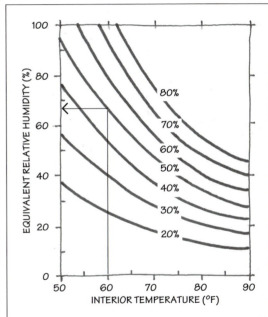

9.8 *Minimum interior relative humidity values that must exist for specifying a vapor retarder in a low-slope roof assembly — corresponding to an interior temperature of 68°F (20°C).*

9.9 *Equivalent interior relative humidity corresponding to an interior temperature of other than 68°F (20°C).*

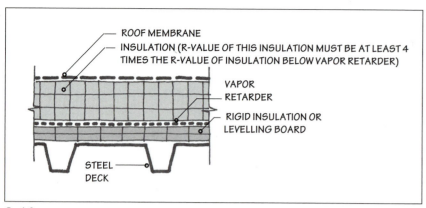

ROOF MEMBRANE

INSULATION (R-VALUE OF THIS INSULATION MUST BE AT LEAST 4 TIMES THE R-VALUE OF INSULATION BELOW VAPOR RETARDER)

VAPOR RETARDER

RIGID INSULATION OR LEVELLING BOARD

STEEL DECK

9.10 *Vapor retarder in a steel deck roof assembly.*

9.4.3 Detailing a Vapor Retarder in a Low-Slope Roof

As stated previously, roof membranes are excellent vapor retarders. Thus, a 2- or 3-ply built-up roof , particularly with coated fiberglass felts, can be used as a vapor retarder. Other commercially available vapor retarders are polyethylene sheet, aluminum foil laminated to vinyl sheets, etc. However, sheet materials, being thin and lightweight, may present installation problems on windy days. They are also vulnerable to punctures due to roofers' traffic on an uneven deck. Punctures compromise the effectiveness of a vapor retarder.

In the particular case of a steel deck, the vapor retarder must be installed on a flat surface, which may be obtained by the use of a wood fiberboard or perlite board laid atop the deck. In fact, a 1/2-in.-thick fiberboard or a 3/4-in.-thick perlite board gives an excellent surface on which to apply a vapor retarder. Insulation can then be laid on the vapor retarder, Figure 9.10.

In such an assembly, it is important to ensure that the R-value of the insulation above the vapor retarder is much greater (at least 4 times greater) than the R-value of the assembly below the vapor retarder. This should ensure that the dew point occurs above the vapor retarder to prevent surface condensation.

TEMPERATURE GRADIENT

The inside and outside air in a building are usually at different temperatrures. The change in temperature from the inside surface to the outside surface of an assembly is gradual and is refereed to as the *temperature gradient*. The temperature gradient is a function of the R-values of various components of the assembly.

Consider an assembly consisting of three components, whose R-values are R_1, R_2, and R_3, respectively, so that the total R-value of the assembly, $R = R_1 + R_2 + R_3$. Let the temperature differential between the inside and outside air be Δt. It can be shown that the temperature drop across Components 1, 2 and 3 (denoted by Δt_1, Δt_2, and Δt_3, respectively) are given by:

$$\Delta t_1 = \left[\frac{R_1}{R}\right]\Delta t \qquad \Delta t_2 = \left[\frac{R_2}{R}\right]\Delta t \qquad \Delta t_3 = \left[\frac{R_3}{R}\right]\Delta t$$

so that, $\Delta t = \Delta t_1 + \Delta t_2 + \Delta t_3$

Example: Draw the temperature gradient through a low-slope roof assembly consisting of three components whose R-values are 1, 10 and 2 respectively. Assume that the inside and outside air temperatures are 70 ^oF and 10 ^oF, respectively. If the relative humidity of inside air is 50%, determine where in the assembly the condensation will occur.

Solution: It is important to include the film resistances of inside and outside air. From Section 4.3.8 in Chapter 4, the inside and outside film resistances are 0.7 and 0.2, respectively. Thus, the total R-value of the assembly is R = 0.7 + 1 + 10 + 2 + 0.2 = 13.9. With two film resistances, the assembly really consists of five components. $\Delta t = 70 - 10 = 60$ ^oF.

Temperature drop across inside air film, $\Delta t_i = \left[\frac{0.7}{13.9}\right]60 = 3.0^oF$

The drop of 3.0°F takes place through the internal air film. Hence, the temperature of the inside surface of assembly = 70 - 3.0 = 67°F.

Temperature drop across Component 1, $\Delta t_1 = \left[\frac{1.0}{13.9}\right]60 = 4.3^oF$ — from 67°F to 62.7°F

Temperature drop across Component 2, $\Delta t_2 = \left[\frac{10.0}{13.9}\right]60 = 43.2^oF$ — from 62.7°F to 19.5°F

Temperature drop across Component 3, $\Delta t_3 = \left[\frac{2.0}{13.9}\right]60 = 8.6^oF$— from 19.5°F to 10.9°F

Temperature drop across outside air film, $\Delta t_o = \left[\frac{0.2}{13.9}\right]60 = 0.9^oF$ — from 10.9°F to 10°F

The temperature gradient is superimposed on the cross-section of the assembly, as shown in the following figure. Note that the temperature drop across each component is directly proportional to the component's R-value. Thus, the temperature drop across Component 1 (with an R-value of 1.0) is 4.3 ^oF. The temperature drop across Component 2 (an R-value of 10.0) is 43.2 ^oF.

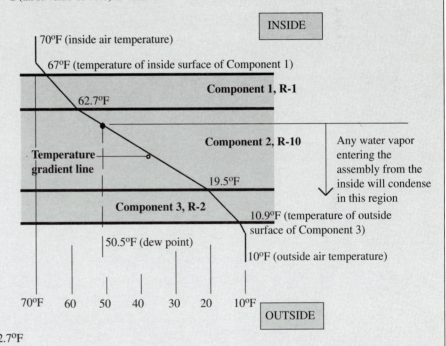

From Table 9.2, the dew point of inside air (70 ^oF and 50% RH) is 50.5 ^oF. The location where this temperature occurs in the assembly is shown by a dot in the above figure. Observe that the dew point occurs in the component with a high R-value — the insulation.

REFERENCES

9.1   Mehta, Madan. *Principles of Building Construction* (Upper Saddle River, NJ: Prentice Hall, 1997), p. 169.

9.2   Tobiasson, W. "General Considerations for Roofs," *Moisture Control in Buildings*, ASTM Manual 18 (1994), p. 291.

10 DETAILS AT TERMINATIONS AND PENETRATIONS

The termination of a roof, which generally occurs over a wall, requires careful detailing. The wall either stops below the roof, in which case the roof terminates into a free edge (e.g., a gravel guard edge), or the wall projects above the roof as a parapet wall. In either case, the differential movement between the roof and the wall, and the higher wind loads at roof terminations, increase the stresses in a roof membrane at a wall-roof junction.

Additional strength is, therefore, required at a roof-wall junction, which is provided by a special sheet material called *flashing*. Flashing also helps to integrate the roof membrane with the wall and further waterproofs the wall-roof junction, which is more vulnerable to leakage than the field-of-roof.

Flashing is also required around penetrations in the roof, such as roof drains,[1] gutters, vent stacks, curbs below skylights and roof-top equipment, expansion joints, area dividers,[2] etc. This chapter deals with the details of the roof at terminations and penetrations.

It is impossible to cover every conceivable detail in such a text without significantly increasing its size. Therefore, only a few commonly used details are presented, which are neither complete nor comprehensive. Several minor but important items of information, such as sheet metal gauge, schedule of fasteners (i.e., type, size, and spacing of fasteners), thickness of flashing, etc., have deliberately been left out for the sake of readability and clarity.

Additionally, most details shown here refer to built-up roofs. The details relating to modified bitumen and single-ply roofs are slightly different, but the basic principles of detailing remain essentially the same. For full coverage, the reader should refer to References 10.1 and 10.2 given at the end of this chapter and the manufacturer-provided details.

---

[1] Details of roof drains are covered in Chapter 6.

[2] Details of roof expansion joints and area dividers are covered in Chapter 5.

10.1 ROOF FLASHINGS

Locations where flashings are needed on a typical roof are shown in Figure 10.1. Flashings may be divided into three basic types:

- Base flashings
- Curb flashings
- Flange flashings

A base flashing occurs at the junction of a roof and a wall that rises above the roof, e.g., a parapet wall, Figure 10.2. A curb flashing occurs at a curb placed around a roof opening, such as around a skylight or under roof-top equipment, Figure 10.3. Both base and curb flashings extend vertically along the wall or the curb, terminating some distance above the roof level.

A flange flashing does not extend vertically, but lies in the plane of the roof. It occurs at a free edge of the roof, e.g., a gravel guard edge, around a vent stack, or around a pipe used for supporting a structural frame under roof-top equipment, Figure 10.4.

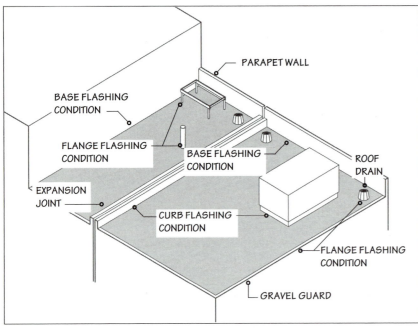

10.1 *Various types of roof flashings.*

10.2 *Base flashing at a parapet wall. The top of the parapet will be covered with a sheet metal coping, see Figures 10.11 amd 10.12. Photo by Madan Mehta.*

CURB FLASHING

10.3 *Examples of curb flashings. Photo by Madan Mehta.*

FLANGE FLASHING

10.4 *Examples of flange flashings. Photo by Madan Mehta.*

10.2 BASE FLASHING AND A LOW-HEIGHT PARAPET

A base flashing consists of two parts: *membrane flashing* and *counterflashing*, Figure 10.5. Membrane flashing provides additional reinforcement to the roof membrane and extends the waterproofing ability of the roof to the highest anticipated water level. Membrane flashing also provides additional waterproofing at the roof-wall junction, which, being under greater stress, is more prone to leakage than the field-of-roof.

Counterflashing is generally made of sheet metal. Galvanized steel is most commonly used for counterflashing, but aluminum, copper, or stainless steel should be specified where greater durability is needed. Counterflashing laps over the top of membrane flashing to prevent the entry of water between the membrane flashing and the parapet wall.

10.2.1 Membrane Flashing Material

Membrane flashing must be compatible with the roof membrane material. Therefore, it is generally of the same or similar material. Membrane flashing must have adequate strength and pliability to withstand minor movement between the wall and the roof. Therefore, the most commonly used membrane flashing material with a built-up roof is an SBS-modified bitumen sheet. An SBS membrane flashing is also used with an SBS-modified bitumen roof.

An SBS-modified membrane flashing is generally a mineral-granule-surfaced sheet. Mineral granules protect the flashing against weathering. This is helpful since gravel protection is not available on the vertical portion of membrane flashing. Some designers specify a back-up layer of felt to add redundancy to flashing.

There are also multilayer built-up flashings consisting of two or more layers of felt or special reinforced membrane flashing material. The layers of flashing are solidly adhered with hot asphalt or flashing cement. Torch-applied flashing sheets are also used, typically with a torch-applied roof membrane. A single-ply flashing material is used with a single-ply roof membrane.

10.2.2 Membrane Flashing Height and Securement

On built-up and SBS-modified roofs, membrane flashing can be hot mopped. Hot mopping has the advantage of speed of application, but it is difficult to apply around small areas. The alternative to hot bitumen is roofer's cement or flashing cement, which because it is at the prevailing air temperature, facilitates its application in corners and other small areas.

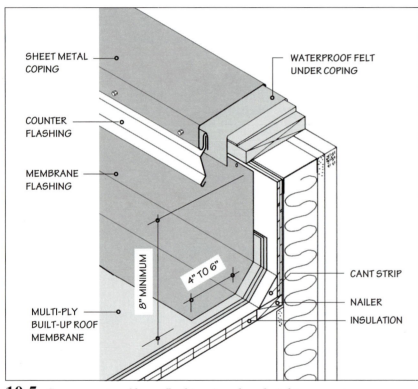

10.5 *Components of base flashing in a low-height parapet.*

Flashing cement is similar to roofer's cement but with greater amounts of mineral fibers and other additives to make it stiffer and more sag resistant. Therefore, flashing cement is used for vertical surface flashings, e.g., base and curb flashings. Roofer's cement is commonly used for horizontal surfaces, e.g., flange flashings, where sag resistance is not a consideration.

On APP-modified bitumen roofs, APP membrane flashing is generally specified, which is typically heat welded. APP membrane flashing can also be used on built-up and SBS-modified roofs. The heat-welding process allows the roofer to direct the heat where needed to ensure adhesion and conformability of membrane flashing to the backup. Single-ply roof flashing is adhered with adhesives provided by the manufacturer.

Field membrane plies should extend slightly above the top of the cant, which effectively turns the waterproofing above the generally prevailing water level. Membrane flashing should generally extend 4 to 6 in. on the flat portion of the roof and at least 8 in. up the parapet wall, see Figure 10.5.

A minimum recommended flashing height of 8 in. establishes the minimum height of a parapet wall or a curb. This provides adequate height to prevent water from entering the interior of the building, even in the "snow belt" region. Membrane flashing must be mechanically fastened to the wall along the top edge of the flashing, Figure 10.6. Fasteners are typically placed 8 in. on center.

10.6 *A roofer fastening granule-covered, SBS-modified membrane flashing to masonry parapet wall with nails and metal caps. Photo by Madan Mehta.*

10.2.3 Cant Strips

Since bituminous materials are relatively brittle, they should not be bent to form a 90° angle, as they will crack during service. A cant strip is, therefore, provided where a built-up or a modified bitumen roof meets a vertical wall, i.e., at the base. Some modified bitumen roofing manufacturers do not require a cant strip with their material, but a good detail should include a cant strip at all base locations, since a gradual upturn also reduces the possibility of voids between the flashing and the backup. Cant strips are, however, not needed in a single-ply roof because of the much greater flexibility of a single-ply membrane.

Cant strips may be of solid (pressure-treated) wood or of a rigid insulating material, such as wood fiberboard or perlite board, Figure 10.7. Perlite or wood fiberboard cants are commonly used and are generally adhered (with hot bitumen or roofer's cement) to the insulation or the base sheet, Figure 10.8.

10.7 *Perlite board cant strip. Photo by Madan Mehta.*

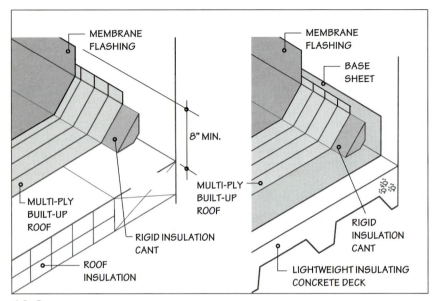

10.8 *(a) Rigid insulation cant mopped to insulation. (b) Rigid insulation cant mopped to a base sheet, which has been applied over a lightweight insulating concrete deck.*

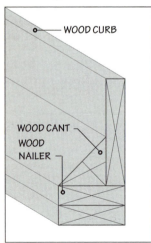

10.9 *A solid wood cant provides stability to a wood curb.*

10.10 *Treated wood nailers at top of a parapet and the roof perimeter. Photo by Madan Mehta.*

Solid wood cants are generally more expensive and more difficult to work with than perlite or wood fiberboard cants. Because of the greater strength of solid wood compared to perlite board or wood fiberboard, wood cants are used where it is necessary for the cant strip to provide strength and stability to a wood curb. In such a case, the cant strip is nailed to the curb and the underlying wood nailer, Figure 10.9. Wood curbs are required at roof expansion joints and area dividers (see Figures 5.31 and 5.32 in Chapter 5) and at some roof-wall junctions (see Figure 10.16).

10.2.4 Wood Nailers

Wood nailers are generally used below the cant strips at the roof perimeter, below curbs, and under parapet wall copings, Figure 10.10. They must be of pressure-treated wood. The top of perimeter nailers should be flush with (i.e., at the same elevation as) the top of the adjoining roof insulation. Nailers add strength and provide a nailable surface to which the membrane, flashing, or copings are fastened.

10.2.5 Counterflashing and Metal Coping

As stated earlier, counterflashing is generally made of galvanized steel, aluminum, copper, or stainless steel. In the case of a low parapet wall (up to a height of 24 in. or so), counterflashing engages into metal coping on the parapet, Figure 10.11. Alternatively, a separate counterflashing may be avoided, and the metal coping used as counterflashing, Figure 10.12. The disadvantage of the latter detail is that the coping has to be replaced with every reroofing operation.

Metal coping wraps over a continuous metal cleat on the outside face of the parapet and is fastened to the parapet nailer with high-domed, gasketed fasteners on the inside face of parapet. A waterproof felt, such as a No. 30 organic felt or a modified bitumen sheet, should be placed under the metal coping, Figure 10.13. This provides additional waterproofing, particularly under the joints in metal coping, Figure 10.14. Joints in metal copings are typically placed at 10 ft on center.

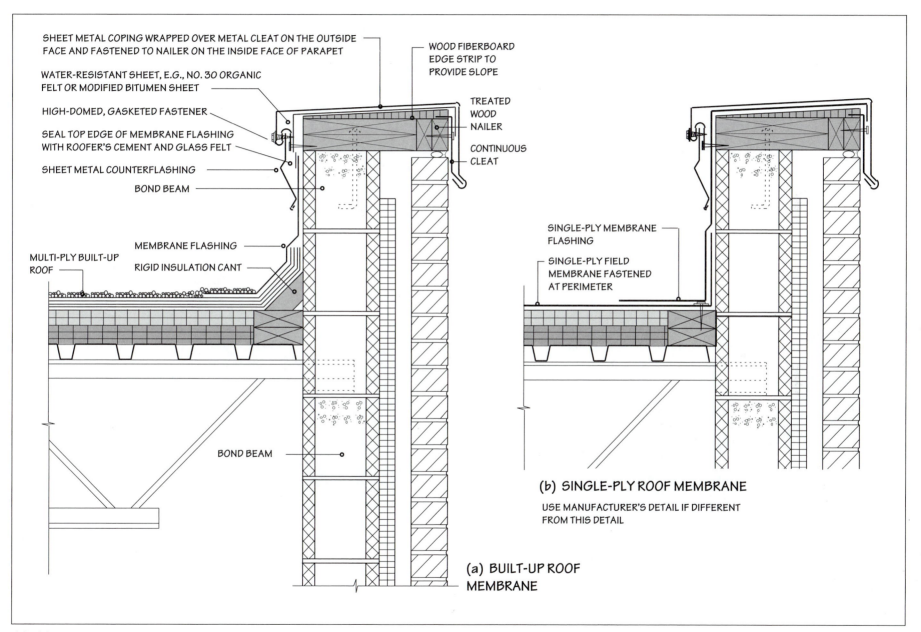

SHEET METAL COPING WRAPPED OVER METAL CLEAT ON THE OUTSIDE FACE AND FASTENED TO NAILER ON THE INSIDE FACE OF PARAPET

WATER-RESISTANT SHEET, E.G., NO. 30 ORGANIC FELT OR MODIFIED BITUMEN SHEET

HIGH-DOMED, GASKETED FASTENER

SEAL TOP EDGE OF MEMBRANE FLASHING WITH ROOFER'S CEMENT AND GLASS FELT

SHEET METAL COUNTERFLASHING

BOND BEAM

MEMBRANE FLASHING

MULTI-PLY BUILT-UP ROOF

RIGID INSULATION CANT

WOOD FIBERBOARD EDGE STRIP TO PROVIDE SLOPE

TREATED WOOD NAILER

CONTINUOUS CLEAT

BOND BEAM

SINGLE-PLY MEMBRANE FLASHING

SINGLE-PLY FIELD MEMBRANE FASTENED AT PERIMETER

(b) SINGLE-PLY ROOF MEMBRANE

USE MANUFACTURER'S DETAIL IF DIFFERENT FROM THIS DETAIL

(a) BUILT-UP ROOF MEMBRANE

10.11 *Base flashing and low-height parapet detail for a wall-supported roof.*

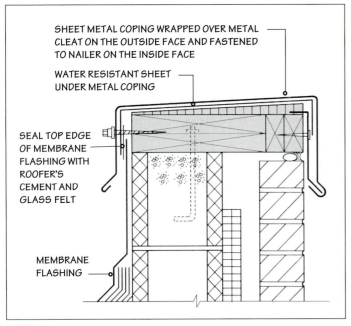

SHEET METAL COPING WRAPPED OVER METAL CLEAT ON THE OUTSIDE FACE AND FASTENED TO NAILER ON THE INSIDE FACE

WATER RESISTANT SHEET UNDER METAL COPING

SEAL TOP EDGE OF MEMBRANE FLASHING WITH ROOFER'S CEMENT AND GLASS FELT

MEMBRANE FLASHING

10.12 *Coping detail. This detail is similar to the coping detail in Figure 10.11(a), except that the coping also serves as a counterflashing in this case.*

10.13 *SBS-modified bitumen sheet as water-resistant layer over top of parapet (under coping). Photo by Madan Mehta.*

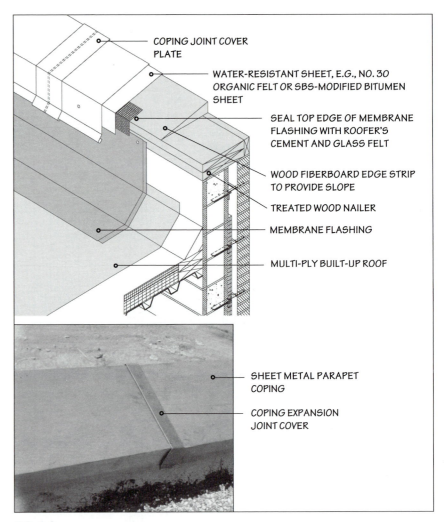

COPING JOINT COVER PLATE

WATER-RESISTANT SHEET, E.G., NO. 30 ORGANIC FELT OR SBS-MODIFIED BITUMEN SHEET

SEAL TOP EDGE OF MEMBRANE FLASHING WITH ROOFER'S CEMENT AND GLASS FELT

WOOD FIBERBOARD EDGE STRIP TO PROVIDE SLOPE

TREATED WOOD NAILER

MEMBRANE FLASHING

MULTI-PLY BUILT-UP ROOF

SHEET METAL PARAPET COPING

COPING EXPANSION JOINT COVER

10.14 *Coping expansion joint cover. Photo by Madan Mehta.*

10.2.6 Prefabricated Copings

In place of the site-fabricated copings shown in Figures 10.11 and 10.12, shop-fabricated sheet metal copings may be specified. Most manufacturers' copings are spring loaded, so that they can be snapped to continuous cleats on both sides of coping, precluding the need for external fasteners, Figure 10.15.

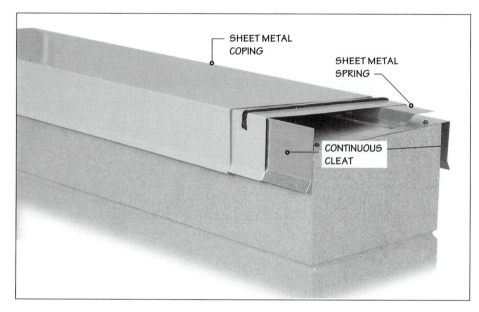

SHEET METAL COPING

SHEET METAL SPRING

CONTINUOUS CLEAT

10.15 *Snapped-in-place coping. Photo courtesy of MM Systems Corporation, Tucker, Georgia.*

10.2.7 Independence of Roof-Wall Movement

In Figure 10.12, the roof is supported on a loadbearing wall. In such a structure, the roof and wall will move in conjunction with each other. On the other hand, if the roof is not supported on the wall but rests on a frame structure, the roof and the wall must be able to move independently of each other to avoid overstressing of the roof membrane. In such a case, the base flashing detail must include a wood curb, a solid wood cant, and fire safing, Figure 10.16. The minimum height of a curb is 8 in., but 2 x 12 treated wood curb is commonly specified.

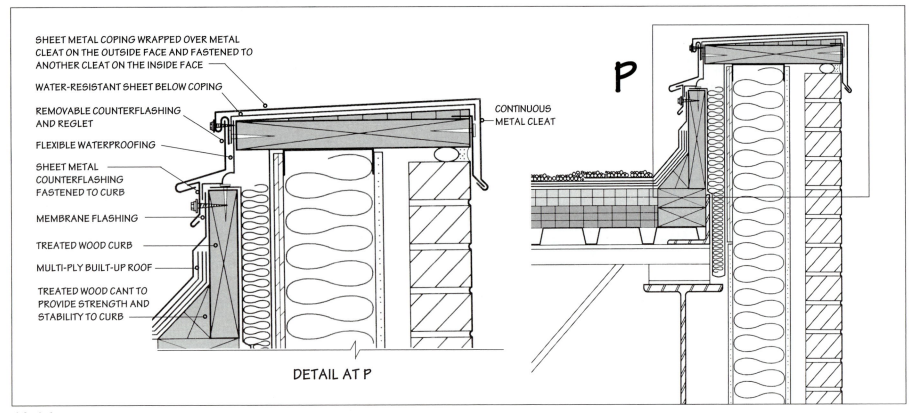

SHEET METAL COPING WRAPPED OVER METAL
CLEAT ON THE OUTSIDE FACE AND FASTENED TO
ANOTHER CLEAT ON THE INSIDE FACE

WATER-RESISTANT SHEET BELOW COPING

REMOVABLE COUNTERFLASHING
AND REGLET

FLEXIBLE WATERPROOFING

SHEET METAL
COUNTERFLASHING
FASTENED TO CURB

MEMBRANE FLASHING

TREATED WOOD CURB

MULTI-PLY BUILT-UP ROOF

TREATED WOOD CANT TO
PROVIDE STRENGTH AND
STABILITY TO CURB

CONTINUOUS
METAL CLEAT

P

DETAIL AT P

10.16 *Base flashing and parapet detail of a non-wall supported roof. This detail should be used where differential movement between the wall and the roof is expected. Items not noted in this diagram are similar to those in Figure 10.11.*

10.3 BASE FLASHING AND A TALL PARAPET WALL

In Figure 10.11, the waterproofing of the inside face of a parapet wall is achieved by extending the membrane flashing over the entire height of the parapet. While this strategy is acceptable for a short parapet wall (typically 2 ft or so in height), it is not a good detail for a tall parapet wall. In a tall parapet wall, the membrane flashing material tends to sag under the effect of the sun's heat, requiring expensive maintenance.

The detail of Figure 10.17 may be used for a tall parapet wall, in which a sheet metal through-wall flashing extends from the bed joint of masonry to the underside of the parapet nailer. However, a through-wall flashing weakens the bed joint and cannot be easily repaired in case of workmanship defects.

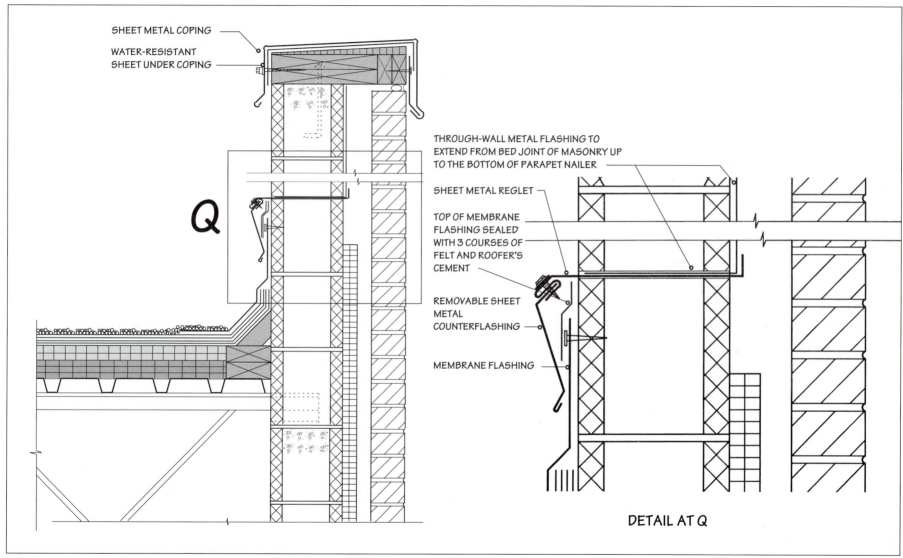

SHEET METAL COPING

WATER-RESISTANT
SHEET UNDER COPING

Q

THROUGH-WALL METAL FLASHING TO
EXTEND FROM BED JOINT OF MASONRY UP
TO THE BOTTOM OF PARAPET NAILER

SHEET METAL REGLET

TOP OF MEMBRANE
FLASHING SEALED
WITH 3 COURSES OF
FELT AND ROOFER'S
CEMENT

REMOVABLE SHEET
METAL
COUNTERFLASHING

MEMBRANE FLASHING

DETAIL AT Q

10.17 *Base flashing and a tall masonry parapet.*

A better detail is is to cover the inside face of the wall with a more permanent material, such as ribbed metal panels, Figures 10.18 and 10.19. The membrane flashing extends up to the bottom of the wall panels and is protected by sheet metal counterflashing tucked under the wall panels. This detail allows the ribbed wall panels to remain in place during reroofing operations.

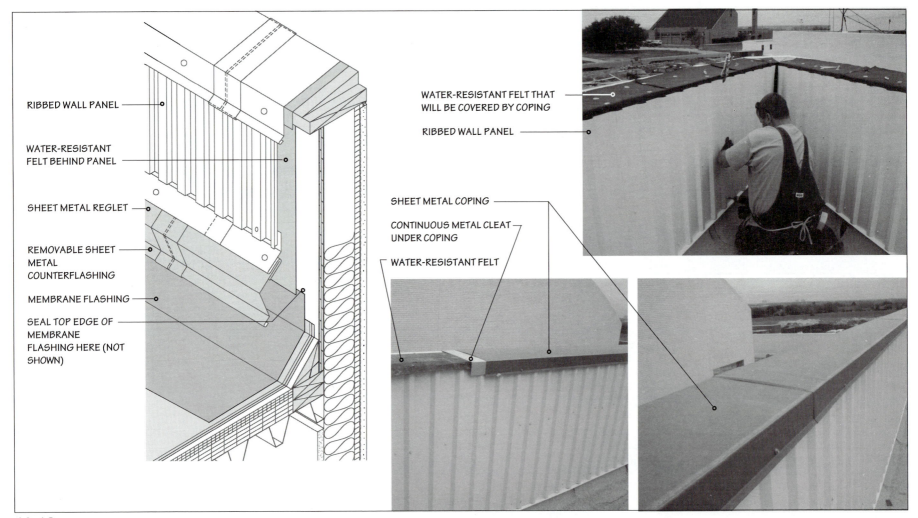

RIBBED WALL PANEL

WATER-RESISTANT FELT BEHIND PANEL

SHEET METAL REGLET

REMOVABLE SHEET METAL COUNTERFLASHING

MEMBRANE FLASHING

SEAL TOP EDGE OF MEMBRANE FLASHING HERE (NOT SHOWN)

WATER-RESISTANT FELT THAT WILL BE COVERED BY COPING

RIBBED WALL PANEL

SHEET METAL COPING

CONTINUOUS METAL CLEAT UNDER COPING

WATER-RESISTANT FELT

10.18 *Ribbed metal panel cladding on the interior face of a parapet wall. Photos by Madan Mehta.*

In the case of a wall that can be waterproofed by other means (e.g., a reinforced concrete wall with integral and/or surface waterproofing), a simple sheet metal counterflashing fastened to the wall may be adequate, Figure 10.20.

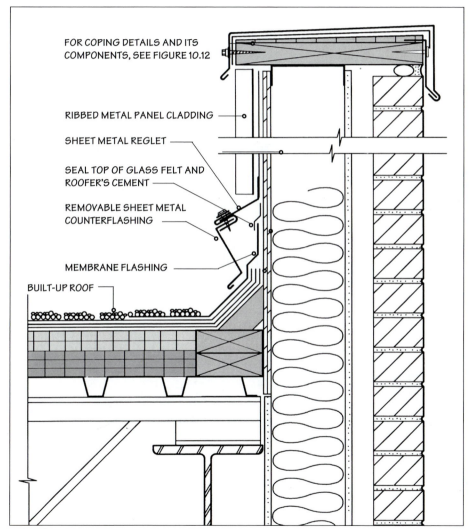

FOR COPING DETAILS AND ITS COMPONENTS, SEE FIGURE 10.12

RIBBED METAL PANEL CLADDING

SHEET METAL REGLET

SEAL TOP OF GLASS FELT AND ROOFER'S CEMENT

REMOVABLE SHEET METAL COUNTERFLASHING

MEMBRANE FLASHING

BUILT-UP ROOF

10.19 *Ribbed metal cladding on the interior face of a tall parapet wall.*

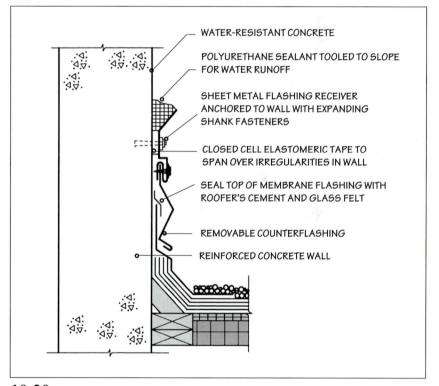

WATER-RESISTANT CONCRETE

POLYURETHANE SEALANT TOOLED TO SLOPE FOR WATER RUNOFF

SHEET METAL FLASHING RECEIVER ANCHORED TO WALL WITH EXPANDING SHANK FASTENERS

CLOSED CELL ELASTOMERIC TAPE TO SPAN OVER IRREGULARITIES IN WALL

SEAL TOP OF MEMBRANE FLASHING WITH ROOFER'S CEMENT AND GLASS FELT

REMOVABLE COUNTERFLASHING

REINFORCED CONCRETE WALL

10.20 *Surface-mounted counterflashing for a water-resistant wall. This detail should be used if the roof is supported by the wall. If the wall does not support the roof, modify this detail as per Figure 10.15, so that the roof and wall can move independently.*

10.4 CURB FLASHING

A typical curb flashing detail is shown in Figure 10.21. It consists of a rectangular frame made of of galvanized steel channel sections supported on treated wood nailers, Figure 10.22. The height of the curb must be a minimum of 8 in. The flashing and counterflashing components are similar to those used in base flashing at a parapet wall. If the weight of the equipment supported by the curbs is light, wood curbs (typically treated 2 x 12 solid wood) may be used instead of steel channel sections.

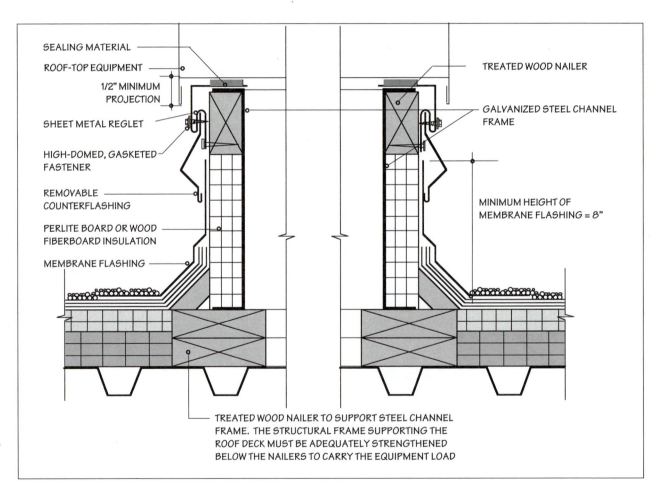

SEALING MATERIAL

ROOF-TOP EQUIPMENT

1/2" MINIMUM PROJECTION

SHEET METAL REGLET

HIGH-DOMED, GASKETED FASTENER

REMOVABLE COUNTERFLASHING

PERLITE BOARD OR WOOD FIBERBOARD INSULATION

MEMBRANE FLASHING

TREATED WOOD NAILER

GALVANIZED STEEL CHANNEL FRAME

MINIMUM HEIGHT OF MEMBRANE FLASHING = 8"

TREATED WOOD NAILER TO SUPPORT STEEL CHANNEL FRAME. THE STRUCTURAL FRAME SUPPORTING THE ROOF DECK MUST BE ADEQUATELY STRENGTHENED BELOW THE NAILERS TO CARRY THE EQUIPMENT LOAD

10.21 *Detail of curb flashing for roof-top equipment.*

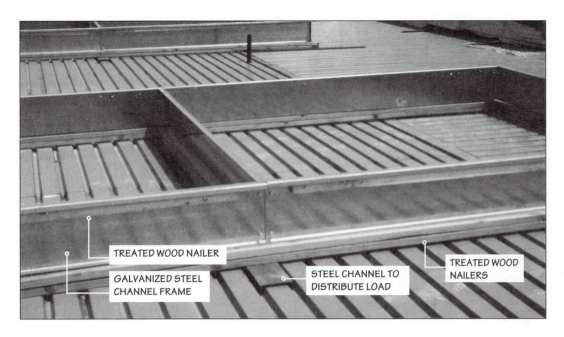

TREATED WOOD NAILER

GALVANIZED STEEL CHANNEL FRAME

STEEL CHANNEL TO DISTRIBUTE LOAD

TREATED WOOD NAILERS

10.22 *Galvanized steel channel frame to support roof-top equipment. The roof deck inside the frame will be cut where required and the uncut parts insulated. Photo by Madan Mehta.*

10.5 FLANGE FLASHING AT ROOF FASCIA

A typical detail of a roof edge that terminates in a metal fascia is shown in Figure 10.23. The commonly used metals for the fascia are aluminum, copper, stainless steel, and galvanized steel. The horizontal flange of the fascia is installed over the the roof membrane and then covered over by membrane flashing. Thus, the metal flange is sandwiched between membrane flashing and the roof membrane, integrating the metal with the roof membrane.

Since the coefficient of thermal expansion of the metal is much higher than that of the roof membrane, a perfect seal between the membrane and the metal is difficult to obtain. Hence, the elevation of the flange of the fascia should be higher than the expected water level on the roof.

In the case of a gravel-covered built-up roof, the raised fascia also functions as a gravel guard — as a barrier to prevent loose aggregate from falling off the roof.

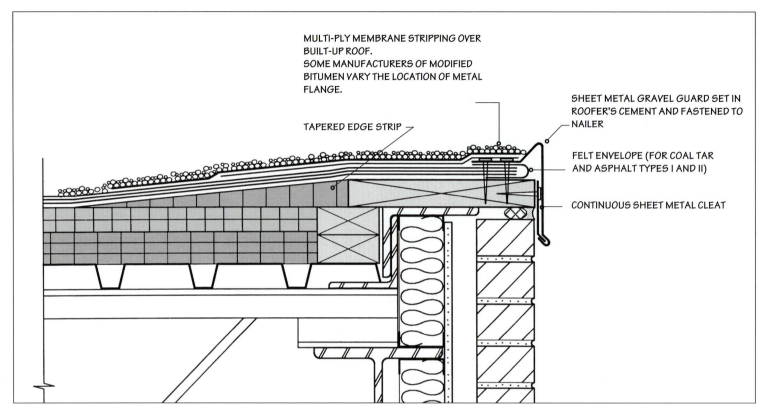

MULTI-PLY MEMBRANE STRIPPING OVER
BUILT-UP ROOF.
SOME MANUFACTURERS OF MODIFIED
BITUMEN VARY THE LOCATION OF METAL
FLANGE.

SHEET METAL GRAVEL GUARD SET IN
ROOFER'S CEMENT AND FASTENED TO
NAILER

TAPERED EDGE STRIP

FELT ENVELOPE (FOR COAL TAR
AND ASPHALT TYPES I AND II)

CONTINUOUS SHEET METAL CLEAT

10.23 *Flange flashing around a gravel guard roof fascia.*

10.5.1 Stripping Plies

If the roof consists of a built-up or a modified bitumen membrane, the metal fascia is nailed to the edge nailer. The flashing that covers the flange of the fascia is referred to as *stripping plies*. Stripping plies consist of a minimum of two plies of built-up roof felts laid in hot bitumen (or with flashing cement). One or two sheets of smooth-surfaced, modified-bitumen sheets may also be used as stripping plies instead of built-up roof felts.

In the case of a single-ply roof membrane, stripping plies are not used, but the metal edge is integrated with the roof membrane by adhering another layer of single-ply membrane flashing over the metal edge, Figure 10.24.

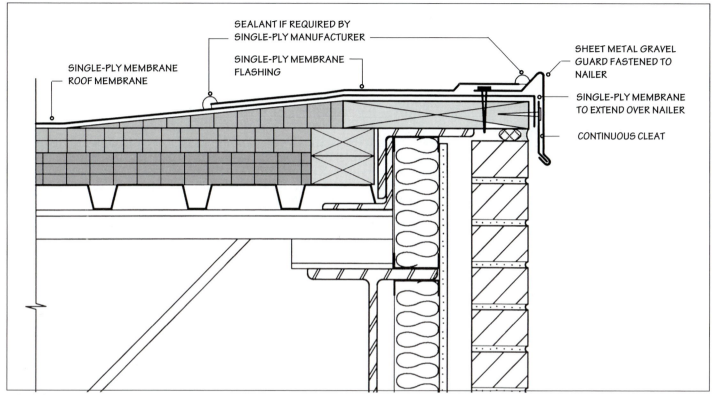

SEALANT IF REQUIRED BY
SINGLE-PLY MANUFACTURER

SINGLE-PLY MEMBRANE
FLASHING

SINGLE-PLY MEMBRANE
ROOF MEMBRANE

SHEET METAL GRAVEL
GUARD FASTENED TO
NAILER

SINGLE-PLY MEMBRANE
TO EXTEND OVER NAILER

CONTINUOUS CLEAT

10.24 *A typical roof edge fascia with a single-ply roof membrane. Manufacturer's detail should be used if it is different from this detail.*

10.5.2 Felt Envelope

Because of the low softening point temperature of coal tar, a felt envelope is required at the edge of a coal tar built-up roof membrane. A felt envelope contains the tar within itself, preventing its drippage at the edge. A felt envelope consists of an impervious felt such as a base sheet, laid at the edge of the roof prior to installing the built-up roof membrane. This sheet extends beyond the edge and is folded over the membrane.

   Perforated built-up roof glass fiber felts should not be used as a felt envelope. A felt envelope is also required if the built-up roof felts are mopped with Type I or Type II asphalt.

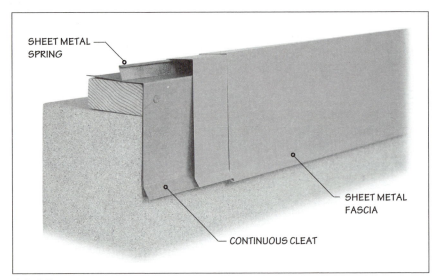

SHEET METAL
SPRING

SHEET METAL
FASCIA

CONTINUOUS CLEAT

10.25 *Prefabricated sheet metal fascia. Photo courtesy of MM Systems Corporation, Tucker, Georgia.*

10.5.3 Prefabricated Fascias

Like prefabricated copings, prefabricated sheet metal fascias are also available, which by virtue of their snap-lock design require either little or no external fastening, Figure 10.25.

10.5.4 Advantage of a Parapet Wall

Although a gravel guard fascia is commonly used over roofs, life safety considerations suggest that a raised parapet, instead of a fascia, should be designed. Several accidents have occurred during roofing or reroofing operations with roofs that do not have a parapet. A parapet, 3 ft or higher, also reduces the wind uplift in addition to providing a safer roof.

10.6 FLASHING AROUND PLUMBING AND EQUIPMENT SUPPORT PIPES

Flange-type flashing is also required around roof openings, such as roof drains, vent stacks, and equipment support stands. Roof drain flashing has been covered in Chapter 6. Two alternative details of vent stack flashing are shown in Figures 10.26 and 10.27. To ensure proper flashing around a vent stack, there must be adequate free space around it. In other words, a vent stack should be at least 12 in. away from a parapet wall, a curb, or another stack.

The details for a typical equipment stand are shown in Figure 10.28. As with a vent stack, adequate (minimum 12 in.) clearance must be provided around an equipment support pipe for good flashing.

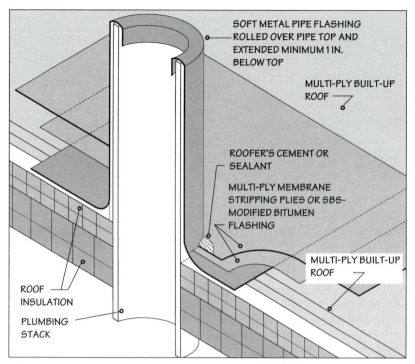

10.26 *Flashing around a plumbing or a vent stack on a built-up roof.*

Labels in 10.26:
SOFT METAL PIPE FLASHING ROLLED OVER PIPE TOP AND EXTENDED MINIMUM 1 IN. BELOW TOP

MULTI-PLY BUILT-UP ROOF

ROOFER'S CEMENT OR SEALANT

MULTI-PLY MEMBRANE STRIPPING PLIES OR SBS-MODIFIED BITUMEN FLASHING

MULTI-PLY BUILT-UP ROOF

ROOF INSULATION

PLUMBING STACK

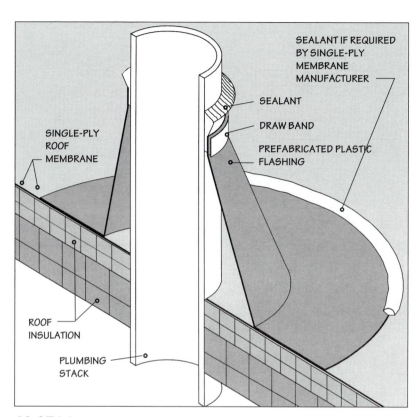

10.27(a) *Flashing around a plumbing or a vent stack on a single-ply roof.*

Labels in 10.27(a):
SEALANT IF REQUIRED BY SINGLE-PLY MEMBRANE MANUFACTURER

SEALANT

DRAW BAND

PREFABRICATED PLASTIC FLASHING

SINGLE-PLY ROOF MEMBRANE

ROOF INSULATION

PLUMBING STACK

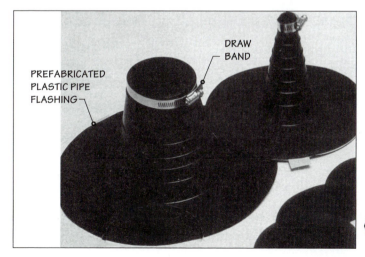

Labels in 10.27(b):
DRAW BAND

PREFABRICATED PLASTIC PIPE FLASHING

10.27(b) *Prefabricated plastic flashing. Photo by Madan Mehta.*

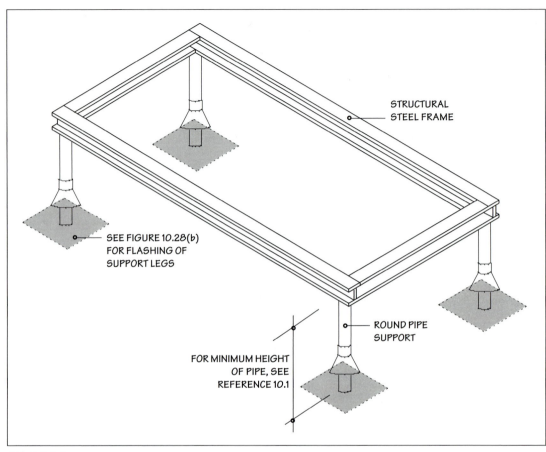

STRUCTURAL
STEEL FRAME

SEE FIGURE 10.28(b)
FOR FLASHING OF
SUPPORT LEGS

ROUND PIPE
SUPPORT

FOR MINIMUM HEIGHT
OF PIPE, SEE
REFERENCE 10.1

10.28(a) *Equipment support stand.*

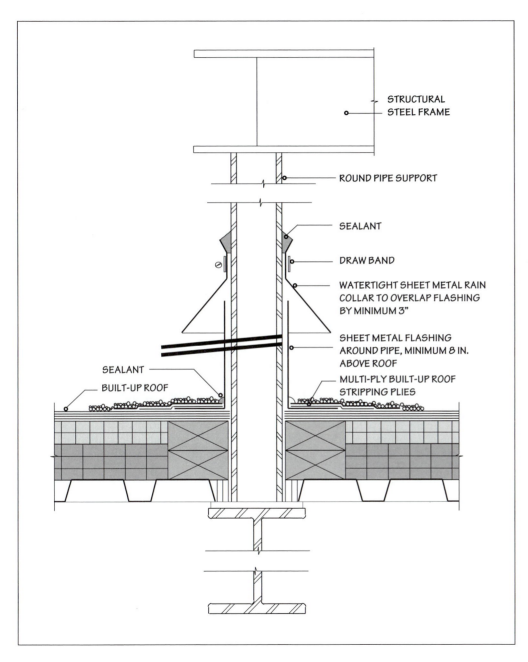

STRUCTURAL STEEL FRAME

ROUND PIPE SUPPORT

SEALANT

DRAW BAND

WATERTIGHT SHEET METAL RAIN COLLAR TO OVERLAP FLASHING BY MINIMUM 3"

SHEET METAL FLASHING AROUND PIPE, MINIMUM 8 IN. ABOVE ROOF

MULTI-PLY BUILT-UP ROOF STRIPPING PLIES

SEALANT

BUILT-UP ROOF

10.28(b)   *Flashing around equipment support stand pipe.*

10.7 VAPOR PRESSURE RELIEF VENTS

In Section 4.9 in Chapter 4, we mentioned the need for vapor pressure relief vents where lightweight insulating concrete is used over a reinforced concrete deck or an unslotted steel deck. A vapor pressure relief vent is made of plastic or aluminum, Figure 10.29. Its purpose is to relieve any build-up of vapor pressure that is generated by the residual water in lightweight insulating concrete turning into water vapor under the effect of the sun's heat.

A vapor pressure relief vent, which is typically 6 in. high, is placed over a hole cut in the base sheet and adhered to it with hot bitumen or roofer's cement. The hole is slightly smaller than the diameter of the vent chamber so that the flange of the vent sits on the uncut part of the base sheet. The water vapor under the base sheet is able to enter the vent chamber, from where it is exhausted to the outside, Figure 10.30.

The vent is designed to allow a one-way exit of water vapor. This is achieved by the diaphragm opening up if the vapor pressure under the base sheet is higher than the outside atmospheric vapor pressure. In the reverse case, i.e., when the atmospheric vapor pressure is higher than the vapor pressure under the base sheet, the diaphragm will close. Vapor pressure relief vents are generally placed on the roof every 1,000 ft^2 of roof area.

10.7.1 Disadvantage of Vapor Pressure Relief Vents

The use of vapor pressure relief vents does have some disadvantages. Because of their relatively close spacing (one every 1,000 ft^2), they can cause roof leakage, particularly if they are not carefully flashed around. Therefore, a prudent design should avoid their use. This implies that lightweight insulating concrete should be used only over decks that allow below-deck venting. Such decks are slotted steel decks and precast concrete decks in which the joints between decks are detailed to allow such ventilation. Lightweight insulating concrete should be avoided over a structural concrete deck, since below-deck venting is not possible with such a deck.

10.29   *A typical vapor pressure relief vent.   Photo by Madan Mehta.*

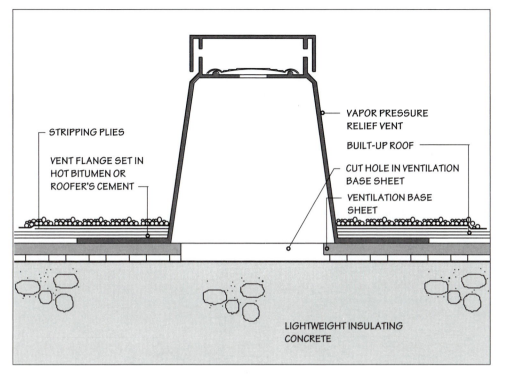

STRIPPING PLIES

VENT FLANGE SET IN
HOT BITUMEN OR
ROOFER'S CEMENT

VAPOR PRESSURE
RELIEF VENT

BUILT-UP ROOF

CUT HOLE IN VENTILATION
BASE SHEET

VENTILATION BASE
SHEET

LIGHTWEIGHT INSULATING
CONCRETE

10.30 *Pressure relief vent over a lightweight insulating concrete deck.*

Wind uplift resistance considerations also apply to gravel stop fascias and parapet copings. Most roof blow-offs commence with failures of fascias or parapet copings. Failure of these elements opens the edges of the membrane flashing to peeling, leading to the peeling of the roof membrane. Therefore, the fascias and copings must be able to resist the applied wind loads.

The key to wind-resistant fascias and coping details is proper anchorage (fastener size and spacing) and thickness of sheet metal components. Generally, a cleat should be one or two gauge thicker than a fascia or coping. Factory Mutual's publication[10.3] and the ANSI/SPRI publication[10.4] give recommendations for wind-resistant design of fascias and copings.

10.8 WIND UPLIFT RESISTANCE OF FASCIAS AND PARAPET COPINGS

REFERENCES

10.1 National Roofing Contractors Association. *NRCA Roofing and Waterproofing Manual* (Rosemont, IL: 1996).

10.2 Sheet Metal and Air Conditioning Contractors National Association, Inc. *Architectural Sheet Metal Manual* (Chantilly, VA: 1993).

10.3 Factory Mutual Research Corporation. *Perimeter Flashing, 1-49* (Norwood, MA: 1996).

10.4 American National Standard Institute. "American National Standard Wind Design Standard for Edge Systems Used With Low Slope Roofing Systems," ANSI/SPRI Publication ES 1-98 (1998).

11 STEEP ROOFING — Asphalt Shingle Roof

As stated in Section 1.2 in Chapter 1, asphalt shingles (also referred to as *asphalt composition shingles*) are the most commonly used roofing material for steep roofs in the United States. They are easy to transport from the factory to the roofing site and easy to install. Although there are a few performance issues, such as premature cracking, long-term wind resistance, and durability, asphalt shingles are relatively trouble free.

Asphalt shingles have been available in the United States since 1914 when F. C. Overbury of the Flintcote Company patented the design. The early asphalt shingles consisted of an organic felt coated with asphalt and covered with crushed slate granules. In the 1970s, manufacturers began to replace the organic felt with fiberglass felt, which is more fire-resistant and also more dimensionally stable since a fiberglass felt does not absorb moisture. Additionally, a fiberglass felt is more resistant to mold and mildew.

This chapter begins with a description of various types of asphalt shingles, followed by the requirements for the roof deck and the underlayment below the shingles. Subsequently the details of shingle installation, flashing around penetrations, and projections through the roof are discussed.

11.1 SHINGLES, DECK, AND UNDERLAYMENT

11.1 *Asphalt shingles with color variations in its granule surface that gives shadow lines to mimic wood or slate roofing. Photo by Madan Mehta.*

Asphalt shingles are manufactured in strips measuring nearly 12 in. x 36 in. with up to five cut-outs. The cut-outs separate a shingle strip into tabs making the strip seem composed of several smaller shingles, which improves the shingle's appearance. Strip shingles (as they are sometimes called) vary in weight from about 200 lb to nearly 400 lb per roof square. The heavier varieties, which consist of two or more layers of shingles laminated together, are generally more durable and aesthetically more pleasant.

Each shingle strip is made from a fiberglass mat, which is coated with asphalt and surfaced with ceramic-coated mineral granules. The granules give the desired surface color to a shingle, which may vary from white, gray, and black to various shades of red, brown, and green. Color combinations on a shingle strip can further enhance the aesthetics of the roof.[1] Shingles with shadow lines are available, which attempt to mimic a wood shingle or a slate roof, Figure 11.1.

Because of the fiberglass mat and the granule surfacing, fire-rated shingles of up to Class A (as per ASTM Standard E 108 or UL 790, see Section 7.3 in Chapter 7) are available. They are delivered to the construction site in bundles. Several bundles are packed together in pallets, Figure 11.2.

The three most commonly used asphalt shingle profiles are shown in Figure 11.3. Each shingle is coated with a line of self-sealing adhesive, which helps to adhere that shingle with the overlying shingle. The adhesion is activated by the sun's heat after the shingles have been installed on the roof. The adhesive line increases the wind resistance of shingles.

Out of the three self-sealing shingle varieties shown in Figure 11.3, the three-tab shingle is the most commonly specified. In addition to self-sealing varieties, a T-shaped interlocking shingle is also specified. The interlocking shingles can provide higher resistance to wind uplift than the self-sealing shingles.

11.1.1 Asphalt Shingles and Roof Deck

The deck under asphalt shingles generally consists of plywood or oriented strandboard (OSB) panels. Tongue-and-groove wood planks and cement fiber decks may also be used, but their use is relatively rare in contemporary construction.

The requirements of a plywood or an OSB deck for a steep roof are essentially the same as those for a low-slope roof (see Section 5.4 in Chapter 5). In other words, each plywood or OSB panel must have a 1/8-in. gap at panel joints, and the joints should be staggered as indicated in Figure 11.4. Additionally, the panels must have the appropriate structural span rating and durability classification. They must be securely fastened to rafters and provided with clips or blocking at unsupported edges.

---

[1] The more uniform the color and texture of shingles, the more visible the irregularities in the deck or shingles.

11.2 *Asphalt shingles at a roofing site. Photos by Madan Mehta.*

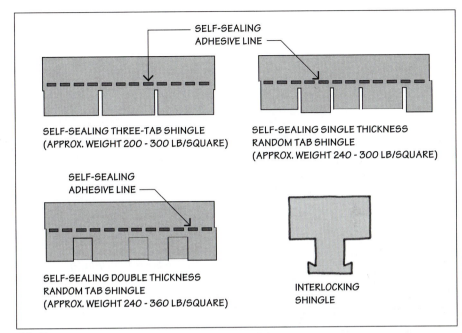

SELF-SEALING THREE-TAB SHINGLE
(APPROX. WEIGHT 200 - 300 LB/SQUARE)

SELF-SEALING SINGLE THICKNESS
RANDOM TAB SHINGLE
(APPROX. WEIGHT 240 - 300 LB/SQUARE)

SELF-SEALING DOUBLE THICKNESS
RANDOM TAB SHINGLE
(APPROX. WEIGHT 240 - 360 LB/SQUARE)

INTERLOCKING
SHINGLE

11.3 *Commonly used asphalt shingle profiles.*

11.4 *Plywood or OSB deck under asphalt shingles. See also Figures 5.22 and 5.23 in Chapter 5.*

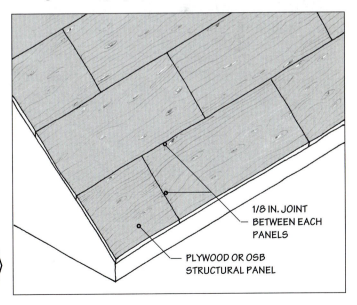

1/8 IN. JOINT
BETWEEN EACH
PANELS

PLYWOOD OR OSB
STRUCTURAL PANEL

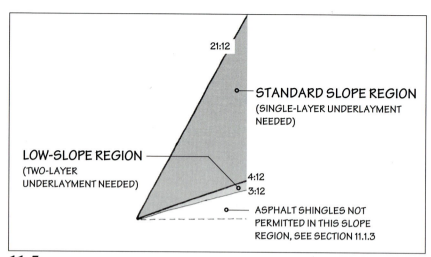

11.5 *Slope and underlayment requirements for asphalt shingle roofs.*

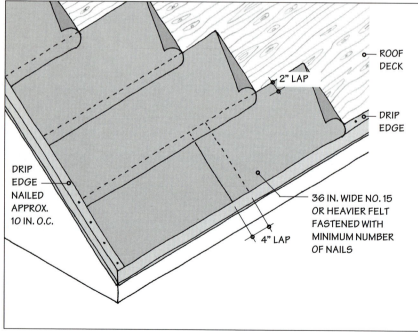

11.6 *Underlayment layout on a standard slope roof deck.*

11.1.2 Underlayment and Ice Dam Protection Membrane on a Standard Slope Roof

The recommended roof slope for asphalt shingles is between 4:12 and 21:12. This is referred to as the *standard slope* for asphalt shingles, since a slope other than the standard slope may also be used, as shown in Figure 11.5.

Regardless of roof slope, an asphalt shingle roof requires a water-resistant sheet placed between the shingles and the deck — called an *underlayment*. The purpose of the underlayment is to keep the deck dry until the shingles are installed. Additionally, the underlayment provides a second line of defense against water penetration in case the shingles are lifted due to wind, allowing the wind-driven rain to find its way under the shingles.

The recommended underlayment is a No. 15 or a heavier (say, No. 30) nonperforated, asphalt-saturated (generally organic) felt, which is typically manufactured in 36-in. wide rolls. The underlayment is applied with 2-in. laps at the edges of the roll and 4-in. laps at the ends of the roll, Figure 11.6. It is nailed to the deck with a minimum number of nails — enough to hold it in place until the shingles are installed. It is essential that the underlayment is turned up the abutting walls or curbs (see Figures 11.30 and 11.31).

The freezing and thawing of snow on a roof can lead to the formation of ice dams, water buildup at the eaves, and consequent roof leakage. In locations where there is such a possibility, an ice dam protection membrane (also referred to as *eave flashing*) is required. Typically, if the average daily temperature in January at a location is ≤ 30°F (- 1°C), the use of an ice dam protection membrane is recommended,[11.1] Figure 11.7.

An ice dam protection membrane on a standard slope roof is typically provided by a proprietary ice dam protection membrane, which is generally a self-adhering modified bitumen sheet, Figure 11.8. It must extend a distance of at least 24 in. from the exterior wall into the interior of the building.

11.1.3 Underlayment and Ice Dam Protection Membrane on a Low-Slope Roof

Asphalt shingles may be used on a low-slope roof (defined as a slope lying between 3:12 and 4:12), but generally the roof's performance is not as good as that on a standard slope. Note, however, that some asphalt shingle manufacturers permit the use of their product on a slope as low as 2:12. The underlayment on a low-slope roof must be a two-layer felt underlayment, applied in shingle fashion (see Section 2.3 in Chapter 2). Thus, each 36-in.-wide felt roll has a 19-in. lap and 17-in. exposure, Figure 11.9.

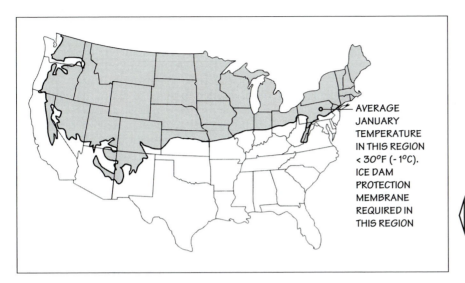

11.7 *Approximate areas of the United States where an ice dam protection membrane is recommended (Reference 11.1).*

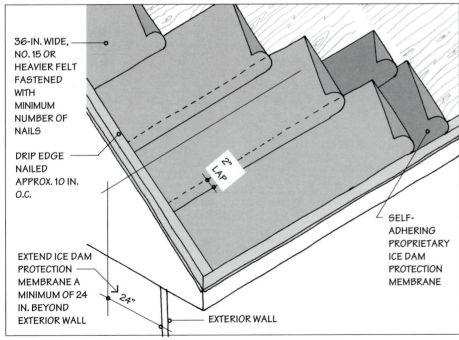

11.8 *Ice dam protection membrane on a standard slope roof deck.*

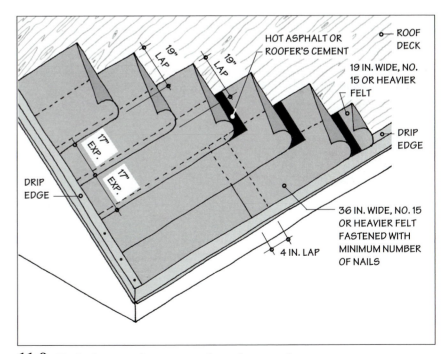

11.9 *Underlayment layout on a low-slope roof.*

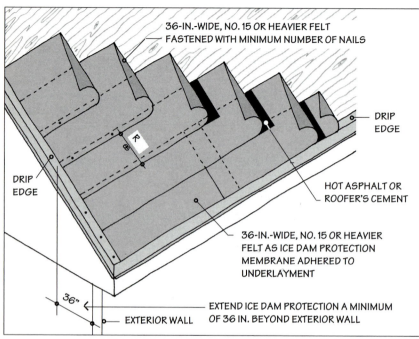

36-IN.-WIDE, NO. 15 OR HEAVIER FELT FASTENED WITH MINIMUM NUMBER OF NAILS

DRIP EDGE

DRIP EDGE

HOT ASPHALT OR ROOFER'S CEMENT

36-IN.-WIDE, NO. 15 OR HEAVIER FELT AS ICE DAM PROTECTION MEMBRANE ADHERED TO UNDERLAYMENT

36"

EXTERIOR WALL

EXTEND ICE DAM PROTECTION A MINIMUM OF 36 IN. BEYOND EXTERIOR WALL

11.10 *Ice dam protection membrane on a low-slope roof.*

An ice dam protection membrane is required at the eaves if there is a possibility of the formation of ice dams. An ice dam protection membrane is provided by cementing (with hot asphalt or roofer's cement) the underlayment layers up to a distance of at least 36 in. from the external wall into the interior of the building, Figure 11.10. Note that the first 19-in.-wide starter strip of underlayment is not cemented but simply nailed in place to avoid the contact of roofer's cement with wood.

As an alternative to Figure 11.10, a proprietary ice dam protection membrane may be applied directly to the deck, which should extend at least 36 in. into the interior of the building, Figure 11.11.

11.1.4 Roof Slope Steeper than 21:12

Asphalt shingles should not be used on a roof slope steeper than 21:12 without conforming to special fastening requirements. There have been numerous problems with asphalt shingles used on such slopes. The self-sealing properties of shingles is reduced on a steep slope due to their tendency to slip downward, necessitating the use of manual sealing (see Section 11.2.1).

11.11 *Ice dam protection membrane on a low-slope roof — an alternative to Figure 11.10.*

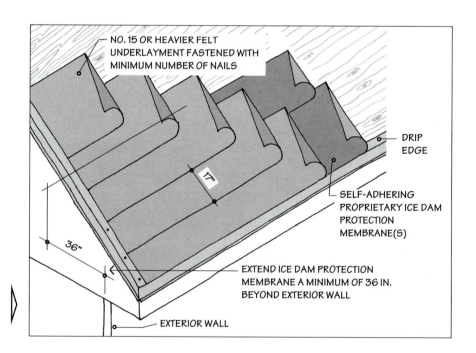

NO. 15 OR HEAVIER FELT UNDERLAYMENT FASTENED WITH MINIMUM NUMBER OF NAILS

DRIP EDGE

SELF-ADHERING PROPRIETARY ICE DAM PROTECTION MEMBRANE(S)

17"

36"

EXTEND ICE DAM PROTECTION MEMBRANE A MINIMUM OF 36 IN. BEYOND EXTERIOR WALL

EXTERIOR WALL

There have also been problems with heavier shingles pulling through the fasteners on steep slopes. Some manufacturers do not recommend the use of their shingles on extremely steep slopes, and it is important to check the slope limitation of the product being used. Additionally, most manufacturers' warranties against wind uplift resistance of their shingles are void for steep slopes.

11.1.5 Perimeter Flashing at Eave and Rake — The Drip Edge

A sheet metal drip edge should be provided at all eaves and rakes and mechanically fastened to the deck at nearly 10 in. on center. Galvanized steel or prefinished metal (minimum 28 gauge) is the most commonly used metal for a drip edge, but stainless steel, copper, or aluminum may also be used for higher durability. On an eave, the drip edge is applied before laying the underlayment. On a rake, on the other hand, it is applied over the underlayment, Figure 11.12.

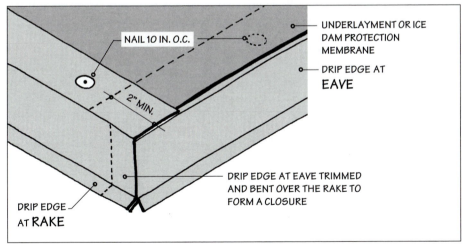

11.12 *Drip edge installation details.*

11.2 INSTALLATION OF SHINGLES

After the underlayment (and ice dam protection membrane, if needed) has been installed, the roof is ready to receive the shingles. The procedure to install various types of shingles (shown in Figure 11.3) is almost identical. Because the three-tab shingles are most commonly used, the installation procedure described below refers to their installation.

The installation of a three-tab shingle begins with the starter course at the eave, which is applied directly over the underlayment or the ice dam protection membrane. A starter course consists of the standard three-tab shingles, whose tabs have been cut off, Figure 11.13(a). The remaining part of each shingle, which is nearly 7 in. wide, is nailed to the deck with the self-sealing adhesive line placed along the outside edge of the eave, Figure 11.13(b).

The self-sealing adhesive line of the starter course bonds with the overlying shingles (of the first course), providing a better wind performance to the roof. The starter course is laid from one end of the roof to the other. The first shingle in the starter course is cut by 3 in., so that the joints in the starter course are offset from the joints in the first course of shingles.

Next the first course of shingles is laid. The first course of shingles fully covers the starter course, and each shingle is a full-length shingle. The second course of shingles is laid so that only the tabs of the first course are exposed. However, the first shingle of the second course is cut in its length by one-half tab (nearly 6 in.). This cut breaks the joints in the upper and lower course of shingles, Figure 11.14.

The first shingle of the third course is cut by one full tab — nearly 12 in. The first shingle of the fourth course is cut by one-and-half tabs, and so on, Figure 11.15. The first shingle in the seventh course, in the thirteenth course, etc., is a full-length shingle, identical to the first course

The pattern of shingles generated by this half-tab offset procedure is referred to as the *6-in. offset method*, since the shingles are offset by one-half tab (6 in.). The layout pattern generated by the 6-in. offset method in the field of the roof is shown in Figure 11.16(a).

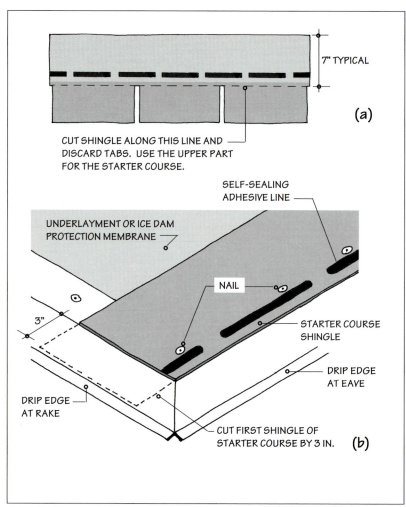

7" TYPICAL

(a)

CUT SHINGLE ALONG THIS LINE AND DISCARD TABS. USE THE UPPER PART FOR THE STARTER COURSE.

SELF-SEALING ADHESIVE LINE

UNDERLAYMENT OR ICE DAM PROTECTION MEMBRANE

NAIL

3"

STARTER COURSE SHINGLE

DRIP EDGE AT EAVE

DRIP EDGE AT RAKE

CUT FIRST SHINGLE OF STARTER COURSE BY 3 IN.   (b)

11.13 *Starter course installation details.*

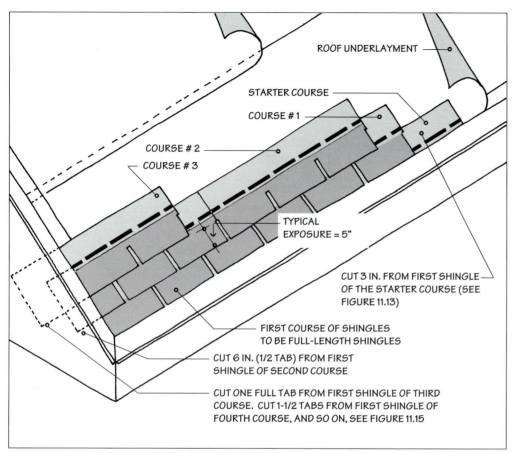

ROOF UNDERLAYMENT

STARTER COURSE

COURSE # 1

COURSE # 2

COURSE # 3

TYPICAL
EXPOSURE = 5"

CUT 3 IN. FROM FIRST SHINGLE
OF THE STARTER COURSE (SEE
FIGURE 11.13)

FIRST COURSE OF SHINGLES
TO BE FULL-LENGTH SHINGLES

CUT 6 IN. (1/2 TAB) FROM FIRST
SHINGLE OF SECOND COURSE

CUT ONE FULL TAB FROM FIRST SHINGLE OF THIRD
COURSE. CUT 1-1/2 TABS FROM FIRST SHINGLE OF
FOURTH COURSE, AND SO ON, SEE FIGURE 11.15

11.14 *Layout of starter course and the first few courses of shingles according to the 6-in. offset method*

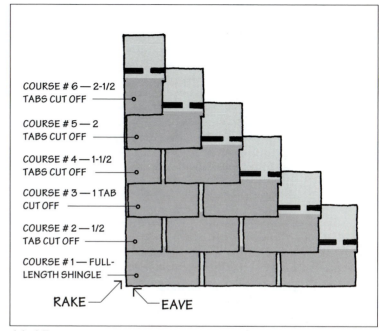

COURSE # 6 — 2-1/2
TABS CUT OFF

COURSE # 5 — 2
TABS CUT OFF

COURSE # 4 — 1-1/2
TABS CUT OFF

COURSE # 3 — 1 TAB
CUT OFF

COURSE # 2 — 1/2
TAB CUT OFF

COURSE # 1 — FULL-
LENGTH SHINGLE

RAKE

EAVE

11.15 *Cut-offs in the first shingle of various courses at the rake according to the 6-in. offset method. Note that course # 1, course # 7, and course # 13 are identical, i.e., they use full-length shingles.*

11.16(a) *The appearance of shingles in the field of the roof when laid according to the 6-in. offset method.*

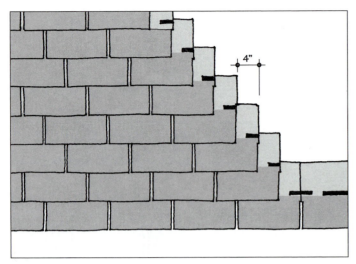

11.16(b) *The appearance of shingles when laid according to the 4-in. offset method.*

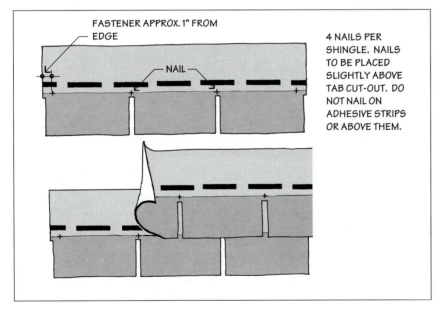

11.18 *Standard fastening pattern of asphalt shingles.*

In addition to the 6-in. offset method, the *3-in. offset method*, *4-in. offset method* and *5-in. offset method* are also used. The shingle layout generated by the 4-in. offset method is shown in Figure 11.16(b).

To improve the performance of the roof, it is desirable (though not mandatory) to include a course of bleeder strips at the rake. A bleeder strip is similar to the starter course at the eave and is applied with self-adhesive lines nearest the rake, Figure 11.17.

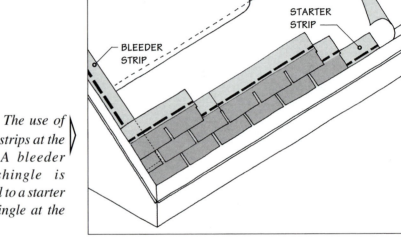

11.17 *The use of bleeder strips at the rake. A bleeder strip shingle is identical to a starter strip shingle at the eave.*

11.2.1 Fasteners for Shingles

Asphalt shingles are fastened to the deck with 11- or 12-gauge galvanized steel roofing nails with 3/8-in. to 7/16-in. diameter nail heads. The nail shanks are barbed to increase their pullout resistance. They should be long enough to penetrate at least 3/4 in. into the plywood, OSB, or solid wood plank deck. Nails may be driven manually or pneumatically. Each shingle strip (nearly 36 in. long) requires a minimum of four nails, placed, as shown in Figure 11.18.

In high wind regions, six nails per shingle strip are needed. In addition to the nails, two daubs of roofer's cement per shingle are manually applied, as shown in Figure 11.19. This fastening pattern is also required for a roof with a slope ≥ 18:12 and on a mansard roof.

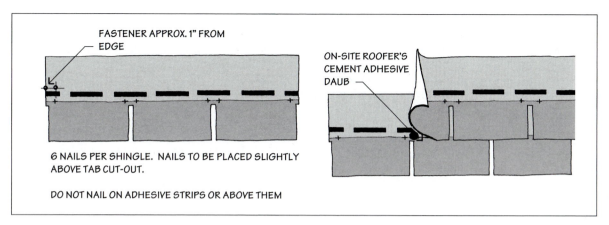

FASTENER APPROX. 1" FROM EDGE

6 NAILS PER SHINGLE. NAILS TO BE PLACED SLIGHTLY ABOVE TAB CUT-OUT.

DO NOT NAIL ON ADHESIVE STRIPS OR ABOVE THEM

ON-SITE ROOFER'S CEMENT ADHESIVE DAUB

11.19 *Fastening pattern of asphalt shingles for high wind regions and on roofs with slope ≥ 18:12.*

A valley occurs where two pitched roofs meet. Because the water from both roofs runs off through the valley, a valley is more prone to leakage than the rest of the roof. The greater vulnerability of the valley is also due to its lower slope compared to the rest of the roof. Therefore, the treatment of a valley is relatively more complex than the rest of the roof. In asphalt shingle roofs, we recognize three types of valley treatments:

- Open valley
- Woven valley (also called closed valley)
- Closed-cut valley

Regardless of the type of valley, each valley requires an underlayment and flashing. Although the flashing material varies with the valley type, the underlayment requirement for each valley is the same. A valley underlayment consists of a full-width (36-in.-wide) roll of No. 15 or heavier, asphalt-saturated, nonperforated (generally organic) felt with the center of the roll laid on the centerline of the valley, Figure 11.20.

The valley underlayment is secured with a minimum number of nails, just as the underlayment on the field of the roof. The underlayment from the field of the roof is cut so that it overlaps the valley underlayment by a minimum of 6 in. Some roofers and designers prefer the use of a self-adhering ice dam protection membrane as the valley underlayment.

11.3 VALLEY TREATMENT

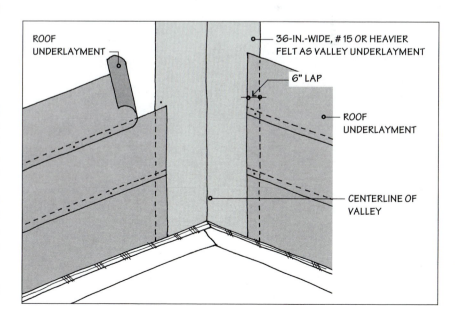

ROOF UNDERLAYMENT

36-IN.-WIDE, # 15 OR HEAVIER FELT AS VALLEY UNDERLAYMENT

6" LAP

ROOF UNDERLAYMENT

CENTERLINE OF VALLEY

11.20 *Valley underlayment.*

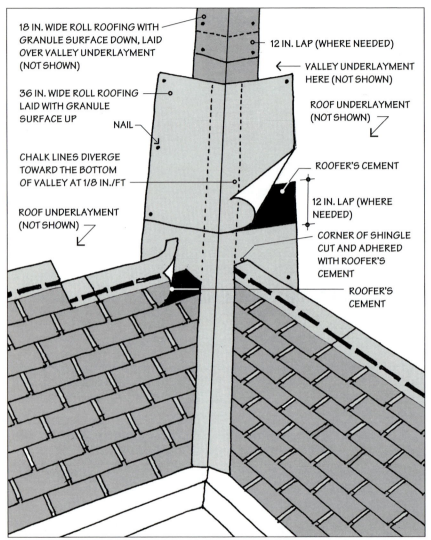

18 IN. WIDE ROLL ROOFING WITH GRANULE SURFACE DOWN, LAID OVER VALLEY UNDERLAYMENT (NOT SHOWN)

36 IN. WIDE ROLL ROOFING LAID WITH GRANULE SURFACE UP

NAIL

CHALK LINES DIVERGE TOWARD THE BOTTOM OF VALLEY AT 1/8 IN./FT

ROOF UNDERLAYMENT (NOT SHOWN)

12 IN. LAP (WHERE NEEDED)

VALLEY UNDERLAYMENT HERE (NOT SHOWN)

ROOF UNDERLAYMENT (NOT SHOWN)

ROOFER'S CEMENT

12 IN. LAP (WHERE NEEDED)

CORNER OF SHINGLE CUT AND ADHERED WITH ROOFER'S CEMENT

ROOFER'S CEMENT

11.21 *Open valley with roll roofing material used as valley flashing.*

11.3.1 Open Valley with Flashing Consisting of Roll Roofing Material

In an open valley, the shingles are held away from the centerline of the valley so that the valley flashing is exposed to view. An open valley provides a relatively smooth and more rapid discharge of water. It may have some benefit over other valley treatments where leaves, twigs, and other foliage material may accumulate on the roof from nearby trees.

The flashing in an open valley may consist of either a roll roofing material or a sheet metal. The construction of an open valley using roll roofing material as valley flashing is shown in Figure 11.21. A roll roofing material is an asphalt-saturated, fiberglass felt whose one surface is smooth and the other surface is covered with mineral granules. It is generally manufactured in 36-in.-wide rolls and weighs nearly 80 lb per roof square.

Roll roofing valley flashing consists of two layers of felt. The first layer, which is laid immediately over the valley underlayment, is an 18-in.-wide roll roofing felt with granule surface facing down. The second layer consists of the same material as the first layer, but it is 36-in. wide. It is laid over the first layer with the mineral granule surface facing up.

In the case of a long valley, which may necessitate overlapping of roll roofing felts, the overlap must be a minimum of 12 in. and treated with roofer's cement. Both layers of roll roofing are secured with a minimum number of nails placed nearly 1 in. from either felt's outer edges.

The width of the exposed part of the flashing should increase at the rate of 1/8 in. per ft toward the bottom of the valley. In practice, this is achieved by placing chalk lines over the valley flashing that converge upward. The minimum width of the exposed part of valley at the top is 6 in. Thus, if the valley is 24 ft long, the width of the exposed part of valley flashing at the bottom should be 9 in.

The shingles are trimmed along chalk lines. The upper corner of each shingle adjacent to the valley is cut and adhered with roofer's cement to prevent water entering under the shingles.

11.3.2 Open Valley with Sheet Metal Flashing

The construction of an open valley using sheet metal flashing is similar to roll roofing flashing. The sheet metal generally consists of a minimum of 24-gauge galvanized steel and must be at least 24-in. wide. It is placed over the valley underlayment, Figure 11.22(a). It is typically not nailed, but secured with special metal clips that allow the sheet metal to expand and contract, Figure 11.22(b). Sheet metal flashing should be used in lengths of no more than 12 ft to reduce their expansion and contraction.

The metal clips, which are located at 8 in. to 24 in. on center, grip the sheet metal flashing at one end. The other end of a clip is nailed to the deck and then folded over to cover the nails. This protects the shingles against damage by any backout of the nails.

While the fastening of metal flashing with clips is generally recommended, the clips can telegraph through a (lightweight) shingle roof, adversely affecting the roof's appearance and performance. In such a case, sheet metal flashing may be nailed at its outer edges. The outer edges may then be stripped in with a self-adhering ice dam protection membrane. An ice dam protection membrane as valley underlayment is also helpful. However, nailing sheet metal flashing can be problematic in regions with large daily or annual temperature variations. That is why an open valley sheet metal flashing is generally not recommended for such areas.

Sheet metal flashing should be profiled to form a W-shaped rib in the center. This reduces the crossover of water from one side of the roof to the other.

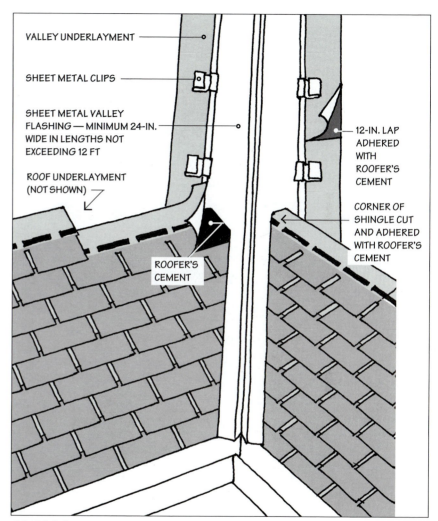

11.22(a) *Open valley with sheet metal used as valley flashing.*

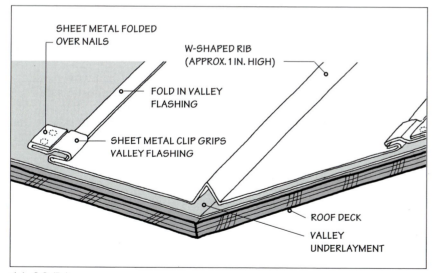

11.22(b) *Detail of the anchorage of sheet metal valley flashing to the deck.*

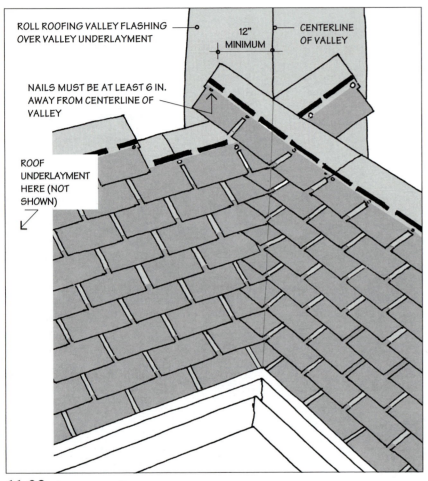

ROLL ROOFING VALLEY FLASHING OVER VALLEY UNDERLAYMENT

12" MINIMUM

CENTERLINE OF VALLEY

NAILS MUST BE AT LEAST 6 IN. AWAY FROM CENTERLINE OF VALLEY

ROOF UNDERLAYMENT HERE (NOT SHOWN)

11.23 *A woven valley.*

11.3.3 Woven Valley

In a woven valley, shingles from the two adjacent roofs weave into each other, covering the valley flashing, Figure 11.23. Because of the weaving of shingles, the thickness of roofing material in a woven valley is greater than in an open valley. Therefore, a woven valley is more durable. It can better withstand the traffic of roofers because they tend to walk in the valley, since the valley's slope is lower than the two adjoining areas of the roof. A woven valley, however, does not work well with heavier weight laminated shingles because these shingles do not bend as much.

The valley flashing in a woven valley consists of roll roofing material and is identical to that provided in an open valley. However, the 18-in.-wide roll roofing sheet shown in Figure 11.21 may be omitted, using only the 36-in.-wide sheet. Sheet metal valley flashing is not to be used in a woven valley.

Once the valley flashing has been installed, shingles are laid starting from the eave upward. The shingles must extend to the opposite side of the valley by at least 12 in.

11.3.4 Closed-Cut Valley

In a closed-cut valley, the shingles from one side of the valley are cut parallel to the line of the valley so that the valley is partially closed, Figure 11.24. A closed-cut valley combines the advantages and disadvantages of the other two valley types and is more commonly used. It is more resistant to roofers' traffic than an open valley, but less than that of a woven valley.

Valley flashing in a closed-cut valley is identical to that in a woven valley. The shingles from one side of the valley must extend to the opposite side by a minimum of 12 in., Figure 11.25. However, the shingles from the other side are trimmed parallel to the centerline of the valley, leaving an overlap of 2 in., as shown in Figure 11.24. To lay the shingles parallel to the valley line, a chalk line is drawn on the roof as a guide, Figure 11.26.

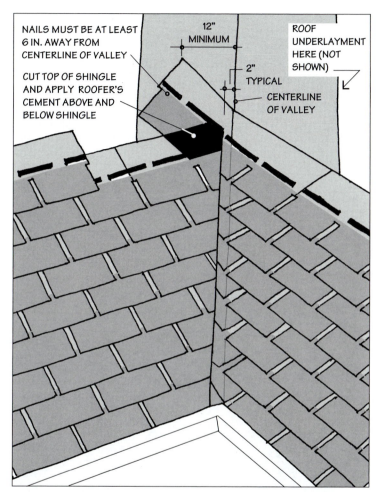

NAILS MUST BE AT LEAST
6 IN. AWAY FROM
CENTERLINE OF VALLEY

CUT TOP OF SHINGLE
AND APPLY ROOFER'S
CEMENT ABOVE AND
BELOW SHINGLE

12"
MINIMUM

2"
TYPICAL

CENTERLINE
OF VALLEY

ROOF
UNDERLAYMENT
HERE (NOT
SHOWN)

11.24 *Layout of shingles in a closed-cut valley.*

11.25 *Shingles being laid in a closed-cut valley. Photo by Madan Mehta.*

11.26 *Chalk line to locate the centerline of the valley. Photo by Madan Mehta.*

11.4 RIDGE AND HIP TREATMENT

Asphalt shingles from both sides of a ridge are butted against each other at the ridge, which is then capped with ridge shingles. Some manufacturers provide special ridge shingles, but these can also be prepared on site from the standard shingles. To do so, a shingle is field trimmed along dashed lines, Figure 11.27. The dashed lines taper slightly away from the cut-outs. The trimming converts a three-tab shingle in three (nearly 12 in. x 12 in.) shingles.

These (smaller) shingles are now bent and placed over the ridge as caps, using two nails per shingle, one on each side of the ridge. A 5-in. exposure is provided, Figure 11.28. In cold weather, the shingles may be warmed somewhat to increase their pliability, since fiberglass shingles are generally brittle. The shingles are applied starting from the end of the ridge that is opposite the prevailing wind direction.

The treatment of a hip is similar to that of a ridge. The hip is capped with the same shingles as a ridge, and the shingles are installed from the bottom of the hip to the top, Figure 11.29.

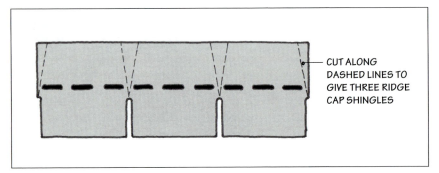

11.27 *Creating ridge (or hip) caps from a standard 3-tab shingle.*

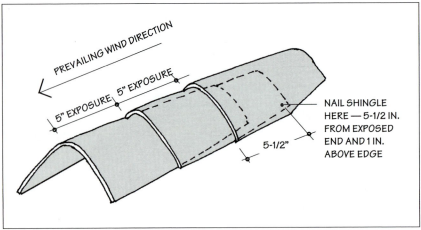

11.28 *Layout and nailing of ridge cap shingles.*

11.29 *Application of ridge and hip shingles. Photo by Madan Mehta.*

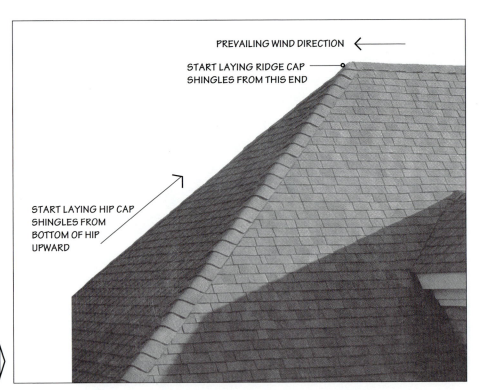

A sloping roof plane that abuts against a vertical side wall is flashed with metal shingles placed over the end of each asphalt shingle course — a flashing system referred to as *step flashing*. Metal shingles are made of galvanized or prepainted sheet steel with a minimum thickness of 24 gauge. Other metals may be used as long as they are compatible with, and have at least the same durability as, the roof shingles.

The profile of a metal shingle is an L-shape, each leg at least 5 in., so that the shingle extends 5 in. in both horizontal and vertical directions. The length of the shingle is 2 in. greater than the exposure of roof shingles. Thus, with the most commonly used three-tab roof shingles that have a 5-in. exposure, 7-in.-long metal shingles are commonly used. With its 7-in. length, and 5-in. exposure, each metal shingle overlaps the underlying metal shingle by 2 in., Figure 11.30.

Each metal shingle is placed slightly up slope of the exposed edge of the roofing shingle that overlaps it. In other words, the horizontal surface of metal shingles is not visible, since each metal shingle is completely covered by the overlying roof shingle. Each metal shingle is secured to the deck by two nails placed at its top edge; the vertical leg of a metal shingle is not fastened. Metal shingles are counterflashed by siding, which should terminate 2 in. above the roof surface.

11.5.1 Flashing Against a Vertical Front Wall

Flashing against a vertical front wall consists of a continuous L-shaped galvanized or prepainted sheet steel flashing, which should extend at least 5 in. vertically and 4 in. over the roof. Roof shingles are applied over the roof in such a way that the last shingle, which abuts against the wall, must be at least 8 in. wide. This may require adjusting the exposure slightly in the previous two or more courses. Metal flashing is applied over the last shingle course by embedding it into roofer's cement and nailing it to the deck; metal flashing is not nailed to the wall. Wall siding provides the counterflashing over the flashing, Figure 11.31.

11.31 *Flashing against a vertical front wall.*

11.5 FLASHING AGAINST VERTICAL WALLS

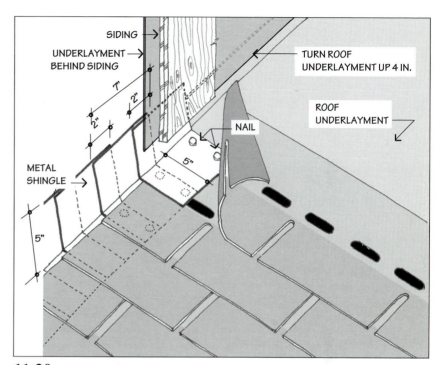

11.30 *Step flashing against a vertical side wall.*

11.6 FLASHING AROUND A CHIMNEY

Flashing around a masonry chimney consists of the following four component sheet metal flashings consisting of prepainted steel, 24 gauge or thicker, or any other compatible metal:

- Apron flashing
- Step flashing
- Cricket flashing
- Counterflashing

Sheet metal apron flashing is placed over the downslope side of chimney and tightly wrapped around it, Figure 11.32(a). This requires prefabricating the flashing to a profile, shown in Figure 11.32(b), and adhering it to the chimney with roofer's cement.

After the apron flashing has been applied, step flashing is installed on the side walls of the chimney in the same way as discussed in Section 11.5. Note that the first step flashing shingle wraps over the apron flashing at the corner by at least 2 in., Figure 11.33. Step flashing is also set with roofer's cement applied to chimney walls.

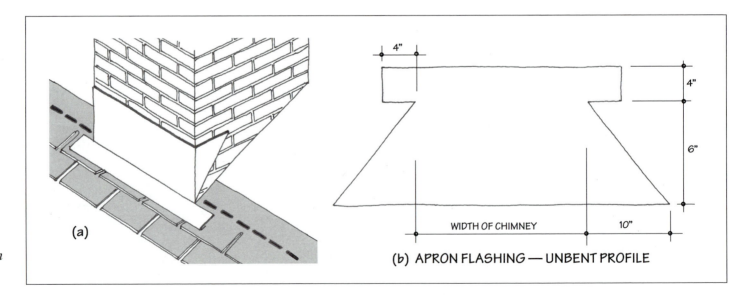

11.32 *Apron flashing — on the front face of a chimney.*

(a)

(b) APRON FLASHING — UNBENT PROFILE

4"

4"

6"

WIDTH OF CHIMNEY   10"

The upslope side (backside) of a chimney requires a cricket. Thus, before installing any metal flashing, roof shingles, or a roof underlayment around a chimney, a cricket is formed with plywood or oriented strandboard, Figure 11.34. Since a chimney is one of the primary sources of leaks on an asphalt shingle roof, a self-adhering ice dam protection membrane should be installed all around the base of the chimney, and its edges turned up the chimney walls. Roof underlayment is subsequently installed on the deck and the ice dam protection membrane.

The flashing over the cricket consists of a prefabricated sheet metal flashing, Figure 11.35. The joints in cricket flashing must be thoroughly soldered. The chimney is now ready to receive sheet metal counterflashing, Figure 11.36.

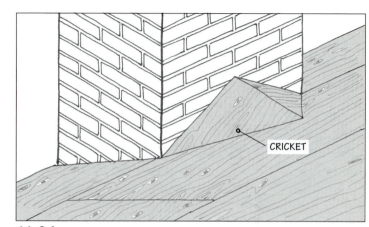

11.34 *Formation of a cricket with roof deck material on the upslope side (back side) of chimney*

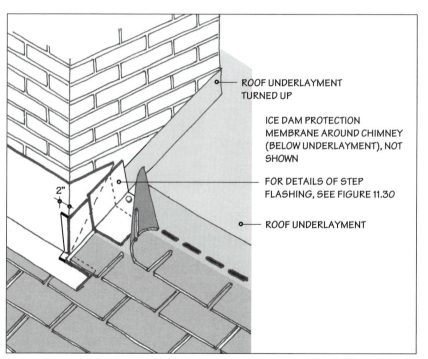

ROOF UNDERLAYMENT TURNED UP

ICE DAM PROTECTION MEMBRANE AROUND CHIMNEY (BELOW UNDERLAYMENT), NOT SHOWN

FOR DETAILS OF STEP FLASHING, SEE FIGURE 11.30

ROOF UNDERLAYMENT

2"

11.33 *Step flashing on the side walls of a masonry chimney.*

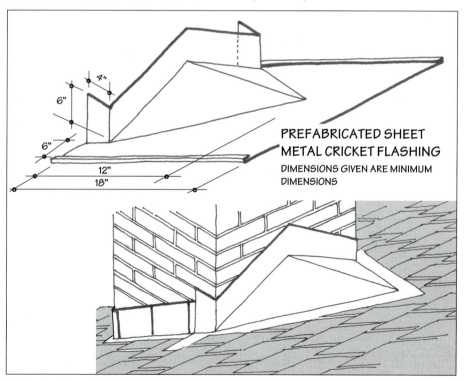

PREFABRICATED SHEET METAL CRICKET FLASHING

DIMENSIONS GIVEN ARE MINIMUM DIMENSIONS

4"

6"

6"

12"

18"

11.35 *Cricket flashing.*

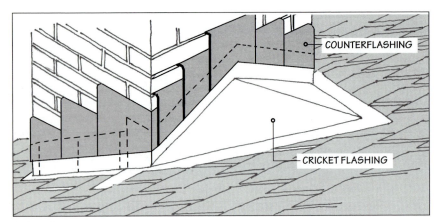

11.36 *Counterflashing over chimney flashing.*

Counterflashing is generally of the same metal as the flashing. One edge of the counterflashing laps over the flashing and the other edge is inset into masonry mortar joints, Figure 11.37. This requires cutting the appropriate mortar joints to a depth of nearly 1.5 in. — a cut that is commonly referred to as a *raggle*.

The inset edge of counterflashing is profiled to fit into the raggle giving a friction fit. Counterflashing is further secured by driving a soft metal wedge into the raggle and finishing the joint with an elastomeric sealant.

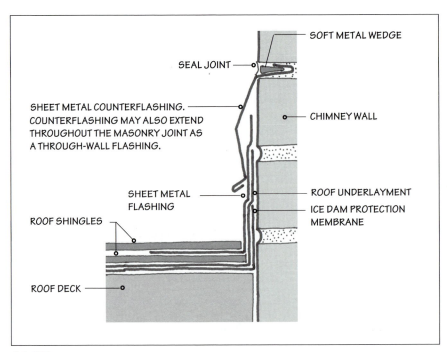

11.37 *Section through counterflashing.*

REFERENCES

11.1 National Roofing Contractors Association. *NRCA Roofing and Waterproofing Manual* (Rosemont, IL: 1996), p. 1028.

12 STEEP ROOFING — Slate Roof

Slate roofs are among the longest lasting of all contemporary roof systems. Properly installed and maintained, these roofs are considered to be permanent roofs, unlike asphalt shingle roofs or any of the low-slope roof varieties such as built-up, modified bitumen, or single-ply roofs. Better varieties of slate can give a roof that could last 75 years or longer. In other words, a properly constructed slate roof is constructed only once.

Slate is a naturally occurring stone, which has been mined for use as a roofing (and flooring) material for centuries. In the United States, active roofing slate quarries exist in New York, Pennsylvania, Vermont, and Virginia. Slate is also imported into the United States from Spain, the United Kingdom, and several other countries.

An effective use of roofing slate requires good detailing with durable underlayments and flashings to optimize the slate's inherent durability. Rarely will the slates themselves fail. Premature failure of slate roofs is generally due to the failure of underlayments or flashings. Therefore, multilayered underlayments, copper, lead-coated copper, or terne-coated stainless steel flashings; drip edges, etc., are generally recommended with slate roofs.

Because the basic principles of all shingle-type roofs are similar, this chapter follows the same format as that of Chapter 11 on asphalt shingles. Wherever the construction requirements for slate roofs is similar to those of asphalt shingle roofs, reference is made to that chapter. Thus, this chapter begins with a discussion of the various types of roofing slates, followed by descriptions of roof underlayment, slate installation, and flashing around roof penetrations.

Photo courtesy of Mickey Miller, The Roof Tile and Slate Company, Carrollton, Texas.

12.1 TYPES OF SLATES AND SLATE ROOFS

Table 12.1 Durability Grades of Roof Slates

Grade	Expected service life (years)
S_1	over 75
S_2	40 - 75
S_3	20 - 40

Table 12.2 Commonly Used Color Nomenclature of Roof Slates

Black	Purple	Red
Blue black	Purple variegated	
	Mottled purple and green	
Gray	Green	
Blue gray	Weathering green — changes to buff or brown	

Slate is a hard and dense stone. Its high density makes it virtually nonabsorbent to water and other chemicals, thus protecting it from damage due to freeze-thaw action and other deteriorating elements.

Being a sedimentary rock, it has naturally occurring cleavage planes, which allow it to be split easily into relatively thin slabs. Slate also possesses natural grain. In roofing slates, the grain runs parallel to the length of slate.

Since slate is a naturally occurring material, it comes in a large number of colors, textures, strengths, and other relevant properties. Based on strength and water absorption, ASTM standard C 406 standardizes roofing slates[12.1] in three durability grades: S_1, S_2, and S_3, see Table 12.1.

The standard excludes slates referred to as "ribbon stock." Ribbon stock slates include narrow ribbons of soft carbonaceous matter, which are much weaker than the slate itself. However, when these ribbons have been cut off and eliminated, the clear slate is acceptable for use.

Although the large number of colors and shades available in slate can make a slate roof look very pleasing, it also makes their selection and specification a difficult exercise. To simplify selection and specification, ASTM Standard C 406 standardizes roofing slates in 10 basic colors, see Table 12.2. However, the color and texture of some slates can change due to weathering. Owners, architects and roof consultants should request information on possible age-related color and texture changes from slate manufacturers and suppliers where this factor is important.

12.1.1 Types of Slate Roofs

As per ASTM Standard C 406, slate roofs are classified under the following three general categories depending on the type of slates used and the appearance of the roof:

* *Standard roof* is a roof that utilizes 3/16-in.- to 1/4-in.-thick slates of uniform lengths and widths with square edges. This is the most commonly used slate roof.

* *Textural roof* is a roof that utilizes slates of various sizes, thickness, and color for architectural effect. The slate surface is generally rough with uneven edges.

* *Graduated roof* is a roof that utilizes a greater range of sizes, thicknesses, and exposed lengths of shingles than a textural roof. An important feature of a graduated slate roof is that the thickest and longest slates are used at the eave, which gradually reduce in thickness and length toward the ridge.

12.1.2 Slate Dimensions and Weight of a Slate Roof

Roofing slates vary in size that typically range in length from 26 in. to 18 in. and in width from 16 in. to 9 in. The most commonly used sizes for the standard slate roof (3/16-in.- to 1/4-in.-thick slates) are given in Table 12.3, which also gives the number of slates required to cover one roof square with a 3-in. head lap.[12.2] Obviously, if the head lap used is greater than 3 in., the number of slates needed to cover one roof square increases.

The weight of slate roof is a function of slate thickness. The standard slate roof, with 3/16-in.- to 1/4-in.-thick slates and a 3-in. head lap, weighs nearly 10 lb per sq ft. Thus, a roof with 1/2-in.-thick slates weighs nearly 20 lb per sq ft.

12.1.3 Imitation Slates

Imitation slates — slates manufactured from mineral fibers, portland cement, and other proprietary materials — are also available. These are somewhat less expensive than the natural slates and look almost like the natural slates, when new. However, the specifier must examine the imitation slate's long-term color fastness, fungal growth due to its greater porosity, and durability.

Table 12.3 Schedule for Standard Slates — 3/16-in.- to 1/4-in.-Thick

Size of slate (L x W) in.	Slates per square	Exposure with head lap = 3 in.	Size of slate (L x W) in.	Slates per square	Exposure with head lap = 3 in.
26 x 14	89	11-1/2	20 x 14	121	8-1/2
			20 x 13	132	8-1/2
24 x 16	86	10-1/2	20 x 12	141	8-1/2
24 x 14	98	10-1/2	20 x 11	154	8-1/2
24 x 13	106	10-1/2	20 x 10	170	8-1/2
24 x 12	114	10-1/2	20 x 9	189	8-1/2
24 x 11	138	10-1/2			
			18 x 14	137	7-1/2
22 x 14	108	9-1/2	18 x 13	148	7-1/2
22 x 13	117	9-1/2	18 x 12	160	7-1/2
22 x 12	126	9-1/2	18 x 11	175	7-1/2
22 x 11	138	9-1/2	18 x 10	192	7-1/2
22 x 10	152	9-1/2	18 x 9	213	7-1/2

Source: Reference 12.2

Approximate weight (per sq ft) of slate roof

1/4-in.-thick slates — 10 psf
1/2-in.-thick slates — 20 psf

The most commonly used deck for a slate roof is a solid wood deck, or a plywood or an oriented strandboard deck with a minimum thickness of 3/4 in. A thicker deck is recommended with thicker slates to obtain a compatible durability.

Perimeter flashing, i.e., a drip edge, is not required with slate roofing because the (rigid) projecting slates at the eave form a good drip edge. However, whenever a sheet metal is used with a slate roof, it should be as durable as the slates. Therefore, if specified, a drip edge should consist of a minimum of 20-oz copper or other equivalent durability metal, applied to the deck in the same way as on an

12.2 ROOF SLOPE AND ROOF UNDERLAYMENT

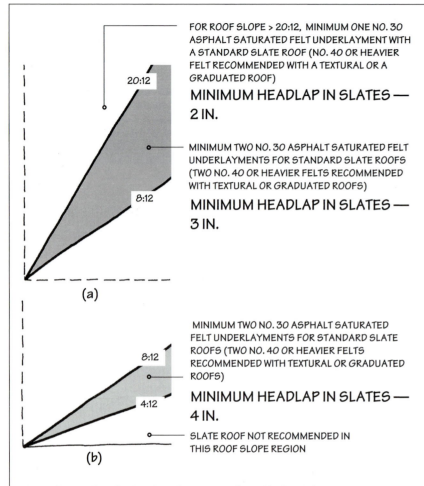

FOR ROOF SLOPE > 20:12, MINIMUM ONE NO. 30 ASPHALT SATURATED FELT UNDERLAYMENT WITH A STANDARD SLATE ROOF (NO. 40 OR HEAVIER FELT RECOMMENDED WITH A TEXTURAL OR A GRADUATED ROOF)

MINIMUM HEADLAP IN SLATES — 2 IN.

MINIMUM TWO NO. 30 ASPHALT SATURATED FELT UNDERLAYMENTS FOR STANDARD SLATE ROOFS (TWO NO. 40 OR HEAVIER FELTS RECOMMENDED WITH TEXTURAL OR GRADUATED ROOFS)

MINIMUM HEADLAP IN SLATES — 3 IN.

(a)

MINIMUM TWO NO. 30 ASPHALT SATURATED FELT UNDERLAYMENTS FOR STANDARD SLATE ROOFS (TWO NO. 40 OR HEAVIER FELTS RECOMMENDED WITH TEXTURAL OR GRADUATED ROOFS)

MINIMUM HEADLAP IN SLATES — 4 IN.

SLATE ROOF NOT RECOMMENDED IN THIS ROOF SLOPE REGION

(b)

SEE THE FOLLOWING FIGURES FOR LAYOUT OF UNDERLAYMENT

SINGLE LAYER — FIGURE 11.6 (CHAPTER 11)
SINGLE LAYER WITH ICE DAM PROTECTION — FIGURE 11.8
DOUBLE LAYER — FIGURE 11.9

DOUBLE LAYER WITH ICE DAM PROTECTION — FIGURE 11.10 OR FIGURE 11.11

asphalt shingle roof, see Figure 11.12 in Chapter 11. The fasteners should be of compatible durability (generally copper), of sufficient gauge, and appropriate spacing for required durability and wind resistance.

The minimum roof slope for slate roofs, as recommended by NRCA,[12.3] is 4:12. However, some slate manufacturers allow their slates to be applied on a deck with a slope less than 4:12, which requires a more careful detailing and an enhanced roof underlayment.

For a deck with a slope greater than 20:12, a minimum of one No. 30 asphalt saturated felt is necessary for a standard slate roof. The slates should be applied with a minimum headlap of 2 in., Figure 12.1(a). Heavier underlayment (No. 45 or heavier felt) should be used with textural or graduated roofs. In the case of a slate roof, the underlayment not only provides the necessary waterproofing but also a cushion to the slates against impact or roof traffic. A heavier underlayment increases the cushioning effect.

In regions frequented by wind-driven rain, two layers of No. 30 felts, laid in shingle fashion, are suggested along with an ice dam protection membrane. An ice dam protection membrane is also recommended for all slate roofs, regardless of roof slope if the average January temperature of the location is less than 30°F. This recommendation is the same as for asphalt shingle roofs, see Figure 11.7.

If the roof slope is less than 20:12 but greater than 8:12, a minimum of two layers of No. 30 asphalt saturated felts are required on a standard slate roof. The slates should be applied with a minimum headlap of 3 in. No. 30 felt should be substituted by heavier felts (e.g., No. 45 or heavier felt) for textural or graduated roofs. An ice dam protection membrane should be used where necessary, as described earlier.

For a roof slope less than 8:12 but greater than 4:12, the underlayment requirements are the same as for a roof slope greater than 8:12, but the headlap in slates must not be less than 4 in., Figure 12.1(b).

The layout of roof underlayment for a slate roof is identical to that for a asphalt shingle roof as given in Figure 12.1. The underlayment is the most inexpensive part of a slate roof. Therefore, providing more than just the minimum underlayment is a good practice. Many roofers will use a minimum of two layers of underlayment with a slate roof, regardless of the slope.

12.1 *Underlayment and headlap requirements for slate roofs with different roof slopes.*

12.2.1 Spaced Deck

Slates can be applied over a spaced deck (open lath) typically with a 1 x 4 or 1 x 6 nominal solid wood lath. Such a deck is generally restricted for use over an unheated building or on a low-slope deck (roof slope less than 4:12). In a typical low-slope application, the deck consists of a solid plywood (or OSB) deck, waterproofed with conventional built-up roof or single-ply membrane, with the open lath installed over the waterproof membrane. The slates are then secured to the lath in the same way as on a solid deck, see Section 12.3.

The slates are applied over the underlayment beginning with a starter course of slates. The starter course slates are smaller than the field slates (full-length slates). The length of the starter course is obtained simply by adding the headlap to the exposure of slates. The minimum headlap is a function of roof slope, as given in Figure 12.1. Thus, if the exposure of slates is 10 in. and the headlap is 4 in., the length of the starter slates is 14 in.

The exposure of slates is obtained by subtracting the headlap from the length of field slates and dividing the resultant by 2. Thus, if the length of slates is 24 in. and the headlap is 4 in., the exposure of slates is (24 - 4)/2 = 10 in.

The starter course slates are applied beginning at the eave so that they project nearly 2 in. beyond the eave to provide a drip edge. A tapered treated wood edge strip is secured to the deck at the eave, Figure 12.2. The location of the edge strip on the deck may need adjustment to tip the starter course to obtain proper inclination of the starter and succeeding slate courses. The edge strip may be applied either below the roof underlayment, as shown in Figure 12.2, or above the underlayment, as shown in Figure 12.4.

Although all other courses of slates are laid with the smooth surface facing down (i.e., toward the deck), the starter course is laid with its smooth surface facing up. Thus, the smooth surface of the starter course and the smooth surface of the first course of slates contact each other. This reduces the space between these two courses, reducing the possibility of wind-driven rain forcing its way through the interface between these courses. The fascia board may also be raised to close the gap between the slates and the deck at the eave caused by the edge strip.

12.3 INSTALLATION OF SLATES

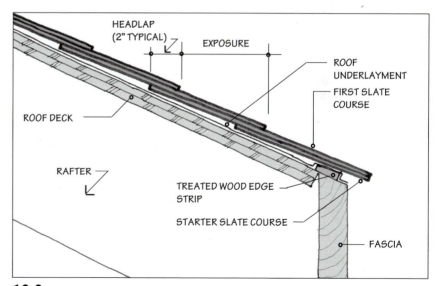

12.2 *Slate application at the eave.*

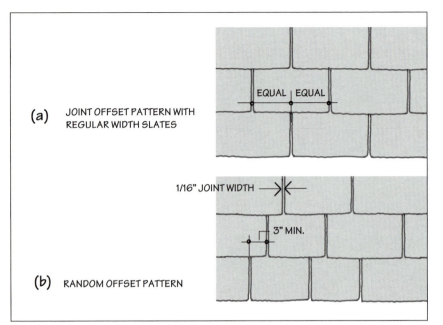

(a) JOINT OFFSET PATTERN WITH REGULAR WIDTH SLATES

EQUAL | EQUAL

1/16" JOINT WIDTH

3" MIN.

(b) RANDOM OFFSET PATTERN

12.3 *Offset between the joints of slate courses.*

The first course is laid above the starter course so that its joints are offset from the starter course. Ideally, the joints between two consecutive courses should be offset by half the slate width, Figure 12.3(a). In any case, the offset should not be less than 3 in., Figure 12.3(b). The slates should be laid with a 1/16-in. gap between adjacent slates to allow for some movement.

12.3.1 Slate Fasteners

For a standard slate roof, each slate is punched with two holes located at a distance of nearly 1/4 the length of slates from the slate's upper edge and between 1-1/2 to 2 in. from the sides, Figure 12.4. In high wind regions, for steep slopes, and/or on roofs with heavier slates (textural or graduated roofs), four holes per slate are recommended. When four holes are used, the two additional holes are punched nearly 2 in. above the regular holes. The holes are generally punched at the quarry. Field punching is necessary only for hip slates, which may need cutting of slates at the roofing site.

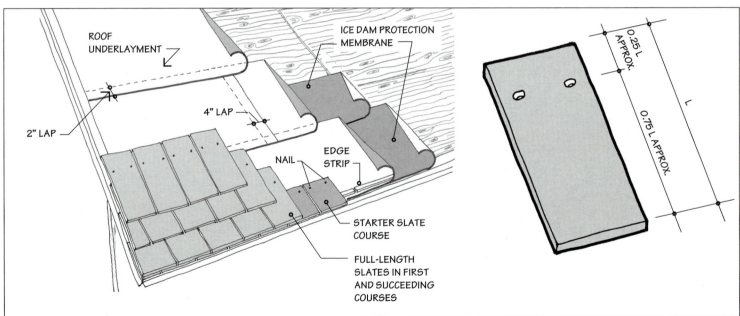

ROOF UNDERLAYMENT

ICE DAM PROTECTION MEMBRANE

4" LAP

2" LAP

NAIL

EDGE STRIP

STARTER SLATE COURSE

FULL-LENGTH SLATES IN FIRST AND SUCCEEDING COURSES

0.25 L APPROX.

0.75 L APPROX.

L

12.4 *Slate application.*

Slates are secured to the deck with nails driven through prepunched holes. As stated previously, copper slating nails are generally recommended, but stainless steel, bronze, or cut brass nails may be used. Copper, being a softer metal, has an advantage over other metals, since the nails can be more easily cut when repairs are needed.

For a standard roof, the minimum shank diameter of copper slating nails is 1/8 in. (3 mm). They should be long enough to penetrate all the way into the plywood or oriented strandboard deck so as to be visible from the underside of the deck. With a solid wood plank deck, the nails should penetrate at least 3/4 in. into the deck.

Another method of attaching slates involves metal clips, usually stainless steel slating clips. Attaching the slates with clips does not require any holes in the slates. The clips not only secure the slates but also provide the necessary space between the adjacent slates, allowing the slates to move, Figure 12.5. Each slate is secured with one clip in the center of its bottom edge. The clip method of securing slates is gaining popularity since improperly seated nails can cause the slates to crack and fail.

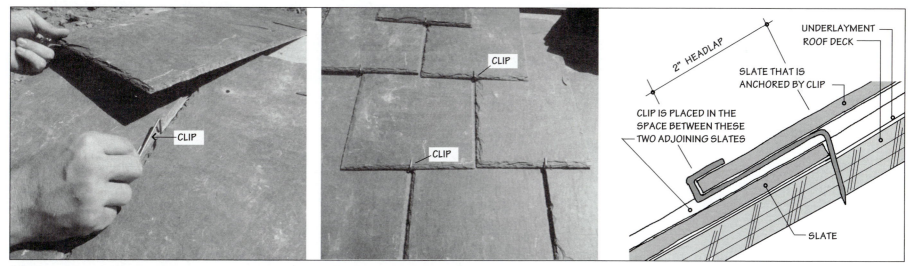

12.5 *Securing slates with the help of slating clips. Photos by Madan Mehta.*

12.4 VALLEY, RIDGE, AND HIP TREATMENTS AND CHIMNEY FLASHING

An open valley, with sheet metal valley flashing, is the most commonly used valley treatment with slate roofs, Figure 12.6. This treatment is similar to the open valley treatment for asphalt shingles except that the valley flashing metal should be a minimum of 20-oz copper and the valley underlayment felt heavier, see Figures 11.20 and 11.22(a) and (b) in Chapter 11. Other valley treatments such as a *closed valley* or a *closed rounded valley* may also be used.[12.4]

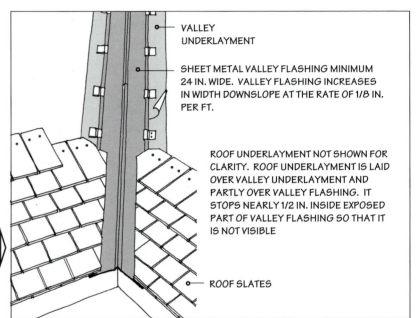

VALLEY
UNDERLAYMENT

SHEET METAL VALLEY FLASHING MINIMUM
24 IN. WIDE. VALLEY FLASHING INCREASES
IN WIDTH DOWNSLOPE AT THE RATE OF 1/8 IN.
PER FT.

ROOF UNDERLAYMENT NOT SHOWN FOR
CLARITY. ROOF UNDERLAYMENT IS LAID
OVER VALLEY UNDERLAYMENT AND
PARTLY OVER VALLEY FLASHING. IT
STOPS NEARLY 1/2 IN. INSIDE EXPOSED
PART OF VALLEY FLASHING SO THAT IT
IS NOT VISIBLE

ROOF SLATES

12.6 *Open valley treatment. This detail is similar to that of Figure 11.22, except that sheet metal flashing must be a minimum 20-oz copper or other equivalent durability metal.*

12.4.1 Ridge Treatment

Several methods may be used to construct a ridge on a slate roof, but the most commonly used method is the *saddle ridge method*, Figure 12.7. Using this method, the last course of field slates from both sides of the roof are brought up flush against wood nailers that are secured to the deck. This last course is nailed to a wood lath, which is a nailer whose thickness is the same as the field slate, so that the slates immediately below the last course of field slates are flush with the lath.

The nailer and the lath are covered over by sheet copper or self-adhering ice dam protection membrane material. Ridge slates from both sides of the roof are placed over the felt with their joints staggered from the last course of field slates. Each ridge slate is nailed to the nailer with four copper slating nails, and the nails are then coated with a sealant. The nails and the sealant are fully shielded by the overlapping ridge slate. The joint between ridge slates abutting from either side of the roof should be sealed with a durable sealant, Figure 12.7(b)

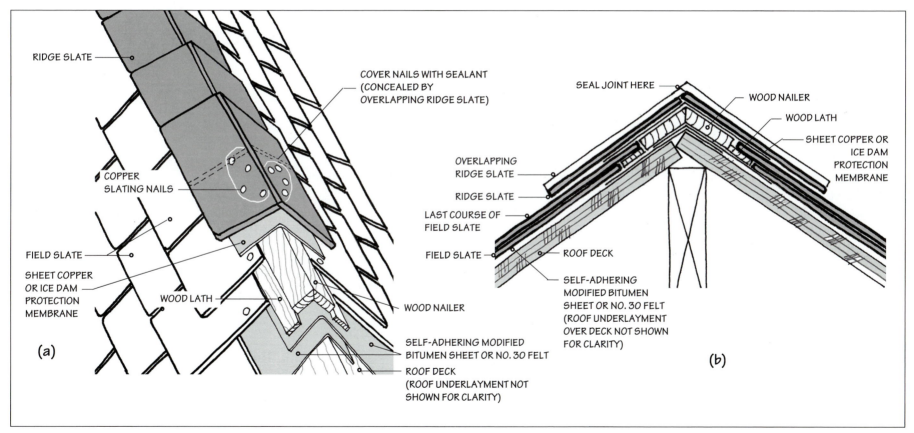

12.7 *Ridge treatment — saddle ridge method.*

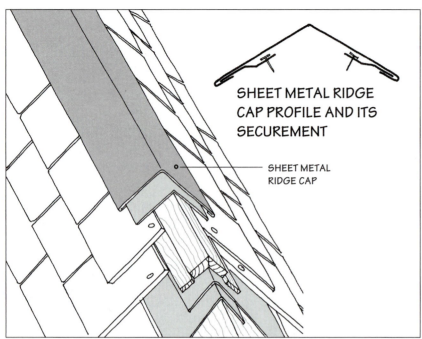

12.8 *Ridge treatment — sheet metal ridge cap. This detail is similar to that of Figure 12.7 except that ridge slates have been substituted by a sheet metal ridge cap.*

Instead of using the ridge slates, a sheet metal ridge cap may be used, Figure 12.8. The metal used for the ridge cap should be copper or stainless steel, and the length of an individual ridge cap should not exceed 10 ft to allow for expansion and contraction. Individual ridge cap lengths should be sufficiently lapped and the lap joint soldered and sealed.

12.4.2 Hip Treatment

The two most commonly used hip treatments for a slate roof are the *saddle hip* and *mitered hip*. A saddle hip is similar to a saddle ridge. It is formed by installing two pieces of wood nailers over the roof underlayment. Field slates are butted against the nailer. The thickness of the nailer is nearly twice the thickness of the slates. Hip slates, which are the same as the field slates, are installed over the wood nailer with the same headlap and exposure as the field slates, Figure 12.9.

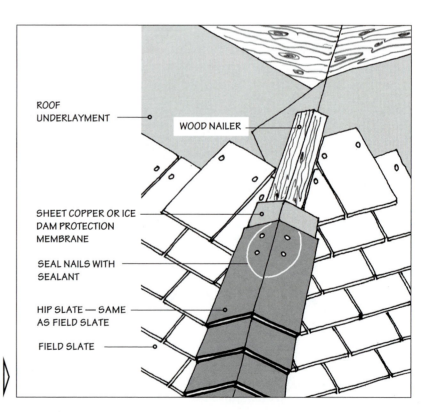

12.9 *Hip treatment — saddle hip.*

An alternative to a saddle hip is the mitered hip in which a soft metal flashing is interwoven between hip slates. The hip slates are made by cutting field slates at the roof site to form tightly abutting mitered joints, Figure 12.10. If the bottom of mitered hip slates is cut to make a fantail, the resulting hip is referred to as a fantail hip.

12.4.3 Flashing Around a Chimney

The details of flashing around a chimney with a slate roof are similar to those of an asphalt shingle roof, see Figures 11.32 through 11.37.

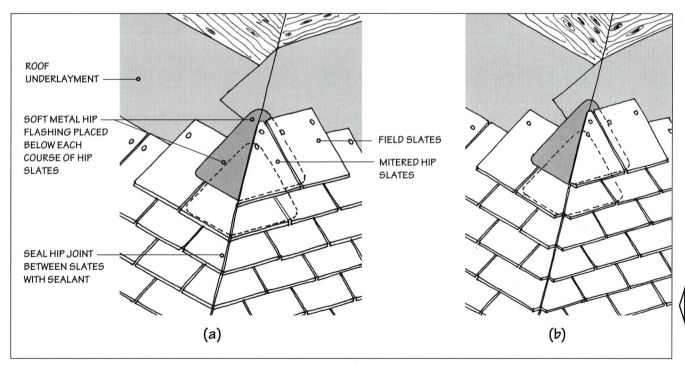

ROOF UNDERLAYMENT

SOFT METAL HIP FLASHING PLACED BELOW EACH COURSE OF HIP SLATES

FIELD SLATES

MITERED HIP SLATES

SEAL HIP JOINT BETWEEN SLATES WITH SEALANT

(a)

(b)

12.10 *Hip treatment: (a) mitered hip, and (b) fantail hip, which is identical to mitered hip except that the hip slates are cut to form a fantail.*

REFERENCES

12.1 American Society for Testing and Materials. "Standard Specification for Roofing Slate," *ASTM Standard C 406 -89* (West Conshohocken, PA: reapproved 1996).

12.2 National Roofing Contractors Association. *NRCA Roofing and Waterproofing Manual* (Rosemont, IL: 1996), p. 1184.

12.3 Ibid., p. 1186.

12.4 Ibid., p. 1207.

13 STEEP ROOFING — Tile Roof

Unlike slates, concrete and clay tiles are manufactured products. Consequently, they are available in a wide variety of types, sizes, shapes, and colors. Although concrete tiles are of relatively recent origin, clay tile roofs have been in use for centuries.

The service life spans of concrete and clay tile roofs are significantly longer than asphalt shingle roofs. Because of their color, texture, and tile profile, they produce handsome looking roofs. That is why in modern construction, concrete and clay tiles are extensively used in low-rise commercial structures and higher-priced homes and apartment buildings.

This chapter examines the type of tiles and the details of their installation. Since the construction fundamentals of all types of steep roofs are similar, the reader is advised to review Chapters 11 and 12 before reading this chapter.

Photo by Madan Mehta.

13.1 TYPES OF CONCRETE AND CLAY TILES

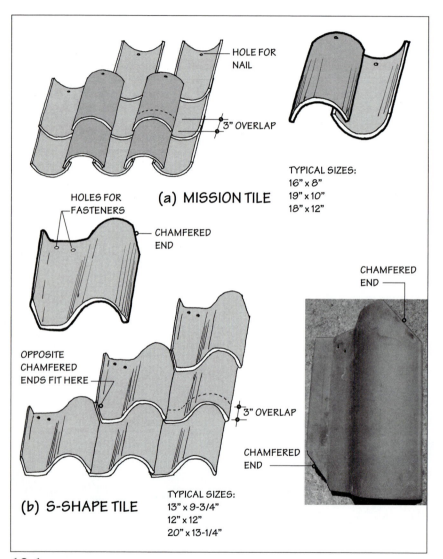

(a) MISSION TILE

HOLE FOR
NAIL

3" OVERLAP

TYPICAL SIZES:
16" x 8"
19" x 10"
18" x 12"

HOLES FOR
FASTENERS

CHAMFERED
END

CHAMFERED
END

OPPOSITE
CHAMFERED
ENDS FIT HERE

3" OVERLAP

CHAMFERED
END

(b) S-SHAPE TILE

TYPICAL SIZES:
13" x 9-3/4"
12" x 12"
20" x 13-1/4"

13.1 *Profiles of (a) mission tile and (b) S-shape tile. Photo by Madan Mehta.*

Tiles come in a large variety of profiles, sizes, and colors, depending on the manufacturer. The clay tile's color is primarily a function of the chemical composition of the clay from which it is made. If any additional color-modifying agent is used, it is added to the clay before firing. Therefore, the color becomes integral to the tile. With its integral color, the color of clay tile weathers only slightly with time, which is caused mainly by the pollutants in the air. Glaze-coated clay tiles are also available. The glaze is applied to the already fired tiles, which are then refired to obtain a durable glaze.

The color of concrete tiles is a function of the color of the portland cement, aggregates, and any pigments, if used. The gradual erosion of the surface of the tile due to running water on the roof exposes the aggregates in a concrete tile, which can create a noticeable change in the tile's color over time. Initial and periodic sealing of the tiles' surface helps retain the color longer.

Concrete tiles can also be factory painted on their exposed surface. Several manufacturers make concrete tiles with the characteristic (brown) terracotta color painted on them to mimic clay tiles. Being an applied finish, the paint tends to fade over time.

13.1.1 Tile Profiles

Because of the enormous variety in the profiles of concrete and clay tiles, it is impossible to discuss all available profiles. Although some profiles are only used with clay tiles and the others with concrete tiles, most tile profiles are essentially similar. Except for flat tile, all tile profiles provide for water channels that direct water down the roof. That is why tiles are generally laid in single coverage with a simple overlap of 3 in. between succeeding courses. This is unlike slate or asphalt shingle roofs that are laid in double coverage with a 2-in. headlap.

One of the oldest and a commonly used profile in clay tiles is the *mission tile*, which consists of an almost semicircular barrel profile. The tiles are laid alternately, one tile in water-holding setting (pan) and the other tile in water-shedding setting (cover), Figure 13.1(a). Both pan and cover tiles are provided with one hole to receive a fastener at the head of each tile.

The commonly available sizes[13.1] in mission tiles are 16 in. x 8 in., 19 in. x 10 in., and 18 in. x 12 in. They are laid with an overlap of 3 in. between adjacent courses. Thus, in a 16-in.-long tile, the exposure is 13 in.

Another commonly used clay tile profile is a derivative of the mission tile. Called *S-shape tile*, a *one-piece barrel*, or an *S-shape mission tile*, it integrates the pan and cover of the mission tile into one unit, Figure 13.1(b). The S-shape tile generally comes with its two opposite ends chamfered to allow for easier drainage of water. The chamfer is generally of the same size as the overlap needed between the adjacent tiles to give a better, more exact fit between them.

The S-shape tiles are also laid with an overlap of 3 in., and each tile is provided with two fastener holes at its head. Typical sizes are 13-1/4 in. x 9-3/4 in., 12 in. x 12 in., and 20 in. x 13-1/4 in.

Other profiles include a flat tile. Flat tiles are laid like asphalt shingles or slates — in double coverage and with a headlap of 2 in., Figure 13.2(a). That is why they are also referred to as *shingle tiles*. Because of its double coverage, the weight of a flat tile roof is higher than the roofs constructed of other tile profiles.

The bottom of a flat tile may be fluted to reduce the weight of the tile, Figure 13.2(b). It may also be provided with a lug, which helps to hang the tile to the underlying wood battens, see Figure 13.7.

A variation of the flat tile is the interlocking tile, Figure 13.3. Interlocking tiles are laid so that the tongues fit into the grooves of adjacent tiles. They are also laid with a simple course-to-course overlap of 3 in. (typical), with the joints between adjacent courses offset by half the width of the tile.

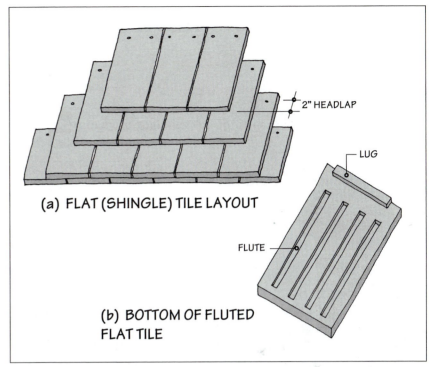

(a) FLAT (SHINGLE) TILE LAYOUT

(b) BOTTOM OF FLUTED FLAT TILE

13.2 *(a) Flat tile layout. (b) Flat tile with flutes and a lug at its underside.*

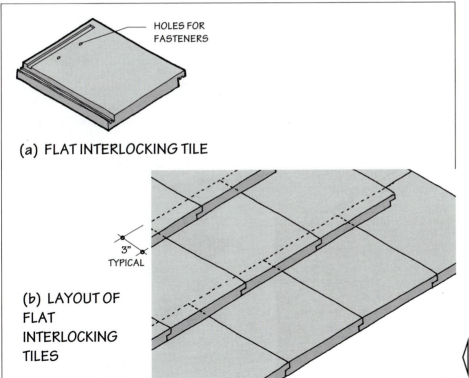

(a) FLAT INTERLOCKING TILE

(b) LAYOUT OF FLAT INTERLOCKING TILES

13.3 *Interlocking flat tile and its layout.*

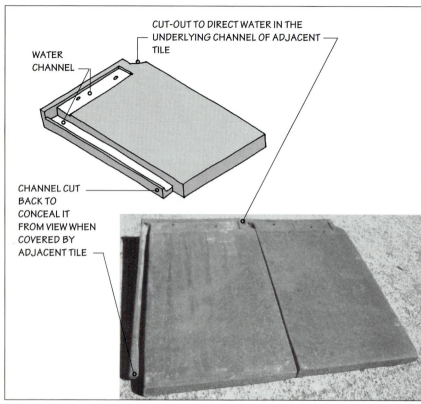

13.4 *Interlocking flat tile with water-diverting channels. Photo by Madan Mehta.*

Some flat interlocking tiles use a more sophisticated design of water-directing channels, Figure 13.4. The interlocking feature is also provided in S-shaped tiles, which may also be ribbed for stiffness and provided with lugs, Figure 13.5.

13.1.2 Water Absorption and Strength of Tiles

Unlike asphalt shingles or slates (whose water absorption is negligible), concrete and clay tiles absorb water. Water absorption increases the weight of the tile roof and leads to freeze-thaw damage of tiles. It also aggravates color degradation tendency as the water-soluble pollutants enter the body of the tile. Less porous tiles are obviously better but are more expensive.

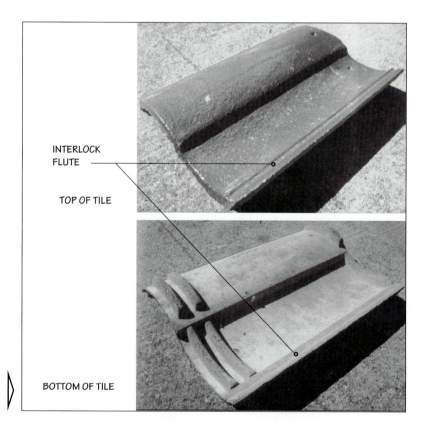

13.5 *S-shape tile with an interlock feature. Photos by Madan Mehta.*

The porosity[13.2] of clay tiles varies from 2% to 10%; concrete tiles, from 3% to 20%. Sealers are generally used to reduce the effect of porosity. The service life of the sealers and the cost of repeat applications must be considered in tile selection. It may be more economical in the long run to specify a denser, albeit more expensive, tile.

Some tiles are graded (Grades 1, 2, or 3) for their freeze-thaw resistance.[13.3] Grade 1 is typically specified in severe freeze-thaw climates, Grade 2 in moderate freeze-thaw climates, and Grade 3 in climates with negligible freeze-thaw activity.

Porosity is not merely an index of the tile's water absorptivity, it also indicates the tile's strength – in fact, the lack of it. A more porous tile is weaker. Strength is an important selection criterion for concrete and clay tiles, because a stronger tile is generally more durable.

13.1.3 Tile Thickness and Weight

Because of their higher porosity and lower strength, clay and concrete tiles need to be much thicker than slates. Concrete and clay tile thickness varies from 1/2 in. to 1-1/2 in. However, because of their layout in single coverage (as compared to double coverage in slate roofs), concrete and clay tile roofs are not much heavier than slate roofs. On the average, a concrete and clay tile roof weighs nearly 10 psf, if the tile thickness is nearly 1/2 in. However, this weight may be substantially exceeded with thicker tiles.

Approximate weight (per sq ft) of tile roof

1/2-in.-thick tiles — 10 psf
1-in.-thick tiles — 20 psf

The most commonly used deck for a tile roof consists of plywood or oriented strandboard panels. Tongue-and-groove solid wood planks are also used but less often. An underlayment is required in all cases. Since a tile roof is a relatively long-lasting roof, the underlayment should match the durability of the tiles. The National Roofing Contractors Association[13.4] recommends the following minimum underlayment specifications:

- *For roofs with a slope greater than 20:12*: A minimum one layer of No. 30 asphalt-saturated felt in moderate climates. In more severe climates, with wind-driven rain or snow, a minimum of two layers of No. 30 or one layer of No. 40 (or heavier) felt should be used, Figure 13.6.

13.2 ROOF SLOPE AND UNDERLAYMENT

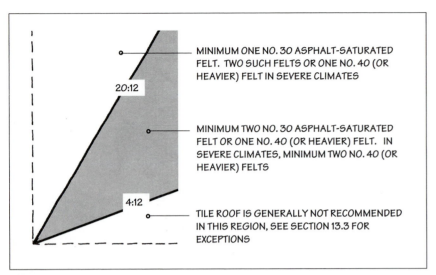

MINIMUM ONE NO. 30 ASPHALT-SATURATED FELT. TWO SUCH FELTS OR ONE NO. 40 (OR HEAVIER) FELT IN SEVERE CLIMATES

20:12

MINIMUM TWO NO. 30 ASPHALT-SATURATED FELT OR ONE NO. 40 (OR HEAVIER) FELT. IN SEVERE CLIMATES, MINIMUM TWO NO. 40 (OR HEAVIER) FELTS

4:12

TILE ROOF IS GENERALLY NOT RECOMMENDED IN THIS REGION, SEE SECTION 13.3 FOR EXCEPTIONS

13.6 *Underlayment requirements for tile roofs with different roof slopes.*

- *For roofs with a slope between 4:12 and 20:12*: A minimum of two layers of No. 30 asphalt-saturated felt or one No. 40 (or heavier) felt should be specified.

- *For roofs with a slope less than 4:12*: Tile roofs are generally not recommended on such low slopes, although some manufacturers promote their product for this slope region.

However, it is prudent to exceed the above requirements as an underlayment adds substantially to the overall durability of the roof, contributing only a small increase in its cost. Most roofers and roofing consultants use a minimum of two layers of underlayment in all cases. When two layers are used, they should be laid in shingle fashion. Underlayment should be laid with a minimum number of nails — to hold them in position until the tiles are installed.

13.2.1 Ice Dam Protection Membrane

In the authors' opinion, an ice dam protection membrane at the eave should be specified in all climates. However, it is particularly important in cold climates. The minimum requirement for an ice dam protection membrane is the same as for the asphalt shingle roofs, see Section 11.1.

13.3 INSTALLATION OF TILES

The easiest and most commonly used method of fastening the tiles is to nail them to the substrate. Except for mission tile, which is provided with only one nail per tile, other tiles are secured with two nails per tile. The nails should be of stainless steel or copper to match the long life of a tile roof.

Except for mission tiles (see Section 13.4), other tiles can be nailed straight to the deck. However, the best installation of tiles is achieved if a network of battens and crossbattens of treated wood is nailed to the deck over the underlayment, Figure 13.7(a). The tiles are then nailed to the (top) battens, which run horizontally, Figure 13.7(b). The horizontal battens should be a minimum of 1 in. x 2 in. (nominal), and the vertical battens should be a minimum of 1/2 in. x 1-1/2 in. nominal.

The vertical battens are generally laid 24 in. on center. The spacing of the horizontal battens is a function of the length of the tile. Thus, with a 3-in. lap between successive courses, the center-to-center spacing of horizontal battens equals the tile length minus 3 in.

The batten network creates a space under the tiles, which allows for a clear drainage of water should the water seep under the tiles. Since the tiles are generally laid in single coverage with only a 3-in. lap, the seepage of water under the tiles in severe weather is not uncommon.

The space under the tiles also permits a more rapid drying of the underlayment. Battens also help to hang the tiles that consist of lugs. A major advantage of a batten and crossbatten network is that such a system can be used with slopes less than 4:12, provided the underlayment is treated like a built-up roof. In that case, the tiles serve simply as a decorative roof covering.

In place of the batten and crossbatten network, a system of one-way (horizontal) battens may be used, Figure 13.8. The battens, minimum 1 in. x 2 in. nominal, are generally laid in 4-ft lengths, separated by a minimum of 1/2-in. space. The 1/2-in. separation allows the drainage of any water trapped by the battens. However, this system does not perform as well as the crossbatten system.

In some regions that do not experience severe storms or earthquakes, and if the roof slope is shallow, tiles with lugs may be hung loose off the battens with minimal nailing, such as the nailing of perimeter tiles. However, building codes must be consulted if any securement below the standard minimum (two nails per tile) is to be used.

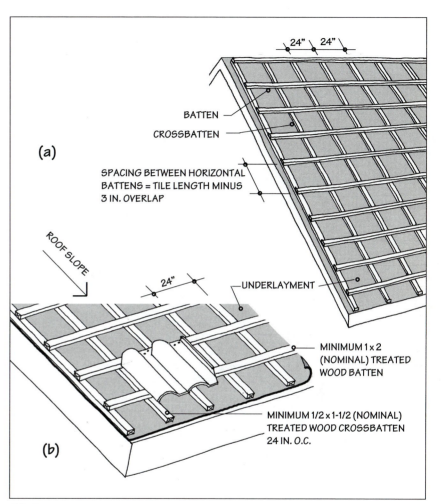

13.7 *Installation of tiles on a network of battens and crossbattens.*

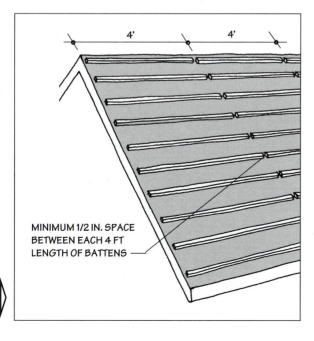

13.8 *A system of one-way battens.*

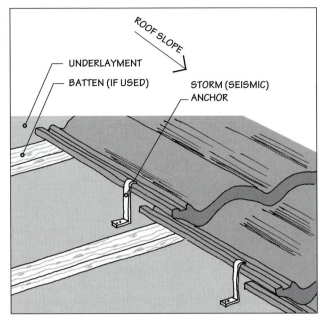

13.9 *Storm (seismic) tile anchor.*

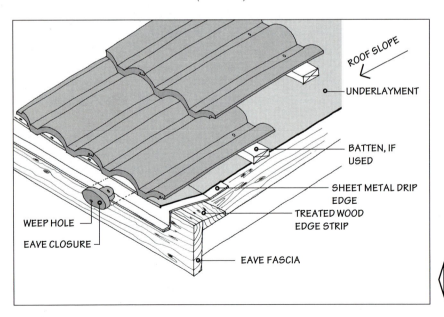

On the other hand, building codes may require additional securement of every tile if the region is subjected to abnormal wind or earthquake activity. This may be provided by storm/seismic anchors in addition to nailing, Figure 13.9.

13.3.1 Eave Treatment

As with a slate roof, the drip edge is not necessary with a tile roof, since the eave tiles can be made to project sufficiently beyond the fascia. However, if a drip edge is used, it should be of durable metal (e.g., 24-oz copper) to match the long life of a tile roof. A treated wood edge strip is also required at the eave to give the correct alignment to the first tile, Figure 13.10. Tile manufacturers also make starter tiles that preclude the need of an edge strip.

If tiles with curvature are used, eave closure pieces are required to fill the space between the tiles and the underlying construction. These specially made closure pieces can be of clay (with clay tiles), concrete, or plastic. They are provided with weep holes to allow the escape of water that may seep under the tiles. The closure pieces are nailed to the deck before setting the tiles at the eave. The closing of the space under the tiles prevents the nesting of birds and insects.

Portland cement mortar may also be used to fill the gap between the eave tiles and the underlying part of the roof, if weep holes are provided in each mortar filling. With flat interlocking tiles, eave closure pieces are obviously not required, Figure 13.11.

13.3.2 Rake, Ridge, and Hip Treatments

The treatment of a rake with a flat tile is similar to that of a slate roof, i.e., the field tiles simply project beyond the rake to protect the fascia. In other words, there is no special rake treatment provided with flat tiles, except a sheet metal flashing if considered necessary. However, with flat interlocking or curved tiles, specially prepared rake tiles are generally used to weatherproof the rake, Figures 13.12 and 13.13.

13.10 *Eave treatment with tiles that are curved in profile.*

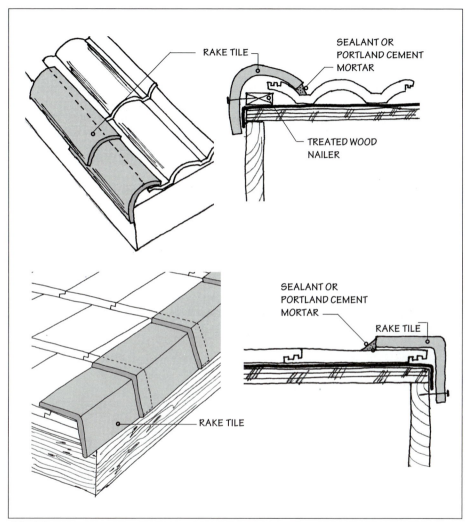

RAKE TILE

SEALANT OR
PORTLAND CEMENT
MORTAR

TREATED WOOD
NAILER

SEALANT OR
PORTLAND CEMENT
MORTAR

RAKE TILE

RAKE TILE

13.12 *Rake treatments with curved and flat interlocking tiles.*

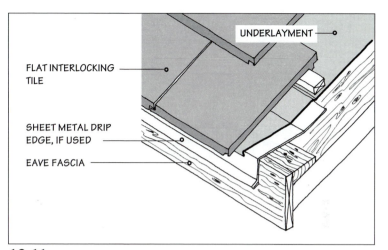

UNDERLAYMENT

FLAT INTERLOCKING
TILE

SHEET METAL DRIP
EDGE, IF USED

EAVE FASCIA

13.11 *Eave treatment with flat interlocking tiles.*

13.13 *Rake and hip treatments. Photo by Madan Mehta.*

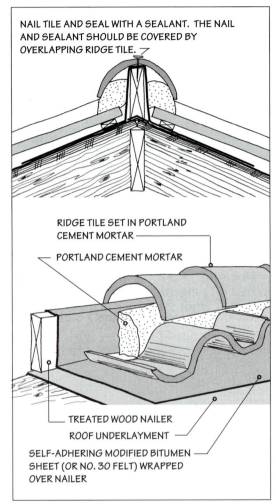

13.14 *A commonly used ridge treatment.*

The construction of a ridge and a hip are similar. With curved tiles, a treated wood nailer is installed at the ridge (or the hip) and a self-adhering modified bitumen sheet (or No. 30 felt) is wrapped over the nailer. Field tiles are brought close to the nailer, and the nailer is covered with special ridge (or hip) tiles set in portland cement mortar. The mortar holds the ridge (or hip) tiles and also closes the gap between the ridge tiles (or hip tiles) and the field tiles, Figures 13.14 and Figure 13.15.

Each ridge (or hip) tile is nailed to the nailer. Although these nails are protected by the overlapping ridge (or hip) tile, it is necessary to seal the nail with roofer's cement or sealant.

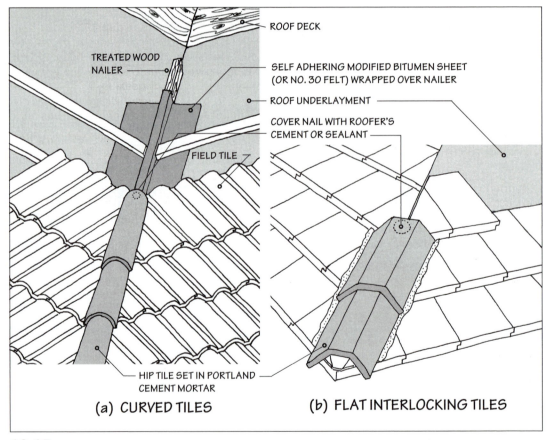

13.15 *Hip treatments with curved and flat interlocking tiles.*

Mission tiles, with their pan and cover pieces, require an entirely different installation system. A treated wood nailer, aligned along the slope of the roof, is placed under every cover piece, and the cover piece is nailed to the nailer, Figure 13.16(a). The nailer is usually either a 2 x 3 or a 2 x 4 (nominal size), depending on the height of the cover piece. The nailer not only helps to secure the tile, it also reduces the possibility of tile breakage when walked on by roofers. The tiles are laid with 3-in. standard overlap as with other tiles.

Eave closure pieces are required, and the rake is covered with the field tiles and rake cover tiles. Additional nailers are needed at the rake, Figure 13.16(b). The construction of a ridge or a hip is similar to that of other tile roofs, Figures 13.17(a) and (b).

13.4 MISSION TILE INSTALLATION

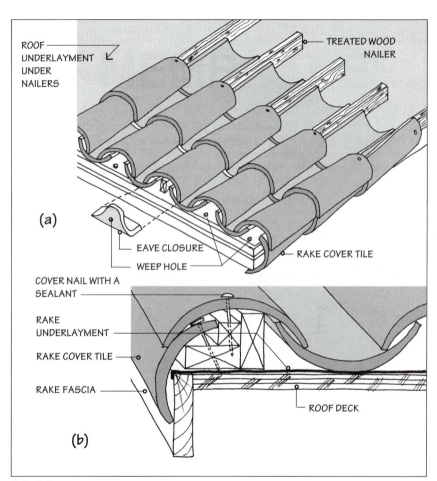

13.16 *Installation of mission tiles.*

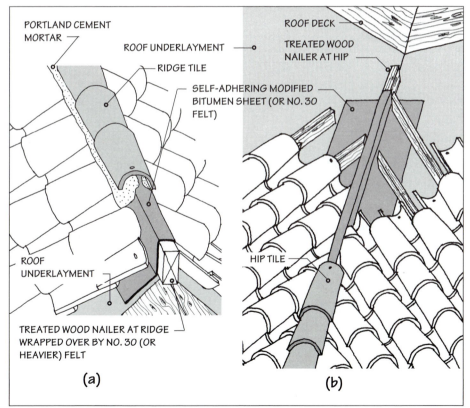

13.17 *Typical ridge and hip treatments with a mission tile roof.*

13.5 VALLEY AND OTHER FLASHINGS

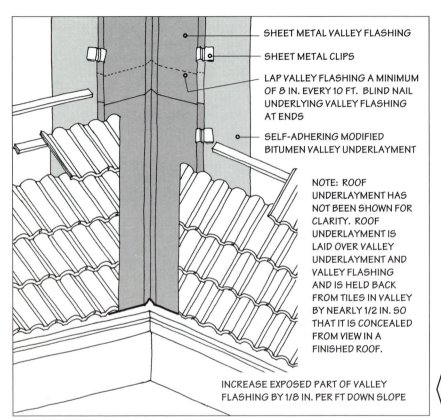

SHEET METAL VALLEY FLASHING

SHEET METAL CLIPS

LAP VALLEY FLASHING A MINIMUM OF 8 IN. EVERY 10 FT. BLIND NAIL UNDERLYING VALLEY FLASHING AT ENDS

SELF-ADHERING MODIFIED BITUMEN VALLEY UNDERLAYMENT

NOTE: ROOF UNDERLAYMENT HAS NOT BEEN SHOWN FOR CLARITY. ROOF UNDERLAYMENT IS LAID OVER VALLEY UNDERLAYMENT AND VALLEY FLASHING AND IS HELD BACK FROM TILES IN VALLEY BY NEARLY 1/2 IN. SO THAT IT IS CONCEALED FROM VIEW IN A FINISHED ROOF.

INCREASE EXPOSED PART OF VALLEY FLASHING BY 1/8 IN. PER FT DOWN SLOPE

As with other steep roofs, a tile roof needs additional waterproofing with the help of flashing at interruptions (such as a change in roof slope), terminations, and around roof penetrations. An important such flashing is valley flashing. Valley in a tile roof can only be flashed with a sheet metal. This is similar to a slate roof.

Because of the long life span of a tile roof, a durable sheet metal, such as 24-oz copper or an equivalent durability stainless steel, should be used for valley flashings. Two types of valleys are generally used with a tile roof: an open valley and a closed valley. Among the two, an open valley is more commonly used, Figure 13.18, because it provides a more rapid discharge of water. A minimum of 8:12 roof slope is recommended for the use of a closed valley.

For a closed valley and flashings at other locations on a tile roof, the reader should refer to other sources[13.5] and manufacturer-recommended details.

13.18 *Open valley flashing.*

REFERENCES

13.1   National Roofing Contractors Association. *NRCA Roofing and Waterproofing Manual* (Rosemont, IL:1996), pp. 1096-1097.

13.2   Ibid., p. 1098.

13.3   Ibid., p. 1099.

13.4   Ibid., p. 1102.

13.5   Ibid., pp. 1115-1123.

14

STEEP ROOFING — Architectural Metal Roof

Sheet metal roofs are increasingly becoming a part of the urban landscape. The development of durable coatings on steel, coupled with a vast array of nonfading coating colors, has increased the popularity of metal roofs. Metal roofs are, therefore, spared of the rapid atmospheric and solar degradation to which other commonly used low-slope roofs (e.g., built-up, modified bitumen, or single-ply roofs) are subjected.

Several owners of commercial buildings, unhappy with frequent replacement of their existing low-slope roofs, are switching to metal roofs when reroofing is needed. This is despite the fact that a change from a low-slope roof to a metal roof on an existing building requires a great deal of additional under-roof components. Sheet metal roofs can be divided under two types:

- Structural

- Architectural

Structural metal roofs double as a roof covering and also as a deck. A separate deck is not provided with such roofs, and the roof panels are supported directly on purlins, which are typically spaced 4 to 5 ft on center. Structural metal roofs are commonly used in low-cost industrial buildings in what are generally referred to as *preengineered metal buildings*. Preengineered metal buildings use highly standardized manufacturer-specific components and assemblies and are out of the scope of this text.

Architectural sheet metal roofs, which are discussed further in this chapter, require a supporting deck and an underlayment. They are meant to be used on steep slopes (slope ≥ 3:12), and may be further subdivided into the following types:

METAL ROOF

Photo by Madan Mehta.

259

- *Traditional metal roofs*: They are typically made from metals that can be soldered and are inherently durable in their natural state, not requiring any protective finish, such as copper or lead-coated copper.

- *Contemporary metal roofs*: They are typically made from steel and aluminum, which have been treated with protective finishes. Thus, the metals commonly used in such roofs are painted steel, metallic-coated steel, and aluminum.

Traditional metal roofs have a long history, since they originate from an era when building construction relied entirely on manual fabrication and assembly. Although adapted to modern industrialized modes of construction, traditional metal roofs still rely to some extent on hand-detailed craftsmanship. That is why traditional metal roofs are also referred to as *custom metal roofs* and are the only metal roofs that can be used on complex roof geometries, including domes and cupolas.

Contemporary metal roofs are manufacturer-specific with hardly any custom-made components. The introduction of industrialized methods of metal forming and the discovery of durable paints and metallic coatings have made contemporary metal roofs an economical alternative to the traditional copper or lead-coated copper roofs. In fact, the durability and color-fastness of paints and coatings are responsible for the acceptance of sheet steel and aluminum as roofing materials.

14.1 ROOFING METALS — TYPES AND PROPERTIES

Historically, copper and lead were the metals commonly used for roofs. In fact, copper and lead have been used for centuries as a roofing material, and copper is still used in architecturally significant buildings. A properly installed copper roof can last 100 years or longer.

14.1.1 Sheet Copper

Copper weathers initially from its shiny brown surface to an earthtone brown color and finally into a blue-green color, referred to as *patina*. Patina, which is a result of the corrosion of copper, is a naturally protective layer that retards further corrosion of copper. It is regarded as a handsome finish.

The time it takes for copper to develop patina is a function of the humidity and pollutants in the air and the slope of the surface. Although the process is noticeable after 2 to 3 years, it takes 10 to 40 years for patina to develop fully depending on the atmosphere and the type of surface.

Steeply sloped surfaces take longer to develop patina. On some vertical surfaces and soffits, and in desert climates, patina may never develop. Apart from the patina, another advantage of copper as a roofing material is its softness and malleability so that it can be bent to shape easily. Copper can also be soldered easily.

Water runoff from weathered copper can stain light-colored building components such as concrete, masonry, limestone, etc. Careful detailing is, therefore, required with copper roofs so that water from the roof does not fall on such surfaces. The commonly used weight for copper roofing panels is 16 oz per sq ft, and 20 oz per sq ft for flashings.

14.1.2 Lead-Coated Copper

Historically, sheet lead was used extensively on roofs in Europe. In the United States, however, lead has had a limited use as a roofing material, although it is used commonly in flashings. The form of lead that is commonly used as a roofing material is lead-coated copper, Figure 14.1.

A lead-coated copper sheet has the appearance of lead with the durability of copper. It is malleable and also solderable. Like lead, lead-coated copper weathers into a soft gray color. Water run-off from lead-coated copper will stain dark colored surfaces.

Lead coating is typically applied over 16- to 20-oz copper sheets. The coating thickness is specified either as Class A or Class B. Class A coating has 12 to 15 lb of lead on both sides of a 100 ft^2 copper sheet; Class B has 20 to 30 lb of lead. Class B is typically specified where pollution from nearby industries is a concern or in dense urban areas that have excessive pollution from automobile exhaust.

14.1.3 Sheet Steel and Other Metals

Factory-painted and/or metallic-coated steel panels are among the most commonly used metal roof panels. The most commonly used metallic coatings consist of zinc (to obtain galvanized steel) or zinc-aluminum alloy, which has been patented as *galvalume* by its manufacturer. Other less commonly used metals are aluminum, stainless steel, and terne-coated stainless steel.

14.1 *The barrel vaults of the Kimbell Art Museum in Fort Worth, Texas (Architect: Louis I. Kahn, 1901-74) were initially (1969-72) roofed with sheet lead, but in 1996, the building was reroofed with lead-coated copper. Roofing consultant: Stephen Patterson. Photographer: Bob Wharton. Photos courtesy of the Kimbell Art Museum, Fort Worth, Texas.*

GALVANIC SERIES

Active	Zinc
	Aluminum
	Steel
	Cast iron
	Lead
	Brass
	Copper
	Bronze
	Stainless steel
	Silver
Noble	Gold

COEFFICIENT OF THERMAL EXPANSION OF COMMONLY USED METALS ($°F^{-1}$)

70×10^{-7} ▭ Steel, galvanized steel, cast iron

95×10^{-7} ▭ Copper

95×10^{-7} ▭ Stainless steel

130×10^{-7} ▭ Aluminum

150×10^{-7} ▭ Lead

175×10^{-7} ▭ Zinc

To calculate the expansion (or contraction) of a given length of a metal component, multiply the coefficient of expansion by the length of the component and the temperature differential. For instance, a 50-ft-long stainless steel component, if heated from 30°F to 130°F (a temperature differential of 100°F) will expand by $(95 \times 10^{-7})(50)(100) = 47.5 \times 10^{-3}$ ft $= 0.57$ in.

14.1.4 Galvanic Corrosion

The consideration of galvanic action is particularly important in metal roofs. Galvanic action implies the corrosion occurring in the presence of moisture between two incompatible metals in contact with each other. In other words, direct contact between incompatible metals should be avoided. As far as possible, all components of a metal roof, such as drip edges, fasteners, flashings, etc., should be of the same or compatible metals.

The compatibility of metals can be assessed from the galvanic series, which lists commonly used metals according to their propensity for atmospheric corrosion. Metals further down the series are less likely to corrode and are considered as *noble metals*. Conversely, metals further up the series are referred to as *active metals*. Thus, silver and gold do not corrode easily. On the other hand, corrosion occurs readily in zinc. That is why zinc coating on steel works as a sacrificial layer.

Two metals that are far off from each other in the series are incompatible. If they are in contact with each other, they will corrode in the presence of moisture. If incompatible metals are used together, they should be separated from each other by an intervening (electrically) nonconducting material, such as a plastic interlayer, a thick paint film, or a bituminous coating.

14.1.5 Expansion and Contraction of Roof Panels

The temperature expansion and contraction of metals is far greater than it is with other conventional roofing materials. Therefore, adequate allowance must be made for the panels to move. Since the length of roofing panels is much greater than their width, the longitudinal movement of panels — from the ridge to the eave — is a concern.

If the individual roof panels are longer than 40 ft, the use of expansion type cleats (see Figure 14.9) are recommended. Expansion cleats are generally two-piece cleats, in which the lower part is fastened to the substrate and the upper part engages into the panel. This allows the panels to float over the substrate, while being restrained against vertical uplift.

When expansion cleats are used, each panel must be fixed at one point along its length, which may be the top of the panel (at the ridge), in the middle, or at the bottom of the panel (at the eave). Whichever point of fixing is chosen, it should be the same for all panels, i.e., the fixing should be along a horizontal line on the roof. This ensures that the movement of panels is consistent throughout the roof.

Expansion of panels must be incorporated at the end that is not fixed. Thus, if the panels are fixed at the ridge, the eave detail must be designed to accommodate the expansion and contraction of the panels.

14.1.6 Oil Canning

Because metals and their coatings are highly reflective (metallic lustre), any distortion of the surface of panels appears exaggerated. The problem, referred to as *oil canning*, is worsened with the use of panels that consist of flat pans. Oil canning is less noticeable in panels that have intermediate stiffening ribs.

Oil canning can result from coils that are not initially flat, poor handling of panels on the roofing site, and the use of thin sheets. Oil canning can also result from excessive expansion and contraction of panels, particularly in copper and lead-coated copper. These metals have a low elastic limit, which means that when they are excessively stressed, they acquire a permanent, visible deformation.

Oil canning can be reduced by increasing the thickness of panels, allowing panels to move, and using matte instead of glossy finishes. Oil canning is less noticeable on metals that weather naturally, such as copper.

Architectural metal roofs require a deck and an underlayment. The deck can be any one of the deck types used in low-slope roof applications, e.g., concrete, steel, plywood (or oriented strandboard), etc. In commercial buildings, in which steel or concrete decks are common, a typical metal roof assembly consists of the structural deck, one or two layers of insulation, a layer of plywood, an underlayment and the metal roof, Figure 14.2.

In this assembly, plywood works as a nail base to which the metal panels are fastened. The underlayment provides the secondary waterproofing and is generally one layer of No. 30 (or heavier) asphalt-saturated organic felt. In some applications, however, the nail base may be omitted, and the metal panels may be fastened to the deck through the insulation.

Because the bitumen from the underlayment tends to bleed on warm days, a layer of slip sheet directly above the underlayment (below the panels) is required. The slip sheet prevents the adhesion of metal panels to the underlayment and allows the panels to move without being restrained by the underlayment. The slip sheet should be a nonbituminous building paper, such as a red rosin paper.

An ice dam protection membrane is also needed, as in other steep roofs. The recommendation for an ice dam protection membrane is the same as for other steep roofs, see Section 11.1 in Chapter 11. In areas with high snow loads, an ice dam protection membrane should be installed over the entire roof. Additionally, continuous ventilation under the plywood nail base should be provided and the roof designed as a cold roof.[14.1]

14.2 DECK AND UNDERLAYMENT

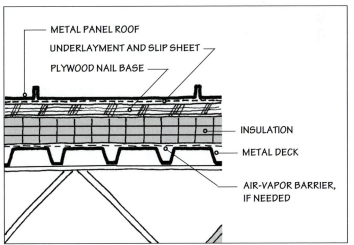

14.2 *A cross-section through an architectural metal panel roof fastened to a plywood nail base.*

Standing seam metal roofs, used in high wind uplift applications, have had problems with meeting wind uplift ratings. Air barriers are, therefore, commonly used in metal roof assemblies to increase their wind uplift resistance. A properly installed air barrier also decreases air infiltration in the building through the roof. If the air barrier is of a material that also functions as a vapor barrier (i.e., an air-vapor barrier), it will also control condensation in roof assembly. Metal roofs are more prone to condensation than other roof coverings.

14.3 PANEL PROFILES AND TYPES OF SEAMS BETWEEN PANELS

Architectural metal roofs are generally of the standing seam type in which each panel has two upturned legs, one at each longitudinal edge of the panel. The upturn is generally 3/4 in. to 1-1/2 in. high, depending on roof slope and the rainfall intensity. A higher upturn is needed where the rainfall intensity is high. The width of the panel varies from 10 in. to 24 in., Figure 14.3. The upturned edges of adjacent panels meet to form a seam, which can be waterproofed in several ways.

The panels are generally fabricated to the required profile at the construction site from a coil of (prefinished) metal, Figure 14.4. This means that panels of almost any length can be used. The longer the panel, the smaller the number of transverse seams.

In many cases, only one length of panel on each side of a sloping roof is needed, completely precluding the use of transverse seams. In such a case, there is only one joint between the two panels from the two opposite slopes of the roof — at the ridge. The length of a panel is limited by its handleability. Panels of 100 ft in length are not uncommon.

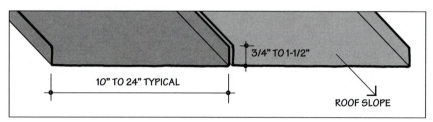

14.3 *Typical metal panel profile.*

Site fabrication of panels reduces the cost of transporting long panels from the factory to the site. In tall buildings, the panel fabricating equipment is generally placed on the roof, which avoids lifting panels from the ground to the roof.

The panels are fastened to the substrate by metal cleats, whose design varies from manufacturer to manufacturer. One such fastening method is shown in Figure 14.5. The center-to-center distance between cleats is a function of the wind uplift on the roof and may vary from 12 in. (or less) to 5 ft. The cleat shown in Figure 14.5 is of a *fixed type* that does not allow any movement in panels. Generally, if panels are longer than 40 ft, *expansion cleats* are recommended. Expansion cleats[1] allow the panels to move.

---

[1] See Figure 14.9 for a typical expansion cleat.

SHEET
METAL ROLL

14.4(a) *Panels are formed at the site from a roll and cut to size. Photo by Madan Mehta.*

14.4(b) *A panel being carried away to make way for the next panel. Photo by Madan Mehta.*

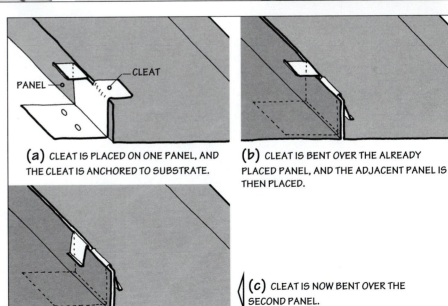

PANEL — CLEAT

(a) CLEAT IS PLACED ON ONE PANEL, AND THE CLEAT IS ANCHORED TO SUBSTRATE.

(b) CLEAT IS BENT OVER THE ALREADY PLACED PANEL, AND THE ADJACENT PANEL IS THEN PLACED.

(c) CLEAT IS NOW BENT OVER THE SECOND PANEL.

14.5 *Anchoring of panels to the substrate through cleats.*

After the panels have been fastened, each seam can be covered with a snap-on cover piece, Figure 14.6(a) to (c). The snap-on cover piece has a factory-applied sealant throughout the length of the cover piece, which squeezes over and around the panel seams, providing additional waterproofing, Figure 14.7.

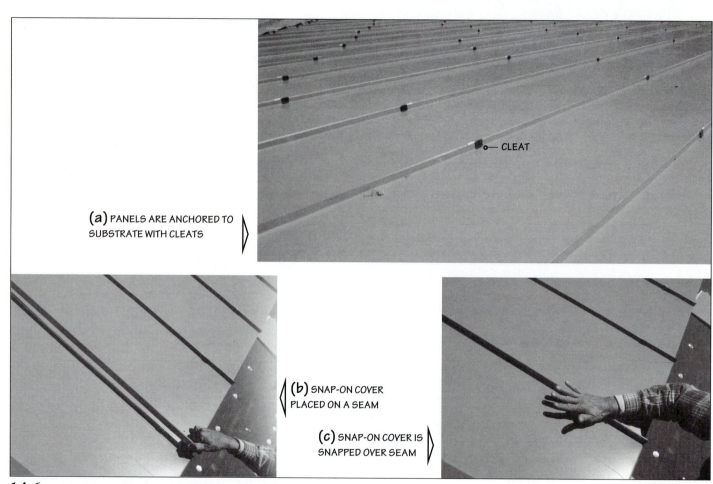

(a) PANELS ARE ANCHORED TO SUBSTRATE WITH CLEATS ▷

— CLEAT

◁ **(b)** SNAP-ON COVER PLACED ON A SEAM

(c) SNAP-ON COVER IS SNAPPED OVER SEAM ▷

14.6 *Snap-on covers on seams. Photos by Madan Mehta.*

14.3.1 Double-Lock Standing Seams

Waterproofing the seams of adjacent panels can be achieved by field-bending the seams, which locks the panels together. A commonly used seam locking method is referred to as double-lock standing seam, Figure 14.8. To achieve a double-lock standing seam, the edges of the adjacent panels are field-bent in two stages by a power seaming machine or manually using tongs. Note that the panels' profile is slightly different from those of Figure 14.3.

Two types of cleats commonly used to anchor the panels to the substrate in a double-lock standing seam roof are shown in Figure 14.9. The cleat shown in Figure 14.9(a) is a fixed cleat, which does not allow the movement of panels. The cleat shown in Figure 14.9(b) — a two-piece cleat — is an expansion cleat. Expansion cleats are recommended if the panels are longer than 40 ft. When expansion cleats are used, each panel must be anchored by one fixed cleat, see Section 14.1.5. The other cleats are all expansion cleats.

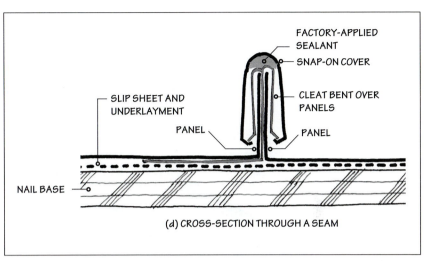

(d) CROSS-SECTION THROUGH A SEAM

14.7 *Section through a seam with a snap-on cover.*

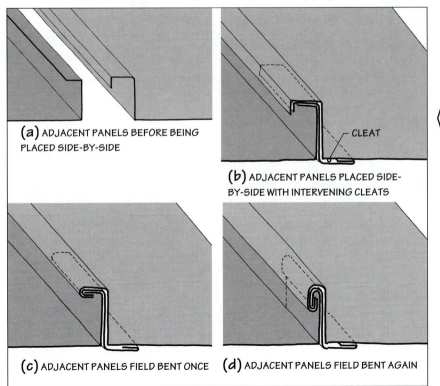

(a) ADJACENT PANELS BEFORE BEING PLACED SIDE-BY-SIDE

(b) ADJACENT PANELS PLACED SIDE-BY-SIDE WITH INTERVENING CLEATS

(c) ADJACENT PANELS FIELD BENT ONCE

(d) ADJACENT PANELS FIELD BENT AGAIN

14.8 *Double-lock standing seam.*

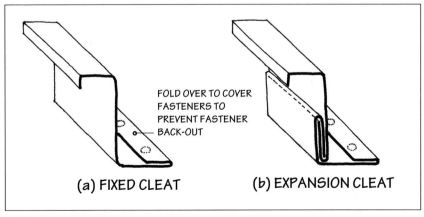

(a) FIXED CLEAT   (b) EXPANSION CLEAT

14.9 *Fixed and expansion cleats used with double-lock standing seams.*

14.3.2 Batten Seams

In place of thin snap-on covers, shown in Figures 14.6 and 14.7, wider snap-on covers are sometimes used to highlight the seams. The wider covers (nearly 2 in. wide) are referred to as *battens*. They are held by cleats that anchor the adjacent panels in addition to engaging the overlying batten. Manufacturers have their own designs for the battens as well as the cleats. One batten seam assembly is shown in Figure 14.10.

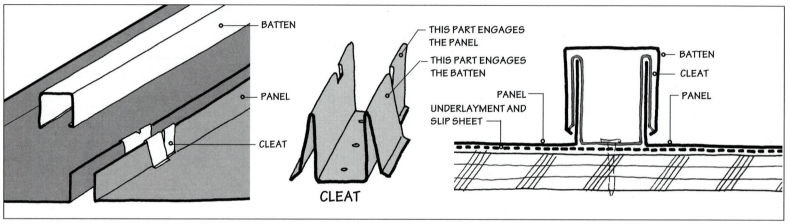

14.10 *Typical prefabricated batten seam roof components.*

The batten seam assembly of Figure 14.10 has its roots in the age-old practice of constructing batten seam copper roofs — a practice that is still used today. In this system, 2 x 2 wood battens separate the adjacent panels that are anchored together by U-shape cleats, Figure 14.11(a). The battens are slightly tapered down to allow for expansion and contraction of panels. A cover sheet wraps over the cleats, Figure 14.11(b). Finally, the cover sheet, panels, and cleats are field-bent, Figure 14.11(c).

14.3.3 Flat Seams

Another method of connecting metal roof panels is by using flat seams. The construction of a flat seam roof is shown in Figure 14.12. It consists of individual panels (which are flat metal sheets) that interlock by engaging folded edges of adjacent sheets into each other. To achieve a flat seam, two adjacent edges of each sheet are folded *over* and the other two adjacent edges are folded *under*. The folds are typically 3/4-in. wide, Figure 14.13.

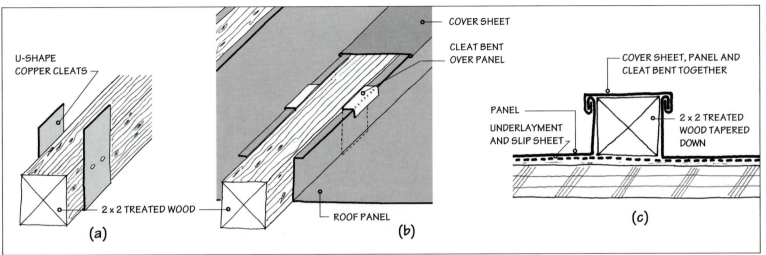

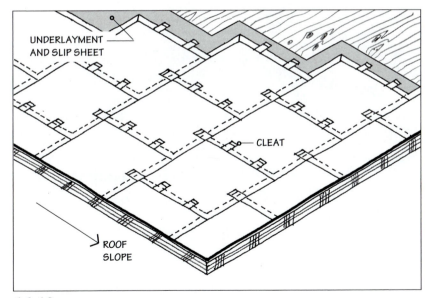

14.11 *Traditional batten seam roof.*

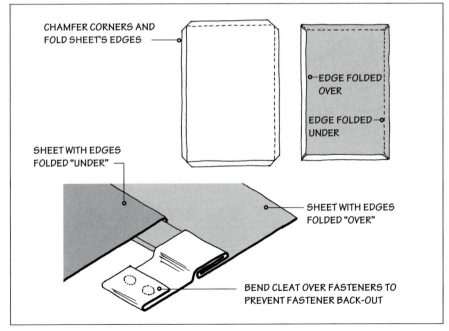

14.12 *Sheet layout with flat seams.*

14.13 *Details of flat seams.*

Cleats are placed in each folded-over edge. The sheets are locked into each other by inserting a folded-under edge of a sheet into the folded-over edge of the adjacent sheet. This process is repeated for each longitudinal and transverse joint. The transverse seams are staggered. Each seam is malleted and soldered. For roof slopes greater than 8:12, the National Roofing Contractors Association[14.2] allows the use of nonsoldered seams.

A flat seam roof is generally used with soft metals such as copper and lead-coated copper. Since standing seam or batten seam roofs cannot be used on a doubly-curved surface, such as a dome or a shell, flat seams are the only system of joining individual metal sheets. When used on a singly-curved surface, such as a barrel vault, flat seams retain the clarity of the roof's form, Figure 14.14.

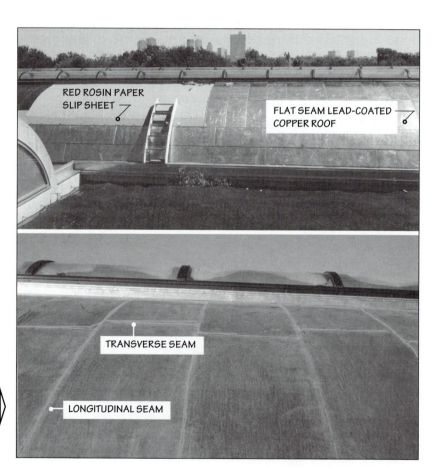

RED ROSIN PAPER
SLIP SHEET

FLAT SEAM LEAD-COATED
COPPER ROOF

TRANSVERSE SEAM

LONGITUDINAL SEAM

14.14 *Reroofing of the Kimbell Art Museum in 1996 (Architect: Louis I. Kahn, 1901-74) with flat seam lead-coated copper sheets. Roofing consultant: Stephen Patterson. Photographer: Larry Eubank. Photos courtesy of the Kimbell Art Museum, Fort Worth, Texas.*

A typical ridge detail is shown in Figure 14.15, which consists of a continuous Z-shape sheet metal closure set in sealant and soldered to the underlying metal panels. A preformed ridge cap engages into the closure. An ice dam protection membrane is adhered over the ridge directly below the roof panels.

Figure 14.16 shows a typical eave detail. Note that the flat portion of roof panels is turned over the eave flashing.

14.4 RIDGE, EAVE, AND FLASHING DETAILS

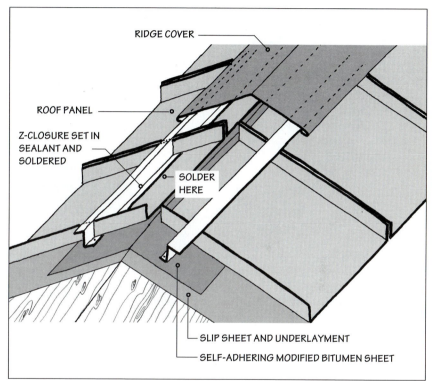

SLIP SHEET AND UNDERLAYMENT

ICE DAM PROTECTION MEMBRANE

EAVE FLASHING, SEE DETAIL BELOW

TURN PANEL'S EDGE OVER EAVE FLASHING

EAVE FLASHING

CONTINUOUS CLEAT

ICE DAM PROTECTION MEMBRANE

SLIP SHEET AND UNDERLAYMENT

RIDGE COVER

ROOF PANEL

Z-CLOSURE SET IN SEALANT AND SOLDERED

SOLDER HERE

SLIP SHEET AND UNDERLAYMENT

SELF-ADHERING MODIFIED BITUMEN SHEET

14.15 *A typical ridge detail.*

14.16 *A typical eave detail.*

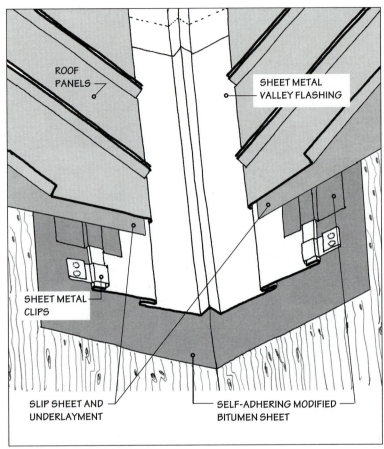

ROOF PANELS

SHEET METAL VALLEY FLASHING

SHEET METAL CLIPS

SLIP SHEET AND UNDERLAYMENT

SELF-ADHERING MODIFIED BITUMEN SHEET

14.17 *A typical valley detail.*

The principles of flashing in valleys and around roof penetrations are similar to those of slate or tile roofs. A typical valley flashing detail is shown in Figure 14.17. The National Roofing Contractors Association[14.3] recommends that the panels overlap valley flashing by at least 4 in., and the minimum exposed width of valley flashing is 5 in. The width of the exposed part of valley flashing may be increased by 1/8 in. per ft toward the bottom of the valley, as in other steep roofs.

REFERENCES

14.1   Mackinlay, I., and Flood, R. "Roof Slopes, Ice Dams and Cold Roofs," *The Construction Specifier* (January 2000), pp. 31-36.

14.2   National Roofing Contractors Association. *NRCA Roofing and Waterproofing Manual* (Rosemont, IL: 1996), p. 1359.

14.3   Ibid., p. 1389.

15

ROOF WARRANTIES

Roof warranties have been a controversial issue in roofing since their introduction in the beginning of the twentieth century. To someone unfamiliar with roof warranties, a roof warranty implies that if the roof fails to perform as warranted, the warrantor (generally the roofing material manufacturer) will do whatever is necessary to bring the roof back to its warranted state of performance. Unfortunately, the reality is far from this implication.

A roof warranty is not only a legal document, it is an intricate legal document. It is generally provided to the owner by the roofing material manufacturer, who by virtue of its financial position, has access to the best legal pundits experienced in construction warranties. A warranty is drafted to generally protect the interest of the manufacturer and to limit its liability.

The architect or the roofing consultant must, therefore, advise the owner to consult an attorney who specializes in such issues to determine what a warranty will (or will not) cover in case the need to invoke the warranty arises. The attorney will also advise whether the warranty being offered by the manufacturer is worth its price, because most worthwhile warranties cost an additional amount to the owner, increasing the initial cost of the roof.

A detailed discussion of roof warranties is obviously outside the scope of this text, since it is addressed primarily to architects, engineers, and roofing consultants. However, even these professionals must understand the fundamentals of roof warranties. In some cases, the roof warranty may impact the selection of the roofing material manufacturer and its particular system.

Usually, a system with a good performance record carries a better warranty. On the other hand, the manufacturer of a new and an untested roofing system may offer a better warranty to induce the buyer.

The aim of this chapter is, therefore, to examine the basics of roof warranties. More specifically, it describes the history of roof warranties, types, lengths of coverage, warrantor's monetary obligations, warranty charges, and typical exclusions.

However, it must be underlined that a roof warranty is not a replacement for a good roof design, construction, on-site quality control, and, above all, good roof maintenance. Indeed, the best overall warranty that an owner can obtain is through sound technical advice and a good maintenance record.

15.1 ROOFING BOND — A PRECURSOR TO ROOF WARRANTIES

When the built-up roof was first introduced in the latter part of the 19th century, the roofing material manufacturers not only provided the materials but also functioned as roof installers. As the built-up roof grew in popularity and use, manufacturers were forced to give up roof installation, concentrating on material manufacturing only. This gave birth to a new trade group called *roofing contractors*.

Although some early roofing contractors were excellent and highly professional, many had little commitment to their trade, and many entered the trade with insufficient or no experience. This led to many roofing problems and premature failures of roofs, in which the distinction between poor material and poor installation was often obscure.

Concerned with the adverse impact of roofing problems on their business, manufacturers introduced a few quality control measures. The first such measure was to standardize built-up roof specifications. This was initiated in 1906 by the Barrett Company, a leading manufacturer at the time. The company compiled a code of good roofing practice,[15.1] called the *Barrett Specifications*.

The second quality control measure was also initiated by the Barrett Company. In 1916, the company introduced the entire line of products to be used in a built-up roof, i.e., the felts, bitumen, flashings, etc. Thus was born the "roofing system" as we know it today. To gain an edge over their competitors, the Barrett Company backed its system with a *roofing bond*.

The roofing bond was not a warranty as per the definition of the term "warranty," but a first step toward it. The bond simply implied that if the manufacturer's system failed to perform as stated in the bond, the manufacturer was financially liable. To strengthen the bond's credibility, the manufacturer arranged to have its financial liability assumed by a bonding agency, generally an insurance company. The bonding agency guaranteed that if the manufacturer became financially incapable of honoring the bond, it would do so on the manufacturer's behalf.

To ensure the success of this new strategy, the Barrett Company introduced a contractor approval program. The roofing bond was only provided for roofs that adopted the Barrett roofing system and had it installed by a Barrett-approved roofing contractor. The Barrett's strategy paid off, and other manufacturers soon followed its course.

Although successful as a marketing strategy, the bond provided little real value to the owner. For instance, the original Barrett's bond cost the owner $1.50 per roof square (100 ft^2) and guaranteed a maximum of $5 per square as the penal sum. In other words, the premium for the bond was a hefty 30% of the value of the bond. Additionally, $5 per square was far less than the amount needed to replace the roof at that time.

Difference Between a Guaranty and a Warranty

Although used interchangeably in everyday language, the terms "guaranty" and "warranty" have a subtle distinction in some legal quarters. Warranty is an undertaking by the warrantor to make good on its liability under the terms and conditions of the warranty. A guaranty is a collateral or separate undertaking that does not impose primary responsibility on the guarantor. The guaranty (and, hence, the guarantor) comes into the picture only when the individual or the business whose performance was guaranteed has defaulted.

Based on these definitions, the early roofing bonds were not warranties. Similarly, in contemporary material and workmanship warranties issued by the manufacturer, the manufacturer, in fact, warrants its materials and guarantees the workmanship of its approved roofing contractor. In other words, the manufacturer warrants the roof "as installed."

Despite its lack of value, the roofing bond was the first attempt by manufacturers to somewhat indemnify owners. Its major advantage lay in that it forced manufacturers to introduce two significant roofing concepts: (1) the roofing system, and (2) the roofing contractor approval — concepts that have survived to this day.

Roofing bonds remained the primary form of warranty until the 1980s when manufacturers dropped bonding agencies as the guarantors. Instead, the manufacturers themselves became the warrantors. Before discussing present-day roof warranties, it is important to distinguish between the following two forms of warranties, which apply to all types of warranties, not just roof warranties:

- Implied

- Express

An implied warranty exists whether or not the goods or service provided carry their own separate warranty. An implied warranty is a statutory obligation imposed by law from the nature of transactions between the two parties. It exists even if neither party mentions anything about it at the time of the transaction. An example of an implied warranty is the one that exists between an owner and building contractor in that the contractor is supposed to perform the work in a workmanlike manner and in accordance with the standards prevailing in the contractor's trade.

Another form of implied warranty is that which exists under the Uniform Commercial Code (UCC). The UCC, which has been incorporated into most state laws, lays down the terms of sale transactions between the buyer and the seller of goods. Under the UCC, the seller of goods is deemed to warrant that the goods are merchantable and are fit for the commonly used purpose for which they are sold. In other words, the seller is deemed to warrant a fair quality of its product that conforms with the description and labeling of the product.

The UCC permits the seller to disclaim in writing any parts of the implied warranty of merchantability and fitness. It is under this provision that an express warranty overrides an implied warranty. For instance, the seller could describe the situations in which its product, if used, is not warranted.

15.2 IMPLIED AND EXPRESS WARRANTIES

In an express warranty, the obligations of both parties under the warranty and the warranty's limitations are expressed (specifically stated). A present-day roof warranty is, in general, a type of express warranty. A valid express warranty may override an implied warranty if it is so stated in the express warranty. For instance, most roof warranties state that the warranty is the "sole and exclusive remedy" available to the owner and is issued in lieu of all other warranties, express or implied. In such a warranty, the owner may gives up his (her) rights under the UCC, other state statutes, or the common law.

15.3 LOW-SLOPE ROOF WARRANTIES

It is important to appreciate that all roof warranties (with few exceptions) only cover defects pertaining to roof leaks, and nothing else. A defect that does not cause a leak is not considered a defect under the terms of a typical roof warranty. Thus, wear and tear of the roof membrane or any other roofing component, loss of granules, wind scouring of ballast, etc., are not covered by the warranty. Similarly, blisters, wrinkles, discolorations, etc., are also not warranted unless they cause a leak.

The National Roofing Contractors Association provides an annual evaluation of roof warranties issued by nearly 100 roofing material manufacturers. It is a valuable resource[15.2] to gain an understanding of the differences between available warranties. In analyzing warranties, NRCA identifies 27 components of information, Table 15.1. Here, we shall focus only on the following few important ones.

15.3.1 Scope of Coverage

In discussing the scope of coverage, two types of warranties may be identified:

- Materials only, i.e., a product warranty

- Material and workmanship, i.e., a systems warranty

A *product warranty* covers leaks caused by defective materials only. It excludes leaks arising from roof installation. Even the materials warranted must be specific to the manufacturer. Since it is usually difficult to distinguish between whether the leak was caused by a defective material or a defective installation, a product warranty is not worthy of any premium charged by the manufacturer.

An alternative to a product warranty is a *materials and workmanship warranty*. It covers both defective installation as well as defective materials, and eliminates the potential conflict between the manufacturer and the contractor. A better materials and workmanship warranty warrants virtually the entire roof assembly, and is generally referred to as the *systems warranty*.

A systems warranty is offered for a roof that is installed by a contractor who is approved by the manufacturer and in accordance with the manufacturer's specifications and details. Contractors are approved based on their experience, financial standing, and the training provided to them by the manufacturer.

A systems warranty typically warrants the roof membrane, the insulation, and the membrane flashing. In any case, manufacturers do not warrant components of the assembly that are not provided by them. Thus, even a systems warranty excludes sheet metal flashings and counterflashings, expansion joint materials, vents, vapor barriers, etc., since these materials are generally not provided by the roofing material manufacturers.

The anomaly, however, is that most leaks occur due to components that are generally excluded from a systems warranty. For instance, leaks are often caused where sheet metal flashing is integrated into the membrane or because of defective counterflashing, or at roof terminations, such as an expansion joint. Some manufacturers are, however, trying to correct this situation. It is likely that in the future, manufacturers will sell sheet metal flashings and also other accessories, and include them as part of their systems warranty.

15.3.2 Title of Warranty

Most warranty documents are two-page documents, printed back-to-back. On the top of the first page, the title of warranty is printed, which states whether it is a "material warranty" or a "systems warranty." In most cases, the title is an accurate description of the warranty's scope, but sometimes, the title may be misleading.

For instance, a warranty carrying the title "labor and material guaranty" may, on the face of it, indicate that it covers defective materials as well as defective installation. However, the warranty details may read otherwise. Generally, such a warranty only covers labor associated with removing and replacing defective materials.

Therefore, it is important to read through the entire warranty document to obtain the correct scope of a warranty's coverage. The title "high performance roofing guarantee" does not explicitly state whether it is a material or a systems warranty. Generally, if the title does not state it as a "systems warranty," it is very likely a "materials only" warranty.

Table 15.1 Components of Information in NRCA's Analysis of Roof Warranties

1. Identity of issuing entity	16. Minimum charge
2. Title, original publication date, and identifying symbol (if any)	17. Ineligible structures or building use
3. Product, specification, or system covered	18. Preconstruction notice and approval requirements
4. Scope of coverage	19. Approved, authorized, or licensed applicators
5. Length of coverage	20. Job inspection policy
6. Nature of remedy	
7. Monetary limitations	21. Contractor's post-installation obligation
8. Notification requirements	22. Backed by a name insurance company or surety company
9. Exclusive or additional remedy	23. Issuing entity manufactures and/or sells products
10. Inclusion of consequential damages	
11. Determination of warranty applicability	24. Conditions for renewal or extension
12. Specific exclusions from coverage	25. Assignability
13. Wind coverage/exclusion	
14. Index of specific conditions to make warranty ineffective or null and void	26. Special features/conditions
15. Cost to obtain	27. Executed by owner

15.3.3 Length of Coverage

The length of coverage refers to the number of years for which the manufacturer warrants the roof. It may vary from 5 to 25 years on a low-slope roof and up to 50 years for some steep roofs. For a low-slope roof, 10 years is the most common warranty period.

Under normal circumstances, most low-slope roof systems can be expected to last 10 years, or made to last 10 years with some maintenance. The risk of failure increases after 10 years. Therefore, longer term warranties (15, 20, or 25 years) provide greater value to the owner and will more likely be utilized than shorter term warranties.

15.3.4 Warranty Charges

Warranty charges are based on a dollar amount per roof square (100 ft^2). This dollar amount increases with the length of coverage. For instance, a 10-year warranty may cost the owner \$5 per roof square, and a 20-year warranty may cost \$15 per square. The decision to select a longer term warranty becomes an economic decision.

The warranty cost may be a better value for a high-rise roof than for a low-rise roof, since it costs more to replace the roof on a high-rise building than on a low-rise building. For example, the replacement cost of roof for a low-rise warehouse may be \$300 per square. To replace an identical roof system on a high-rise building may cost \$1,500 per square or more. The warranty charges for both roofs will generally be the same.

15.3.5 Monetary Limitations

The monetary value of a warranty, which is the maximum sum the manufacturer promises to spend for the repair of a roof during the entire warranty period, is referred to as the *penal sum* or the *maximum monetary obligation*. The penal sum in some warranties may be a certain dollar amount per roof square. In product warranties (materials only), this sum is generally limited to the original purchase price of the materials.

In a systems warranty, a similar agreement limits the manufacturer's monetary obligation to the original installed cost of the roof, referred to as the *OIC warranty*. Since the monetary obligation in an OIC warranty does not include inflation, the real value of the warranty depreciates with time.

In some warranties, there is no limit on the penal sum, referred to as *no dollar limit* (NDL) warranty. In such a warranty, the manufacturer will spend whatever amount is necessary to repair the roof within the warranty period. In an NDL warranty, the manufacturer will generally enter the phrase "none stated" under the "monetary obligation" column. If other conditions in the warranty are acceptable, an NDL warranty is the only warranty that will be of real value to the owner if the need arises.

15.3.6 Exclusions from Coverage

The exclusions from coverage are of two kinds: legal and technical. The legal exclusions have already been discussed in Section 15.2. For instance, almost all warranties exclude recovery available to the owner under other legal theories of recovery by containing the clause that this warranty is the "sole and exclusive" remedy available to the owner.

As for the technical exclusions, the NRCA lists several exclusions commonly used by manufacturers to void the warranty, Table 15.2. Not all exclusions listed in Table 15.2 are contained in every warranty, since exclusions depend on whether the warranty is a product or a systems warranty. In any case, even the better warranties contain the first 8 to 10 exclusions of Table 15.2.

Exclusion due to wind is generally treated as a separate exclusion and not listed as a part of exclusion due to natural disaster, see Item 1 of Table 15.2. This is because the term "wind" needs further definition as to its speed. Some manufacturers' warranties exclude damage caused to the roof from wind (regardless of the speed of wind). Other manufacturers cover wind-caused damage up to a certain wind speed.

Manufacturers generally specify wind speeds according to the Beaufort Scale,[1] e.g., gale, strong gale, storm, etc. Thus, a warranty may exclude wind damage caused by a gale (wind speed between 39 to 46 mph) or a higher wind speed. The better warranties cover wind damage up to (but not including) hurricane wind speed (72 mph).

Table 15.2 Typical Exclusions from Roof Warranties

1. Natural disasters such as lightning, tornadoes, earthquakes, and hail.
2. Failure of roof caused by negligence, abuse, or misuse.
3. Failure of roof caused by accidents, vandalism, civil disobedience, and war.
4. Failure of roof due to the failure or damage to building's structure.
5. Repairs or alterations to roof, and the addition of fixtures on or through the roof.
6. Change in the usage of building.
7. Traffic or storage of materials on roof.
8. Inadequate drainage and roof ponding.
9. Negligence in regular maintenance of roof.
10. Moisture entering the roof through walls, copings, and other parts of the building, including adjacent buildings.
11. Defective insulation and roof deck or any other underlying component
12. Environmental fallout, chemical attack, or use of hazardous materials inside the building.
13. Discoloration or change of appearance of the roofing material.
14. Repairs performed or materials furnished by others.
15. Fire
16. Faulty construction or design of building including copings, parapet walls, chimneys, skylights, etc.
17. Exposure to contaminants not preapproved by the manufacturer.
18. Materials not applied per the manufacturer's specifications and application instructions.
19. Installation of roof membrane.
20. Abnormal climatic conditions.
21. Infiltration or condensation of moisture within the roof assembly.
22. Damage caused by falling objects.
23. Acts of parties other than the manufacturer and/or roofing contractor.
24. Growth of vegetation on roof.

Some Beaufort Scale Terms

Description	Wind speed (mph)	Description	Wind speed (mph)
Moderate breeze	13 - 18	Strong gale	47 - 54
Fresh breeze	19 - 24	Storm	55 - 63
Strong breeze	25 - 31	Violent storm	64 - 72
Moderate (or near gale)	32 - 38	Hurricane	73 - 136
Gale	39 - 46		

---

[1] The wind speed in Beaufort Scale is the fastest mile wind speed, not the 3-second gust speed, see Section 8.2.2 in Chapter 8.

15.4 ASPHALT SHINGLE WARRANTIES

Because an asphalt shingle roof is the most commonly used roof in the United States, a few words about the nature of asphalt shingle warranties are necessary. Asphalt shingles generally carry a 20- to 40-year warranty, depending on the type of shingles and the manufacturer. Thus, "25-year shingles" or "40-year shingles" are terms commonly used by the manufacturers.

Manufacturers generally do not charge any extra amount for the warranty; any warranty charge is included in the price of shingles. Almost all shingle warranties are "materials only" warranties. In other words, they do not cover defective installation.

Most manufacturers cover the replacement of defective shingles and the installation of new ones. However, hardly any manufacturer covers the disposal of defective shingles.

The labor cost associated with the replacement of defective shingles and the installation of new ones is generally limited to the first few years of the warranty period — generally up to 10 years even in the case of the 40-year shingles. After this initial period, the manufacturer will only replace defective shingles, but not pay for their disposal or the installation of new shingles.

Virtually all shingle manufacturers have some prorating formula for replacement shingles. This means that the value of the warranty decreases over time. Thus, after 15 years in a 30-year shingles, the manufacturer will pay only half the original cost of the replacement shingles. The present worth of these shingles may be three times of their original cost. In other words, the owner will get only one-sixth the present cost of the shingles!

Shingle manufacturers also limit coverage for damage caused by high winds. Generally, the damage caused by winds exceeding 60 mph is not covered. Some manufactures use 54 mph wind speed in place of 60 mph. The wind speed in windstorms and hurricanes often exceeds these values.

In substance, the length of a warranty should not be used as a criterion for selecting asphalt shingles. The selection should be based on the installed cost, aesthetics, weight of shingles, and the remedy available to recover cost for shingle replacement and their disposal.

As stated earlier, a roof warranty is a complicated legal document, of which only a few important issues have been discussed here. Several other important issues must be considered for a comprehensive coverage. For instance, the owner should be aware of the financial status of the manufacturer to ensure that the manufacturer will be able to honor its obligations under the warranty. For instance, an important information to find out is the manufacturer's financial standing and its insurance coverage.

Although an experienced attorney is the owner's best guide, an experienced architect or roofing consultant is a good source of information about the manufacturer's reputation and the manufacturer's record with respect to servicing the warranty. Generally, a large and established roofing manufacturer will be more generous to the owner.

Additionally, a manufacturer may agree to modify and negotiate the warranty terms, if requested. For instance, one roofing consultant requires the built-up roof to carry a 20-year systems warranty, including an initial 5-year warranty during which all labor, materials, and workmanship required to repair blisters, ridges, wrinkles, etc., is covered regardless of whether a leak occurs or not.

In any case, the manufacturer's aim, in general, is to limit its liability. Therefore, its warranty is an instrument to achieve that end. In some cases, particularly in a "materials only" warranty, the owner may be better off not being a party to any warranty document, because such a document may exclude his (her) recovery remedies under the common law or other statutes.

On the other hand, some warranties are definitely worthwhile. While providing coverage for repairs, they also provide some indirect benefits to the owner. For instance, most systems warranties require a roof maintenance program to keep the warranty in force,. This impels the owner to maintain the roof. Without this requirement, most owners tend to neglect and abuse the roof. Because the manufacturer has a stake in the warranted roof, it generally provides its own periodic roof inspection — another advantage of the warranty.

The approved contractor requirement is another indirect benefit to the owner. This improves the quality of work because the contractor and its crew go through a regular training program established by the contractor.

15.5 FINAL COMMENTS

REFERENCES

15.1   National Roofing Contractors Association. *100 Years of Roofing in America* (Rosemont, IL: 1986), pp. 70-71.

15.2   National Roofing Contractors Association. *NRCA Roofing and Waterproofing Manual* (Rosemont, IL: 1996).

REVIEW QUESTIONS

1

Introduction to Roofing

1.1 Discuss the basic differences between a low-slope roof and a steep roof.

1.2 With the help of a sketch, outline the important components of a steep roof.

1.3 With the help of a sketch, outline the important components of a low-slope roof.

1.4 List various types of coverings used on a steep roof. Which of these roof coverings are more commonly used?

1.5 What is the purpose of an underlayment in a steep roof? Which material is commonly used for the purpose?

1.6 With the help of a sketch, explain why and under what conditions an ice dam will form on a steep roof.

1.7 What is a flashing? Where is it used on a steep roof?

1.8 List the commonly used roof membranes on a low-slope roof.

1.9 List two more commonly used single-ply roof membranes.

1.10 List the commonly used roof deck materials for a low-slope roof.

1.11 List some of the important factors that must be considered in the design and selection of a low-slope roof.

2

Built-up Roof Membranes

2.1 With the help of a sketch, explain the composition of a built-up roof membrane.

2.2 Explain the individual functions of the felts and the bitumen in a built-up roof membrane.

2.3 Discuss the advantages and disadvantages of organic and inorganic felts. Which of these is commonly used in a built-up roof. Why?

2.4 What are the typical dimensions of a built-up roof felt roll?

2.5 Explain what is meant by a No. 15 felt? A No. 30 felt?

2.6 Discuss various types of fiberglass felts used in a built-up roof membrane.

2.7 With the help of a sketch and notes, explain in detail the type of built-up roof you will specify for a building where the roof's durability is important. Give the specification of each component of the roof membrane.

2.8 With the help of a sketch, explain what is meant by the terms "exposure" and "headlap" in the layout of built-up roof felts.

2.9 How much are the headlap and exposure of felts in a 3-ply built-up roof? A 4-ply built-up roof?

2.10 With the help of sketches and notes, explain the difference between the built-up roof felts in a shingle application and in a phased application.

2.11 Explain why built-up roof felts are generally laid in shingle fashion.

2.12 What is meant by the term "roof square"?

2.13 Write notes on (1) base sheet, (2) ventilation sheet, and (3) cap sheet.

2.14 Discuss the advantages and disadvantages of an asphalt built-up roof versus a coal tar built-up roof.

2.15 What are the important differences between various types of asphalts used in a built-up roof?

2.16 Which type of asphalt would you specify for interply application in a built-up roof in a warm climate, such as in Phoenix, Arizona? In a cold climate, such as in Buffalo, New York?

2.17 Which type of asphalt would you specify for the flood coat in a built-up roof in a warm climate, such as in Phoenix, Arizona? In a cold climate, such as in Buffalo, New York?

2.18 What are the important differences between various types of coal tars used in a built-up roof?

2.19 List various types of materials used in the flood coat of a built-up roof, giving their function and typical weights.

2.20 List some of the nonaggregate surfacings used in a built-up roof.

2.21 In which situations, would you specify a built-up roof with a flood coat and gravel? A built-up roof with a cap sheet?

2.22 Write notes on (1) cutback asphalt, (2) roofer's cement, and (3) asphalt emulsion.

3

Modified Bitumen and Single-Ply Roof Membranes

3.1 What are the advantages of using a modified bitumen instead of an unmodified bitumen in roofing?

3.2 List the types of modified asphalts used in modified bitumen sheets. Give their relative advantages and disadvantages.

3.3 With the help of a sketch, explain the anatomy of a modified bitumen sheet.

3.4 What is the width of a typical modified bitumen sheet?

3.5 What are the essential differences between an SBS-modified bitumen sheet and an APP-modified bitumen sheet?

3.6 Explain which type of asphalt is commonly used as interply bitumen in an SBS-modified bitumen roof? Why?

3.7 With the help of a sketch, explain the anatomy of a typical 2-ply SBS-modified bitumen roof laid over a steel deck.

3.8 With the help of a sketch, explain the anatomy of a typical 3-ply SBS-modified bitumen roof laid over a steel deck.

3.9 With the help of a sketch, explain the anatomy of a 3-ply SBS-modified bitumen roof laid over a plywood deck.

3.10 With the help of a sketch, explain the anatomy of a hybrid modified bitumen roof.

3.11 Explain why an SBS-modified bitumen sheet is commonly used as flashing material in a built-up or an SBS-modified bitumen roof.

3.12 A 4-ply built-up roof is to be applied using cold adhesives. Give the specifications for the roof.

3.13 Discuss the advantages and disadvantages of a cold-applied built-up roof versus a conventional hot-applied built-up roof.

3.14 Discuss the advantages and disadvantages of a torch-applied modified bitumen roof versus a mop-applied modified bitumen roof.

3.15 Explain how the lap seams in a torch-applied modified bitumen roof are treated.

3.16 What is the difference between a thermoplastic and a thermosetting plastic? Which of the commonly used single-ply roof membranes are thermoplastics? Which are thermosetting plastics?

3.17 Discuss the advantages and disadvantages of a single-ply roof over a built-up roof.

3.18 What do the following acronyms stand for? (1) EPDM, (2) PVC, (3) CSPE, and (4) TPO.

3.19 List the two more commonly used single-ply roof membranes. Which of these has a greater market share?

3.20 Compare the performances of EPDM and PVC roofs with respect to fire resistance, ultraviolet degradation, and resistance to kitchen oils.

3.21 How are the lap seams in an EPDM roof membrane typically adhered together?

3.22 How are the lap seams in a PVC roof membrane typically adhered together?

3.23 List materials with which the following roof membranes are not compatible: (1) EPDM, and (2) PVC.

3.24 List the three commonly used methods of securing a single-ply roof membrane to the substrate.

3.25 What are the advantages and limitations of a ballasted single-ply roof?

3.26 What are the advantages and limitations of a mechanically fastened single-ply roof?

3.27 What are the advantages and limitations of a fully adhered single-ply roof?

3.28 With the help of a sketch, explain the installation of a mechanically attached EPDM roof membrane with small width rolls.

3.29 With the help of a sketch, explain the installation of a mechanically attached EPDM roof membrane with large-width rolls.

4

Roof Insulation

4.1 Explain how insulation affects the durability of a low-slope roof.

4.2 Discuss the advantages and disadvantages of insulating a low-slope roof.

4.3 Draw the typically used graphic notations for flexible and rigid insulations.

4.4 With the help of a sketch, explain how all three modes of heat transfer through a building component generally occur simultaneously.

4.5 Using Table 4.1, determine the R-value of:
(1) an 8-in. nominal (7.625 in. actual) brick wall,
(2) a 2-in.-thick EPS board, and
(3) a 2- in.-thick polyisocyanurate board.

4.6 Which insulating materials have HCFC gas trapped in their cell cavities?

4.7 Explain what is meant by the term "aged R-value." To which materials does this apply?

4.8 What is meant by surface resistance? Explain.

4.9 What is the R-value of a skylight consisting of a single sheet of glass?

4.10 What is emissivity? Explain.

4.11 Which material is commonly used to retard heat transfer across a cavity space? What is the mechanism by which it does so?

4.12 What is the approximate R-value of a typical attic cavity in a steep roof?

4.13 Sketch a low-slope roof with the following components and determine its U-value: steel deck, 3-in.-thick isocyanurate board, 1-in.-thick perlite board, and a gravel-covered, built-up roof.

4.14 Sketch a typical steep roof with asphalt shingles, plywood deck, 10-in.-thick fiberglass insulation in attic cavity, and 1/2-in.-thick gypsum board ceiling. Determine the U-value for this roof-ceiling assembly.

4.15 With the help of a sketch, explain how a mechanically fastened roof membrane is better able to accommodate the dimensional instability of the substrate than a fully adhered membrane.

4.16 With the help of sketches and notes, explain the difference between an expanded polystyrene and an extruded polystyrene board.

4.17 Which of the plastic foam insulations has the highest fire resistance?

4.18 List the commonly used rigid board insulations in low-slope roofs.

4.19 With the help a sketch and notes, show all of the components of a low-slope roof that you would recommend for the following conditions:
(1) a built-up roof on a steel deck with intervening insulation,
(2) a mechanically fastened single-ply roof on a steel deck with intervening insulation,
(3) a built-up roof on a poured-in-place concrete deck and intervening insulation, and
(4) a built-up roof on a precast concrete deck with intervening insulation.

4.20 Explain the composition of lightweight insulating concrete.

4.21 With the help of a sketch and notes, show all of the components of a built-up roof over a lightweight insulating concrete deck.

4.22 Explain the difference between lightweight aggregate insulating concrete and foamed concrete.

4.23 With the help of sketches and notes, explain the construction of a protected membrane roof.

4.24 With reference to Appendix B, determine the minimum amount of roof insulation you would recommend for an office building in Chicago, Illinois, with a low-slope roof.

4.25 With reference to Appendix B, determine the minimum amount of insulation you would recommend for an apartment building in Chicago, Illinois, with a steep roof in which the insulation is to be provided in the attic.

5

Roof Deck

5.1 List the commonly used roof decks in low-slope roofs.

5.2 Which of the commonly used roof decks are considered nailable? Which are considered nonnailable?

5.3 Explain why the assembly consisting of an insulating concrete fill over a steel deck is generally considered as a roof deck.

5.4 What is the typical center-to-center spacing of ribs in a steel deck?

5.5 With the help of sketches, explain the three different classifications of steel decks based on their rib profiles.

5.6 What is the typical thickness of sheet steel used in making steel decks?

5.7 Which type of steel deck would you recommend for a coastal region?

5.8 What is meant by the term "G 90"?

5.9 Sketch a typical fastener used to fasten insulation to a steel deck.

5.10 As far as roofing is concerned, what is the primary difference between a sitecast concrete deck and a precast concrete deck consisting of single or double tees?

5.11 With the help of a sketch, explain how you would secure rigid board insulation to a sitecast concrete deck.

5.12 With the help of a sketch, explain how you would secure insulation to a precast concrete deck.

5.13 Explain why a nonbituminous separator sheet is commonly used between a solid lumber deck and the insulation, or between the solid lumber deck and a base sheet.

5.14 List the commonly used wood panel roof decks.

5.15 What is the composition of a cement fiber deck? Name the major manufacturer of cement fiber decks.

5.16 List some of the advantages and limitations of cement fiber decks.

5.17 What is the typical width of a building expansion joint?

5.18 With the help of a sketch, explain the critical locations of expansion joints in a building.

5.19 What is the difference between a roof expansion joint and a roof area divider? Explain.

5.20 Sketch a typical roof expansion joint showing its various components.

6

Design for Drainage

6.1 What are the advantages and disadvantages of increasing the slope of a low-slope roof beyond the minimum requirement of 1/4:12?

6.2 What is backnailing of felts? Where is it typically required? Explain with the help of a sketch.

6.3 With the help of sketches and notes, explain the difference between internal and external drainage of low-slope roofs.

6.4 Discuss the advantages and disadvantages of using tapered insulation to create slope in a low-slope roof.

6.5 With the help of sketches, explain how crickets can help to drain a roof that slopes to a valley in the center of the roof.

6.6 Explain the concepts of primary and secondary drainage.

6.7 Using Tables 6.1 and 6.2 and Appendix C, determine the number and size of primary roof drains required for a low-slope roof measuring 300 ft x 120 ft in New Orleans, Louisiana.

6.8 Repeat problem 6.7 for the secondary drainage.

6.9 Provide a sketch of the layout of drains and the required crickets for the drainage system in Problems 6.7 and 6.8.

6.10 Using Appendix D, recommend the difference in the inlet levels of primary and secondary drains in Problem 6.9.

6.11 Repeat Problems 6.7 through 6.10 for Las Vegas, Nevada.

6.12 Discuss the pros and cons of using through-wall scuppers as primary drainage elements.

7

Design for Fire

7.1 Provide the names of two U.S. organizations that test roof assemblies for fire-related properties and establish standards to that end.

7.2 List the properties of a roof assembly that are critical to its performance against a fire originating inside the building.

7.3 What design strategy is generally employed to improve the safety of a building against fire?

7.4 What is the unit of fire-resistance rating of a component?

7.5 List the categories in which the UL test for interior fire spread rates roof assemblies.

7.6 List the categories in which the FM test for interior fire spread rates roof assemblies.

7.7 Which types of decks are required to be subjected to the interior flame spread test?

7.8 List the tests to which a roof assembly is subjected to determine its performance with respect to an exterior fire. Are these tests required of all types of decks?

7.9 List the categories in which the standard test for exterior fire exposure rates roof assemblies.

7.10 What does the term "FM Class 1A" roof mean? Explain.

7.11 How does the slope of a roof affect its fire performance? Explain.

8

Design for Wind and Hail

8.1 Explain what is meant by the FM classification "1-180" of a low-slope roof assembly.

8.2 Is a low-slope roof subjected to an upward (suction) pressure or downward pressure?

8.3 How is the uplift pressure on a roof related to the wind speed?

8.4 Explain why the wind speeds in tornadoes are generally not considered in determining the design wind speed for a location.

8.5 List the ground roughness (exposure) categories that are used in determining wind loads on buildings.

8.6 Explain what a ballooning effect is.

8.7 Determine the wind load on the corners, perimeter, and the field-of-roof of a low-slope roof of a 100 ft x 100 ft office building in Boston, Massachusetts. Exposure category is B. The building is 20 stories tall with a roof height = 250 ft. The building is fully glazed on all sides with glass that can withstand the design wind load.

8.8 With the help of a sketch, show the dimensions of the perimeter and the corners of the roof in Problem 8.7.

8.9 Determine the wind load on the corners, perimeter, and the field-of-roof of a low-slope roof on a 100 ft x 200 ft hotel lounge and conference facility in Miami, Florida. The building is one story tall with a roof height = 20 ft and faces the ocean. All walls have glazed openings with glass area nearly 15% of each wall area. The glazed openings are designed to withstand wind loads but are not missile impact resistant.

8.10 With the help of a sketch, show the dimensions of the perimeter and the corners of the roof in Problem 8.9.

8.11 List the categories in which Factory Mutual divides low-slope roof assemblies with respect to hail resistance.

9

Design for Water Vapor Control

9.1 Define the relative humidity of air.

9.2 What is the dew point of air if the air temperature is 85°F and the air's RH = 55%.

9.3 A low-slope roof is composed of the following elements: 5-ply built-up roof, 1-in.-thick perlite board, 3-in.-thick iso board, and steel deck. The inside air temperature is 70°F, and the external air temperature is 10°F. Draw the temperature gradient through the assembly.

9.4. If the relative humidity of inside air is 50%, determine where the dew point will occur within the assembly in Problem 9.3.

9.5 With the help of a sketch, explain where a vapor retarder should be placed in a low-slope roof assembly.

9.6 The interior air temperature and relative humidity of air in an office building in Chicago, Illinois, is maintained at 70°F and 40% respectively. Determine if a vapor retarder is required in the low-slope roof of this building.

9.7 The interior air temperature and relative humidity of air in an indoor swimming pool building in Chicago, Illinois, is generally at 75°F and 80% respectively. Determine if a vapor retarder is required in the (low-slope) roof of this building.

9.8 If a vapor retarder is required in the roof in Problem 9.7, explain where it should be located in the assembly and what material it should be. The other components of the roof assembly are a metal deck, insulation, and a 4-ply built-up roof.

10

Details at Terminations and Penetrations

10.1 With the help of sketches, explain where in a low-slope roof, the following flashings are required: (1) base flashing, (2) curb flashing, and (3) flange flashing.

10.2 What is a cant strip? Where is it required?

10.3 Which material will you specify for membrane flashing in (1) a built-up roof? (2) SBS-modified bitumen roof? (3) APP-modified bitumen roof? (4) single-ply roof?

10.4 Sketch a detail showing the junction of a low-slope built-up roof with the parapet wall. Assume that the parapet is 18 in. high and the roof deck (steel deck) is supported on bar joists that rest on the masonry wall.

10.5 Repeat Problem 10.4 if the bar joists rest on a steel spandrel beam.

10.6 Repeat Problem 10.4 if the parapet wall is 42 in. high.

10.7 Sketch a typical detail of a low-slope roof with a fascia and gravel guard.

10.8 Sketch a typical detail for a curb-mounted mechanical equipment on a low-slope roof.

10.9 With the help of a sketch, explain how the penetration around a pipe is typically waterproofed on a low-slope roof.

11

Steep Roofing — Asphalt Shingle Roof

11.1 Sketch some of the commonly available asphalt shingle profiles.

11.2 Discuss the requirements for the underlayment on asphalt shingle roofs.

11.3 Discuss the requirements for the ice dam protection membrane on asphalt shingle roofs.

11.4 Which material is commonly used for the ice dam protection membrane?

11.5 Sketch the eave detail of a typical asphalt shingle roof.

11.6 Sketch the detail at the corner of an eave and rake showing the installation of a metal drip edge.

11.7 What is a starter course of asphalt shingles? Explain with the help of a sketch.

11.8 What is a bleeder strip? Explain with the help of a sketch.

11.9 How are the asphalt shingles secured to the deck? With the help of a sketch, show the typical location and number of fasteners used per shingle strip.

11.10 With the help of a sketch, explain the construction of an open valley in an asphalt shingle roof.

11.11 With the help of a sketch, show where a cricket may be needed on a steep roof.

11.12 List the various flashings that are required to waterproof the junction of a chimney with a steep roof.

12

Steep Roofing — Slate Roof

12.1 What is the fundamental distinction between the underlayment requirements for an asphalt shingle roof and a slate roof? Explain.

12.2 List the types of roofing slates commonly used.

12.3 List the durability grades in which roofing slates are divided.

12.4 What is the most commonly used thickness of roofing slates?

12.5 What is the weight per square foot of commonly used roofing slates?

12.6 How are slates commonly secured to the deck? Explain with the help of a sketch.

12.7 What are slating clips? How do they secure slates to the deck? Explain with the help of a sketch.

12.8 What is the most commonly used valley treatment with slate roofs?

12.9 Sketch a commonly used eave treatment with a slate roof.

13

Steep Roofing — Tile Roof

13.1 What is the fundamental distinction between the underlayment requirements for an asphalt shingle roof and a tile roof? Explain.

13.2 Sketch in three dimensions the following tiles: (1) mission tile, (2) S-shape tile, and (3) flat interlocking tile.

13.3 With the help of a sketch explain the purpose of a lug that is provided in some tiles.

13.4 With the help of a sketch, explain the installation of a tile roof using a system of battens and crossbattens.

13.5 What is the alternative to batten and crossbatten system? Explain.

13.6 With the help of a sketch, explain the commonly used eave treatment with a tile roof.

13.7 With the help of a sketch, explain the commonly used ridge treatment with a tile roof.

14

Steep Roofing — Architectural Metal Roof

14.1 Explain the difference between a structural sheet metal roof and an architectural sheet metal roof.

14.2 What is the commonly used thickness of copper sheet used in copper roofs?

14.3 Explain what oil canning is.

14.4 With the help of sketches, explain the construction of a typical standing seam metal roof.

14.5 With the help of sketches, explain the construction of a typical double-lock standing seam metal roof.

14.6 Explain how the expansion and contraction of metal roof panels is accommodated.

14.7 With the help of sketches, explain the construction of a typical batten seam metal roof.

14.8 With the help of sketches, explain the construction of a typical flat seam metal roof.

15

Roof Warranties

15.1 Explain the term "roofing bond."

15.2 What is the difference between an implied warranty and an express warranty? Explain.

15.3 Explain the difference between: (1) a material only warranty and (2) a systems warranty.

15.4 What type of defect is usually covered in a roof warranty?

15.5 What is meant by an OIC warranty? An NDL warranty?

15.6 For how long does a manufacturer typically warrant a low-slope roof?

Appendix A   Systems of Units

The system of measurement (or units) commonly used at the present time in the United States building industry is the foot-pound-second (FPS) system. In this system, the length is measured in the foot, or its multiples — the yard and the mile, or its submultiple — the inch. Weight is measured in pounds, ounces, or grains. Time is measured in seconds.

Although the United States was the first country to establish the decimal currency in 1785, it is one of the few countries where the nondecimal FPS system is still used. Therefore, the FPS system, earlier known as the *Imperial System of Units*, is now commonly known as the *U.S. System of Units*.

The system of units used by most other countries is the SI system. It is this system to which the United States has committed to change through the 1975 Metric Conversion Act, as amended by the Omnibus Trade and Competitiveness Act of 1988. These two acts establish the SI system as the preferred system of measurement in the United States and require that, to the extent feasible, the SI system shall be used in all federally funded projects and business-related activities. With its growing acceptance, it is expected that the SI system will completely replace the FPS system in the U.S. building industry in the next few years.

The SI system, popularly known as the *International System*, is an acronym for Le Systeme International d'Unites, a name given by the 36 nations' meeting at the 11th General Conference on Weights and Measures (CGPM, an acronym for Conference Generale des Poids et Measures) in 1960 in Paris. The SI system is a rationalized meter-kilogram-second system (MKS) system and has been modified several times since the 1960 CGPM meeting.

The advantage of using the SI system is that the multiples and submultiples of each unit (the secondary units) have a decimal relationship with each other that makes computations easier and less susceptible to errors. For instance, the secondary unit of length — the centimeter — is related to the base unit — the meter — by 10^{-2}, since 1 cm = 10^{-2} meter. By contrast, the length unit in the U.S. system — the foot — does not bear a decimal relationship with its secondary units — the inch, the yard, or the mile.

Twelve prefixes have been standardized for use with the base unit to make the secondary units. These prefixes along with their symbols are given in Table A.1 The SI system uses seven base quantities: length, mass, time, temperature, electric current, luminous intensity, and the amount of substance.

The units corresponding to the base quantities are listed in Table A.2. Of these, only the first four quantities are of concern to architects and builders: length, mass, time, and temperature.

Quantities other than the base quantities — such as force, stress, pressure, velocity, acceleration, energy, etc., and their units — are derived from a combination of two or more base quantities. For example, acceleration is the rate of change of velocity, which, in turn, is the rate of change of distance. Consequently, the units for acceleration are meters per second square (m/s^2).

Another advantage of the SI system is that there is one, and only one, unit for each quantity — the meter for length, kilogram for mass, second for time, and so on. This is not so in the U.S. system where multiple units are often used. For instance, power is measured in Btu per hour and also in horsepower.

Table A.1 Prefixes in the SI System

Factor	Prefix	Symbol
10^{12}	tera	T
10^{9}	giga	G
10^{6}	mega	M
10^{3}	kilo	k
10^{2}	hecto	h
10	deka	da
10^{-1}	deci	d
10^{-2}	centi	c
10^{-3}	milli	m
10^{-6}	micro	μ
10^{-9}	nano	n
10^{-12}	pico	p

Table A.2 Base Quantities and Their Symbols in the SI System

Quantity	Unit name	Symbol
Length	meter	m
Mass	kilogram	kg
Time	second	s
Temperature	Kelvin	K
Electric current	Ampere	A
Luminous intensity	candela	cd
Amount of substance	mole	mol

A.1 Rules of Grammar in the SI System

The symbols of units in the SI system are always used in lowercase unless the unit is after the name of a person, such as Newton, Pascal, or Kelvin, in which case the first letter of the symbol is in uppercase, and the second letter in the lowercase, as in Pa. The exception is, however, made in the case of the litre which, although not after the name of a person, is given the symbol in the uppercase letter "L."

Multiples of base units must be given with a single prefix. Double prefixes are not allowed. Thus, megakilometer (Mkm) is incorrect; instead, we use gigameter (Gm). Use prefixes as given in Table A.1 in which the prefixes are in uppercase for magnitudes 10^6 and greater and in lowercase for magnitudes 10^3 and lower. No space should be left between a prefix and a symbol. Thus, use km, not k m.

The product of two or more units in symbolic form is given by using a dot between individual symbols (example N.m). Mixing a symbol and the full name of a unit is incorrect (example N.meter).

Plurals are not used in symbols. For instance, we use 1 m and 50 m. Periods are not used after symbols except at the end of a sentence.

A space must be left between the numerical value and the unit symbol. Thus, use 300 m, not 300m. No space, however, is left between degree and Celsius.

In architectural drawings, dimensions should preferably be given in millimeters. When that is done, the use of mm should be avoided. For instance, the measurements of a floor tile are given as 300 x 300, not as 300 mm x 300 mm. Larger dimensions may be given in meters, if considered necessary. For instance, a building may be dimensioned as 30.800 m x 50.600 m in plan, but it is preferable to dimension it as 30,800 x 50,600.

A.2 Length, Thickness, Area, and Volume

In the U.S. system, the standard unit of length is the foot: 1 ft = 12 in. Long distances are measured in miles. In the SI system, the standard unit of length is the meter. Most dimensions in the SI system are given in millimeters (mm), where 1 mm = 10^{-3} m. Long distances are given in kilometers (km).

    1 ft = 0.3048 m; 1 m = 3.281 ft = 39.37 in; 1 in. = 25.4 mm
    1 mile = 1.609 km

A.3 Mass, Force, and Weight

In the U.S. system, the unit of mass is the pound (lb); the corresponding unit in the SI system is the kilogram (kg).

    1 lb = 16 ounces (oz) = 7,000 grains (gr) = 0.4536 kg
    1 kg = 2.205 lb

Force is defined as mass times acceleration. Since the unit of acceleration in the U.S. system is ft/second^2 (ft/s^2), the unit of force is (lb.ft/s^2). This unit is called pound-force, but is usually referred to as the pound. In the SI system, the unit of force is (kg.m)/s2. This complex unit is called the Newton (N), after the famous physicist Isaac Newton.

Since the weight of an object is the force exerted on it by the gravitational pull of the earth, the weight of an object is equal to (mass) x (acceleration due to gravity). The acceleration due to gravity on earth's surface is 9.8 m/s^2. Therefore, the weight of an object whose mass is 1 kg is 9.8 (kg.m)/s^2, or 9.8 N.

In the SI system, there is a clear distinction between the units of mass and the weight of an object. The distinction between the mass and the weight in the U.S. system is rather obscure because the pound is used as the unit for both the mass and the weight of an object.

    1 kilogram-force = 9.8 N; 1 lb = 4.448 N; 1 N = 0.2248 lb
    1 kilopound (kip) = 1,000 lb = 4.448 kN; 1 kN = 0.2248 kip

A.4 Pressure and Stress

Since pressure or stress is defined as force per unit area, the unit for pressure or stress in the U.S. system is lb/ft^2 (psf). Other units commonly used are pounds per square inch (psi) and kilopounds per square inch (ksi). In the SI system, the unit of pressure or stress is N/m^2. This unit is called the Pascal (Pa), after the physicist Blaise Pascal. Thus, 1 N/m^2 = 1 Pa.

    1 psf = 47.880 Pa; 1Pa = 0.208 85 psf
    1 psi = 6.895 kPa; 1 kPa = 0.1450 psi

In weather-related topics, the unit of pressure is the atmosphere (atm); 1 atm is the standard atmospheric pressure at sea level.

    1 atm = 760 mm of mercury (Hg) = 29.92 in. of Hg = 14.69 psi = 2,115.4 psf = 101.3 kPa. For all practical purposes, the atmospheric pressure may be taken as 2,100 psf, or 101 kPa.

A.5 Temperature and Energy

In the U.S. system, temperature is measured in degrees Fahrenheit ($^{\circ}$F). This scale was introduced during the early 18th century. Zero on the Fahrenheit scale was established based on the lowest obtainable temperature at the time and 100°F, on the basis of human body temperature as it was then considered to be.

On the Celsius scale ($^{\circ}$C), earlier known as the *Centigrade scale*, the zero refers to the freezing point of water, and 100 $^{\circ}$C is the boiling point of water.

The unit of temperature in the SI system is the Kelvin (K). The preference for Kelvin over Celsius is that on the Kelvin scale, the temperature is always positive. This is not so on the Celsius or the Fahrenheit scales on which the temperature may be positive or negative. In other words, zero Kelvin (as we know it now) is the lowest obtainable temperature. A temperature of 0 K is therefore called the *absolute zero temperature*. The relationship between Kelvin and Celsius temperatures is:

T $^{\circ}$C = (T + 273.15) K

In other words, 20°C = 293.15 K. Other relationships are:

T $^{\circ}$F = [(1.8) T + 32] $^{\circ}$C; T $^{\circ}$C = [(0.555)(T - 32)] $^{\circ}$F.

The intervals in both the Kelvin and the Celsius scales are equal. Therefore, the Celsius and Kelvin scales start at different points, but their subdivisions are equal. Note that the prefix "degree" is not used on the Kelvin scale. Although Kelvin is the appropriate scale to use in the SI system, $^{\circ}$C is also used because of the smaller numbers associated with the Celsius scale.

A comprehensive list of conversion factors to convert from the U.S. system to the SI system is given in Table A.3.

Table A.3 Unit Conversion Factors

Quantity	To convert from	To	Multiply by
Length	mile	km	1.609 344*
	yard	m	0.9144*
	foot	m	0.304 8*
	foot	mm	304.8*
	inch	mm	25.4*
Area	square mile	km^2	2.590 00*
	acre	m^2	4 046.87
	acre	ha**	0.404 687
	sq ft	m^2	0.092 903 04*
	sq in.	mm^2	645.16*
Volume	cu yard	m^3	0.764 555
	cu ft	m^3	0.028 3168
	100 board feet	m^3	0.235 974
	gal	L	3.785 41
	cu in.	cm^3	16.387 064
	cu in.	mm^3	16 387.064
Velocity	ft/s	m/s	0.3048
Rate of fluid flow	ft^3/s	m^3/s	0.028 3168
	gal/h	mL/s	1.051 50
Acceleration	ft/s^2	m/s^2	0.3048
Mass	lb	kg	0.453 59
Mass per unit area	psf	kg/m^2	4.882 43
Mass density	pcf	kg/m^3	16.018 5
Force	lb	N	4.448 22
Force per unit length	plf	N/m	14.593 9
Pressure, stress	psf	Pa	47.880 26
	psi	kPa	6.894 76
	in. of mercury (in.Hg)	kPa	3.386 38
	in. of Hg (in.Hg)	psf	70.72
	atmosphere***	kPa	101.325

Quantity	To convert from	To	Multiply by
Temperature	^{o}F	^{o}C	5/9(^{o}F - 32)
	^{o}F	K	(^{o}F + 459.7)/1.8
Quantity of heat	Btu	J	1055.056
Power	ton (refrigeration)	kW	3.517
	Btu/h	W	0.293 07
	hp	W	745.7
	$Btu/(h.ft^2)$	W/m^2	3.154 59
Thermal conductivity	$Btu.in/(ft^2.h.^{o}F)$	$W/(m.^{o}C)$	0.144 2
Thermal conductance, or Thermal transmittance, U	$Btu/(ft^2.h.^{o}F)$	$W/(m^2.^{o}C)$	5.678 263
Thermal resistance	$(ft^2.h.^{o}F)/Btu$	$(m^2.^{o}C)/W$	0.176 110
Thermal capacity	$Btu/(ft^2.^{o}F)$	$kJ/(m^2.^{o}C)$	20.44
Specific heat	$Btu/(lb.^{o}F)$	$J/(kg.^{o}C)$	4.186 8
Vapor permeability	perm.in	ng/(Pa.m.s)	1.459 29
Vapor permeance	perm	$ng/(Pa.m^2.s)$	57.213 5
Angle	degree	radian	0.017 453

*   Denotes exact conversion
**   1 hectare (ha) = 100 m x 100 m
***   1 atmosphere = 29.92 in. of mercury

Appendix B   Maximum U-Values for Roof Assemblies

Tables B.1 to B.4 give the minimum amount of insulation required for a roof assembly of any building except a low-rise residential building.[B.1] The minimum insulation is given in terms of the maximum U-value (U_{max}).

U_{max} is obviously a function of the severity of the external climate of the location. The more severe the climate, the greater the amount of insulation needed (i.e., the smaller the value of U_{max}). The severity of the external climate of a location is measured in terms of the heating degree days and the cooling degree days. Thus, U_{max} values are given in terms of HDD and CDD data for a given location.

Assumptions Made in the Data of Tables B.1 to B.4

The values given in Table B.1 are prescriptive values. They are based on the assumptions that (1) the vertical glazing area in the building is less than or equal to 50% of the total wall area, and (2) the roof skylight area is less than or equal to 5% of the roof area.

There also requirements for the U-values and solar heat gain coefficient (SHGC) of windows and skylights. However, these values are not excessively demanding, and commonly used windows and skylights would generally satisfy these requirements. For additional information, the reader is referred to Reference B.1.

If a building does not satisfy the assumptions given above, a detailed study of the energy use performance of the building is recommended.

HDD 65 and CDD 50

"HDD 65" is an acronym for heating degree days with a base temperature of 65°F. It refers to the number of days in the entire year on which the average daily external air temperature at a location is less than 65°F. Thus, if the average air temperature on a particular day at a location is 60°F, then that day contributes 5 heating degree days (HDD), which is obtained by subtracting 60 from 65. If on another day, the average external air temperature is 55°F, then that day will contribute 10 HDD.

If the average external air temperature on a day is ≥ 65°F, that day does not contribute to HDD 65. When we sum all HDD contributions for the entire year, we obtain the HDD 65 value for that location.

The choice of 65°F as the base temperature is a function of the fact that when the average external air temperature on a day is less than 65°F, interior heating is generally required on that day.

Similarly, CDD 50 implies the number of cooling degree days with 50°F as the base temperature. Thus, when the average external air temperature on a day is greater than 50°F, that day will contribute to CDD 50. In other words, a day with an average external temperature of 64°F will contribute 14 cooling degree days. The sum of all cooling degree day contributions for a year gives the value of CDD 50 for a location.

REFERENCE B.1   American Society of Heating, Refrigerating and Air Conditioning Engineers. *Energy Standard for Buildings Except Lowrise Residential Buildings*, ASHRAE/IESNA Standard 90.1-1999 (Atlanta, GA: 1999).

Table B.1 Values of U_{max} for the Roof of a Nonresidential Building with Insulation Above the Deck

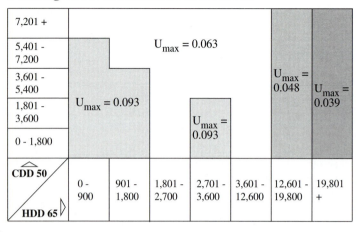

Chart axes: CDD 50 (horizontal): 0 - 900 | 901 - 1,800 | 1,801 - 2,700 | 2,701 - 3,600 | 3,601 - 12,600 | 12,601 - 19,800 | 19,801 +. HDD 65 (vertical): 7,201 + | 5,401 - 7,200 | 3,601 - 5,400 | 1,801 - 3,600 | 0 - 1,800.

Regions: $U_{max} = 0.063$; $U_{max} = 0.093$; $U_{max} = 0.048$; $U_{max} = 0.039$.

Table B.2 Values of U_{max} for the Roof of a Residential Building (Except a Low-Rise Residential Building) with Insulation Above the Deck

Chart axes: CDD 50 (horizontal): 0 - 900 | 901 - 9,000 | 9,001 - 10,800 | 10,801 +. HDD 65 (vertical): 10,801 + | 1,801 - 10,800 | 0 - 1,800.

Regions: $U_{max} = 0.048$; $U_{max} = 0.063$.

Table B.3 Values of U_{max} for the Roof of a Nonresidential Building with Insulation in the Attic

Chart axes: CDD 50 (horizontal): 0 - 5,400 | 5,401 - 7,200 | 7,201 - 9,000 | 9,001 - 19,800 | 19,801 +. HDD 65 (vertical): 5,401 + | 3,601 - 5,400 | 1,801 - 3,600 | 0 - 1,800.

Regions: $U_{max} = 0.027$; $U_{max} = 0.034$; $U_{max} = 0.017$.

Table B.4 Values of U_{max} for the Roof of a Residential Building (Except a Low-Rise Residential Building) with Insulation in the Attic

Chart axes: CDD 50 (horizontal): 0 - 1,800 | 1,801 - 2,700 | 1,801 - 2,700 | 2,701 - 3,600 | 3,601 - 7,200 | 7,201 - 19,800 | 19,801 +. HDD 65 (vertical): 7,201 + | 5,401 - 7,200 | 3,601 - 5,400 | 1,801 - 3,600 | 0 - 1,800.

Regions: $U_{max} = 0.027$; $U_{max} = 0.034$; $U_{max} = 0.017$.

Example B.1: Determine the minimum insulation required for the roof of an office building in Phoenix, Arizona in which the insulation is to be provided above the deck.

Solution: From Table B.5, for Phoenix, HDD 65 = 1,350 and CDD 50 = 8425. From Table B.1, U_{max} = 0.063. Hence, total R-value = 1/0.063 = 16. Assuming R-1 to be provided by inside and outside film resistances (see Section 4.3.1 in Chapter 4), the minimum amount of insulation for this roof = R-15.

Example B.2: Determine the minimum insulation required for the roof of a motel building in Phoenix, Arizona, in which the insulation is provided in the attic space.

Solution: From Table B.4, U_{max} = 0.027. Hence, total R-value = 1/0.027 = 37. Assuming R-2.5 to be provided by the attic cavity (see Section 4.4.2), the R-value of attic insulation = 37 - 2.5 = 34.5, or say R-35.

Table B.5 Climatic Data (HDD 65 and CDD 50) for Selected U.S. Cities

City	HDD	CDD	City	HDD	CDD	City	HDD	CDD	City	HDD	CDD
Alabama			**Connecticut**			**Indiana**			**Maryland**		
Birmingham	2,920	5,210	Bridgeport	5,540	3,000	Evansville	4,710	4,070	Baltimore	4,710	3,710
Huntsville	3,320	4,860	Hartford	6,160	2,770	Fort Wayne	6,270	3,080	Hagerstown	5,290	3,340
Mobile	1,700	6,760				Indianapolis	5,620	3,450	Salisbury	4,030	4,000
Montgomery	2,220	5,990	**Delaware**								
			Dover	4,340	3,890	**Iowa**			**Massachusetts**		
Alaska			Wilmington	4,940	3,560	Des Moines	6,500	3,370	Boston	5,640	2,900
Anchorage	10,570	0				Dubuque	7,330	2,670	Springfield	5,750	3,040
Fairbanks	13,940	0	**District of Columbia**			Sioux City	6,890	3,150			
			Washington	4,710	3,710				**Michigan**		
Arizona						**Kansas**			Detroit	6,170	3,050
Flagstaff	7,130	1,660	**Florida**			Dodge City	5,000	4,090	Grand Rapids	6,970	2,540
Nogales	2,930	4,550	Jacksonville	1,430	6,850	Topeka	5,270	3,880			
Phoenix	1,350	8,430	Miami	200	9,470	Wichita	4,790	4,350	Lansing	7,100	2,450
Yuma	930	8,900	Pensacola	1,620	6,820				Sault Ste. Marie	9,320	1,420
			Tampa	730	8,240	**Kentucky**					
Arkansas						Ashland	5,220	3,280	**Minnesota**		
Fort Smith	3,480	5,080	**Georgia**			Lexington	4,780	3,750	Duluth	9,820	1,540
Little Rock	3,160	5,300	Atlanta	2,990	5,040	Louisville	4,510	4,000	Minneapolis	7,980	2,680
Texarkana	2,300	6,150	Dalton	3,550	4,550	Paducah	4,280	4,320	Rochester	8,250	2,380
			Macon	350	2,330						
California			Savannah	50	1,850	**Louisiana**			**Mississippi**		
Crescent City	4,400	1,630				Alexandria	2,000	6,410	Biloxi	1,90	6,950
Fresno	2,560	5,350	**Hawaii**			Baton Rouge	1,670	6,850	Jackson	2,470	5,900
Los Angeles	1,460	4,780	Hilo	0	8,760	Lafayette	1,590	6,880	Vicksburg	2,200	6,060
San Diego	1,260	5,220	Honolulu	0	9,950	New Orleans	1,510	6,910			
San Francisco	3,020	2,880				Shreveport	2,260	6,170	**Missouri**		
Yreka	2,630	5,390	**Idaho**						Columbia	5,210	3,750
			Boise	5,860	2,810	**Maine**			Kansas City	5,390	3,850
Colorado			Lewiston	6,750	2,170	Bangor	7,930	1,920	Rolla	4,750	4,190
Boulder	5,550	2,820				Lewiston	7,240	2,260	St. Louis	4,760	4,280
Denver	6,020	2,730	**Illinois**			Portland	7,380	2,180			
Pueblo	4,640	5,410	Chicago	6,180	3,250				**Montana**		
			Peoria	6,150	3,340				Billings	7,610	2,470
			Rockford	6,970	2,850				Kalispell	8,380	1,350
			Springfield	5,690	3,640				Livingston	7,220	1,900

Table B.5 (continued) Climatic Data (HDD 65 and CDD 50) for Selected U.S. Cities

City	HDD	CDD	City	HDD	CDD	City	HDD	CDD	City	HDD	CDD
Nebraska			**North Carolina**			**South Carolina**			**Virginia**		
Lincoln	6,280	3,460	Asheville	4,310	3,370	Charleston	1,870	6,300	Charlottesville	4,220	3,900
Norfolk	6,870	3,070	Charlotte	3,340	4,700	Columbia	2,650	5,510	Lynchburg	4,340	3,730
			Greensboro	3,870	4,140	Greenville	3,270	4,630	Norfolk	3,500	4,480
Omaha	6,300	3,400	Wilmington	2,470	5,560				Richmond	3,960	4,220
Scottsbluff	6,730	2,680				**South Dakota**					
			North Dakota			Pierre	7,410	2,940	**Washington**		
Nevada			Bismarck	8,970	2,140	Rapid City	7,300	2,410	Port Angeles	5,700	1,260
Elko	7,080	2,140	Devils Lake	9,950	1,970	Sioux Falls	7,810	2,740	Seattle	4,610	2,120
Ely	7,620	1,720	Fargo	9,250	2,290				Spokane	6,840	2,030
Las Vegas	2,410	6,750	Jamestown	9,170	2,260	**Tennessee**			Yakima	5,970	2,350
Reno	5,670	2,500				Chattanooga	3,590	4,610			
			Ohio			Knoxville	3,940	4,160	**West Virginia**		
New Hampshire			Cincinnati	4,990	3,730	Memphis	3,080	5,570	Charleston	4,650	3,660
Berlin	8,650	1,720	Cleveland	6,200	2,760	Nashville	3,730	4,690	Morgantown	5,360	3,160
Concord	7,550	2,090	Columbus	5,710	3,120						
			Toledo	6,580	2,720	**Texas**			**Wisconsin**		
New Jersey						Abilene	2,580	6,050	Appleton	7,690	2,510
Atlantic City	5,170	3,200	**Oklahoma**			Amarillo	4,260	4,130	La Crosse	7,490	2,790
Newark	4,890	3,750	Norman	3,300	5,270	Brownsville	640	8,780	Madison	7,670	2,390
			Oklahoma City	3,660	4,970	Dallas	2,260	6,590			
New Mexico			Stillwater	4,030	4,720	El Paso	2,710	5,490	**Wyoming**		
Albuquerque	4,420	3,910				Fort Worth	2,300	6,560	Cheyenne	7,330	1,890
Hobbs	2,850	5,160	**Oregon**			Houston	1,600	6,880	Evanston	8,850	1,290
Roswell	3,270	4,960	Baker	7,160	1,740	Lubbock	3,430	4,830	New Castle	7,270	2,520
			Eugene	4,550	2,350	San Antonio	1,640	7,140	Sheridan	7,800	2,020
New York			Portland	4,520	2,520						
Albany	6,890	2,530				**Utah**					
Binghamton	7,270	2,190	**Pennsylvania**			Cedar City	5,960	2,770			
Buffalo	6,750	2,470	Erie	6,280	2,650	Salt Lake City	5,770	3,280			
New York	4,810	3,630	Harrisburg	5,350	3,360						
Rochester	6,730	2,410	Philadelphia	4,950	3,620	**Vermont**					
			Pittsburgh	5,970	2,840	Burlington	7,770	2,230			
						Norfolk	3,500	4,480			
						Richmond	3,960	4,220			

Appendix C 100-Year, 1-Hour Peak Rainfall Intensities (in inches) for Selected U.S. Cities

Alabama
Birmingham	3.8
Huntsville	3.6
Mobile	4.6
Montgomery	4.2

Alaska
Fairbanks	1.0
Juneau	0.6

Arizona
Flagstaff	2.4
Nogales	3.1
Phoenix	2.5
Yuma	1.6

Arkansas
Fort Smith	3.5
Little Rock	3.7
Texarkana	3.8

California
Barstow	1.4
Crescent City	1.5
Fresno	1.1
Los Angeles	2.1
Needles	1.6
Placerville	1.5
San Fernando	2.3
San Francisco	1.5
Yreka	1.4

Colorado
Craig	1.5
Denver	2.4
Durango	1.8
Grand Junction	1.7
Lamar	3.0
Pueblo	2.5

Connecticut
Hartford	2.7
New Haven	2.8
Putnam	2.6

Delaware
Georgetown	3.0
Wilmington	3.1

District of Columbia
Washington	3.2

Florida
Jacksonville	4.3
Key West	4.3
Miami	4.7
Pensacola	4.6
Tampa	4.5

Georgia
Atlanta	3.7
Dalton	3.4
Macon	3.9
Savannah	4.3
Thomasville	4.3

Hawaii
Hilo	6.2
Honolulu	3.0
Wailuku	3.0

Idaho
Boise	0.9
Lewiston	1.1
Pocatello	1.2

Illinois
Cairo	3.3
Chicago	3.0
Peoria	3.3
Rockford	3.2
Springfield	3.3

Indiana
Evansville	3.2
Fort Wayne	2.9
Indianapolis	3.1

Iowa
Davenport	3.3
Des Moines	3.4
Dubuque	3.3
Sioux City	3.6

Kansas
Atwood	3.3
Dodge City	3.3
Topeka	3.7
Wichita	3.7

Kentucky
Ashland	3.0
Lexington	3.1
Louisville	3.2
Middlesboro	3.2
Paducah	3.3

Louisiana
Alexandria	4.2
Lake Providence	4.0
New Orleans	4.8
Shreveport	3.9

Maine
Bangor	2.2
Houlton	2.1
Portland	2.4

Maryland
Baltimore	3.2
Hagerstown	2.8
Oakland	2.7
Salisbury	3.1

Massachusetts
Boston	2.5
Pittsfield	2.8
Worcester	2.7

Michigan
Alpena	2.5
Detroit	2.7
Lansing	2.8
Grand Rapids	2.6
Marquette	2.4
Sault Ste. Marie	2.2

Minnesota
Duluth	2.8
Grand Marais	2.3
Minneapolis	3.1
Moorhead	3.2
Worthington	3.5

Mississippi
Biloxi	4.7
Columbus	3.9
Corinth	3.6
Natchez	4.4
Vicksburg	4.1

Missouri
Columbia	3.2
Kansas City	3.6
Springfield	3.4
St. Louis	3.2

Montana
Ekalaka	2.5
Havre	1.6
Helena	1.5
Kalispell	1.2
Missoula	1.3

Nebraska
North Platte	3.3
Omaha	3.8
Scottsbluff	3.1
Valentine	3.2

Nevada

Elko	1.0
Ely	1.1
Las Vegas	1.4
Reno	1.1

New Hampshire

Berlin	2.5
Concord	2.5
Keene	2.4

New Jersey

Atlantic City	2.9
Newark	3.1
Trenton	3.1

New Mexico

Albuquerque	2.0
Hobbs	3.0
Raton	2.5
Roswell	2.6
Silver City	1.9

New York

Albany	2.5
Binghamton	2.3
Buffalo	2.3
Kingston	2.7
New York	3.0
Rochester	2.2

North Carolina

Asheville	4.1
Charlotte	3.7
Greensboro	3.4
Wilmington	4.2

North Dakota

Bismarck	2.8
Devils Lake	2.9
Fargo	3.1
Williston	2.6

Ohio

Cincinnati	2.9
Cleveland	2.6
Columbus	2.8
Toledo	2.8

Oklahoma

Altus	3.7
Boise City	3.3
Durant	3.8
Oklahoma City	3.8

Oregon

Baker	0.9
Coos Bay	1.5
Eugene	1.3
Portland	1.2

Pennsylvania

Erie	2.6
Harrisburg	2.8
Philadelphia	3.1
Pittsburg	2.6
Scranton	2.7

South Carolina

Charleston	4.3
Columbia	4.0
Greenville	4.1

South Dakota

Buffalo	2.8
Huron	3.3
Pierre	3.1
Rapid City	2.9
Yankton	3.6

Tennessee

Chattanooga	3.5
Knoxville	3.2
Memphis	3.7
Nashville	3.3

Texas

Abilene	3.6
Amarillo	3.5
Brownsville	4.5
Dallas	4.0
Del Rio	4.0
El Paso	2.3
Fort Worth	4.0
Houston	4.6
Lubbock	3.3
Odessa	3.2
Pecos	3.0
San Antonio	4.2

Utah

Brigham City	1.2
Roosevelt	1.3
Salt Lake City	1.3
St. George	1.7

Vermont

Barre	2.3
Bratteboro	2.7
Burlington	2.1
Rutland	2.5

Virginia

Bristol	
Charlottesville	2.8
Lynchburg	3.2
Norfolk	3.4
Richmond	3.3

Washington

Omak	1.1
Port Angeles	1.1
Seattle	1.4
Spokane	1.0
Yakima	1.1

West Virginia

Charleston	2.8
Morgantown	2.7

Wisconsin

Ashland	2.5
Eau Claire	2.9
Green Bay	2.6
La Crosse	3.1
Madison	3.0
Milwaukee	3.0

Wyoming

Cheyenne	2.2
Fort Bridger	1.3
Lander	1.5
New Castle	2.5
Sheridan	1.7
Yellowstone Park	1.4

Appendix D   Head of Water over Roof Drains and Scuppers, and Roof Ponding Load

In Chapter 6, we observed that the design of the primary and secondary drainage systems is based on the flow capacities of roof drains. For instance, in Table 6.1, the flow capacity of a 4-in. roof drain is given as 18,400 ft^2, for a rainfall of 1 in. per hour (1 in./h). Since 1 in. = 1/12 ft, this corresponds to a drainage capacity of (18,400/12) = 1,533.3 ft^3 per hour (ft^3/h).

In some plumbing literature, the flow capacities of roof drains are expressed in gallons per minute (gpm) instead of square feet of roof area. Since 1 ft^3 = 7.48 gallons, the flow capacities can be converted from ft^3/h to gpm. Thus, 1 gpm = 8.02 ft^3/h. With this conversion factor, the capacity of a 4-in. roof drain is 1,533.3/8.02 = 191 gpm.

Thus, more generic roof drainage design values are those given in Table D.1. Note that unlike Table 6.1, this table is independent of rainfall intensity, and the values given in Tables 6.1 or 6.2 can be derived from the values in Table D.1.

To determine the number of roof drains, N, needed to drain A ft^2 of roof area, using Table D.1, we use the following expression:

$$N = \frac{0.0104 \, AI}{Q} \qquad (D.1)$$

where I = rainfall intensity (in./h) and Q = drainage capacity (in gpm) of the selected roof drain.

Example D.1: Use Table D.1 to obtain the number of 4-in.-diameter roof drains for the roof in Example 6.1, Chapter 6.

Solution: From Example 6.1, the area of roof, A = 30,000 ft^2, I = 4 in./h, and Q = 191 gpm. Hence, from Equation D.1,

$$N = \frac{0.0104 \, (30,000) \, 4}{191} = 6.53$$

Note that this is the same value obtained in Example 6.1.

Table D.1 Drainage Capacities (in gpm) of Roof Drains, Vertical Leaders, and Horizontal Drainage Pipes

Pipe diameter (in.)	Flow capacity (gpm) of roof drains or vertical leaders	Flow capacity (gpm) of horizontal drainage pipes Slope (in./ft)		
		1/8	1/4	1/2
2	30			
3	91	34	48	68
4	191	78	110	156
5	359	139	195	278
6	561	222	314	445
8	1205	478	677	956
10		860	1,214	1,783
12		1,384	1,953	2,768

To convert values in this table to those in Tables 6.1 and 6.2, multiply the above values by 96.25.

1 ft^3/h = 7.48 gph = (7.48/60) gpm = 0.1247 gpm. Hence, 1 gpm = 1/0.1247 ft^3/h = 8.02 ft^3/h

With a rainfall intensity of I in./h, the amount of water collecting on a roof with an area of A ft^2 = (AI/12) ft^3/h = 0.1247(AI)/(12) gpm = 0.0104(AI) gpm

If the drainage capacity of one drain is Q gpm, the number of drains, N, required are N = 0.0104(AI)/Q

Head of Water over Roof Drains

The values given in Table D.1 assume the existence of a certain head of water above the inlet level of roof drains. For instance, to achieve a flow of 191 gpm through a 4-in. drain, slightly more than 2.5-in. head of water above the drain inlet is needed. If the head of water is less than 2.5 in., the flow through a 4-in. drain will be smaller. The amount of flow through roof drains (or vertical leaders) for various haudraulic heads is given in Table D.2.

Table D.2 can be used to determine the ponding load on the roof when the primary system is choked. Alternatively, it can be used to limit the ponding load on the roof, as illustrated by the following examples. In either case, a roof's drainage design must be fully coordinated with its structural design.

Table D.2 Drainage Capacities (in gpm) of Roof Drains and Vertical Leaders at Various Hydraulic Heads

Roof drain diameter (in.)	Hydraulic head (in.)						
	1	2	2.5	3	3.5	4.0	4.5
4	80	170	180				
6	100	190	270	380	540		
8	125	230	340	560	850	1,100	1,170

Interpolation is appropriate, including between roof drains.

Source: American Society of Civil Engineers. *Minimum Design Loads for Buildings and Other Structures*, ASCE Standard 7-98 (New York: 1998).

Example D.2: Determine the head of water that will accumulate above the inlet of primary drains of the roof in Example 6.1.

Solution: From Example 6.1, design rainfall intensity = 4.0 in./h, diameter of each drain = 4 in., and each drain serves a roof area of 3,750 ft^2. In other words, each drain carries (3,750 x 4/12) = 1,250 ft^3/h of water, or (1,250/8.02) = 156 gpm.

From Table D.2, we note that the head of water lies between 1 and 2 in. By interpolating the values in Table D.2, the head of water on a roof drain is

$$1 + \frac{(156 - 80)}{(170 - 80)} = 1.8 \text{ in.}$$

Example D.3: Determine the difference in elevation that you would recommend between the inlet levels of primary and secondary drains of the roof in Example 6.1.

Solution: Because the secondary drains become operative only if the primary drains are choked, the inlet level of the secondary drains must be above the the maximum head of water over the primary drains. Although there is no mandated requirement, it is suggested that the inlet level of secondary drains = inlet level of primary drains + head of water + 1.0 in. The 1.0-in. factor is arbitrary, which further ensures that the secondary drains will not be operative unless the primary drains are flooded.

From Example D.2, head of water = 1.8 in. Hence, a level difference of 1.8 + 1.0 = 2.8 in., or say 2.75 in., should be provided between the primary and secondary drain's inlet levels.

Example D.4: Determine the ponding load on the roof in Example D.3 if the primary drains are choked. Assume that the secondary drains are 2.75 in. above the primary drains.

Solution: Because the primary roof drains are choked, the head of water over the secondary drains is 1.8 in., giving a total depth of water at the lowest level of the roof (i.e., at the sump) = 2.75 + 1.80 = 4.55 in.

From Example 6.1, the roof slopes 1/4 in./ft. With a 4.55-in. depth of water at the roof's lowest level, the build-up of water on the roof extends to (4.55 x 4) = 18 ft from the sump, Figure D.1. Assuming an average depth of

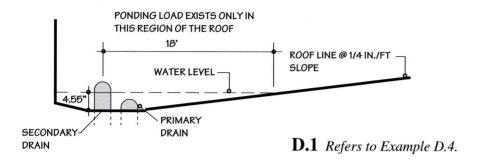

D.1 *Refers to Example D.4.*

(4.55/2) = 2.3 in., the average ponding load = (2.3)5.2 = 12 psf, and the maximum ponding load = 24 psf.[1] Note that the ponding load exists only within 18 ft region of the sump.

Example D.5: If the maximum head of water over the primary drains of the roof in Example 6.1 is required to be only 1 in., determine the number of 4-in.-diameter roof drains required.

Solution: From Table D.2, a 4-in. roof drain allows 80 gpm of water through it under a head of 1 in. of water. Therefore, from Equation D.1, the number of 4-in. roof drains required are

$$N = \frac{0.0104\ (30,000)\ 4}{80} = 15.6,\ \text{or say } 16$$

Example D.6: If the maximum head of water over the primary drains of the roof in Example 6.1 is required to be only 1 in., determine the number of 5-in.-diameter roof drains required.

Solution: By interpolation from Table D.2, a 5-in. roof drain allows 90 gpm of water under a head of 1 in. of water. Therefore, from Equation D.1, the number of 5-in. roof drains required are

$$N = \frac{0.0104\ (30,000)\ 4}{90} = 13.9,\ \text{or say } 14$$

---

[1] Because water weighs 62.5 lb/ft^3, a 1-in.-deep pond of water weighs 62.5/12 = 5.2 psf.

Determining Scupper Size and Roof's Ponding Load

The flow through a scupper is a weir-type flow, as shown in Figure D.2(a), unlike a pipe-type flow through a roof drain. Two types of roof scuppers are used: an edge scupper, or a through-wall scupper (see Figure 6.36 in Chapter 6). In terms of its flow characteristics, a through-wall scupper behaves the same as an edge scupper if the scupper opening's height is greater than the head of water, so that there is some clearance above the top of the water level, Figure D.2(b).

A minimum of 1-in. clearance above the maximum expected head of water in a scupper is generally recommended. A 1-in. clearance, even in an edge scupper is important, since it ensures no overflow above the roof's edge. The drainage capacity of a scupper can be obtained from Table D.3, or from the following expression:

$$Q = 2.9bH^{1.5} \tag{D.2}$$

where Q = drainage capacity of scupper (in gpm), b = width of scupper in inches, and H = hydraulic head in inches.

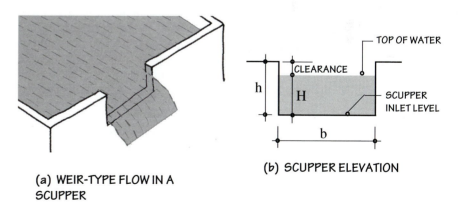

(a) WEIR-TYPE FLOW IN A SCUPPER

(b) SCUPPER ELEVATION

D.2 *Flow of water through a scupper.*

Table D.3 Drainage Capacity of Scuppers (in gpm)

Head of water, H (in.)	Width of scupper, b (in.)			
	6	8	12	24
1	18	24	36	72
2	50	66	100	200
3	90	120	180	360
4	140	186	280	560
5	194	258	388	776
6	255	340	510	1,020
7	321	428	642	1,284
8	393	522	786	1,572

Example D.7: If the overflow drainage for the roof in Example 6.1 is to be provided by through-wall scuppers, located adjacent to roof drains, determine the scuppers' size.

Solution: Because the scuppers are located adjacent to roof drains, each scupper serves the same area of roof as the drain, i.e., 3,750 ft². Because the design rainfall intensity is 4 in./h, each scupper must have a capacity of $3,750(4/12) = 1,250$ ft³/h = 156 gpm. From Table D.3, a 4-in. x 8-in. scupper opening has a capacity of 186 gpm. Increase the scupper opening height to 5 in. to allow 1-in. clearance above the 4-in. head of water. Hence, use 5 in. x 8 in. scuppers.

Example D.8: The International Plumbing Code requires that the opening of an overflow scupper be three times the area of the corresponding primary roof drain. Compare the scupper opening size obtained in Example D.7 with that of the primary roof drain in Example 6.1.

Solution: From Example 6.1, the primary drains are 4 in. in diameter. Hence, the area of each drain = $\pi(2.0)^2 = 12.56$ in². Thus, the required overflow scupper, as obtained from Example D.7 (5 in. x 8 in. = 40 in.²) is 3.2 times the area of primary roof drain — almost the same as that required by the International Plumbing Code.

Example D.9: Determine the ponding load on the roof in Example 6.1, in which the secondary drainage consists of 5 in. x 8 in. scuppers. Assume that the primary roof drains are located adjacent to the scuppers.

Solution: From Example D.3, the bottom of the scuppers' inlet should be 2.75 in. above the primary drains. With a 4-in. head of water in the scupper, there will be a 6.75-in. build-up of water on the roof at the scuppers' location. With 1/4 in./ft slope, the water will extend back to 27 ft from the scuppers, Figure D.3. The average depth of water is 6.75/2 = 3.4 in., which gives an average ponding load of 3.4(5.2) = 17.7 psf. The maximum ponding load on the roof = 6.75(5.2) = 35.4 psf.

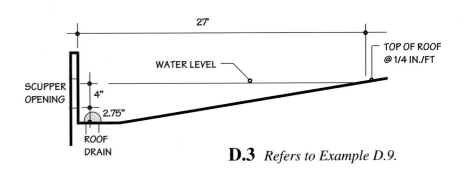

D.3 *Refers to Example D.9.*

Example D.10: The primary drainage in a 100 ft x 100 ft roof is provided by four roof drains, as shown in Figure D.4. The roof slopes at the rate of 1/4 in./ft toward the drains. The overflow is provided by four through-wall scuppers at the roof perimeter. Determine the size of the scuppers, if the design rainfall intensity is 4 in./h.

Solution: Each scupper serves a roof area of 2,500 ft². With a rainfall of 4 in./h, the amount of water to be drained = $2,500(4/12) = 833.3$ ft³/h = 104 gpm. From Table D.3, the required scupper size is 3 in. x 8 in., with a 3-in. head of water. Thus, provide four scuppers, each with an opening of 4 in. x 8 in.

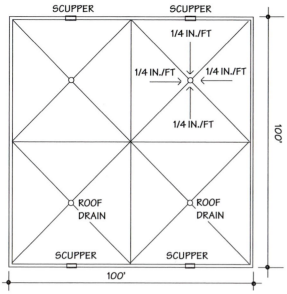

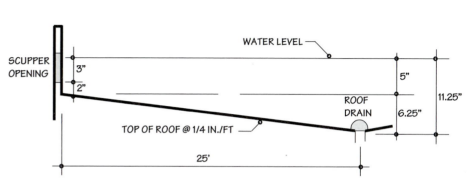

D.4 *Refers to Example D.10.*

D.5 *Refers to Example D.11.*

Example D.11: If the inlet level of each scupper in Example D.10 is 2 in. above the adjacent roof level, Figure D.5, determine the ponding load on the roof.

Solution: Because the roof slopes at 1/4 in./ft and the distance between the highest and the lowest elevations of the roof is 25 ft, the drains are depressed by $25/4 = 6.25$ in. below the roof level at the edges. Because the scuppers are 2 in. above the roof's edge and there is a 3-in. head of water at the scuppers, there will be a 11.25-in. build-up of water, Figure D.5.

Thus, the maximum ponding load $= 11.25(5.2) = 58.5$ psf. The average ponding load, as seen in Figure D.5, is $= (6.25/2)5.2 + 5(5.2) = 42.3$ psf. This is an extremely heavy ponding load, which illustrates the importance of the architect and/or the roofing consultant coordinating the design of the roof with the structural engineer.

This example also illustrates the fundamental flaw in the roof drainage design in Figure D.4, where the separation between the scuppers and the roof drains is large.

Appendix E Effect of an Escarpment or a Hill on Wind Loads on a Roof

When the wind flowing over a relatively flat ground encounters a topographic feature such as a ridge (i.e., hill) or an escarpment, the blockage effect caused by such a feature increases the wind speed close to the feature, Figure E.1. Wind speed far away from the feature is relatively unaffected. This is called the *speed-up effect*. The speed-up effect is maximum at the ground level and decreases with increasing height above the ground.

The speed-up effect is accounted for by the speed-up factor, K_{zt}. In the absence of a topographic feature, $K_{zt} = 1.0$. If, however, a topographic feature is present, K_{zt} is greater than 1.0, and must be determined based on the height of the feature, its shape, etc. For additional details, consult Reference 8.1 in Chapter 8.

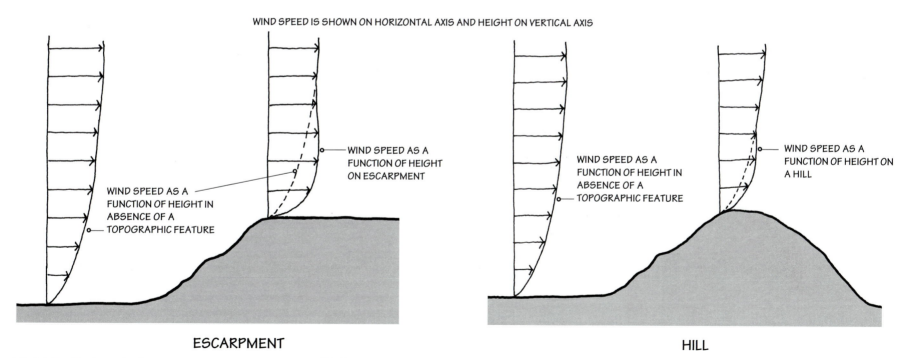

WIND SPEED IS SHOWN ON HORIZONTAL AXIS AND HEIGHT ON VERTICAL AXIS

WIND SPEED AS A FUNCTION OF HEIGHT ON ESCARPMENT

WIND SPEED AS A FUNCTION OF HEIGHT IN ABSENCE OF A TOPOGRAPHIC FEATURE

WIND SPEED AS A FUNCTION OF HEIGHT IN ABSENCE OF A TOPOGRAPHIC FEATURE

WIND SPEED AS A FUNCTION OF HEIGHT ON A HILL

ESCARPMENT

HILL

E.1 *Windload profiles on a hill and escarpment.*

Glossary of Roofing Terms

AIA — American Institute of Architects.

Alligatoring — Shrinkage cracking of the surface of a bituminous material, which produces a pattern similar to that of an alligator's hide. The cracks may or may not extend through the bitumen surface.

Ambient temperature —The temperature of surrounding air.

APP — See Attactic polypropylene.

Apron flashing — Sheet metal flashing used at the junction of a steep roof and a vertical wall (or a steeply sloped surface) abutting the roof.

Area divider — A raised projection in the middle of a low-slope roof that divides a large roof area in two parts. It is provided for stress relief in the roof, where a building expansion joint has not been provided. An area divider may also be needed to facilitate the installation of tapered insulation.

ARMA — Asphalt Roofing Manufacturers Association.

ASCE — American Society of Civil Engineers.

ASHRAE — American Society of Heating, Refrigerating and Air Conditioning Engineers.

Asphalt — A dark brown to black substance left as a residue from the refining of crude oil. For roofing purposes, this residue is further processed to provide four types of roofing asphalts: Type I, Type II, Type III, and Type IV.

Asphalt emulsion — A mixture of asphalt, water, and an emulsifying agent such as bentonite clay. An asphalt emulsion is used as a coating on a built-up roof.

Asphalt felt — A felt treated with asphalt. A treated organic felt is called a *saturated felt*, because organic felt fibers absorb asphalt. A treated glass fiber felt is called an *impregnated felt*, because glass fibers cannot absorb asphalt.

Asphalt primer — See Primer.

Asphalt roof cement, or roofer's cement — A trowelable mixture of bitumen, solvent, mineral stabilizers, fillers, and/or fibers. *ASTM D 4586-92: Asphalt Roof Cement* classifies asphalt roof cement under Types I and II. Type I, generally called *plastic* or *roofer's cement*, is self-sealing, adhesive, and ductile. Type II is referred to as *vertical grade flashing cement*. It has a lower ductility than Type I. See also Plastic cement and Flashing cement.

Asphalt shingle — Small units of roofing made of asphalt saturated fiberglass felt.

ASTM — American Society for Testing and Materials.

Attactic polypropylene — A high molecular weight polymer formed by the polymerization of propylene. Attactic propylene is used to favorably modify the properties of asphalt.

Backnailing — Nailing the back edge of a roof membrane, roof felt, or other component in a manner that it is covered by the next sequential membrane or felt. Backnailing is done to prevent the slippage of sheets or felts on a roof with an excessive slope.

Ballast — A material generally used over a loose-laid single-ply roof membrane to resist wind uplift. Commonly used ballast materials are gravel, crushed stone, or precast concrete pavers.

Bar joist, open web joist, or steel joist — A shop-fabricated, truss-like member used for the support of floors and low-slope roofs. The web of the truss consists of round steel bars (hence, the name "bar joist"). The top chord of the truss consists of a pair of steel angles, and the bottom chord may consist of a pair of steel angles or round steel bars.

Base flashing — Plies or strips of roof membrane material used for sealing the junction between a low-slope roof and an abutting wall, curb, or parapet. See also Flashing.

Base sheet or base ply — A bitumen-impregnated fiberglass felt, which is further coated with bitumen; or a bitumen-saturated organic felt, which is further coated with bitumen. A base sheet is thicker than a normal built-up roof felt and is used as the first ply in some built-up roofs.

Batt insulation — Fiberglass or mineral wool insulation cut to rectangular sizes and packed flat into bundles rather than in a roll form. The roll form is called a *blanket*. Batts and blankets are made from the same material. The only difference between a batt and a blanket is the format in which they are packaged.

Batten — Usually a wood strip, used between rigid insulation boards to secure roof felts or roof membrane in a low-slope roof. Wood battens are also used to anchor to and elevate slate or roof tiles above an underlying roof membrane. Such a slate or tile roof is generally used if the roof pitch is small. The term is also used to describe a wood or metal strip in metal roofing, e.g., a batten seam metal roof.

Batten bar or batten strip — A thin metal or plastic strip used to fasten a single-ply roof membrane to the deck.

Bitumen — A generic term in roofing that implies either asphalt or coal tar.

Bituminous emulsion — An emulsion of either asphalt or coal tar. See also Asphalt emulsion.

Blanket insulation — See Batt insulation.

Bleeder strip — Asphalt shingles with tabs cut, used as a starter course on the rake of a steep roof. The term is also used to describe felt envelope. See also Rake starter.

Blindnailing — see Backnailing.

Blister — A pocket of air, or air and water-vapor mixture, trapped between a roof felt or a sheet during the felt's or sheet's installation.

Blocking — Solid wood members used across rafters (or floor joists) under the unsupported edges of plywood or oriented strandboard. The term is also used for nailers on a roof.

Blowing agent — Air or a gas (of a low thermal conductivity) used in the manufacture of a plastic foam insulation such as extruded polystyrene or foamed polyisocyanurate.

British thermal unit (Btu) — A unit of energy in the U.S. customary system of units. One Btu is the amount of heat required to raise the temperature of 1 lb of water by 1°F.

Built-up roof membrane — A continuous multi-ply roof membrane consisting of three to five plies of bitumen impregnated (or saturated) felts adhered together with interply bitumen.

Cant strip — A strip of wood, wood fiber, perlite, or other material with a triangular profile. It is used as a transition piece between a low-slope roof surface and an abutting wall, parapet, or curb. Cant strips are generally not needed with a single-ply roof membrane due to the membrane's flexibility.

Cap flashing or counterflashing — Generally a sheet metal flashing to cover and protect the upper edges of a membrane base flashing or an underlying metal flashing from weather.

Cap sheet — A mineral-granule-surfaced, modified bitumen sheet, used as the last ply in a modified bitumen roof or a built-up roof.

Caulk — A semisolid sealing compound used for filling joints where the compound need not be elastomeric.

Chlorinated polyethylene (CPE) — A flexible rubberlike material used as single-ply roof membrane. The flexibility results from chlorinating polyethylene molecules, which in an unchlorinated state yield a rigid material. It is a thermoplastic; hence, the seams in CPE roof membranes can be heat-welded.

Chlorosulfonated polyethylene (CSPE) — A flexible rubberlike material used as a single-ply roof membrane, in which the polyethylene molecules have been sulfonated as well as chlorinated. In roofing industry, CSPE is better known as "Hypalon" — a trade name for the DuPont Company's CSPE membrane.

Cleat — A continuous metal plate or a metal angle piece (clip) used to secure two components together. A continuous cleat is commonly used to secure metal copings on masonry walls.

Closed-cut valley — A method of constructing the valley in an asphalt shingle roof, where the shingles from one side of the valley extend beyond the valley centerline, and the shingles from the other side are cut back nearly 2 in. from the valley centerline.

Coal tar — A dark brown to black semisolid substance obtained from the distillation of coal. It is also referred to as *coal tar pitch*, or simply *pitch*.

Coal tar felt — A fiberglass or organic felt impregnated or saturated with coal tar. See also Asphalt felt.

Coal tar roof cement — A trowelable compound of coal tar, solvents, and mineral fillers and fibers, similar to asphalt roof cement.

Coated base sheet — See Base sheet.

Coated felt — Same as Coated base sheet.

Cold flow — A relatively slow deformation of material at room or below room temperature. See also Creep.

Cold process roof — A roof in which hot asphalt or torch adhesion is replaced by asphalt roof cement or adhesive, which is at ambient temperature.

Composition shingle — Same as Asphalt shingle.

Coping — A metal, masonry, or stone component that covers the top of a wall or parapet to protect it from rain.

Copolymerization — A chemical reaction between two monomers, which yields a new substance with long chain molecules.

Counterflashing — See Cap flashing.

Course — Basically implies a layer, such as a course of masonry. In roofing, a row of shingles is referred to as a course of shingles. Similarly, flashing may consists of several courses. A five-course flashing consists of a layer of bitumen, a layer of felt, a layer of bitumen, a layer of felt, and finally a layer of bitumen.

Cover board — An insulating or a noninsulating rigid board placed under a built-up or modified bitumen membrane that can withstand the high temperature of bitumen and is chemically compatible with it.

CPA — Copolymer alloy.

CPE — See Chlorinated polyethylene.

Creep — A permanent, inelastic deformation of a material subjected to a constant compressive force, following an initial elastic deformation. In roofing, the insulation can experience creep at the location of fasteners. Creep at room temperature is sometimes called *cold flow*.

Cricket — An elevated area of roof constructed to divert rainwater to drains or to divert water away from a chimney, curb, or a wall. See also Saddle.

CSPE — See Chlorosulfonated polyethylene.

Curb — A raised projection over a low-slope roof to support mechanical equipment, skylight, a hatch door, etc., or to form a roof expansion joint or an area divider.

Cutback asphalt — An asphalt thinned by a solvent, used in the making of roofer's cement and coatings for built-up roofs.

Dead-level asphalt — Type I roofing asphalt. See also Asphalt.

Dew point temperature or dew point — The temperature at which the water vapor in air condenses into bulk water.

Diffusion — The flow of water vapor through a building component, caused by the vapor pressure difference across the two sides of a component.

Dimensional shingle — An asphalt shingle that is textured, layered, or laminated to produce a three-dimensional effect.

Dimensional stability — The ability of a material to resist change in its dimensions caused by a changes in its temperature, moisture, stresses, etc.

Double coverage — A term used with roof shingles in which the roof has at least two layers of shingles at any point on the roof.

Double-lock standing seam — See Standing seam.

Downspout — A vertical pipe to carry water from a roof scupper or a roof gutter.

Drain or roof drain — An outlet on a low-slope roof for the discharge of rainwater.

Eave — The edge of a steep roof that may or may not project beyond the supporting wall.

Elastomeric — The property of a material to deform under the action of a force and return to its original dimensions after the force is removed, such as rubber.

Elastomeric sealant — A compound used for filling joints between materials or components. An elastomeric sealant should remain pliable throughout its service life.

Emulsion — A product resulting from mixing two otherwise immiscible products, such as emulsifying butter by mixing it with water. See also Asphalt emulsion.

EPDM — Ethylene propylene diene monomer, a commonly used single-ply roof membrane.

Epoxy — A synthetic thermosetting resin that produces a hard, chemical-resistant coating and adhesive.

EPS — Expanded polystyrene. An EPS board is an insulation board, consisting of beads of polystyrene, also called a *bead board*. Note that an EPS board is different from an extruded polystyrene (XEPS) board.

Equiviscous temperature (EVT) —The temperature at which bitumen achieves the required viscosity for built-up roof application. Manufacturers of asphalt and coal tar provide the EVT of their product.

Extruded polystyrene — A plastic foam insulation board, which has HCFC gas trapped within its foam cavities.

Factory Mutual Research Corporation (FMRC, or simply FM) — A research and testing organization that evaluates roofing products for their resistance to wind, fire, traffic, and hail. Factory Mutual affiliated insurance companies in the U.S. require that a roofing design meets FM standards.

Felt — A thin flexible sheet made by rolling under pressure wood pulp, glass fibers, or polyester fibers. The process of manufacture of a felt is similar to that of making paper. A felt made from wood pulp is called an *organic felt*; that made from glass fibers is called an *inorganic* or *fiberglass felt*. A felt is subsequently treated with asphalt or coal tar. See also Asphalt felt.

Felt envelope — In roofing terminology, a continuous seal at the edge of a built-up roof in which the base sheet extends beyond the roof's edge. After the roof membrane is laid, the base sheet is folded over and adhered to prevent bitumen's drippage from the edge of the roof.

Field-of-roof — The central or main part of a roof excluding roof perimeter, corners, and roof penetrations.

Fire resistance — The ability of a building component to resist fire and contain it within the compartment of its origin.

Fishmouth — A half-cylindrical or half-conical shape (like the mouth of a fish) formed due to the wrinkling of built-up roof felts at edge seams.

Flash point — The temperature of a combustible liquid (such as asphalt, coal tar, solvents, and adhesives) at which it gives off vapors that ignite in the presence of air.

Flashing — Additional waterproofing components placed above or below the roof membrane to create a watertight seal at the roof perimeter, at the junction of a roof with an abutting wall, around roof penetrations, and at a roof expansion joint.

Flashing cement — A trowelable mixture of bitumen (coal tar or asphalt), solvent, and mineral fillers and fibers. Generally, flashing cement is a special type of roofer's cement intended for use on vertical surfaces. See also Asphalt roof cement.

Flat asphalt — Type II asphalt.

Flood coat — A layer of bitumen poured over a built-up roof, which is subsequently covered with aggregate.

FM — See Factory Mutual Research Corporation.

Foaming agent — See Blowing agent.

G 90 — A specification of zinc coating on galvanized steel sheets. The designation G 90 implies that the weight of zinc on 1 sq ft of the sheet is 0.90 oz. Because the sheet is coated on both surfaces, it implies that the weight of zinc on one side of the sheet is 0.45 oz. Similarly, G 60 implies that the sheet has 0.60 oz of zinc coating per sq ft.

Galvanic action — An electrolytic reaction between dissimilar metals in the presence of moisture.

Galvanize — To coat with zinc for corrosion resistance.

Gauge — A measure of the thickness of metal sheets or wires.

Glass felt — Same as fiberglass felt. See also Felt.

Glaze coat — The top layer of bitumen on a smooth-surfaced, built-up roof, or a thin protective coating of bitumen applied during the construction of a built-up roof when the subsequent layers of the built-up roof are expected to be delayed. In the latter case, the glaze coat provides temporary protection until the roof is completed.

Grain — A unit to measure the mass of water vapor. 1 lb = 7,000 grains.

Gravel — A rounded stone aggregate formed by natural erosion of stone by flowing water, typically obtained from river beds.

Gravel stop — A sheet metal or extruded metal flashing with upward projecting metal edge that stops the migration of gravel or bitumen on a built-up roof. A gravel stop is used at the perimeter of a built-up roof and around roof drains.

Hand tabbing — A method of applying spots of roofer's cement to asphalt shingles to improve their adhesion to the substrate for greater wind resistance.

Headlap — The overlap between the uppermost and lowest shingles at a point in a steep roof. When roofing felts are laid like shingles, such a layout is called *shingled felt layout*.

Heat seaming — Adhering the overlapping seams of thermoplastic single-ply roof membranes with hot air. In roofing vernacular, the process is also referred to as *heat welding*.

Hem — The edge created by folding a sheet metal over itself.

Hip — The edge in a sloping roof formed by the intersection of two sloping roof planes.

Hip roof — A roof that includes hips.

HVAC — Heating, ventilating, and air conditioning.

Hydrocarbon — A compound that contains carbon and hydrogen atoms. Asphalt and coal tar are hydrocarbons.

Hygroscopic — A material that absorbs moisture from the air and retains it.

Hypalon —See Chlorosulfonated polyethylene.

Ice dam — A collection of melted snow that refreezes, typically at the projecting eave of a sloping roof. The ice dam causes the water from melting snow to back up under roof shingles.

Incline — See Roof slope.

Inorganic — A compound that does not contain carbon.

Insulation — A material specially formulated to retard the flow of heat.

Interlocking shingles — Asphalt shingles that mechanically lock into each other to provide greater wind resistance.

Inverted roof membrane assembly (IRMA^{TM}) — A patented assembly by Dow Chemicals Company in which Styrofoam brand insulation and ballast are placed above the roof membrane. The generic name for such an assembly is *protected membrane roof.*

Iso board — A rigid polyisocyanurate insulation board.

Laminated shingles — See Dimensional shingle.

Loose-laid membrane — A roof membrane that is not attached to the deck but held down by the weight of ballast, which may consist of crushed stone, water-worn gravel, or precast concrete pavers.

Low temperature flexibility — The ability of a membrane to resist cracking and remain flexible when bent at a low temperature.

Mastic — Same as roofer's cement or plastic cement. See also Asphalt roof cement.

Mechanically fastened membrane — A single-ply roof membrane that is secured to roof deck with fasteners, usually in conjunction with metal or plastic plates or batten bars.

Membrane — A single-ply or multi-ply flexible or semiflexible sheet used for waterproofing the roof.

Membrane flashing — Flashing made from a roof membrane material. See also Flashing.

Mil — A unit of thickness. 1 mil = 0.001 in.

Mineral fibers — Fibers of material mined from the earth that do not contain carbon, e.g., glass fibers (or fiberglass), rock wool, slag wool, etc.

Mineral granules — Stone crushed to small particle sizes.

Mineral stabilizer — Finely ground stone, sand, and/or mineral fibers used with bitumen (asphalt or coal tar) to improve bitumen's stability and flow characteristics.

Mineral-surfaced sheet — A bituminous felt that is surfaced with mineral granules to improve its weatherability. See also Cap sheet.

Miter, or mitered joint — A joint created by joining two pieces at right angles to each other in such a way that the ends of both pieces are diagonally cut.

Modified bitumen — Roofing asphalt or coal tar that has been modified by the inclusion of a polymer to provide greater weatherability to bitumen. Two most commonly used polymer modifiers are attactic polypropylene (APP) and styrene butadiene styrene (SBS).

Moisture relief vent — A device installed on a roof that penetrates through the membrane and the insulation to allow the moisture in the roof assembly to exit through the vent.

Moisture scan — The detection of moisture in a roof assembly by using an electromechanical device.

Monolithic — A building component without joints or seams.

Monomer — A single molecule that has the ability to chemically combine with several identical molecules to form a chain of molecules, referred to as a polymer.

Mop — A device consisting of a straight bar, whose one end consists of a bundle of fibrous rags.

Mop-and-flop — A procedure of applying a roofing sheet (or an insulation board) in which the sheet (or insulation) is placed upside down, coated with the adhesive, and then turned over and placed on the substrate.

Mopping — The process of applying bitumen or other adhesive on the substrate using a mop. Mopping may be of three types: solid mopping, spot mopping, or strip mopping. Solid mopping consists of an uninterrupted spread of bitumen or adhesive. Spot mopping consists of nearly circular areas of bitumen or adhesive separated by unmopped areas. Strip mopping consists of linear strips of bitumen separated by unmopped areas.

Mud cracking — The cracked pattern of a roof that looks like dry, cracked earth.

Nailer — A wood member provided in a roof assembly to nail a roof membrane or flashing, or any other roof component to it. See also Blocking.

Neoprene — A synthetic rubber (polychloroprene).

No-cutout shingles — Asphalt shingles with a single solid strip with no cut-outs.

NRCA — National Roofing Contractors Association.

Open valley — A method of valley construction in a steep roof, where the shingles from either side of the valley are laid away from the valley centerline to expose the valley flashing.

Organic — A material that has carbon atoms, e.g., plant or animal matter. In roofing literature, it generally means cellulosic (wood-pulp-based) material.

Organic felt — A sheet made from cellulosic fibers. It is generally treated with asphalt or coal tar to yield a treated organic felt.

Organic shingle — An asphalt shingle made from cellulosic fibers and asphalt.

Pallet — A wooden platform to store materials for shipping purposes.

Parapet wall or parapet — The portion of a wall at the end of a building that projects above the roof.

Pascal — The unit of stress or pressure in the SI system of units.

Peel strength — The force (usually expressed as force per unit width of a membrane or sheet, e.g., pounds per inch or Newtons per meter) required to peel the membrane from the substrate to which it is adhered.

Penetration — In roofing terminology, penetration implies the resistance of a bituminous material to a standard needle penetrating vertically into it under standard test conditions of duration of loading, ambient temperature, etc.

Perlite — A volcanic rock, used in the manufacture of perlite boards.

Perm — A unit of water vapor diffusion (flow) through a building component. 1 perm = 1 grain of water vapor flowing through 1 ft^2 of component in one hour under a vapor pressure difference of 1 in. of mercury between the two sides of the component.

Permeance — The rate of water vapor diffusion through a component measured in perms, also referred to as *perm rating*.

pH — A measure of acidity/alkalinity of an aqueous solution. The measure pH 7 is neutral; a lower value means an acidic solution, and a higher value means an alkaline solution.

Phased application — Installation of roofing in which there is a deliberate time interval between two successive membranes.

PIMA — Polyisocyanurate Insulation Manufacturers Association.

Pipe boot — A prefabricated flashing used on a round, vertical penetration through a roof.

Pitch pocket or pitch pan — A flanged open bottom sheet metal enclosure placed around a drain or a penetration through a low-slope built-up roof.

Plastic cement — A trowelable cement, made from Type I asphalt, solvent, and mineral fillers and fibers, generally used on horizontal or low-slope surfaces. See also Roofer's cement. For vertical surfaces, a similar product, known as *flashing cement*, is used.

Plasticizer — A compound added to a polymeric substance to improve its pliability and extensibility.

Ply — A layer of felt, sheet, or reinforcement in a roof membrane.

PMR — See Protected membrane roof.

Polychloroprene — See Neoprene.

Polyester — A lightweight flexible polymer used in roofing sheets and garments.

Polyisobutylene (PIB) — A compound obtained from polymerizing isobutylene.

Polymer-modified bitumen — See Modified bitumen.

Polypropylene — A tough, lightweight plastic made from the polymerization of propylene gas.

Polyvinyl chloride (PVC) — A thermoplastic material obtained from polymerizing vinyl chloride. PVC roof membranes are used as single-ply membranes in low-slope roofs.

Primer — A thin, bituminous liquid applied to a roof substrate to improve the adhesion of bitumen to it. The term "primer" is also used with single-ply membranes in which the membrane seams are primed before applying adhesive or double sided tape to the seams. The primer cleans the seams and prepares them to give a good shear and peel strength to the finished seam.

Protected membrane roof — A roof assembly consisting of a membrane installed directly on the deck. The membrane is protected by an overlying loose-laid insulation, which is held down by ballast.

PVC — See Polyvinyl chloride.

R-value — A measure of the resistance to heat transfer through a component, i.e., a measure of the insulating property of a component.

Racking — A method of asphalt shingle application in which shingle courses are applied vertically up the roof rather than laterally, also called a *straight-up method*.

Rafter — A sloped repetitive member in a roof over which the roof deck (e.g., plywood or oriented strandboard panels) are applied.

Raggle — A groove cut in a masonry or concrete wall for inserting counterflashing in it.

Rake — The edge of a roof over a gable end.

Rake starter — A shingle strip applied at the rake of a roof. See also Bleeder strip.

RCI — Roof Consultants Institute.

Re-cover — The addition of a new roof membrane over an existing roof assembly.

Reglet — A sheet metal receiver inserted into a concrete wall (before pouring concrete) or in a slot created in masonry joint (raggle) to receive counterflashing. A metal component attached to the surface of a concrete or masonry wall, to receive counterflashing, is also called a *reglet*.

Reinforced membrane — A roofing membrane that has been strengthened with strengthening materials such as fiberglass, polyester, or polyethylene mat or scrim.

Relative humidity — The ratio of the weight of water vapor in air and the weight of dry air, expressed in percentage form.

Release tape (film or strip) — A thin plastic sheet applied to the back of a roof membrane or to the back of a shingle to prevent the membrane roll from sticking to itself or to prevent the shingles from sticking to each other when packed together.

Ridge cap — A special type of shingle that is applied on the ridge of a steep roof.

Ridge vent — A ridge cap that allows ventilation at the ridge to allow the escape of air and water vapor in the attic.

Ridging — Buckling of roofing felts or sheets.

RIEI — Roofing Industry Educational Institute.

Roll roofing — Smooth-surfaced or mineral-granule-surfaced bituminous felt typically used for temporary roofing.

Roof curb — See Curb.

Roof diaphragm — The structural action of a roof deck by which it resists lateral loads and integrates the walls and the roof deck into an integral building unit.

Roof slope — The inclination of a roof expressed as a ratio of the units of vertical rise to the units of horizontal run, e.g., 4:12. It may also be expressed as percentage, e.g., 33%.

Roofer — A craftsperson who installs or repairs the roof.

Roofer's cement — Same as Asphalt roof cement.

Rosin paper, or rosin-sized sheathing paper — A nonbituminous building paper used to prevent bitumen drippage or as a separator in some roofs.

Saddle, or cricket — A raised substrate over a roof deck to direct water to roof drains in low-slope roofs or to direct water away from roof projections in a steep roof.

Saturated felt — A felt that has been saturated with asphalt or coal tar, generally used with organic felts. See also Asphalt felt.

SBS — Styrene butadiene styrene, a rubberlike plastic.

Scrim — A woven, nonwoven, or knitted fabric composed of continuous strands (not fibers) of a material, used as reinforcing material in a roof membrane.

SDI — Steel Deck Institute.

Sealer — A liquid coating that is applied on a surface to prevent the absorption of extraneous liquids into that surface.

Seam — A joint formed by mating two separate sections of a material. Seams are sealed in modified bitumen and single-ply membranes in a number of ways.

Seam strength — The tensile force applied to tear off the seam by one sheet, usually expressed as pounds per inch.

Self-adhering membrane — A membrane that will adhere to a substrate or to itself without any applied adhesive. The undersurface of such a membrane is typically covered with a release film.

Self-drilling screw — A screw that drills its own hole during application.

Self-sealing shingle — An asphalt shingle that contains strips of asphalt at its back surface to improve its adhesion to the underlying shingle.

Self-tapping screw — A screw that drills its own hole and makes receiving threads into the material in which it is inserted.

Selvage edge — A term normally used with a mineral-granule-surfaced roofing sheet on which the sheet's longitudinal edges is not surfaced with granules to allow better adhesion of two similar sheets at overlaps. The overlapping sheets form a seam at the selvage edge, which is adhered with bitumen.

Shingle — A general term used with small units of steep roofing that overlap each other to shed water off the roof.

Shingling, or in shingle fashion — The application of shingles or rolls of felts that are applied with overlaps similar to steep roof shingles.

SI system of units — The international system of units (Le Systeme International d'Unites).

Siding — The exterior wall finish, consisting of horizontal or vertical panels or strips.

Sieve — An apparatus with uniform-size openings used for separating large-size particles of a material from small-size particles. The small-size particles pass through the openings of the sieve, while the large-size particles are retained on the sieve.

Single-lock standing seam — A standing seam in a metal roof that uses one overlapping interlock between two seam panels. See also Standing seam.

Single-ply roof membrane — A low-slope roofing system in which only one waterproofing sheet is used.

Slag — A hard aggregate obtained as waste product from iron ore melting furnaces, used as surfacing material in some built-up roofs.

Slate — A hard, dense rock used as steep roofing material.

Slating hook — A metal hook used to fasten slates on a steep roof, as an alternative to nailing the slates to the deck.

Slip sheet — A sheet material such as a building paper, rosin paper, polyester scrim, or polyethylene sheet placed between two low-slope roof components (e.g., between membrane and insulation, or between insulation and deck) to prevent an adverse chemical reaction between the components or to prevent adhesion between them.

SMACNA — Sheet Metal and Air Conditioning Contractors National Association.

Softening point — The temperature at which asphalt or coal tar becomes soft enough to flow as determined by a standard test procedure.

Solder — A process similar to welding in which a lead and tin mixture is used to bond metal pieces under the action of heat.

Solid mopping — See Mopping.

Solids content — The percentage of nonvolatile contents in a coating or asphalt roof cement.

Solvent — A liquid that dissolves a solid or thins a viscous liquid and evaporates during the drying process.

Special steep asphalt — Type IV roofing asphalt.

SPF — Sprayed polyurethane foam, used in urethane roofs.

Splash block — A concrete or plastic unit placed at ground level directly under a vertical downspout to reduce the splashing of rainwater.

Splice tape — A double-sided, plastic adhesive tape placed between the seams of two single-ply roof membranes.

Spot mopping — See Mopping.

Sprayed polyurethane foam — See SPF.

SPRI — Single Ply Roofing Institute.

Square or roof square — 100 sq ft of roof area.

Standing seam — A metal panel roof system consisting of upturned ribs that overlap or interlock.

Starter course — The first layer of shingles, applied at the downslope perimeter of a roof.

Starter sheet — Felt, ply, or shingle strips that are made or cut to width narrower than the standard width of the material. A starter felt is used in built-up roofing at the edge of a roof when the felts are laid in shingle fashion.

Steel joist — See Bar joist.

Steep asphalt — Type III asphalt. See also Asphalt.

Steep roof — A roof whose slope is greater than 3:12.

Steep-slope roof — Same as Steep roof.

Step flashing — Individual pieces of L-shaped sheet metal used as flashing around chimneys, dormer windows, etc., in a steep roof.

Strain — Ratio of change in length to the original length of a component.

Stress — Internal resistance of a material to an applied external force, measured as force divided by the cross-sectional area of the component.

Strip mopping — See Mopping.

Stripping in — Application of strips of roof plies to embed sheet metal flashing within the roof membrane.

Styrene butadiene styrene — A polymer that has rubberlike properties. See also SBS.

Sump — An intentional depression around a roof drain or scupper.

Tab — The exposed portion of asphalt shingles, demarcated by cut-outs.

Tar — Same as coal tar.

Test cut — A sample cut from an existing roof that may contain only the membrane or membrane and the insulation. A test cut is required to analyze the roof in the event of a roof failure.

Thermal insulation — In roofing terminology, same as insulation.

Thermoplastic — A plastic that softens on heating and hardens when cooled.

Thermoplastic olefin (TPO) — A thermoplastic blend of polypropylene and ethylene-propylene polymers.

Thermoset — A plastic that does not become soft on heating.

Through-wall flashing — A water-resistant sheet that extends through the entire width of a masonry wall to capture the rainwater entering the wall from above the flashing and divert it to the wall's exterior.

TIMA — Thermal Insulation Manufacturers Association.

U-value — Inverse of R-value, i.e., $U = 1/R$.

Underlayment — An asphalt-saturated felt or other sheet installed between the roof deck and the roofing material, usually in a steep roof to provide a second line of defense against water leakage through the roof.

Underwriters Laboratories, Inc. (UL) — An organization that tests and rates roof assemblies for resistance to fire, wind uplift, etc.

Vapor pressure — Pressure exerted by water vapor.

Vapor retarder — A sheet material specifically designed to greatly reduce the flow of water vapor through it.

Vermiculite — Expanded mica, used as aggregate in lightweight insulating concrete.

Vulcanization — A treatment process by which a synthetic rubber is made more elastomeric.

Woven valley — A method of valley construction in a steep roof in which shingles from one side of the valley extend into the other side.

Index